It Happened in Brooklyn

MYRNA KATZ FROMMER AND HARVEY FROMMER

It Happened in Brooklyn

AN ORAL HISTORY

OF GROWING UP IN THE BOROUGH IN THE

1940s, 1950s, AND 1960s

Harcourt Brace & Company

NEW YORK   SAN DIEGO   LONDON

Library of Congress Cataloging-in-Publication Data
Frommer, Myrna.
It happened in Brooklyn: an oral history of growing up
in the borough in the 1940s, 1950s, and 1960s/
Myrna Katz Frommer and Harvey Frommer.—1st ed.
p.   cm.
Includes bibliographical references and index.
ISBN 0-15-114366-8
1. Brooklyn (New York, N.Y.)—Social life and customs.
2. New York (N.Y.)—Social life and customs.
3. Interviews—New York (N.Y.) I. Frommer, Harvey. II. Title.
F129.B7F76   1993
974.7'23—dc20   93-19356

Designed by Trina Stahl
Printed in the United States of America
First edition
A B C D E

FOR JENNIFER, OUR DAUGHTER,
THE ONLY ONE OF OUR CHILDREN TO HAVE
BEEN BORN IN BROOKLYN

Contents

PART ONE
WHEN WE WERE A COUPLE OF KIDS

1. THE STREETS WERE OUR SANCTUARY   18

A tidy neighborhood life of courtyard, schoolyard, and sidewalk play, of stickball and stoopball and double-dutch jump rope; exploring the borough by bike, train, and foot; pastoral pastimes at Prospect Park; Saturday afternoons at the movies; Broadway on the other side of the bridge; baseball bliss in Dodger Blue at Ebbets Field.

2. SCHOOL DAYS   42

Perfect penmanship and Permanent Records; patriotic assemblies in red, white, and blue; sparrows and robins; teachers tender and tyrannical; IQ exams and Open School Nights; nuns in the classroom and on the volleyball court; the pleasures and terrors of elementary school.

the shorefront from swanky Manhattan Beach to swampy Canarsie; watching the boats come into the harbor along the bustling docks.

PART THREE
THE DAYS OF OUR GLORY

(and the crinolines went swish, swish, swish); staking out at Bay 2; making out at Plum Beach; standing in line for the rock 'n' roll shows; fighting for turf with zip guns and knives; battling on the basketball court; and moving up to Brooklyn College—all you needed was the grades.

Introduction

We are speaking here of a time as well as a place: the three decades at mid-century, bracketed by two wars. If you lived it, your address said Brooklyn, New York—but you really came from Bensonhurst, Brownsville, Bay Ridge, Borough Park, Brooklyn Heights, Prospect Heights, Manhattan Beach, or Midwood if your family was rich; Williamsburg or Red Hook if it was poor.

Your playing fields were baroque lobbies or concrete courtyards of apartment houses, wide sidewalks where you drew your potsy or skelly grids, sewer-studded gutters where legendary stickball games took place, steep stoops of four-family homes where the intricacies of Russian or Chinese handball were perfected.

You attended a neighborhood elementary school known only by its number preceded by the initials *P. S.* Then with thousands of students you went on to a high school that may have been named after a figure famous in American history, like Abraham Lincoln, Thomas Jefferson, Marquis de Lafayette, or James Madison. Your hangouts were cavernous cafeterias like the Famous or Dubrow's and massive movie palaces like the Kingsway or Loew's Oriental, where you spent the Saturday afternoons of your childhood and the Saturday nights of your teens.

Your favorite foods are still the foods of your Brooklyn childhood: a half-sour pickle straight from the barrel, a charlotte russe from the bakery in the wintertime, ice cream scooped by the man in the candy store into a sugar cone, long skinny pretzels, lime rickeys, and malted milks.

Trolleys glided under the McDonald Avenue el to Coney Island; safe and clean subways had names like the West End Local and the Sea Beach Express. For a seven-cent fare, you could go everywhere: to Bay Parkway, Ocean Parkway, and Eastern Parkway—expansive thoroughfares lined with luxurious "elevator" apartment houses suggestive of European promenades—to bustling Pitkin Avenue, chic Kings Highway, boisterous Thirteenth Avenue, or downtown Brooklyn, with department stores like Martin's, Russek's, and A & S. Or you could take the Flatbush Avenue bus and cut straight through the length of the borough, from the East River to the Rockaway Inlet shore.

In the fourth grade, you learned that the Dutch originally settled Brooklyn, and though you probably didn't give it much thought after studying about Henry Hudson and the *Half-Moon* and how they bought Manhattan from the Indians for twenty-four dollars worth of trinkets, your childhood was nevertheless stamped by the Dutch presence. Even modest walk-up apartment houses had the requisite front garden enclosed by a neat privet hedge. Towering maple and oak and sycamore trees drenched summer streets in greenery. Neighborhoods were punctuated by pastoral parks. And the calm uniformity of rectangular blocks gave to your vision a sense of order and predictability.

Manhattan was another world: "the city" where your father worked and your mother took you to buy clothes or see the Christmas show at Radio City Music Hall. The Bronx was some hilly terrain up north, Queens an indistinct wilderness, and Staten Island a place somewhere across the water that you had to take a ferry boat to reach. Whatever you wanted and needed was there, right at home, in Brooklyn.

By the time you grew up, nearly everything had changed. The 1960s brought Vietnam, civil unrest, riots, new rules, new games. The beloved Dodgers had done the unbelievable—moved away, and to California of all places. The few surviving movie palaces were divided into multiplex theaters. The old hangouts had closed down.

There are compensations enough. Your freezer has more delicacies than the corner candy store ever stocked. Watching rented movies on the projection-screen TV beats sitting near a stranger at the crowded Commodore. A steamy summer night is better spent in an air-conditioned bedroom than on a sweltering stoop. And how can the Coney Island steambath compete with the private pleasures of a sauna or Jacuzzi?

But for some reason, Brooklyn stays with you—that special time, that special place. It keeps coming back like a song.

The Voices

ISAAC ABRAHAM is a member of the Satmar Hasidic community, a community activist, and a businessman.

MARTY ADLER was an assistant principal at the Jackie Robinson Intermediate School, in Brooklyn.

SOLOMON AIDELSON is assistant rabbi and educational director of Temple Hillel, in North Woodmere, Long Island.

MEL ALLEN is the former "Voice of the New York Yankees."

BOB ARNESEN was a social studies teacher at Far Rockaway High School, in Queens, for many years.

PAT AULETTA was a longtime Coney Island resident who operated a sporting-goods business there.

ANGELO BADALAMENTI is a composer whose credits include the scores for *Blue Velvet* and *Twin Peaks*.

FRANK BARBARO is the state assemblyman for Brooklyn's Forty-seventh District.

JOEL BERGER is a professor of science education at the College of Staten Island, City University of New York.

JUDY BERGER is an assistant principal at FDR High School, in Brooklyn.

HERB BERNSTEIN is a composer, arranger, and musical accompanist.

KARL BERNSTEIN was an assistant principal at Meyer Levin Junior High School, in Brooklyn.

MARNIE BERNSTEIN is the pseudonym of an author who lives in Long Island.

POLLY BERNSTEIN was a longtime employee at A & S department store in downtown Brooklyn.

SAM BERNSTEIN is a retired furrier.

ALAN BLANKSTEIN is an associate at Kenneth-John Productions.

FRANCES BLUM is a paraprofessional in special education and a lifelong Bensonhurst resident.

TOM BOORAS is a Long Island businessman.

JULIE BUDD is a recording and performing artist who has sung on television, on stage, and in nightclubs.

MARCO CARCICH is a businessman who resides in Queens.

LOUIS COHEN was a longtime executive at Macy's Herald Square.

SYLVIA COLE is a writer and former English teacher.

LUIS COLMENARES is a Greenpoint resident and college student.

BETTY COMDEN is a writer of books, lyrics, and screenplays, along with her partner, Bronx-born Adolph Green.

PAT COOPER is a comedian and television, radio, and nightclub personality.

WILLIAM CUNNINGHAM is a well-known figure in Irish circles in Brooklyn.

ANNETTE DELUCIA-CLARK is an administrative assistant at New York City Technical College, in Brooklyn.

JOHN DOWNIE was a ticket taker at Ebbets Field.

PAUL DOYLE was a professor of English at New York City Technical College, in Brooklyn, from its inception in 1947.

JACK EAGLE is a comedian who, for many years, was Brother Dominic in the Xerox commercials.

GAIL EISEMAN BERNSTEIN is a teacher at Samuel J. Tilden High School, in Brooklyn.

BOB ERTEL is a Long Island resident and Manhattan businessman.

PHIL FAGIN is an administrator at New York City Technical College, in Brooklyn.

BILL FEIGENBAUM is president and creative director of Bill Feigenbaum Designs.

IRVING FIELDS is a pianist, arranger, and composer of many songs, including "The Miami Beach Rumba."

BARRY FRANK is the longtime director of entertainment at the Raleigh Hotel in the Catskills.

HELEN FRIED GOLDSTEIN is a professor of speech at Kingsborough Community College and the Jewish Theological Seminary.

MORRIS FRIEDMAN is the rabbi of Temple Hillel, in North Woodmere, Long Island.

STARR FROST GOLDBERG is the owner of Trail's End Camp, along with her husband, Stan Goldberg.

PEARL GASARCH is the secretary of the Professional Staff Congress at CUNY and a professor of English at New York City Technical College.

RALPH GASARCH was an assistant principal at Shallow Junior High School, in Brooklyn.

DONNA GEFFNER is a professor of speech at St. John's University, in Queens.

BOB GERARDI is a television actor.

FREDDIE GERSHON is a producer of Broadway shows whose credits include *Evita* and *La Cage aux Folles*.

HENRY GERSHON is a retired garment worker.

STAN GOLDBERG is the co-owner of Trail's End Camp and was the inspiration for the character Alan in the TV series *Brooklyn Bridge*.

RICHARD GOLDSTEIN is an editor in the sports department of *The New York Times*.

ROGER GREEN is the state assemblyman for Brooklyn's Fifty-seventh District.

HERBY GREISSMAN is president and CEO of a wholesale produce company.

ELLIOT GUNTY is a talent representative and agent.

BILL HANDWERKER is senior vice-president of Nathan's Famous and a grandson of its founder, Nathan Handwerker.

DOROTHY HANDWERKER is an art collector and the wife of Murray Handwerker.

MURRAY HANDWERKER was, for many years, the CEO of Nathan's Famous, founded by his father, Nathan Handwerker.

CLIFF HESSE is chairman of the Speech and Theater Department at Kingsborough Community College, in Brooklyn.

CHARLES HYNES is the district attorney of Brooklyn.

LONNY IRGENS is an artist who lives in New Jersey.

HOWARD JONES is first vice-president of the Professional Staff Congress, CUNY.

MARVIN KAPLAN is an actor familiar to audiences for his role in the TV series *Alice*.

CAROLINE KATZ MOUNT is the director of immigrant services for the United Jewish Appeal—Federation of Jewish Philanthropies of New York.

RICHARD KEHOE is a priest and professor of speech at St. John's University, in Queens.

MATT KENNEDY is the executive secretary of the Coney Island Chamber of Commerce.

EVERETT KERNER was principal of Samuel J. Tilden High School, in Brooklyn.

DICK KITTRELL is an attorney and longtime Brooklyn resident.

MIRIAM KITTRELL is a professor of biology at Kingsborough Community College, in Brooklyn.

JUDITH KURIANSKY is a clinical psychologist and TV personality.

CLEM LABINE is a former Brooklyn Dodger pitcher.

ABE LASS is a writer and the former principal of Abraham Lincoln High School, in Brooklyn.

ALAN LELCHUK is a Brooklyn-born novelist whose works include *Brooklyn Boy* and *American Mischief*.

BOB LEVY is a Long Island businessman.

AL LEWIS is an actor best known for his role as Grandpa in *The Munsters*.

BOB LIFF is a reporter for the City Hall bureau of *New York Newsday*.

DAN LURIE is a former Mr. America whose stores specialize in physical fitness equipment.

JOEL MARTIN is a Long Island cable TV personality.

JOAN MAYNARD is the executive director of the Weeksville Society, in Bedford-Stuyvesant, Brooklyn.

ROBERT MERRILL is a star baritone of the Metropolitan Opera Company, in New York.

DORIS MODELL TIPOGRAPH is the daughter of Henry Modell, founder of Modell's, and the company's corporate archivist.

PETER NERO is an arranger, conductor, and pianist and the head of the Philly Pops Orchestra.

CLARENCE NORMAN, SR., is pastor of the First Baptist Church of Crown Heights.

TERRY PERNA ARNESEN was, for many years, a teacher of accounting.

IRWIN POLISHOOK is the president of the Professional Staff Congress of CUNY.

HOWARD RAPP is a partner in Charles Rapp Enterprises, the talent-booking agency.

JOAN RIBAUDO is district leader and state committeewoman for the Forty-seventh Assembly District, in Brooklyn.

RACHEL ROBINSON is the widow of Jackie Robinson and head of the foundation that bears his name.

ELIZABETH RONCKETTI is a longtime Greenpoint resident involved in community life.

IRVING RUDD is a former public relations director for the Brooklyn Dodgers.

TOBY SCHOM GROSSMAN is a teacher and interior decorator.

NEIL SEDAKA is a singer, pianist, and composer.

JOYCE SHAPIRO FEIGENBAUM is vice-president and executive producer of Bill Feigenbaum Designs.

JOE SIGLER is the CEO of a computer consulting firm.

WADE SILER is a former bartender and nightclub singer.

JIM SLEEPER is a columnist at *The New York Daily News* and author of *The Closest of Strangers: Liberalism and the Politics of Race in New York*.

MARTIN SPITZER is a community activist and court reporter for the office of the Brooklyn district attorney.

NORMAN SPIZZ is one of the principal partners of Steven Scott Music and Entertainment.

ROZ STARR is a celebrity sleuth.

JERRY STILLER is an entertainer and one-half of the comedy team Stiller and Meara.

STEWIE STONE is a comedian who has appeared on the nightclub circuit and television.

LARRY STRICKLER is an assistant principal at Edward R. Murrow High School, in Brooklyn, and director of activities at Kutsher's, in the Catskills.

SHELLY STRICKLER is a news broadcaster for WOR radio, in New York City.

WILLIAM THOMPSON is associate justice of the Appellate Division Second Department, New York State.

NORMAN TIPOGRAPH is a retired sporting-goods business owner.

ALBERT VANN is the state assemblyman for Brooklyn's Fifty-sixth District.

ELI WALLACH is an actor whose career spans many years on stage, screen, radio, and television.

MAX WECHSLER is the pseudonym of an author who resides on Long Island.

It Happened in Brooklyn

A Future to Behold

PAT COOPER: *Red Hook, in South Brooklyn, was a nice Italian neighborhood near the Gowanus Canal. There were apartment houses, brownstones, yards in the back, trucks all over the place, garbage guys taking the garbage away, kids jumping rope, kids making their own skateboards and scooters by nailing a two-by-four to a pear box, breaking a skate in half, and putting two wheels on the front and two on the back. There were a lot of moms screaming out the window: "Come home, come on. The macaroni's on. Get up here." "Tony, where are you? Bring the dog in."*

You went to school, you had your three meals a day—that was the norm. When a woman had a package, you ran over and helped her. She offered you a nickel, you never took it. You respected the neighborhood cop. If the policeman said, "You—move," you moved. If he said, "Hey you, what are you doing out at seven o'clock?" and you answered, "None of your business," he'd throw you through the wall and take you to your father. And what would your father do? He'd beat your brains in for hurting the policeman's hand. The cop was worried about you. That was his job, for thirty-six dollars a week.

*Every Sunday in the summertime, everybody had their windows open and their radios tuned to the same station. It was like a stereo, an Italian station with all the Italian songs playing—*Cheno luna mezza mama . . . *the melody Milton Berle sang as "Lucky lucky lucky me." Or songs like "I'll Be Seeing You in All the Old Familiar Places" during the war. You'd smell the aroma of the tomatoes cooking, the smoke of the cigars from the old men outside talking about the old hometown. Your father's sitting on the stoop, and you're eating a lemon ice. You thought you had nothing; you had everything. . . .*

BARRY FRANK: December 7, 1941, a Sunday afternoon—we were visiting my aunt on Remsen Avenue when someone called with the news. We put the radio on right away. Everybody started screaming. Even though it was wintertime, we ran out into the street; it was filled with people. I was not quite sure of what was going on, but I understood something had taken place that would change all of our lives.

SAM BERNSTEIN: Somewhere I read that Brooklyn gave more men to the armed forces than thirty-eight states. I was one of them. My sister gave birth to a baby girl in a little hospital on Bay Parkway. They didn't allow any visitors, but since I was set to be shipped overseas, I got special permission to see the new mother and daughter and say good-bye.

ELIZABETH RONCKETTI: My aunt Eleanor joined the WACs and got stationed in North Carolina. It was quite unusual for women to be in the service then, but Eleanor had a mind of her own. We all thought she looked so smart in her uniform. She had a gorgeous pair of legs and loved to show them off.

The merchant ships let off at Noble Street in Greenpoint. The guys on the crews always seemed to find their way to our house—maybe because my grandfather had been in the Merchant Marine. Everybody had stories to tell, and I always got a lot of presents.

TOM BOORAS: We went down to the Navy Yard to watch the big ships being built. We stood at the docks and saw them going out to sea. I was so impressed. It was hard to believe something so big was sitting in the water.

FREDDIE GERSHON: You could see the aircraft carriers and destroyers moving out through the Narrows. In Brighton, where we lived, people patrolled the beaches for fear that German subs might try to land. Once a mine rolled onto the shore and had to be exploded.

BILL FEIGENBAUM: The boardwalk in Coney Island was filled with soldiers and sailors. Music blared from the penny arcades. Even though all those terrible things were going on, the mood was up, patriotic.

JERRY STILLER: Banners crisscrossed the streets. They put up plaques with the names of the fighting men. If somebody died, people put out a gold star.

BOB ERTEL: We played on this vacant lot on East Fifth Street that had some big trees, which made it great for war games. Farther down at the dead end was a trench called the cut. That was where the Long Island Railroad commercial spur ran from the Brooklyn Army Terminal out east to Long Island. When we'd hear a train, we'd drop everything and run to the cut to watch the troop trains carrying tanks and jeeps and army trucks. On our block almost every young man of military age was in the armed forces. The war was very close to home.

MAX WECHSLER: My father was a former boxer and a tough guy, but he spent the war working in the shipyards. "I was too young for World War I, and now I'm too old for World War II," he used to tell everyone. I guess he felt funny because so many other fathers were away. But he pasted an American flag on his black lunch pail to show his support.

POLLY BERNSTEIN: Our son couldn't remember his father. He would say, "All the children on the block have their fathers. Where's my father?" I told him, "He's in the army." I showed him a picture. Whenever I put him to sleep, he'd say, "Mommy, tell me a story about Daddy." And I'd say, "Some day your father will come home, and we'll buy a car, and we'll go any place that you want."

There was a drugstore on Bay Parkway. The owner was my friend, and every time I came in with Marvin, he'd say, "What a nice boy. Too bad your husband is away. Let's hope he'll come back." Mike, the neighborhood grocer, would call me up: "Polly, do you need something?" He felt sorry for me because Sam wasn't around.

JOAN RIBAUDO: My father became an air-raid warden. His hat looked like an upside-down washbasin. With flashlight in hand and a band around his arm, he and another gentleman in our building would go up to the roof every night.

The Brooklyn waterfront brought the war close to home.

Brooklyn dockworkers united behind the war effort.

KARL BERNSTEIN: As soon as the sirens sounded, we pulled down the black shades on all the windows and went into the dinette, the only room in the house without a window. My father had put a lamp with a blue light bulb on the kitchen table, and we sat around it until the all-clear. I was very frightened of the blackouts, the sirens, the searchlights in the sky.

BOB ARNESEN: My mother and I went to a Norwegian restaurant on Eighth Avenue in Bay Ridge. On the menu was a Norwegian flag and an American flag and the words "VEE VILL VIN" and underneath, in Norwegian, "Can you ever forget old Norway?"

JOAN MAYNARD: On Sunday afternoons, my mother would take me to the Brooklyn Botanic Garden. My favorite place had always been the Japanese Garden. How disappointed I was when they closed it down during the war.

KARL BERNSTEIN: Grandpa Louie and I would plant seeds that I got in packets from school in our backyard Victory Garden and in cottage-cheese boxes filled with earth. We grew grapes, carrots, radishes. For fertilizer, we would go to the bridle path on Ocean Parkway, just a block away, and shovel up the horse manure into a pail.

Grandma Yetta worked at a place called Economy Auto Fabrics, sewing seat covers for army vehicles. She brought home leftover material. It was real thick canvas, and at night working in the basement on the old treadle sewing machine, she made book bags for me. You couldn't get them during the war.

TERRY PERNA ARNESEN: I was one of the first of the fifty women hired by the Brooklyn Navy Yard. We worked among thousands of men, making templates.

JACK EAGLE: At the age of sixteen, I began my career as a trumpet player. The bands had kids my age, men over fifty, and no one in between. I became well known in Brooklyn because I could hit the high D on the end of "In the Mood" and hold it. If you could do that in those days, you were open for all kinds of jobs. I was a busy little kid.

MARVIN KAPLAN: To show you the kind of misfit I was, I belonged to the Interscholastic German Glee Club, which performed Strauss songs and German folk songs at concerts and outings. Later we found out the organization was really a Bundist front to raise money for the Nazi party.

JERRY STILLER: We collected fat from the butcher, melted it down, and put it in a can. Then we brought it to the entrance to Ebbets Field and got into the Dodger game for nothing. It seemed every kid in Brooklyn was there for Fat Day.

Victory gardens were all over Brooklyn, including these at the Brooklyn Botanic Garden.

KARL BERNSTEIN: We collected wire for the war from glass milk bottles, saved newspapers and fat, which we exchanged for additional blue ration stamps. My mother sent me to the store with the stamps. The grocer would raise the glass in the dairy cabinet and precisely cut the quarter-pound of butter you were allowed from a big wooden tub.

ALAN LELCHUK: At night, I'd sit on my father's lap, and we'd listen to Gabriel Heattor and H. V. Kaltenborn on the radio. We would go over the war map in *The New York Times*: the dotted lines versus the solid black lines, the Allies versus the Axis.

RICHARD KEHOE: In my second-year Latin class at St. John's Prep, we were studying Caesar's *Gallic Wars* at the same time the American troops were fighting their way through France. We read about Caesar's battles on the plains of southern France, following the same patterns the Allies were taking.

SAM BERNSTEIN: In the spring of 1945, we crossed the Channel from England to France and were moving on to Germany. All the news was out during the crossing, but as soon as we reached land, we learned FDR had died. For us, it was such a calamity. Who's Truman? We never heard of Truman. The war will never end, we thought.

KARL BERNSTEIN: My mother called out the window that Roosevelt had died. I was almost eleven years old, and in my short lifetime President Roosevelt was *the* president. There never had been another. President Roosevelt—the words seemed to fit together. During the 1944 election, every grown-up I knew was voting for him. All the kids were for him, too. The big rumor was if Dewey became president we would have to go to school on Saturdays and Sundays.

POLLY BERNSTEIN: When I heard the news on the radio, I got Marvin dressed and put him in the stroller. And I walked up Bay Parkway about two miles, all the way to the bay. "What's going to happen now?" I thought. "Is Sam ever going to come home? Will Marvin ever see his father?" Tears were just coming down my face. It seemed the world was over.

ALAN LELCHUK: My father was Russian-born, and although very left wing, he worshiped Roosevelt. He was the head of the Brownsville air raid wardens and had received a letter signed by the president encouraging the wardens' efforts. That gave me a sense that somehow this man Roosevelt was connected to Brownsville. I believed he was such a paragon of justice and optimism. When my mother came up Ralph Avenue to tell me he had died, the world as I knew it fell out from beneath me.

MARNIE BERNSTEIN: We had a book with a red cover from *The New York Post*, a picture history of America. At the end was a photo gallery of the presidents, four to a page, in chronological order. But the last one was President Roosevelt, and his face took up an entire page. I could not imagine a world without him.

About a month later, I was sick in bed, and my mother said, "You have to hurry up and get well in time for VE day." It was coming— VE day! I didn't quite understand what it meant—victory in Europe but the war not over, my uncles not coming home yet. Still, I could feel the momentum. On the other side of the building, the Rutts were planning a welcome-home party for their son Mel. All the furniture was moved out of the apartment into the hall. The big stairwell windows that faced the courtyard were open wide to the springtime air. My friend Barbara lived next door to the Rutts, and we went together into the foyer of their apartment. It was empty, big, waiting. There was so much anticipation.

POLLY BERNSTEIN: Our bedroom window faced Sixty-third Street. The night of September 2, we were asleep when all of a sudden I heard such a big commotion—you have no idea. I got up and pulled

A USO facility in Manhattan Beach.

up the shade, and I saw the street was full of people, yelling, crying, hugging each other. Everyone was shouting, "The war is over, the war is over!" It seemed whoever had someone in the army had come running out into the street. My little son, who was three years old then, woke up. "What's happening, Mommy?" I said, "The war is over." And he said, "Is Daddy coming home?"

"Yes," I told him, "your daddy is coming home."

KARL BERNSTEIN: When my Uncle Herb went away to the war, we all said good-bye in front of the house. Then we stood there and watched him walk down East Seventh Street toward Kings Highway. At the corner, he looked back once, waved, and turned the corner. Now he phoned and told us to wait in front of the house. So we all went out and stood there, and in a little while, there he was, turning the corner from Kings Highway onto East Seventh, coming back just the way he had left.

JOE SIGLER: Sometimes on Saturdays, my father took me along with him to his accounts. We were at a mirror place, and outside all these tanks and trucks were lined up, ready for the big parade to celebrate the end of the war. The soldiers took me inside the tanks. Thrills, these were thrills.

PAT COOPER: In the neighborhood, there was a block party every night for a year. Sackett Street and Henry, President Street and Henry, Clinton and First Place. They'd put up a little platform or we'd use the back of a truck. There was a festive feeling. Everybody kissed each other. People hung flags and signs from their windows.

I worked block parties seven nights a week. They'd give me a dollar, two dollars. People would say, "Get Pat up here." I'd do impressions of James Cagney, Peter Lorre, Sidney Greenstreet. My father would say, "You're makin' stupid again? Can't you sing opera?" But the crowd said, "Go get 'em Pat, we love ya." They didn't want to hear opera.

JOAN RIBAUDO: Christmas lights were strung across the streets. Tables were set up in front of the buildings and in the middle of the street. People shared all the different ethnic dishes. There was music, and everyone was dancing and singing.

MARNIE BERNSTEIN: I remember it as the first time I was out at night—it was odd to see the blocks lit by street lamps, the sky so dark. A parade came down Sixty-third Street: three people like a

Yankee Doodle Dandy pageant, with a fife-and-drum and a huge American flag. Then a woman in a short skirt twirling a baton, and behind her, a brass band.

The street was filled with people in costume. Mrs. Unger, who lived upstairs, was dressed in black Chinese pajamas and had strange-looking colors on her eyelids.

We moved with the crowd down the block and around the corner, onto Sixty-fourth Street. The porch of one of the houses was set up like a stage, with a little band and a microphone. People were entertaining. A few days before, I had been at a birthday party where someone sang "Don't Fence Me In." That gave me the idea. They put me up on a chair so I could reach the microphone, and I sang that song.

There were loudspeakers all over the area, and my father, walking past Feder's Drug Store a block away, stopped to listen. Someone told him, "Don't you know who that is? It's Marnie." He ran down the block and around the corner, and reached the porch just as I finished the song. And while everybody was applauding, they handed me down the steps over to him.

LOUIS COHEN: I came home at the end of 1946. On a Friday night, I was standing on a street corner in my uniform, with all the nice medals on my jacket. A girl walked by, pointed to one, and said, "Can I ask you what that medal is for?" We got to talking, and I walked her home. She lived in East New York. I started taking her with me when I played handball in Brighton. She would say, "Louie, you're some ball player." I ended up marrying that girl.

DOROTHY HANDWERKER: When Murray came home from the army, you couldn't get an apartment for love or money. There had been no construction at all during the war. We moved in with my parents; lots of people did that. It was a beautiful three-bedroom, two-bathroom apartment overlooking the ocean in Brighton. But we were seven people living together: my parents; Murray and me; my sister and brother-in-law, who just got out of the air force; and my nephew, who was just born. And I was pregnant. Still, we were so happy to be together.

NORMAN TIPOGRAPH: They built four "veterans' preference" apartment houses for young married couples on Ocean Avenue between Avenues X and Y. We got a three-room apartment for twenty-five dollars a room. Everybody in the place had served in a branch of the armed forces. Buddy Rich and Harvey Lembeck lived there.

ALAN LELCHUK: The boys coming home were treated like heroes. Some were given free suits on Pitkin Avenue and free meals.

NORMAN TIPOGRAPH: Henry Modell had sales day just for veterans at his downtown Brooklyn store. On Veterans Day 1948, he opened up the store only for veterans. He started a school under the GI Bill of Rights, training them in selling and merchandising. Some went on to work for him at Modell's, many others started their own businesses.

Henry bought merchandise that the government wanted to dispose of: underwear, insect repellent, shoes, sweaters, hats. There was no end to all the utility items available. One of the hottest numbers in Modell's was U.S. Navy shoes: a black oxford. Everybody and his brother bought them, they were so cheap and useful.

MATT KENNEDY: The Depression was over, and now the war was over. There was more money. The soldiers and sailors and Marines coming home helped bring about the resurgence of Coney Island. They'd come off the subway at Stillwell Avenue and rush to the places they frequented, spreading out to the rides. They loved the Cyclone —especially the Air Force people. They'd spend every nickel that they had, and the rides were a nickel then. If they didn't have any

Borough president John Cashmore presents diplomas to graduates of Modell's Veterans' Training Center.

money left for carfare, they'd go to the Sixtieth Precinct, where the police had a special fund to help them.

MURRAY HANDWERKER: At that time, Nathan's was just hot dogs, hamburgers, french fries, soft drinks, chow mein. I had just gotten out of the army, and I saw all the uniformed people coming to Coney Island. I realized the American soldier had been exposed to French food, his tastes had become more sophisticated. I wanted to put in a seafood counter. My father was afraid. Our frankfurter wasn't kosher, but it was kosher-style: all beef, no pork. He was afraid if I put in shrimp and clams, people wouldn't like it. After a while, he said, "All right, if you want to do it, do it. I'm not gonna be around. Do it while I'm away in Florida." So I tried it, and it was a success, and then I brought in delicatessen.

The postwar years were a turning point, you could say—a time of expansion. Tastes were changing. And I, coming home from the war and going into the business, was part of that scene.

PAUL DOYLE: February 5, 1947, was the first day of classes at the experimental New York State Institute of Applied Arts and Sciences. The students were primarily demobilized veterans. The war had made everyone aware we were living in a world of new inventions and sophisticated technology, and this school was designed to prepare people for the future with a combination of technical training and general education. Our slogan was: "Earn a living, and live a life."

P.S. 15 was the original site of what would become New York City Technical College of the City University of New York.

For the first few months, classes were held at P.S. 15, at the corner of Schermerhorn Street and Third Avenue. The GIs sat on top of the small grade-school desks. That spring we moved into our permanent site on Pearl Street. Most of our equipment was surplus war stuff. The only way you could get fifteen file cabinets was also to take twenty-five ship chronometers or maybe forty ship anchors. We had three radar trucks in our parking lot that we had to take in order to get inkwells. Young families moved into the trucks and set up house-keeping.

I taught psychology and sociology. Some of us were not totally familiar with our subjects and kept just a chapter or two ahead of the students. But none of that seemed to matter. We felt what we were part of would bring the benefits of science and technology to everyone, and that was going to make for a better future.

FRANK BARBARO: When I started working on the waterfront, the longshoremen and the sons of the longshoremen had come back from war. They remembered the tremendous oppression they or their fathers endured at the hands of the Mob during the Depression. Like, if you want to work, your daughter has to go to bed with me or your wife has to clean my house or you have to kick back. There had been open terror, subjugation.

Now the Second World War is over. The violence, the intimidation, the corruption—are still there, but different. The people are different. Many saw their friends die. All believe in democracy.

A boss on the pier gives a guy a hard time. The guy goes home, gets his gun, goes back and says, "You son of a bitch, you mess with me, and I'll kill you. You think I went to war to come back and take this from you?" The boss never bothers him again.

The men are cheated out of their time, and they walk off. Nothing striking at the heart of the power structure—just basic elements of common decency, a developing rank-and-file struggle for decency in the union. Coming off the Second World War, a lot of people were saying, "We just fought a war, and it's time for a better life for working people."

MAX WECHSLER: For a week or more, the word was going around the neighborhood: the candy store on Havemeyer Street was getting a shipment of Fleer's Double Bubble Gum. When it finally arrived, the line stretched almost a block and a half. Adults were there along with the kids. The price was at least ten times what it had been before the war. Still, people were jumping the line, bumping the line. They sold the gum direct from cartons stacked up outside the store, and people were in a panic to get to that sweet chewy taste. I guess it made us feel things were getting back to the way they used to be.

KARL BERNSTEIN: Bubble gum was so expensive, we would put it into a glass of water overnight so we could chew it the next day. Rubber came back into production, and so did Spaldings. We finally got rid of those hard balls that didn't bounce. We could get Duncan yo-yos again. Everyone was doing all kinds of tricks with them, like the Windmill, Around the World, the Walk. They became such a distraction that if a kid brought his yo-yo to school, he could get expelled. We had been through the blackouts, the rations, but now everything was coming back. My father even got a new car.

But best of all, the war was over. Now there was a United Nations to make sure there would never be another one. In school, we sang:

> United Nations on the march with flags unfurled.
> Together fight for victory, a brave new world.

Our teacher at Seth Low Junior High School took the class to Greenwich Village for a lesson in Esperanto, the universal language. Once everyone could speak the same language, they told us, there would be no more misunderstandings.

JOAN MAYNARD: With all the world upheaval, people had come into Brooklyn by the bushel, and there was hope and a spirit of optimism, a feeling we had made it, had come through the Depression and the war. We went out to Fulton Street to shop and left the iron gate to our brownstone in Bedford-Stuyvesant open. We went to dances and parties and came back at three in the morning, and there'd be singing in the street, and the milkman would wave to us.

WILLIAM THOMPSON: I came back to my family's home on Putnam Avenue in Bedford-Stuyvesant after serving in the segregated Ninety-second Infantry Division. Bed-Stuy was a fabulous area then, an integrated neighborhood. I started Brooklyn Law School and joined the segregated United Action Democratic Club. When a judge died, we asked that a black man be nominated as his replacement, since the neighborhood was turning black. We were told power does not concede. They took a white man from out of the area, moved him onto

Macon Street, and said, "This is your candidate for judge." At which point a whole bunch of us got together and backed Louis S. Flagg.

They don't hand power to you just because you happen to be there. We spent a lot of money. It was a hard fight. And Flagg won. Then we started opening doors.

ROGER GREEN: There'd be a banging on the front door of our house on Madison Street, and us kids would come running. We knew it was my grandfather up to visit from North Carolina, smelling of Old Spice and his leather suitcase. We'd jump all over him, and he'd cry, "Great Gugga Mugga! Great day in the morning!" And next thing he would say was, "When are we gonna see the Dodgers? I gotta see my man Jackie."

Jackie Robinson breaking through the color line in the years following the war gave folks the perception that there was something different about Brooklyn, that it was a special kind of place.

ALAN LELCHUK: During Robinson's first season, a very close friend of mine named Burt would pick me up at P.S. 189 one hour earlier than the regular let-out time and take me to Ebbets Field. Burt had been shot down during the war and had a Purple Heart. As soon as the ushers saw this uniformed soldier with a Purple Heart, they immediately gave him a box.

Together with Burt, I watched the Brooklyn Dodgers, a team that had been one of comedy and futility now, suddenly, with the introduction and acceptance of Robinson and then other black players, become one of the two great teams of the postwar era.

In the years after the war, nothing symbolized the feeling of hope and optimism more than the Brooklyn Dodgers. By taking in blacks and making them part of the team, Branch Rickey made the Dodgers truly representative of the borough, which at that time flourished as a unique place. The team stood for aspirations at a time when the people of the city were ready for a future of rightness.

For us in Brooklyn, there was the feeling that not only had we made it through—we were on the way up. We had a lot of motivation, we children of immigrants. There was a tremendous amount of talent pooled together to be the smartest, the best, the wittiest, the most mischievous. We had the desire to work hard plus the belief we could do anything. The myth of invincibility was very important. After a great victory in war, there was a feeling that merit would be recognized. It was like coming into a bright light.

PART ONE

When We
Were a Couple of Kids

THE STREETS WERE OUR SANCTUARY

SCHOOL DAYS

LOOK, MA, I'M DANCING!

ONE BIG HAPPY FAMILY

CHAPTER 1

The Streets
Were Our Sanctuary

2 GOOD
+2 BE
4 GOTTEN

—Autograph album, J.H.S. 265

STAN GOLDBERG: Most of us came from blue-collar families, from fathers who had to give up college educations to go to work. My father was a mailman. "I don't mind being a worker," he would tell my brother, Gary, and me. "It's OK. I don't care that I'm not a leader. You two, I want you to do whatever you want to do." He made us really believe that we could be anything in this world that we wanted, that we could succeed in anything. But we couldn't go on the subway alone.

And we had to have our milk and cookies at three o'clock. School days, I came home, had my milk and cookies, and went back to the schoolyard. Weekends, my grandma brought the milk and cookies to the schoolyard. The score is tied? Bases are loaded, and Stanley is up? Grandma Jennie comes by and stops the game. That was bad enough, but she brought a napkin yet. And my grandfather would stop football games to bring me a jacket. In the middle of the play, he would call me to the sidelines. "Grandpa," I explained, "I'm the quarterback. The quarterback doesn't wear a jacket."

FREDDIE GERSHON: Every neighbor looked out for you. If your parents were away, you could not get into trouble, because twenty other mothers were looking out the window. I never experienced that again.

ALAN LELCHUK: It was a very tidy neighborhood life where I grew up, on the border of Brownsville and East Flatbush. For four–six blocks around, I knew practically every face. When I was about seven, my sister said she was not going to baby-sit any longer, and as my parents went out a great deal, I was on my own nearly every evening. If I needed something, I ran across the landing and knocked on a neighbor's door.

ROGER GREEN: When my parents were working and I was outside playing, Mrs. Haskins, who lived down the street, was always looking out for me. At night, I would get the litany from the intelligence network: "Well, Mrs. Haskins said so-and-so."

STAN GOLDBERG: Laura, one of my mother's friends, would have been great in the CIA. You climbed the fence to get the ball, and of course the spy saw. Immediately the word went out if you said the four-letter word. I'd walk in the door and my mother would say, "You cursed!"

"How'd you find out?"

"Laura said."

We knew all the grown-ups in the neighborhood and what to expect from them. Even Silvio, the kid who ruled the schoolyard, knew. Silvio was an older boy who took collections: two cents, three cents, whatever people would give him. He collected just because you were there—until we got wise and stopped going to the schoolyard with money. One day, I was playing third base, and Silvio came over.

"Goldberg, what you got for me today?"

I said, "Nothing."

He checked my pockets and found a quarter. "You lied to me. You have a quarter."

"My mother gave it to me for a rye bread."

"A rye bread's twenty-one cents." He took the quarter and gave me back twenty-one cents. He knew better than to risk my coming home without the rye bread; my mother or, worse, grandma would be after him. Still, I was surprised. I didn't think he knew how to make change.

JULIE BUDD: If my mother wasn't around, I knew the neighbors would take care of me. I could go eat at the Caracaffas', or Lilly Simon's, or Sandy Warren's. In the warm weather, they were all out sitting on their porches, and the kids would stay outside, wait for the ice-cream man, play in the street till eleven o'clock at night.

JUDY BERGER: We played on the streets till our mothers leaned out the window and yelled it was time to come in. The Prince spaghetti commercial that takes place in Boston is really a Brooklyn scene.

ANGELO BADALAMENTI: I had loads of friends—twenty, thirty really good friends, the kids on our block. We went to school together and then played outside together on the streets of the neighborhood.

ROGER GREEN: We played stickball, punchball, hide-and-go-seek, and of course, basketball and softball till after dark. Our block was known for that kind of street activity.

JERRY STILLER: We played ringolevio and kickety-can-hide-go, which means you kick the can and hide before the guy who's It picks up the can. And Johnny-on-the-pony, where guys would line up with their heads against each other's tushes, and someone would take a flying leap, trying to get as far as he could over the line of backs. Then the last guy on the line would try to get on top of the first guy. It ended up a pile of kids.

LUIS COLMENARES: We played "kings" with a Spalding ball in the alley between the houses. If you lost, you were the target. You got your ass up against the wall, and everybody had five throws at you with the ball. I got whacked pretty good.

MARTIN SPITZER: With a piece of chalk, we would draw a big geometric grid on the sidewalk. We'd fill bottle caps with clay or gum or melted crayons and flick the caps into boxes on the grid. That was skelly. Or we used a cigar box and a marble. You'd cut out holes and each hole would be worth so many. People would come with their marbles and if they got it in the hole, I'd have to pay them off, and vice versa. That was the first type of gambling. I made a lot of marbles.

ANGELO BADALAMENTI: We played "heels" with heels gotten off old shoes or from the shoe store. The idea was to throw the heel so it landed on a line of the sidewalk. If it did, the next kid would try to get his heel on top of it. We played "land," flipping a knife onto the strip of earth that lined the sidewalk.

JOYCE SHAPIRO FEIGENBAUM: We played potsy and hop-scotch and jump rope and double-dutch jump rope—the stuff that kids who spent all their time in the streets did. I lived in this crowded little apartment that was so small and stifling. I remember the yelling and all that. I spent every moment I could outside, even in the win-tertime. The streets were my sanctuary.

HELEN FRIED GOLDSTEIN: Winters seemed so fierce when I was a kid. There would be so much snow. They didn't clear it for weeks, and it would be piled up in high mounds on the edge of the streets. Bay Ridge, where we lived, has a lot of hills. We all had sleds, some big enough for several kids, and we would toboggan down the big hill on Forty-fifth Street from Seventh Avenue to Fourth Avenue. At the bottom of each street, we had a monitor posted to watch the traffic. If it was clear, he'd signal us to go through. If not, he'd motion for us to get over to the ash pile on the left. The hill continued below Fourth Avenue, but we stopped there, because we had to carry our sleds back up the hill. We were a crowd of boys and girls, different ethnic groups, all friends, playing outdoors in the cold, brisk air. It felt so healthy and invigorating. Except if Mike, a very fat kid, was on your sled. We bellied, one kid laying on top of another. No one wanted to be under Mike.

HERBY GREISSMAN: On rainy days, we sat on the hard marble steps in the building, flipping baseball cards off the wall, trading joke books, playing cards, pitching pennies, shooting dice. We'd steal two or three cigarettes from our parents' packs, go under the steps by the mailbox, and smoke.

MARNIE BERNSTEIN: The halls of the apartment house were like a theater. Marble staircases led up to tile floors—a stage, perfect for performing. The audience sat on the steps below. Acoustics in that old building were wonderful; your voice bounced off the walls, echo upon echo. The hallways were also great for playing hide-and-seek.

There were so many entrances and alcoves and stairwells where you could hide.

TOBY SCHOM GROSSMAN: We played a game on the lobby floor we called alligator. Most of the floor tiles were white, but there was a green border going around. You had to walk on the green tiles, and if you fell into the white tiles, the alligators would get you.

On Halloween, we got dressed up in costumes, but we never left the building. We'd go from one side of the building to the other. Everyone knew us and gave us treats.

JOYCE SHAPIRO FEIGENBAUM: We avoided the cellar. It was a dark and forbidding place, with many locked rooms. Still, it held a certain fascination.

CAROLINE KATZ MOUNT: The cellar was one of those foreign and frightening elements that intruded every once in a while into my otherwise safe and circumscribed world. When we had to go from the courtyard to the backyard through the corridor that divided the cellar in two parts, we ran in a blind panic. A man named Jeffrey, who did odd jobs for our super, lived down there. Sometimes he hung around with his friends. I'd see them laughing and drinking. None of them ever so much as spoke to me; still, I was very afraid of Jeffrey and the cellar.

FRANCES BLUM: The big courtyard that separated my building from the one next door had benches along the walls and a couple of trees. The mothers would come out with the baby carriages, and all the little toddlers would be running around. There were children of all ages. We never lacked for friends. In the summer, my mother would let us out early in the morning, call us in for lunch, and let us out again to play till suppertime. In the middle of the afternoon, the ice-cream truck came along. You could get chocolate or white—I didn't know it was called vanilla until years later. We bought dixie cups with pictures of movie stars on the lids. After you licked off the ice cream, you had a picture for your collection. We used to trade them: a June Haver for an Alan Ladd. I would trade everyone but Betty Grable. I loved her. I think I saw every Betty Grable picture there was.

We played house with our dolls and doll carriages and toy dishes and pots and pans. We put on talent shows. The kids who took lessons dressed up in their costumes and tap-danced. I mostly used to watch. If the boys didn't have enough for their punchball game, they'd grab one of us: "You're on first base, you're on second base, you're in the outfield."

IRWIN POLISHOOK: I used to explore the old apartment houses in the neighborhood, climbing in the narrow spaces between the buildings—crevices barely wide enough for a child to crawl through. At the end of the war, there were a number of empty buildings we used for war games. I crawled through one, fell down, and cut my hand. I still have the scar.

JOYCE SHAPIRO FEIGENBAUM: In back of my apartment house was a labyrinth of alleys, and beyond them, the backs of other houses. They were two-family or private houses—a whole other world to me.

MIRIAM KITTRELL: We used to play in the alley that runs a full block between the backs of the houses on East Second and Third streets between Quentin Road and Avenue P. Someone planted a row of magnolia trees there. I remember the pink blossoms in the spring-time. Occasionally, there was such a scent of magnolia.

KARL BERNSTEIN: The trees on our block were part of our punch-ball games. When we were younger, if the ball hit a tree, you were out. If the ball went into Mrs. Capricilli's garden across the street, we never saw it again—even during the war, when Spaldings were treasures. Mrs. Capricilli would be out the door in a flash and cut it up.

HELEN FRIED GOLDSTEIN: There must have been at least twenty steps on the stoop of our brownstone, perfect for stoopball. You tried to hit the ball off the corner of the step and catch it before it bounced.

STAN GOLDBERG: We lived and breathed to play ball. If I wasn't in the schoolyard, I was in the backyard. I left the house in the morning, the ball was in my hand. I'd walk down the block and hit every stoop along the way. All my friends were ball players. My mother wanted me to be friends with Gary Stein. "Ma," I said, "I can't. He doesn't like to play ball." She said, "Don't worry. Someday he'll be something." Today he's a heart surgeon in Boston.

In the schoolyard—P.S. 205, Twentieth Avenue between Sixty-sixth and Sixty-seventh—you were on your own. You developed a code that was a great carryover to later life: covering up for each other in certain situations, sharing—whether sharing for a game, or sharing a stickball bat, or sharing a Spalding ball that everyone chipped in for. You didn't want to lose that ball. When it rolled down the street and went into the sewer—that was it, you were finished. You didn't have a quarter for another one. You got a wire hanger, made a loop in it, and fished down to get the ball in the loop and bring it up. Sometimes, you put gum on a stick. No one thought of how to wash it off.

MARTY ADLER: We broke a broom or mop handle under a car's wheel to make it the right length for stickball. It never came off clean, and we were always getting splinters. But that was it. There was no such thing as a store-bought bat.

STAN GOLDBERG: Some women in the neighborhood spent a little more money for a better mop. We cased them. Mrs. Aronowitz bought a very good mop. She hung the mop out the window. It was so tempting. I took it, passed it to my friend Billy Levine. He cut it off at the curb, and Billy and I shared it.

PETER NERO: None of us had the money for a football, so we improvised. We played association football—that was touch football with a Spalding. Aluminum foil was becoming popular just then. We would save it, bunch it up until we got something the size of a golf ball, maybe a little bigger. We'd hit that with our bare hands. It was easy to hit long fly balls that would hang up in the air and not break any windows, either.

ROBERT MERRILL: We scrunched the cellophane and silver paper from cigarette packs into a ball and wrapped electricians' tape around it. That became the ball for a stickball game.

MARTY ADLER: Choosing sides for a game, we would toss the bat vertically. One of the guys would grab it as high up at the top as he could. You added your hand on top of his. The person who was able to hold on to the highest part while turning the bat around his head three times, have his opponent kick it, and still hold on to it was allowed to choose sides first.

FREDDIE GERSHON: I was a fat child and not a great athlete. I was always the person least desired on either team, so I was made to play home plate.

ANGELO BADALAMENTI: Our favorite game, "sewers," was played at an intersection with sewers at each of the four corners. The ball would be thrown to the batter at home plate—one of the sewers —on a bounce, and he would try to slap it through the infielders, run around the other three sewers, and literally slide on the cement of the gutter into home. I can't remember how many times I ripped my pants and ended up with my legs down the sewer. On Sunday mornings, when the fourteen- and fifteen-year-old boys played, it was serious business, with a little side betting for sodas or malteds.

MARTY ADLER: If we had four guys, the sewer was home plate in our stickball games. The pitcher would throw fast to a catcher, who played without benefit of mask or glove. If you hit the ball as far as one sewer down the block, it was a single; two sewers, it was a double. Another kind of stickball was one-on-one, where the batter stood in a box drawn in chalk, and the pitcher threw fast against the wall behind. Another kind was where you hit the ball yourself down the block. Since you were generating your own power, you could get a three-sewer hit.

STEWIE STONE: People from Brooklyn ask, "How many sewers could you hit the ball?" A sewer was every sixty or eighty feet. Anyone who tells you he could hit two sewers is either King Kong or a liar. Ted Kluszewski couldn't hit two sewers.

We played on a narrow street and made up markers—ground rules. If the ball went a certain distance on the sidewalk to the left, it was good. If it went under the sewer, it was a foul ball. If it went past the Chevrolet on the fly, it was a double. If you could hit past the Ford, a triple.

JOEL BERGER: If a car came down the street, we'd yell, "Ship ahoy!" If a guy tried to park, we'd say, "Hey mister, could you move your car? You're on second base." He'd always move.

HERBY GREISSMAN: The cars didn't bother us much because not too many people had cars in those days. If someone drove a Lincoln Continental, it was like the end of the world. We would stop and stare.

MARTY ADLER: The Blumberg brothers from East New York came to play stickball against me, Larry Freidman, Harvey Kaufman, Herbie Young, and Renato Guidice. We set up the game on Fiftieth Street, off Eleventh Avenue. Somebody scrounged up a piece of chalk so we could keep score in the gutter. In the second inning, Larry Freidman hit one smack into Mrs. Myers's window. She came out screaming. Her husband, who happened to be home because he worked nights in the post office, came out, too. Everybody scattered. The cops came. Mrs. Myers pointed her finger and screamed—we're loafers, we're hooligans. A fire engine came driving down the block. People were looking out of their windows, crying, "What the hell is going on?"

"We lived and breathed to play ball."

When it was all over, every one of us had to chip in for the broken window. The Blumberg brothers never returned. That was the first shot heard round the world.

ALAN LELCHUK: We had a regular team, with club jackets. They were purple and white, and reversible—wool on one side, satin on the other. The club's name, the Charantes—which we got from an Indian tribe in the "Dick Tracy" comic strip—was on the back, and our own names were on the breast pocket. We saved for about four years to get those jackets. They cost about eighteen or twenty dollars—a monstrous amount of money in those days.

BOB LEVY: We had kelly-green-and-gold jackets and basketball shirts and shorts. The club's name was the Deuces, and each of us had nicknames. Mine was "Bread," for Levy's bread. We played basketball and schoolyard softball and challenged all the schools in the area. Right next to P.S. 161 was the Crown Heights Yeshiva. We played basketball against the yeshiva kids, and they beat us all the time.

BOB ERTEL: We played football, baseball, or stickball against kids from other neighborhoods. The whole team would ride on bikes halfway across Brooklyn to play those games. Those kids who didn't have a bike sat on the handlebars.

IRWIN POLISHOOK: I explored all over Brooklyn on my Schwinn bike. It was an adventure. I rode to Red Hook and the Navy Yard, where my friend's grandfather owned a junk yard where my father worked during the war. I bicycled ten miles down Shore Parkway to Coney Island.

I had a yen to know what all the different areas of Brooklyn were like. Even as a little boy, I would go around on the subway. I used to wonder what was above me. What kind of people lived there? What kind of neighborhood was I riding underneath?

KARL BERNSTEIN: You'd begin riding the trains and buses and trolleys by yourself when you were a little kid—seven, eight years old. Before I knew how to read, I could identify all the subway trains by the colored lights at the front. The West End line was green and white, the Sea Beach was red and white, the Culver was green and orange, the Brighton was red and green, the Fourth Avenue Local was green and green. I loved the elevated subway trains; you could open the top windows, stand on your knees, look out and feel the wind on your face. They were the old brown trains with rattan seats that stuck to your legs in the summertime when you wore short pants.

JUDY BERGER: The Culver line didn't link up to the rest of the system, so we always had to change trains. Our station had a floor-to-ceiling turnstile, like a revolving door. A family of three could squash into one compartment for a nickel—which a lot of people did, as there was no agent at that station. I was never one for looking down from a height, and when you looked down from the elevator platform, you saw right through to the street. My little sister used to stand at the edge, and I would panic.

CLIFF HESSE: On Sunday afternoons, my sister and I went for these long walks. We picked a direction we never had been before and walked that way. We wandered into new neighborhoods and never worried about it.

LUIS COLMENARES: I lived on Pineapple Street in Brooklyn Heights, and my friend Tommy Antanasio, a Greek kid, lived on Henry Street. We were playing poker. I had taken him for a couple of dollars, and we had nothing else to do that night, a beautiful clear summer night, so we decided to walk over the Brooklyn Bridge. I used to see the city across the river, but I had never gone there. Manhattan was a strange land, a forbidding place. I wondered what it would be like.

So we walked and talked and got to the other side of the Brooklyn Bridge. It was no big deal. All we saw were some official-looking buildings that didn't seem so interesting. So we headed back to Brooklyn, which was our world. We came home close to midnight, and my mother whipped my ass. I found out later on that Tommy's father punched him in the mouth. The walk wasn't worth it.

ANNETTE DE LUCIA-CLARK: My friends and I would walk from the community center on Baltic Street in Gowanus up to Court Street and all the way down the promenade in Brooklyn Heights to the end, somewhere around Pineapple Street. We'd get off and go over to downtown Brooklyn, where we'd go shopping at A & S, Martin's, the big stores. Not real shopping, just looking around. The only thing I ever bought was a lipstick.

ELIZABETH RONCKETTI: In Greenpoint, all the kids roller-skated together, great bunches of us skating down the streets. Some went long distances, all the way into Queens.

HELEN FRIED GOLDSTEIN: I was the best roller skater around. My mother gave me money to take the trolley to my piano lessons. I pocketed it and roller-skated all the way instead. How many times would I come to my piano teacher all out of breath, with a scraped knee. But what a great trip, so free and out in the open.

JOEL MARTIN: In the summer, my friend Warren and I rode our bikes at crazy speeds around Greenwood Cemetery. It was a wonderful place for bike riding—long and pretty and peaceful, with all those big trees. Some of the old gravestones went back hundreds of years. Occasionally, we would get chased by a caretaker or someone in uniform. We'd move out fast, not knowing what they would do to us if they caught us.

I biked only up to a certain point. I had boundaries in my mind. I knew there had to be a Seventeenth Avenue, an Eighteenth Avenue, but I never went past Sixteenth Avenue. Like the guys who sailed with Columbus, I always had this feeling that I would fall off the earth if I went beyond.

When I was about eleven, we ran away from home to Prospect Park, taking along boxes of sugar-coated cereal and a canteen of water. We stayed till one or two in the morning. When we got home, don't ask what happened. They beat the hell out of my friend. Me they just yelled at. My mother said, "Why didn't you tell us you were running away? I would have packed you a good lunch."

FRANCES BLUM: In the springtime, we spent nice Saturday or Sunday afternoons at Prospect Park. We went in one of my uncles' cars, or we met my aunt and cousins and took the train. There were different ways to enter the park. One way, we passed the band shell, and we'd stop off and listen to the band play marching music. Another way took us through the zoo. My aunt would bring along a wicker picnic basket lined with red checkered cloth that she filled with sandwiches and fruit. We brought along big blankets that we spread out on the great lawn. While the grown-ups lay down and relaxed, we ran around on the grass, or played ball. My mother would take us out on the lake in one of the swan boats. Sometimes my father or one of my uncles would rent a rowboat and let us try the oars.

WILLIAM CUNNINGHAM: Donnegal Hill, right near the main gate of Prospect Park off Flatbush Avenue, was named after a county in Ireland. On a Sunday it would be filled with people from all over Ireland. Kids would run up and down the hill, young people would meet and walk around.

JOE SIGLER: Prospect Park was my playground, my front yard and my backyard. When I looked out the window of our apartment, I saw the park, the trees, the grass. Right across the street were the toilets, in a nice big stone building. In those days custodians took care of it, and there was no graffiti. Right down the street, three blocks away, were the Parade Grounds, at the southernmost tip of the park. Everybody came there to play baseball.

A pair of crowd pleasers at the Prospect Park zoo.

MARTY ADLER: Officiated, organized league games were played at the Parade Grounds. There were all these leagues: Babe Ruth, Ty Cobb, Gowanus International. Koufax played there, the Aspromonte brothers, the Torre brothers.

CHARLES HYNES: The Parade Grounds were broken up into thirteen baseball fields. Diamond one and diamond thirteen were the major fields, because they were enclosed.

MARTY ADLER: You had to wear a uniform to play on fields one and thirteen. When I got to play there, it was the first time in my life I put on sanitary whites. My mother said, "You're putting socks on socks."

"That's the way they do it in the big leagues, Mom."

A family spending a blissful Sunday afternoon in Prospect Park.

JOE SIGLER: When I went to P.S. 92, on Parkside Avenue, the schools were crowded, and there were split sessions. If you had the morning session, it was great. We'd have lunch and then meet in Prospect Park. We'd race down the hills. We'd roller-skate on the asphalt-paved playground, play stickball, go look at the animals in the zoo. We rowed on the lake in the summer, ice-skated on it in the winter. When it snowed, we'd go sleigh riding down Lookout Mountain.

My aunt Florence had a brother Nat who was in the cavalry in the First World War. He decided his sons, Sid and George, and my cousin Jay and I should take riding lessons. We took indoor lessons every

Saturday for five dollars an hour in the winter, and by the spring we were riding the bridle paths in Prospect Park. We learned to handle the horses English-style. It was beautiful, but we weren't interested in the trees, only in how fast we could go without getting caught. There were mounted police to keep everybody calm, and the instructors were watching us. We couldn't go off by ourselves, but of course we tried to break away a little.

DORIS MODELL TIPOGRAPH: On Saturdays I took the train from Brighton Beach to Prospect Park wearing a beautiful riding outfit that I got from the Modell Riding Store in Manhattan. I'd rent a horse from the Black and White Stables and take the bridle path on Ocean Parkway, beginning at Prospect Park and going all the way down to Brighton Beach. When I reached the end, I'd turn the horse around and ride all the way back to Prospect Park. Then I'd buy a pretzel for a penny and an ice cream for a nickel, and take the subway back to the Brighton Beach stop.

JUDY BERGER: Riding horses through Prospect Park was pretty passive; we just followed the guide through the trails. I preferred roller skating at the Park Circle rink, right outside the park. They had organ music, and you rented shoe skates instead of the iron skates you used on the streets, the ones with keys that expanded as your feet grew. Of course, we'd have to wait outside on a long line for the two o'clock Saturday afternoon session, but it was worth it.

JOE SIGLER: Most Saturday afternoons, my aunt got rid of us by packing up lunches and candy bars and sending us to the movies. Within walking distance were the Flatbush Movie Theater (which also had big bands performing, and the last of the vaudeville acts) and the Kenmore on Flatbush Avenue, the Paramount, the Patio (which had fish ponds in the lobby), and the Parkside farther down. Near Erasmus Hall High School, there was the Astor, which showed foreign movies; past that, the Albemare; and past that, the Rialto. They were unbelievable: art deco, gorgeous.

HERBY GREISSMAN: My mother used to give me a dollar on Saturday afternoons to go to the Marboro Theater, on Bay Parkway. I walked up Sixty-fifth Street with my friends, and we would stop off at the delicatessen, where we each got a hot dog, a knish, and a soda. We got enough change from that for the movie and a piece of candy.

When they raised the price to get into the Marboro to twenty-six cents, a bunch of maybe ten guys would go, and one guy would go in for twenty-six cents. He'd go to the exit doors and open them, and all nine of us would run in and scatter in all different directions. The matron would come after us with her flashlight, but she couldn't run after everyone.

BILL FEIGENBAUM: Every Saturday we went to the Surf Theater, in Coney Island. We'd buy our candy before we went in because it was five cents in the candy store and seven cents in the theater. Admission was a quarter—fourteen cents during the week—for a main feature, a western, a newsreel, cartoons, and something called the weekly races, usually bicycle races. They used to give out free tickets based on having the right number on your stub. Howie Shumsky, whose big brother was the head usher, won all the time.

CHARLES HYNES: Because my mother was working, her drill most summer weekdays was to drop me off at the Beverly Movie Theater, on Church and McDonald, in the morning and pick me up after work. I think I knew every line in *Guadalcanal Diary*. On Wednesdays there was a drawing. Since I was there so often, I had more chances than others. Twice I got to go up on the stage and collect a Monopoly set.

ALAN BLANKSTEIN: The movie theaters were the first places to be air-conditioned. In the summer we stayed there the whole afternoon. I'd come out from the cold, dark theater into the blinding sunlight, and it felt like I was being hit by a brick of hot air.

FRANCES BLUM: I went with my friends to the Walker Theater, on Eighteenth Avenue, every Saturday. Then we'd come home and play the movie we had just seen. Once we saw Esther Williams and Ricardo Montalban in a movie about bullfighters. Sandra wanted to play Esther Williams. This one time I put up a fight: "I'm tired of playing the mother. I'm going to be Esther Williams."

KARL BERNSTEIN: In those days before television, our entertainment was from either the movies or the radio. My cousin Bill and I loved the radio mystery programs: *The Shadow* and *The Green Hornet*. There was a large brick fireplace in the basement of our house, and we spent countless hours tapping every brick in that fireplace, looking for one that would open the secret panel.

PETER NERO: My grandfather had a little tailor's shop right across the street from Junior High School 149, on Sutter and Vermont, and sometimes I'd bring a lunch from home and eat with him. But most of the time, I would run home and gobble down my sandwich. Neither of my parents were at home at that hour, and I had the radio all to myself. My friends also ran home to listen to the programs, and we compared notes.

MARVIN KAPLAN: I lived inside that radio tube. On Sunday night, there were all the comedy shows: Jack Benny, Fred Allen, Edgar Bergen and Charlie McCarthy, George Burns and Gracie Allen.

MIRIAM KITTRELL: The radio was on all the time. We had a big radio in the living room and a small one on the table in the kitchen. We'd be having dinner when Stan Lomax came on at 6:45, and there'd be a big silence. We lived for the Texaco broadcasts of the Metropolitan Opera on the radio on Saturday afternoons.

CAROLINE KATZ MOUNT: My father heard Ezio Pinza singing "This Nearly Was Mine" from *South Pacific* on the radio, and he couldn't get over how beautiful it was. He bought a new victrola with the 33⅓ LP speed just so he could play the record from that show. And then he decided we had to see it. That became a tradition. Every year, my mother, father, sister, and I, and usually a relative and friend or two, went to see a Broadway show. We saw *Kismet*, *The Pajama Game*, *Can-Can*. We went by subway to a Saturday matinee, and afterward we had a bite at Chock Full O'Nuts.

JULIE BUDD: My sister Jill took me to see my first Broadway show, *Fiddler on the Roof*. That was the beauty of it. We were two kids— Jill was thirteen and I was nine—and we just got on the subway, the

Number 2 express to Forty-second Street, and then got out and walked. I was so impressed that there were kids in it. After that we saw a whole bunch of shows, Broadway, off-Broadway.

BETTY COMDEN: My parents loved music, and we had the traditional records: the Caruso, the Galli-Curci, the Misha Elman. The Metropolitan Opera and the Philharmonic gave performances at the Brooklyn Academy of Music at that time, and that's where I saw my first opera, heard my first symphony. You could have a very rich cultural life without even going across the Brooklyn Bridge.

Our apartment on Park Place and Kingston Avenue, in the Bedford section, was opposite a small park where the Brooklyn Children's Museum is situated. At that time it was in an old Victorian building that was quite wonderful. It had a library, stuffed animals and birds, wonderful dioramas of different periods of history, rooms depicting the way people lived. They showed old silent movies. Since it was right across the street, I went there all the time.

JOE SIGLER: One of my favorite places in Brooklyn was the library at Grand Army Plaza. I was always reading, always curious, and that library had every book, every magazine that you would want. Often I went there all by myself, and then I'd go over to the Brooklyn Museum, which is right down the street. That was another world. The Flatbush Avenue trolley car dropped me off right in front of the library, and in those days it was a nickel. I could have taken the subway, but with the trolley you could see things.

JOEL BERGER: I could take the trolley or the bus, but usually I took the Brighton line and switched to the Franklin Avenue Shuttle to get to my favorite place in all of Brooklyn: Ebbets Field. I'd walk out of the train station, and immediately I'd be hit by the aroma of baking bread from the Taystee factory. It would follow me all the way to the ballpark. I'd see the crowds descending, hear the yelling and screaming, and smell the bread—a total sensory experience.

CHARLES HYNES: We got off at the Prospect Station of the BMT to go to Ebbets Field. The voice of the guy selling programs would get stronger as we came closer: "The Dodgers are going to win. . . . The Dodgers are going to win."

JOE SIGLER: We'd walk seven long blocks on the other side of the Botanic Garden to Ebbets Field and wait outside the main gate. Friday was businessman's night. If a businessman had tickets for somebody who didn't show up, he'd give them to us kids. And not only that, he'd treat us so nice—buy us hot dogs, soda.

DICK KITTRELL: Our apartment house, on President and Bedford, was so close to Ebbets Field, we snuck in on a regular basis. We dearly loved the Dodgers, except when people who drove to the games parked their cars on our block and interfered with our punchball games. There were no parking lots around Ebbets Field, so people had to park in the streets.

AL LEWIS: I was a great walker and would walk home from Ebbets Field on Bedford Avenue, straight down Eastern Parkway to Brownsville. You know what kind of a walk that is? But when the Dodgers won, it wasn't walking. It was flying.

What did I want when I was a kid? I wanted the Dodgers to win the pennant.

JOEL BERGER: During the 1950 baseball season, the Philadelphia Whiz Kids took the lead and were holding on. The Dodgers were something like seven games out with nine games to play. There was a doubleheader; I didn't get to hear it, but the Dodgers won both and picked up a game and a half. The next day, again I didn't get to hear the game, and again they won, and the Phillies lost. This convinced me if I had anything to do with the game, it would be a loss. But if I did not hear it, the Dodgers would win.

The pressure started to mount. The Phillies came into Ebbets Field for the last two games of the season. If the Dodgers won, they'd win the pennant. Everybody, everywhere was listening to the game. But

The elaborate interior of one of Brooklyn's movie palaces. INSET: A pretty pose before a double-feature billboard.

LEFT: That great little bandbox of a ball park where so many "waited for next year."

RIGHT: The Brooklyn Dodgers in their glory when "next year" finally arrived.

I went to the movies. There I was with a bunch of old women in the Claridge Movie Theater on Avenue P. I came out:

"What happened?"

"The Dodgers won."

The last game, I went to the Kingsway Movie Theater. That was the game in which Cal Abrams was thrown out at the plate. At least I knew I was not responsible.

Why was I a Dodger fan? Naturally, all the good people were Dodger fans. If a guy was a Yankee fan, you knew he was a nerd, out of touch. He was probably anti-union, not for good causes, had a rich uncle somewhere. If someone was a Giant fan, he was mixed up, like an anarchist, a nihilist—he was doing it to spite his family, his friends. A Giant fan. Who could be a Giant fan? Dodger fans were the salt of the earth, the common folk who believed in social progress, the American way, the underdog. Where did Jackie Robinson come to if not to Brooklyn? The Dodgers lived in Brooklyn. They could be your neighbors. You actually got to see them out of uniform, on the streets, doing things ordinary people did.

CLEM LABINE: After the kids were out of school, my family came down, and we rented a house in Bay Ridge. Quite a few of the Dodger contingent lived in that area: Pee Wee Reese, Duke Snider, Carl Erskine, Russ Meyer. Preacher Roe lived in the Seventies. Gil Hodges lived on Bedford Avenue.

BILL FEIGENBAUM: We used to see Gil Hodges on the way to junior high school. We saw him wash his car. His wife complained to the principal to please have the kids stop coming around.

JOEL MARTIN: Walking by Gil Hodges's house on Bedford Avenue, we'd jump up and try to look in the windows, which we never could; or walk back and forth; or stand across the street for hours waiting for someone to come out.

MAX WECHSLER: When school was out, I sometimes went with my father in his taxi. One summer morning, we were driving in East Flatbush, down Snyder Avenue, when he pointed out a dark red brick house with a high porch. "I think Jackie Robinson lives there," he said. He parked across the street, and we got out of the cab, stood on the sidewalk, and looked at it.

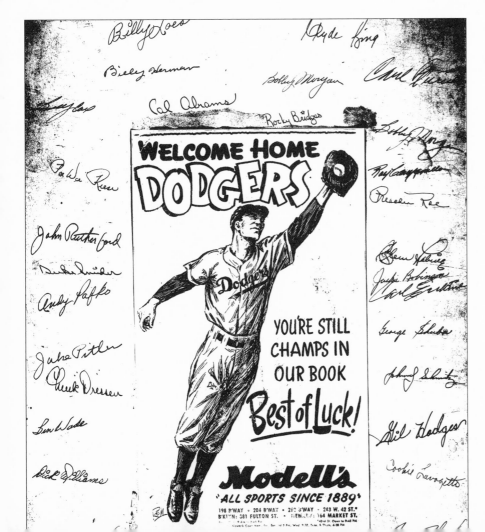

Suddenly the front door opened. A black man in a short-sleeved shirt stepped out. I didn't believe it. Here we were on a quiet street on a summer morning. No one else was around. This man was not wearing the baggy, ice-cream-white uniform of the Brooklyn Dodgers that accentuated his blackness. He was dressed in regular clothes, coming out of a regular house in a regular Brooklyn neighborhood, a guy like anyone else, going for a newspaper or a bottle of milk.

Then incredibly, he crossed the street and came right toward me. Seeing that unmistakable pigeon-toed walk, the rock of the shoulders and hips I had seen so many times on the baseball field, I had no doubt who it was.

"Hi Jackie, I'm one of your biggest fans," I said self-consciously. "Do you think the Dodgers are gonna win the pennant this year?"

His handsome face looked sternly down at me. "We'll try our best," he said.

"Good luck," I said.

"Thanks." He put his big hand out, and I took it. We shook hands, and I felt the strength and firmness of his grip.

I was a nervy kid, but I didn't ask for an autograph or think to prolong the conversation. I just watched as he walked away down the street.

HERBY GREISSMAN: It was a tremendous treat if my father would give up his time and take me to a baseball game. Once we were next to a priest. My father struck up a conversation with him, and he ended up buying beers for everyone in the whole area. There was that kind of feeling at Ebbets Field. Except when the Giants came. Then it was war.

STEWIE STONE: It was like your father's a Democrat, you're a Democrat. My father was a Giants fan, I was a Giants fan. Sal Maglie to me was scary, with that beard. But I loved him; he was a Giant. Until they traded him to the Dodgers. Then I hated him.

It was great to argue with the kids in the neighborhood because they were all Dodger fans. If the Giants lost, they would all come into the alley and yell up to my window, "Hey Stewie, we really got you today, ha-ha-ha." When Bobby Thomson hit the home run that gave the Giants the pennant in 1951, I ran down the street to my father's dance studio to tell him. I was the only one in the street who was happy. Brooklyn was dead.

JOHN DOWNIE: It was the rare kid in Brooklyn who wasn't a Dodger fan. They knew everything about them, felt so close to them they called them by nicknames: Oisk for Erskine, Skoonj for Furillo, Ski for Hermanski, Cookie for Harry Lavagetto.

MAX WECHSLER: In those days, before baseball encyclopedias and readily available stats, baseball knowledge came from newspapers, scorecards, baseball cards. The facts were stored in our heads. On the steamy summer nights, we played all kinds of baseball word games. "Initials" was a game where one guy would stand on the top of the stoop, and a bunch of kids on the sidewalk would shout out initials: "JR" (Jackie Robinson), "VR" (Vic Raschi)—that was the easy stuff. The more rabid baseball types would have a supply of the same initials for different players and would fire them off to the kid on the stoop: "DL" (Don Liddle), "DL again" (Dick Littlefield). One set of initials referred to fourteen players. Then there were the variations. One was "reverse initials": "RJ" (Ransom Jackson, John Roseboro). Another was replacing initials with nicknames. Virtually every Dodger player had a nickname. "The Reading Rifle" (Carl Furillo), "Shotgun" (George Shuba). In another version, "geog-raphy," you'd shoot off the name of a town, and the guy on the stoop had to name the player who came from there. The kid on the stoop was on top, he was king of the hill, and the ones below had to stump him to knock him off. If he missed, he was out, and someone from the sidewalk took his place. We played for hours and for pennies. But it wasn't for pennies, it was for pride. Growing up in Brooklyn, you were nobody if you couldn't show off your baseball knowledge.

School Days

**REMEMBER THE ROW,
REMEMBER THE SEAT,
REMEMBER THE WAY
WE USED TO CHEAT.**

—Autograph album, P.S. 226

CAROLINE KATZ MOUNT: Every spring, my father was worried and unhappy. He was a furrier, and that was his slack season. But one spring morning when I was seven years old and he was at home because there was no work, he decided to walk me to school. Our neighbor Frieda leaned out her kitchen window, which faced the street. We stopped off to say good morning, and my father said, "Look how pretty Caroline is." He held my hand all the way, down the block and around the corner, past the two-family houses with their neat front gardens. Then we crossed Sixty-fifth Street and walked by the big empty lot that was filled with spiky little daisies and dandelions and other wildflowers. All the children were walking to school this beautiful morning, carrying their books; the boys fooling around, the girls giggling with each other. And there I was in a little white sun dress with red flowers and a matching jacket, walking hand-in-hand with my father, who suddenly seemed very happy.

JOAN RIBAUDO: There were no school buses, and no one was driven to school by car. You'd see a march of mothers with children in hand, walking to school.

STEWIE STONE: You'd meet kids along the way, wait on the corner for your friends from down the block. Everybody would gather and walk together in a little crowd. If during the school day it started to rain, the mothers showed up at dismissal with umbrellas and galoshes.

BOB LEVY: P.S. 161 was directly across from our apartment on Crown Street. Our living room faced the schoolyard. I was in that schoolyard every Saturday and Sunday morning at 7:00 A.M., because if you didn't get there early you weren't chosen into the games. But school days, I had to walk all the way down to the corner and wait to be crossed by the crossing guard. I was late every day.

MIRIAM KITTRELL: P.S. 177, on Avenue P and West First Street, was typical of the schools built in the 1920s: four or five stories, dark red brick. The roof was enclosed by some kind of iron latticework, like a big dome. On nice days we had gym classes up there, and when we looked out, we could see as far as the parachute at Coney Island.

My mother took me to kindergarten class the first day of school and saw the children playing. "What do the children do here?" she asked.

"They play, and they learn," the teacher told her.

"Play? She could play at home," said my mother.

I never went to kindergarten.

Out of the classroom but still in uniform, elementary school teachers enjoy moments of rare repose.

CAROLINE KATZ MOUNT: My sister started school before me. I was terribly jealous. My first day, my mother and I walked up this great marble staircase. It was so beautiful. We went into the principal's office. I said, "What's my teacher's name?"

The woman said, "If I tell you, will you say good morning to her?"

I said, "Of course." It was funny because my mother was very quiet, and I was four and a half years old. But I felt very much at home. There was nothing scary about it.

Yet, at the same time, school *was* scary. The teachers could be intimidating; they had so much power. In first grade, my job was to set the table in the back of the room. I kept forgetting which was my right and which was my left, and sometimes I put the fork on the right side. One day the teacher yelled at me, "If you do this one more time, you'll lose this job." The next day was the only day in my life that I played hooky. I told my mother I had a stomachache, because I was so afraid I would not remember which was my right and which my left. Later, when I banged my finger in the door and one of my right nails became misshapen, I was glad, because now I had a sign for which was my right.

MARNIE BERNSTEIN: In the second grade, I had a teacher who had just come into the school. Mrs. Winters was young, tall, and attractive, but I felt there was something cold about her. One afternoon, we were lined up to leave, standing along the wardrobe wall, and my friend Ruthie said to me, "You called me a lucky dog." I said, "I did not." Mrs. Winters heard me talking, and she made me get off the line and go back to my seat. "You wait there till I come back," she said. She marched out with the other children, and I remained behind.

Back then, I was very much afraid of being left alone, and there I was, all alone, I thought, in the whole school. It was very quiet.

I must have panicked, because I bolted from the room and raced down the single flight of stairs and out the door. My mother was waiting for me by the schoolyard gate with my sister in the baby carriage, puzzled by why I wasn't there with the rest of the class. Mrs. Winters was nearby, seeing the children off. When she noticed me, she came over and made some kind of explanation to my mother. There was never anything said or done about it afterward. But for Christmas, my father bought Mrs. Winters a box of handkerchiefs. She was very nice to me after that.

CAROLINE KATZ MOUNT: I wore glasses, and in fourth grade, the teacher sat us alphabetically. I ended up in the back and told her I couldn't see the board from there, but she didn't seem to care. My mother wrote her a note, and she still didn't do anything. Finally, my mother went to see her. "Of course we'll change her seat," the teacher said. "You know, we teachers are not monsters."

In sixth grade, our teacher taught us to make an *X* without lifting the pen. There was a little boy from Czechoslovakia in our class, and one time she chided him for lifting his pen. He said, "But Mrs. Fisher, you do it." And she said, "I do not. Do I, class?" We all said, "No, Mrs. Fisher." But we lied. She did lift her pen. We were afraid to tell the truth.

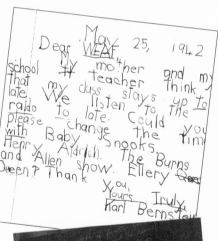

DORIS MODELL TIPOGRAPH: P.S. 99—"It stands for all that's helpful and everything that's fine"—was on East Tenth between Avenues K and L. In the eighth grade, all the girls had to sew their graduation dresses. I had gotten this beautiful organza material at Namm-Loeser's, but I had trouble sewing the French seams. You had to stitch it, turn it over, and stitch it again. So my grandmother did the first stitching on the machine, and I did the other stitching by hand. Miss McCarthy, my gray-haired, pinched-faced teacher, who always wore black, examined my work and spotted the machine stitch. She made me stand in front of the whole class while she ripped the dress open.

JUDY BERGER: Woody Allen named the character Mia Farrow played in *Zelig* after Eudora Fletcher, the principal of P.S. 99, and the photographer in the movie after the husband of Mrs. Degay, who taught sixth grade. Miss Fletcher must have been at P.S. 99 for forty years. She wore bolero-type jackets with frog fasteners. Her hair was pulled back into not one but two buns. She ruled that school with an iron fist. All the teachers were in fear of her.

MARNIE BERNSTEIN: P.S. 177 was run like a military academy. It was right after the war, so that was the influence. We were put through marching drills: right-face, left-face, mark time in place. The whole system of student monitors was based on the military. There were the line and stair guards, and then the officers: sergeant, lieutenant, and captain; separate sets for boys and girls. We had badges. It was a prestigious thing to be in the guards, and most prestigious to be one of the officers. I was Sergeant of the Girl Guards in the sixth grade and got to blow a whistle and say, "On line!" and the kids had to assemble on lines. And then we'd say, "Lines forward," and the lines would proceed from the gym or, in nice weather, the yard to their classrooms—in total silence. If you spoke, one of the guards might spot you and give you a Guard Report, which was noted on your Permanent Record. I was never quite sure what the Permanent Record was, but I knew it was something very significant that would stay with you for your entire life.

TOBY SCHOM GROSSMAN: The times I felt bad at school were when they did census reports. This woman would go around to each class and say, "Anybody not born in the United States, please stand up." I was usually the only one.

STAN GOLDBERG: Unlike a lot of my friends' parents, both my parents were born here. In fifth grade, when my mother came up on Open School Day, the teacher said to her, "I'm surprised to see you're one of the American mothers. From your son's handwriting, I'd never know it."

MARNIE BERNSTEIN: Many of us were first-generation Americans, and we were given strong doses of patriotic indoctrination. We sang songs like "Columbia the Gem of the Ocean," "Our Flag Is the Flag for Me," and "This Is My Country." Assemblies began with a color guard processional, with one of the bigger boys carrying a huge American flag set into a holder strapped around his waist.

Miss Harrington was the assistant principal of P.S. 177. She had silver hair that was perfectly waved and wore a lace handkerchief pulled through her wristwatch. "I wish I had a camera so I could take a photograph of you," she would tell us as she stood on the stage of the auditorium, with a picture of George Washington on one side and Abraham Lincoln on the other. We were dressed all alike for assembly day: girls in white middy blouses with red ties and navy pleated skirts, boys in white shirts, red ties, and navy pants.

LONNY IRGENS: I felt the sense of being American through the assemblies every Thursday. I loved singing the patriotic songs and dressing up in red, white, and blue.

MARNIE BERNSTEIN: Each assembly, one class put on a play, and another class did a choral reading of a psalm. In addition to the patriotic songs, we sang a lot of hymns: "The Lord's Prayer," "The Lord Is My Shepherd" set to music, and "We Gather Together" at Thanksgiving. We also sang all the Christmas carols, even though at least half the children were Jewish. But no one seemed to mind.

ANGELO BADALAMENTI: All the teachers at P.S. 177 loved my playing of "Argonnaise." It was my piece, one of the numbers I performed regularly at assemblies. But one day, in the middle of the piece, I looked up into the auditorium and saw all the kids, all the white shirts and middy blouses and red ties, and I stopped. "I can't perform," I said, and ran out of the auditorium crying. Mrs. Doyle, my sixth-grade teacher, came after me. "Angelo, you have to go back," she said. She wouldn't let me give it up. The next week, I went back, played it through, and got a standing ovation.

Every morning I would walk up to the corner and wait for Mrs. Mary Doyle. She'd come down Avenue P from the Stillwell Avenue

**P.S. 177, the school run like
a military academy.**

bus stop, passing my corner at 8:20 A.M. We would walk the next seven blocks to school together, talking about this and that. She was very Irish, not terribly warm in her approach. But I loved her.

MIRIAM KITTRELL: Many of the teachers were Irish women. There was Miss O'Donald the art teacher, Miss Williams, Mrs. Cunningham, Mrs. Doyle. After I graduated and moved on, I realized they all wore the Hunter College ring. And they all loved baseball and the Brooklyn Dodgers. World Series time they would bring in radios, and we would stop classes to listen to the games.

"The teachers knew their job. Whatever they said was right."

JUDY BERGER: Sometimes the whole game was broadcast over the PA. At the very least, we'd get the score at the end of each half-inning.

MAX WECHSLER: Nobody could take my job away during World Series time: putting the score up, half-inning by half-inning, on the blackboard. I'd get the boards ready by washing them with water and black ink, so the chalk would show off, and I'd use two different colors to distinguish between the Dodgers and the Yankees. That gave the teachers something nice to say about me when my mother came up on Open School Night.

MIRIAM KITTRELL: My parents did not come on Open School nights. They didn't want to be bothered. The teachers knew their job. Whatever they said was right. I just had to bring home a good report card. PTA meetings—forget it. I had to pay the dues myself. The teachers used to make us crazy. They had to have 100 percent PTA so they could hang up those pennants in the window of the classroom door. I used to save up the nickels I got to buy Mounds bars to pay the dues.

JOEL BERGER: In first grade, the teacher sat behind the piano and called you up one at a time to sing while she played a little song. You were pronounced either a robin or a sparrow—a singer or a listener—a judgment that followed you all through elementary school. Most of the people I knew were listeners.

IRWIN POLISHOOK: I was a sparrow. I didn't sing. But I would whistle a lot.

GAIL EISEMAN BERNSTEIN: I was a P.S. 181 listener. I couldn't carry a tune. I also have a dead ear. The robins sang, "Remember your name and address and telephone number too. . . ." or "Let the ball roll, let the ball roll no matter where it may go. . . ." We learned a lot of those safety songs. The teacher walked around the room. "One of the robins or sparrows is not doing what he or she is supposed to," she said, trying to catch the singing sparrow. That was me. When she came near, I shut up. As soon as she moved on, I sang along, off-key.

MARNIE BERNSTEIN: We were three robins who regularly sang the same songs, party after party, term after term. I did the World War II ballad "Mamselle." Ruthie Freedman, a dynamic little brunette, did "The Rich Maharaja of Macador," and Barbara Sanders—who was cool, blonde, and beautiful even in fourth grade—sang "Ah, Sweet Mystery of Life" in a lovely, lyric soprano voice.

Mrs. Marcus, who played the piano for all the assemblies, was our fifth-grade teacher. She was tall and pretty and wore her short dark hair in what they used to call the feather-cut. She dressed in "New Look" outfits—long, swirly skirts and blouses with ruffles around the neck and sleeves. For Christmas, we put on a musical play in which the children represented toys from all over the world. Barbara Sanders was the nurse doll, Ruthie Freedman was the French doll in gorgeous pink organza, and I was the Dutch doll in an authentic costume—courtesy of the Netherlands Board of Trade—right down to the clunky wooden shoes.

ANGELO BADALAMENTI: Emma Marcus was the wife of Colonel Mickey Marcus, the only American buried at West Point who died in the service of another country. He was killed in the Israeli War of

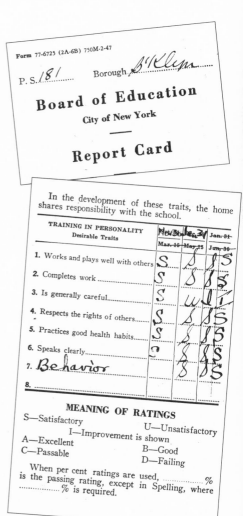

Independence. I remember reading about it in the papers that morning, and when I came into class, there she was with all the other teachers around her, hugging her and crying.

MARNIE BERNSTEIN: Mrs. Conan was another music teacher, and a great lover of Gilbert and Sullivan. In sixth grade, we had club periods. She was in charge of the glee club. For graduation, we put on *The Pirates of Penzance*. Imagine, an operetta in elementary school.

BETTY COMDEN: I went to a wonderful school that no longer exists: the Brooklyn Ethical Culture School, begun by the people who started the Ethical Culture Society. They were pacifists, gentle and wonderful people. The school was new when I entered at the age of five. I was in the first class. They added a class every year, so I was always in the top class. The school was across the street from Prospect Park, on Prospect Park West and First Street. We did our athletics in the park and had spring festivals there. We didn't celebrate Christmas or Easter, since this was an ecumenical school. Instead we had a winter festival, a spring festival—like Old England: yule logs, that kind of thing.

We were encouraged to express ourselves. I was excused from arithmetic if I felt like writing a poem. We studied things in themes. If it was Greek history, for example, we had a Greek festival, studied Greek art and literature. One teacher I remember clearly, Delia Stebbens, encouraged us to take different books and dramatize them. I did *Ivanhoe*.

JOE SIGLER: I had tough, motivating teachers in elementary school. We had to read "The News of the Week in Review" in *The New York Times* every Sunday, and we were tested on it every Monday. For the most part, the teachers lived in the neighborhood. They had a neighborhood interest in us. It was like a small town in that way. You didn't cut school, because someone would see you and tell your parents; you couldn't go to the movies, because no kid was allowed in the movies until after three o'clock.

KARL BERNSTEIN: When he discovered I could play the cello, Mr. Levy drafted me into the Seth Low Junior High School orchestra. It was made up of thirty trumpets, four violins, a clarinet, and now, a cello. Mr. Levy played the violin and conducted at the same time. The setup offended me. I spent the better part of my two and a half years at Seth Low hiding from him. In front of my class, he would say I had no school spirit.

P S 181 BKLYN
KG AM
JAN 1946

STAN GOLDBERG: The black teacher on the TV show *Brooklyn Bridge* is modeled after Mr. Webb, who was an English teacher and later an assistant principal at Seth Low Junior High. Here we were, all white, mostly Jewish kids, and our two role models were Mr. Webb and Jackie Robinson.

CAROLINE KATZ MOUNT: Mr. Webb was so smart, he made literature so exciting. Also, he was much younger than most of the other teachers, and tall and thin—a handsome, elegant man.

I was active in student government at Seth Low, and Arnold Webb was the faculty advisor. It was the time of Little Rock. We had a meeting in the principal's office about it. We must have had an assembly program or some kind of protest, but all I remember is wondering whether Mr. Webb wasn't embarrassed over the whole situation. Here we were so concerned that something bad was going on in Little Rock. Yet nobody seemed to notice that aside from Mr. Webb, there wasn't one black person in the whole school.

CLARENCE NORMAN, SR.: I moved up from a small town near Fort Bragg, North Carolina, to the Williamsburg section of Brooklyn. I really suffered from culture shock coming from a segregated southern school to P.S. 122, on Harrison Avenue, which was nearly all white.

The children were friendly. The teachers, who were all white, were friendly too. They really bent over backward to try to involve me. They made me a hall monitor. Needless to say, the entire time I was in elementary school, I got As in conduct. I was the nicest kid in class, but I was very unhappy. The first summer I went back to North Carolina with the intention of remaining. It had been too much of a sudden change, going from a small rural farming community to Brooklyn. But the irony was that after the summer, I realized that I liked Brooklyn more than I thought I did. I actually begged my mother to bring me back.

ROGER GREEN: I always felt, from first grade on, very oppressed and repressed in the public school system. When I attended P.S. 44, on Madison Street in Bedford-Stuyvesant, all the kids were black, but the whole power structure was white except for one African-American teacher. The class categorizations in the school were almost always color-conscious even within the context of an African-American population. We had 1-A, which might have been the smartest, and those children were the lightest-skinned, etc. When I went to P.S. 221 in Crown Heights and Winthrop Junior High School, it was the same kind of thing: the white students were always in the smarter classes and the black students in the so-called slower classes. It really implanted in the minds of some of the children this subliminal message that you're just not as bright.

I took the IQ exam and scored poorly on it. As a result of that one test, they wanted to put me in one of the slower classes. My mother was a fighter, and she challenged it. She said, "I don't know if one test can determine intelligence. At home he's reading everything. Maybe he just can't take tests."

CLARENCE NORMAN, SR.: I was sent to George Washington Vocational High School because it appeared on paper, from my test scores and grades, that I might have been rather slow, that I was not college material. I was looked upon as one of those children who was going to be a failure. The best thing for me, according to the guidance counselors, was to take up a vocational trade. I was to be relegated to the trash pile. What did I say about it? I felt they were the experts. They knew more about what was best for me than I did.

ROGER GREEN: I was in the second or third grade when some young folks broke into the school building, got into an office, and stole some materials. The following week, my class was getting ready to go on a trip when I was pulled out of the class line and sent into a classroom where there were three white police officers. At first I wasn't scared, because I didn't know what it was about. But I will never forget it. They sat me down, surrounded me, and were very abusive, shouting and cursing. It frightened me very much. I told my father, and he was very upset. He came up to the school and challenged the principal and the teacher. He said if there was any question as to whether I had done anything wrong, he should have been notified.

What happened was that a student in what we would now define as a Special Ed class had said I was part of the group that broke into the school. It was interesting because he was in Special Ed because, among other things, he was visually impaired. Earlier I had been in the playground when some kids were belittling and demeaning him. Now I have a clear understanding of the anger and frustration that he must have felt. At that time, though, I was so traumatized that for about two to three weeks I played hooky. My parents didn't know.

PAT COOPER: The teacher at P.S. 242 said, "All right, Pasquale, get up here. Tell us about Christopher Columbus." I got up in front of the room. "The guy had bloomers on," I said. I made Christopher Columbus so funny that she hit me.

Your father and mother always found out. "Did you say Christopher Columbus wore bloomers? What kind of respect is that?" my father said.

Next day, I'd be black and blue. "What happened?" the teacher asked.

If all the boys were across the sea
What a swimmer Jail would be

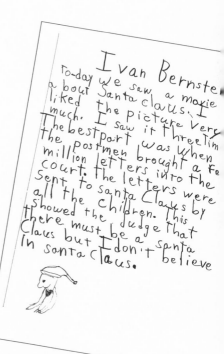

Ivan Bernste[...]
To-day we saw a movie about Santa claus. I liked the picture very much. I saw it three Tim[...] The best part was when the postmen brought a fe[...] million letters into the court. the letters were sent to santa claus by all the children. This showed the judge that there must be a santa Claus but I don't believe In santa Claus.

CLASS
OF
JUNE 1952
P.S. 181
6-1

"My father threw me out the window."

"Oh," she said. "OK."

"Just make sure the teacher don't call me to come to school and I lose a day's work," my father would say. "Or I'll electrocute you. Get a chair, a nice wire, and boom!"

ANNETTE DE LUCIA-CLARK: In the late 1950s, when my parents separated, we moved from the Bronx to the fourteen-story Gowanus Housing Project at 417 Baltic Street. We didn't live well in the Bronx, but moving to the projects in Brooklyn was going down in the world.

My older sister and I were placed in the CRMD class at P.S. 6 —that's for children with mental and medical disabilities. We shared the same clothes even though she was larger than me. Nothing ever fit. The clothes would be basted, or I'd wear a belt around the waist, or a rope. At night we'd wash what I wore, take out the basting, and my sister would wear it the next day. Most of the time at school we slept on cots and did recess. Miss Henry, one of the good teachers there, taught arts and crafts to a class of forty. She taught us how to sew. Guys would ask, "What do we need this for?" And she would tell them, "One of these days you'll thank me for giving you a skill." Some of those guys became tailors. Some of those girls became seamstresses.

The Catholic church felt we shouldn't be in that type of surrounding. St. Agnes Church, on Hoyt Street, took us for a year. Sister Margaret seemed very tall, but I was only four-foot-nine, and anyone seemed tall to me. One day she took a young man who was causing trouble, threw him against the wall, and beat him up. But she did not terrify me. What could scare me? I was a prisoner of life.

CHARLES HYNES: I went to Immaculate Heart of Mary, on Caton Avenue and East Third. I used to think the street was named after Father Caton, the pastor. We were taught by the St. Joseph sisters, who wore the old traditional habit and were very strict. Sister Jeanne DeLourdes, who taught fifth grade, hit very hard. I complained to my mother. But even though she was so protective she took me to and from school every day, she let the sister complete whatever discipline cycle was started. My mother's youngest sister had died shortly after her birth, and Sister Jeanne would have been the same age, which is maybe why my mother became very fond of her. By the time I left Immaculate Heart, in sixth grade, Sister Jeanne had become a fixture in our family.

TOM BOORAS: We were parishioners of St. Charles Borromeo, on Sydney Place in Brooklyn Heights, and I attended its grammar school, which was directly across from our house. I was taught by the sisters, who wore the long black habits and covered their hair with big winged headdresses.

Under their capes, they carried little metal castanets, the kind you used to get as prizes in Cracker Jack boxes. The class would go into church and all the kids would be finding seats in the pews, and you'd hear this *CLICK*. Everyone froze. *CLICK* again. Everyone stood up. *CLICK* one more time. Everyone genuflected. The nuns were very big on group discipline. They liked it when everybody did the same thing at the exact same time.

They were also big on penmanship. Your handwriting had to have this perfect slant. And if you were a lefty, forget it. To this day I write with my right hand although I was born a lefty. While we practiced our penmanship, the nuns would walk up and down the aisle with a ruler. You'd sense this black figure hovering over you as you struggled to get the correct slant. Sometimes you'd get a smack right across your knuckles. What for? You didn't dot your *i*.

But out in the yard, the sisters were terrific. We were seven, eight years old; they were twenty-two, twenty-three. They played everything with us: basketball, volleyball, handball. And some of them were great athletes. Running across the court with their big habits flapping around, the sleeves of their capes wide as wings, they looked to me like giant black birds.

A bevy of "little brides" dressed for their first communion.

JOAN RIBAUDO: Two o'clock on Wednesday afternoons, we were dismissed from P.S. 247 to go to St. Anthanasius for religious instruc-

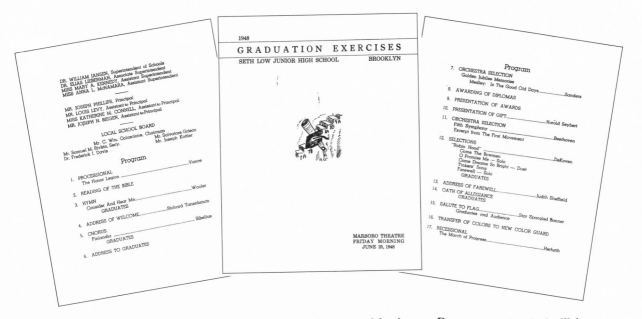

tion. We were maybe twenty kids running the fourteen blocks up Bay Parkway to get there on time. No matter what the weather—there could be four inches of snow, our feet could be frostbitten—we made sure we got there before the bell.

The reason was the principal. She'd stand in the doorway—a stern, short woman, no more than five feet tall. Behind her, the hallway was dark. All you would see was this little figure in the black habit with a ruler in her hand. If you came late, she'd give you a whack across the knuckles with the ruler.

We had only one hour of religious instruction a week in preparation for our communion and confirmation. There weren't too many explanations given or answers to questions. Whatever it said in the Bible, that was it.

I could never understand why so many of the nuns had men's names, like Sister Thomas Aquinas. They took saints' names, I guess, because they sounded holier than their own. Some of them were nice, though. One was young, very sweet to everyone. She used to tell us to be on our best behavior when she thought the principal was roaming the halls. She didn't want to get reprimanded either.

My communion was on a beautiful spring day. There were over a hundred of us, little brides dressed in white dresses and veils. The custom was that after your communion, your parents presented you with a little bouquet of nosegays. But I remember coming out of the church and seeing my father, his arms filled with a massive bouquet of orange gladioli. I ran over to him, and he put this enormous beautiful bouquet in my arms. It was almost as big as I was, and I thought to myself, "Look at this. Aren't I swell?"

Seth Low Junior High School's 1948 graduation ceremony included the transfer of the colors to the new color guard.

CHAPTER 3

Look, Ma, I'm Dancing!

PLAY IT ON THE PIANO,
BANG IT ON THE DRUM,
LOOK OUT, MISTER,
HERE I COME.
—Jump-rope rhyme

KARL BERNSTEIN: All over Brooklyn there were kids banging away on pianos, blowing horns, scratching out melodies on violins, singing up and down the scales: "do-re-mi-fa-sol-la-ti-do."

NORMAN SPIZZ: Every kid on my block played an instrument. When you walked down the block after school was out, you would hear them all at the same time: trumpets, saxophones, clarinets, drums, pianos, accordions, cellos, violins—each playing something different. I took up the trumpet. The very first song I learned was "You Belong to Me."

LARRY STRICKLER: The immigrant parents wanted to enhance their children's lives and believed that culture was the way. Not that they wanted their children to become artists or musicians; they wanted them to become doctors and lawyers. But they had a picture of a successful person, and that included culture.

FREDDIE GERSHON: My mother bought an old upright piano for a dollar. I picked out the melody of "Buttons and Bows," which I'd heard in a Bob Hope movie. I was able to get it because the melody is the five black notes. My mother thought Mozart had been reborn in her home. A local music teacher was not good enough for me—I had to go to Juilliard.

NEIL SEDAKA: I was fascinated with an accordion that one of my uncles brought back from the war. When I was in the second grade, I was picked to lead the class in singing, and the teacher told my mother she thought I had musical talent. Then my mother saw I could play melodies by ear on a neighbor's piano. So when I was eight years old, I started taking piano lessons, together with my sister. We practiced on Myra Auerbach's piano in her sixth-floor apartment. But after a while, my mother got a job as a saleswoman at A & S for a year and made enough money to buy me a secondhand piano.

I practiced the piano five hours a day. I loved it. I was a shy and introverted kid. I didn't play ball, I was always playing music. I planned to be a concert pianist. After my first year of lessons, my teacher said I was too advanced for him and that I should go to a school that could really develop my talent. So my mother started taking me on the subway up to Juilliard every Saturday.

FREDDIE GERSHON: I'm not sure I would have stayed at Juilliard if not for my buddy Neil Sedaka. After a while, we started traveling alone, and every Saturday became an adventure. Neil was so small and frail-looking that he actually was able to get in under the turnstile and not pay the nickel to get on the BMT. We counted stops on the train. Sometimes we stood in the front car and watched the tracks and lights. But mainly we looked at faces to keep ourselves occupied. We tried to imagine who each person was and made up stories about them.

PETER NERO: I picked out tunes on a one-octave toy xylophone my parents bought me—which probably cost eight cents in those days. At night, I'd sing myself to sleep tapping on the bed with my knuckles. I did not come face-to-face with a piano until I was seven years old. We were visiting a relative, and I just started to play on their upright the way I had played the xylophone. My grandmother convinced the relatives they didn't need the piano anymore. It barely fit into our apartment.

When I was seven, my father bought a forty-year-old reconditioned Steinway on the advice of a teacher for one hundred dollars. We lived in a four-family, two-story dwelling, and it was impossible to get the piano up the stairs. It had to be hoisted up to the second floor by a lift anchored on the roof of the building.

From the time I was seven until I was eleven, my father went with me for my lessons every Saturday. We took the subway to either the Grand Army Plaza station or Kingston Avenue. After, we visited the Brooklyn Botanic Garden, the Brooklyn Museum, Prospect Park. I don't know how many pictures were taken of me as a child in Prospect Park. In 1945, at age eleven, I made my official concert debut at the Brooklyn Academy of Music.

ROBERT MERRILL: My mother wanted me to grow up and be a big fat opera singer. She was careful of what I ate. In those days they would buy boiled beef on the bone. She'd not only have the beef, she'd make a big soup with the marrow of the bone melted in. It was quite nourishing. My mother could feed my kid brother, my father, and me for five bucks a week.

We lived in a tenement flat in Williamsburg with no heat except from the stove. My mother didn't like me breathing the polluted air; she thought it would harm my voice. She gave a tugboat captain a couple of dollars to take me out on the water with him so I could breathe the fresh air of the East River.

She sang around professionally under the name of Lillian Miller. She brought music into the home, got a piano for peanuts that someone was throwing out. Once she borrowed a hand-pumped Victrola and got a Caruso recording. I used to shut the windows when she put those records on, so my friends downstairs wouldn't hear. They would have

"All over Brooklyn, there were kids banging away on pianos, blowing horns, scratching out melodies on violins, singing up and down the scales."

called me a fag, because listening to classical music was considered a sissy thing to do. But when I listened to "O sole mio" or "Vesti la giubba" from *Pagliacci*, instinctively I felt something. I tried to imitate it. I did not want to tell anyone how I felt, not even my mother, because I wanted to play baseball—that was the big thing in my life. But listening to Caruso, something stirred in me.

ANGELO BADALAMENTI: I grew up listening to Enrico Caruso, Carlo Buti, all the Neapolitan and classical songs on the old 78-rpm, twelve-inch records. There was always music in the house. My father was an amateur singer. My older brother played the trumpet. It was his idea that I take up piano. We could barely afford the old upright, a player piano with the works taken out.

I started lessons when I was eight. When I was eleven, I wanted to stop, because practicing interfered with stickball games. My father was thrilled that he could save the three dollars a week, but my brother insisted I continue. Then, in the first year of junior high, I began to notice the girls would come over and sit next to me on the piano bench when I played. After that you couldn't get me away from the piano.

KARL BERNSTEIN: First I took piano lessons from Miss Leitman, who came to the house. When I was in fifth grade, I went to the Brooklyn Music School, on St. Felix Street. Then I stopped the piano and took cello lessons. My father was a violinist, although a lousy one, and my mother was a very fine pianist. They needed a cellist in order to have a trio.

LEONA ANTEL DANCE STUDIO

presents

VARIETY REVUE

Thursday Evening, June 7th, 1951
at 7:30 o'clock

BROOKLYN ACADEMY OF MUSIC

———

PROGRAM

Entire production created by Leona Antel

ACT ONE

1. OPENING — Song ———————— Frank Alesi and Rochelle Brodsky,
   Lavern Brown, Patricia Brown, Norma Farca, Ilene Greisman,
   Carolyn Katz, Angela Panarello, Annette Passamonte, Adrianne
   Passamonte, Susan Kunen, Gloria Polansky, Karen Sorci, Lila
   Goldstein, Cynthia La Rocca
   Words of Opening song by James Selva, Music by Dave Ringle
   1A. DANCE ———————————— Gae Blau, Joyce Fantelli,
   Angela Friscia, Marie Anne Friscia, Yvette Jaeger, Carolyn Saiya,
   Barbara Gellerman, Joan Winston, Joan Legrand, Brenda Kaftal,
   Sheryl Shapiro, Barbara Pasternack
2. GOOD MORNING ———————— Cynthia La Rocca, Lila Goldstein
3. SONG AND DANCE ———————— Barbara Trepidie,
4. WILAMENIA — Song & Dance ———— Joyce Shapiro
   Joseph Trepiedi, Frank Alesi
5. DAINTY MISSES ———————— Dianne Glatzer, Judith Wollock
6. PRE-SCHOOL TAP ——— Marylin Freetman, Betty Giarusso,
   Sharon Kaplan, Barbara Kreismans, Anna Pantrello, Ginger Rollo
   6A. TWO GOBS ———————— Carol Poppiceno, Charles Marmo
   7. MODERN MOOD ——————— Sheryl Shapiro
   8. LET'S DO IT AGAIN — Song & Dance —— Beginners Tap
   Rochelle Brodsky, Lavern Brown, Patricia Brown, Carolyn Katz,
   Norma Farca, Ilene Greisman, Susan Kunen, Angela Panarello,
   Annette Passamonte, Adrianne Passamonte, Gloria Polansky, Karen
   Sorci, Lila Goldstein, Cynthia La Rocca
9. CLAP YOUR HANDS ———————— Arlene Ryman

PROGRAM - continued

9A. PONY BALLET —————————— Adv. Toe Group
   Angela Friscia, Marie Anne Friscia, Dianne Glatzer,
   Marylin Silverberg, Maxine Richland, Yvette Jaeger, Laurel Sikoro-
   wicz, Joan Winston
10. DIANNNE ———————————— Joan Winston
11. TEA FOR TWO ———————— Joan Legrand
12. SOME OF THESE DAYS — Song —— Debra Roth
14. TAP DANCE ———————— Ellen Kaufman
   14A. PIZZACATO ———————— Susette Haber
15. CHALLENGE ———————— Carol May, Joan Epifania
   Gae Blau, Joyce Fantelli, Angela Friscia, Marie Anne Friscia, Yvette
16. LITTLE BIT OF HEAVEN — Song & Dance —— Friday Adv. Tap
17. IRISH JIG ———— Carolyn Saiya, Barbara Gellerman, Joan Winston
18. AIR DE BALLET ———————— Chris Salvo
   18A. PURPLE BUTTERFLIES ———— Pearl Dee Lichtman
   Joan Ackerman, Lorraine Boriello, Barbara Elbaum, Gloria
   Krieger, Rosylin Golding, Arlene Ryman, Myra Schaer,
   Carol Sokol, Dianne Sokol, Joyce Cohen, Susan Wollock
19. LOVER — Tap Dance ———————— Wed. Beg. Ballet
20. RHYTHM DANCE ———————— Brenda Kaftal
21. MOONLIGHT SONATA ———————— Saundra Steinbrecker
   Roberta Golding ———— Judith Holtzman, Harriet Barcon,
22. SHIEK OF ARABY ———— Ronnie Kemilhor & Joy Belletti, Joan Epifania,
   Elaine Genger, Lila Gutfeld, Sandra Josephthal, Debra Roth, Marylin
   Silverberg
23. TAPS IN TIME ———————— Yvette Jaeger
24. HINDOO SCENE — Persian Market —— Monday Semi-Adv. Tap
   Barbara Pasternack, Joan Legrand, Terry Mizrachi, Sarah Soloway,
   Sheryl Shapiro, Dianne Glatzer, Joyce Shapiro, Brenda Kaftal
   24A. LAZY RIVER ———————— Barbara Gellerman, Bertha Abadi,
   24B. TAHITI NATIVE DANCE ———— Monday Semi-Adv. Tap
   Barbara Pasternack, Joan Legrand, Terry Mizrachi, Sarah Soloway,
   24C. WHIRLING DERVISH —— Dianne Glatzer, Joyce Shapiro, Brenda Kaftal
   25. HUNGARIAN CZARDAS ———————— Pat Parks
   25A. TAP ACROBATICS ———————— Marylin Silverberg
   26. YOU LOVE ME — Song ———————— Henry Jim
   27. TAPPING MISS ———————— Francis Fallon
   28. PIANO ROLL BLUES — Song —— Barbara Pasternack
   29. HAMP'S BOOGIE WOOGIE ———— Betty Lynn Jensen
   Angela Friscia, Marie Anne Friscia, Gae Blau, Advanced Tap Group
   Jaeger, Joyce Fantelli, Barbara Gellerman, Carolyn Saiya, Yvette
   30. ABA-DABA HONEY MOON ———————— Joan Winston
   Carol Pappiceno, Arlene Scofield, Mathilda Waldron, Ruby Winston,
   James Krieger, Angelina Calo, Joseph Calo, Charles Marmo
   31. NEVERTHELESS — Soft Shoe ———— Saturday Tap
   Roberta Barandes, Mary Anne Celano, Catherine Tuea, Inter. Group
   Haber, Shiela Kantorman, Patricia Borden, Arlene Ryman, Anita
   Schwartz, Rose Weiss, Lida Wunderlich
   32. VALSE BLUE ———————— Joy Belletti, Joan Epifania
   33. THRU THE YEARS — Song —— Maxine Richland
   34. HAWAIIAN WAR CHANT ———— Dorothy Carley
   35. I LOVE YOU — Tap Dance —— Terry Mizrachi
   36. BE A CLOWN — Song & Dance —— Gae Blau
   37. INTERMEDIATE BOOGIE ———— Pat & Stanley Tap
   Joy Beletti, Joan Epifania, Elaine Genger, Lila Gutfeld, Friday Tap
   Josephthal, Ronnie Kemilhor, Debra Roth, Marylin Silverberg

HERB BERNSTEIN: When I was four years old, I saw a violin in a store and fell in love with it. My mother bought me one, and I took lessons, a dollar a lesson, till the age of ten. We never had any money. I think his best year, my father earned $150 a week. But you know how parents are: I wanted music lessons, I got them.

JACK EAGLE: My parents didn't have me until they were married thirteen years. As they say in Yiddish, I was an *ain in aintzika*—one of one. They were very protective, didn't want me to play ball or roller-skate for fear I would get hurt. Instead, they bought me a trumpet. I took lessons from the New York Band Instrument Company, near the St. George Hotel, starting with a little mouthpiece. I moved on to a bugle and started doing bugle calls. Then my mother got me a really good horn.

MARNIE BERNSTEIN: At one time, I took accordion lessons from Mr. Haber, who came to the apartment. I was an advanced student then, and he gave me a difficult arrangement of "Begin the Beguine" that had different rhythms for the left and right hands. He told me, "You know, if you play both hands with the same rhythm, no one may notice. But that's the difference between someone who takes the easy way and the real musician."

My first accordion teacher was Laura Petri, who together with her husband gave music lessons out of their house. She taught piano and accordion in the living room; Mr. Petri taught everything else in a converted closet. I was invited to join the Petri band, and once, when I was about eleven, I went over on a Saturday afternoon. It was a hodgepodge of brass, woodwind, percussion, and one accordion playing "Winter Wonderland." I was the only girl out of about twenty musicians, but just a little too young to appreciate what a nice situation that was.

Mrs. Petri taught from a book called *Everybody's Favorite Accordion Pieces.* She'd assign a different song each week, and as soon as I learned it, I had to perform it for my father. He waited and waited for me to learn "Ave Maria." Finally, he asked Mrs. Petri why she kept skipping it. She explained it was a Catholic hymn. "So what?" my father said. "It's beautiful music."

HOWARD RAPP: My mother heard someone play "The Anniversary Waltz" on the accordion, and she loved it. She wanted to be able to hear it whenever she liked. So she decided my brother would take accordion lessons and learn to play that song. Since we couldn't afford two instruments, I had to take accordion lessons, too. Our teacher came by subway. He got off the train and walked ten blocks to our house. My brother hated the accordion and begged my mother to stop the lessons. But she wanted him to play. Finally, he arranged for a bunch of his friends to meet the teacher on his way and beat him up. The teacher refused to come back again.

Our dancing lessons were another thing. We took tap at the Fred Astaire Dance Studios right under the el on Broadway, in Williamsburg. They got you to pay a year in advance, and they placed you on *The Merry Mailman Show*. I was on three times, once with a bunch of eight other guys, all of us dressed in top hats and canes, singing the Johnny Ray hit "Walking My Baby Back Home."

One day the people who ran the studio absconded with everybody's money. Fred Astaire came down to straighten things out; his name on the line. He taught a class or two to us. Imagine, Fred Astaire in Brooklyn, teaching Howard Rapp to dance.

CAROLINE KATZ MOUNT: In our one-bedroom apartment, there was no room for a piano, so my sister got to take accordion lessons. Since I was little, they decided the accordion was too heavy for me, but my parents felt I had to do something. That's how I wound up at Leona Antel's Dance Studio on Bay Parkway.

Leona Antel was a tough-looking, heavily made-up blonde who gave lessons in every kind of dance you could imagine: ballet, tap, acrobatics, and flamenco with castanets. For advanced students there was Mrs. Antel's specialty: tap-on-toe, where a tap was affixed to the bottom of a toe shoe. I can still hear the *tap-tap-tap* on the wooden floor of that long, narrow, mirror-lined room.

The big event of the season was our recital at the Brooklyn Academy of Music. Mrs. Antel, in the spirit of Busby Berkeley, had choreographed a spectacular opening. All eighteen of the girls in my troupe were positioned in a horizontal line. The curtain was supposed to rise in three stages. First it would reveal just our dancing feet in silver tap shoes doing a shuffle step, then up to our knees, and finally the rest of us. We got through the first stage all right. But when the curtain stopped at our knees, somehow, in the pressure of the moment, we thought it got stuck. In a panic, we crawled under and out in front of the partially raised curtain. There was a jumble of arms and legs. We all bumped into each other. The music played on, but all through the number we couldn't manage to get back in line and step. Maybe I should have taken the accordion after all.

STEWIE STONE: My father, who had been a hoofer in the George White Scandals and the Ziegfeld Follies, ran the Robert Stone Dance

The program for the Leona Antel Dance Studio's annual recital. As noted, the program was always subject to change.

PROGRAM - continued

38. ACROBATICS
Lydia Belopolsky, Carol Pappiceno, Saundra Steinbreeker ———— Tuesday Acro.
Soloway, Charles Marmo, Henry Jim, Josephine Fuchs, Sheldon Fuchs, Sidney Ruben-
stein, Arline Ryman, Joan Winston

INTERMISSION — FIVE MINUTES
PROGRAM SUBJECT TO CHANGE

ACT TWO

1. PRECISION TOE DANCE
Bertha Abadi, Joyce Fantelli, Barbara Gellerman ———— Monday & Friday Tap Group
Joan Winston, Patricia Vailson, Josephine Rosenblatt, Carol Peteszil,
land, Lida Wunderlich, Judith Wollock, Jane Schneider, Debra
Roth, Joan Epifania, Pearl Dee Lichtman, Carol May, Patricia
Miscelli
1A. BEGINNERS BOGGIA
Mary Anne Celano, Catherine Curley, Sucette Haber, Roberta Barandes,
man, Patricia Borden, Arlene Ryman, Anita Schwartz, Rose Weiss,
Lida Wunderlick
2. SONG & DANCE
3. TO A WILD ROSE
4. WALK WITHOUT YOU BABY —— Tap Dance —— Beginners Tap Group
Rochelle Brodsky, Lavern Brown, Patricia Brown, Norma Farese,
Ilene Greissman, Carolyn Katz, Susan Kunen, Angela Panarello,
Annette Passamonte, Adrianne Passamonte, Gloria Polansky, Karen
Sarci, Lila Goldstein, Cynthia La Rocca
5. ECHOES OF SPAIN:
(a) LA CORRIDA
(b) BESA ME MUCHO — Song ———— Gae Blau
(c) MOORISH DANCE ———— Nora Connor
(d) TANGO ———— Bertha Abadi
(e) GRANADA — Song ———— Barbara Arno, Royce Greenberg,
(f) ESPANA CANI ———— Barbara Jensen
(g) A MATADOR — Song & Dance ———— Angela & Marie Anne Friscia
(h) BEGIN THE BEGUIN — Song ———— Carolyn Saiya
(j) BEGUIN THE BEGIN — Dance ———— Evelyn Wallace
Barbara Pasternack, Joan Legrand, Terry Mizrachi, Sarah
Soloway, Sheryl Shapiro, Joyce Shapiro, Dianne Glatzer,
Brenda Kaftal ———— Monday Tap Group
6. TOO YOUNG — Song ———— Sheryl Shapiro
6A. MIRILITONS
7. TAPS ON TOE ———— Nora Connor
8. RAGGEDY ANNE ———— Laurel Sikorwicz
9. TOE STRUT ———— Joyce Fantelli
10. DARK TOWN STRUTTERS BALL ———— Joan Winston
11. ONE OF THOSE THINGS — Dance ———— Carol Peteril
12. INVITATION TO THE WALTZ ———— Saundra Steinbreeker
14. MATINATA — Song ———— Barbara Gellerman
15. WALTZ FROM SLEEPING BEAUTY ———— Yvette Jaeger
16. MOSKOWISKIS WALTZ ———— Chris Salvo
17. NONE BUT THE LONELY HEART ———— Angela Hunter
18. SUR LE POINT ———— (Assistant Teacher)
———— Patricia Miscelli
———— Carol Peterzil
———— Marylin Silverberg

PROGRAM - continued

19. FLOWERS OF THE SEASON:
GARDEN FANTASIE
(a) WALTZ OF THE FLOWERS ———— Carolyn Saiya
(b) SPRING DAFFODILS ———— Monday Ballet
Sally Aaher, Brenda Behat, Clare Cohen, Sandra Josephthal,
Phyllis Kaplan, Bunny Price, Barbara Touritz
(d) RAINBOW ———— Angela & Marie Anne Friscia
(e) ONLY A ROSE — Song ———— Barbara Jensen
(f) SUMMER ROSES — Pink ———— Wed. Ballet Group
Lydia Belopolsky, Susan Bierstein, Gladys Cutler, Ella
Jacobs, Nedra Levit, Linda Koenigsberg, Pauline Mesagcane,
Rose Weiss
SOLO'S: JOAN LE GRAND
AMY ABRAHAM ———— Friday Ballet
(g) AUTUMN ROSES ———— Pearl Dee
Catherine Curley, Joan Epifania, Lila Gutfeld, Debra Roth, Jane
Lichtman, Carol May, Patricia Miscelli, Judith Wollock, Lida Wunderlich
(h) MOONLIGHT ———— Judith Holtzman, Harriet Barcon
Roberta Golding
MOONLIGHT & ROSES — Song ———— Evelyn Wallace
(j) WINTER POINSETTAS ———— Angela Friscia, Marie Anne
Bertha Abadi, Joyce Fantelli, Angela Friscia, Marie Anne
Friscia, Barbara Gellerman, Dianne Glatzer, Yvette Jaeger,
Carol Peterzil, Maxine Richland, Josephine Rosenblatt,
Carolyn Saiya, Laurel Sikorwicz, Marylin Silverberg,
Patricia Vailson, Joan Winston
20. EYES FOR YOU — Song ———— Dorothy Carley
21. NOVELTY SONG & DANCE ———— Pat Parks
22. MODERN DANCE ———— Angela Hunter
(Assistant Teacher)
23. MY SUNFLOWER — Song ———— Frances Fallon
24. ECCENTRIC DANCE ———— Stanley Parks
25. GRAND FINALE: GARDEN POTPURI
BUTTERFLIES — DAFFODILS — ROSES — MOONLIGHT — POINSETTAS
ENTIRE CAST

At this time let me express my sincerest appreciation to the parents for their cooperation in making this recital a success.
SINGING DIRECTION ———— JOSEPHINE DE BUERIS
ACROBATICS DIRECTION ———— JOE PRICE
PIANIST ———— CONNI HALL
ASSISTANT TEACHER ———— ANGELA HUNTER
CLASSES CONTINUED DURING THE MONTH OF JUNE
STUDIO OPEN ALL SUMMER
DANCE SHOES & ACCESSORIES
SELVA & SON — 1607 Broadway
COSTUMES — RAY KAHN AND IRENE PYZNAR
MEMBER: Dancing Masters of America — Dance Educators, N. Y. Society
Dance Teacher, Chicago National Dance Teachers Assoc.,
N.A.D.A. of Hollywood & New York.

Studio for tap dancing and ballroom for more than forty years. It was only a little place with a linoleum floor, but he taught people like Jeff Chandler and Susan Hayward, as well as all the kids in my high school who took up tap.

He said, "Listen, we have no money. But I can give you five dollars a week to go for drum lessons."

I said, "What's that gonna do for me in my life?"

He said, "You play drums and you practice, every summer you can go away and have a free vacation playing in a band. You'll have enough money to put yourself through college. No matter what you do, you can always augment your income playing on weekends. Playing the drums will open a lot of doors for you."

I started on a practice pad. Then he bought me a snare drum, then a bass drum, then the high hats, then the cymbals. I practiced in the apartment. The neighbors threw rocks through the window. Finally, my father cut a deal. They allowed me to practice from 3:30 to 5:30. After I got a full set of drums, I joined a band. We'd go to one guy's house, and we'd all practice together. It sounded a lot better.

You hear a guy practice the drums, you hate it. You hear a guy practice the trumpet, you hate it. But put it all together in a band, it's not that bad.

JULIE BUDD: When I was four or five, I had a lemonade stand. My father was in the soda business, so I figured I knew how to do this. There were construction workers putting up some houses on Avenue J, and I thought I could do some business. There was no problem going away from the house in those days. The only thing I couldn't do was cross Utica Avenue—that was the big street. When I was finally allowed to cross it, I knew I was a mensch.

Anyway, the first day I made a few dollars. That gave me an idea. The next day I put on my holiday dress, the one I was only supposed to wear on Rosh Hashanah and Yom Kippur, with forty-seven crinolines. I put on my patent leather shoes and ruffle socks. And I went around the neighborhood door-to-door, ringing the bells.

"What are you doing all dressed up today?" the neighbors asked.

I said, "I'm here to sing a song for you, but if I sing, you've gotta give me a nickel."

The next day, different dress—I knew, even then, give the audience a surprise. They said, "Are you back?"

"This time," I said, "it's two for a quarter."

BARRY FRANK: I began my career singing for ice cream. Neighbors asked for a song, and I would do "Amapola" or "Zippity-Doo-Dah." I ate so much ice cream, I became a little chubbette. From the streets, I moved on to the department stores in downtown Brooklyn, where they had amateur contests that were broadcast over the radio.

IRVING FIELDS: I began playing the piano when I was eight years old. We moved from Coney Island to Bensonhurst around then, but I had gotten my taste for show business from Coney Island, from hearing the singers and musicians in the Bowery saloons and the bands that played at Steeplechase.

I entered those amateur contests that used to be held in movie theaters all over Brooklyn. They were terrific openings for people who had talent. Then I hit the big one: the Fred Allen Amateur Contest, which was coast-to-coast on radio. I won first prize playing my arrangement of "The Continental" and got a week's engagement at the Roxy for fifty dollars plus fifty dollars prize money. I took all single bills, came home to Brooklyn, threw them all in the air, and said, "Mama, Papa, it's all for you."

PAT COOPER: The boys on the corner would wait for me. "Where's Pat? When's Pat coming down?" I'd do impressions of the instruments of Glenn Miller, Charlie Barnett, Tommy Dorsey. I won the Fox Theater's Monday Night at the Amateurs in '48 or '49. I beat my sister, knocked her brains out.

She sang "Ave Maria." While she was on, everybody was very quiet. People said, "She's gonna win." Then I went out there and did my impressions. Tore the house down.

Productions on the stages of school auditoriums gave Brooklyn kids like "Fidgety-Ben" a chance to show their stuff.

I got the twenty-five dollars. My sister got the watch that never worked. My father got mad at me. "Your sister sings about Jesus Christ and Mother Mary. You, stupid, make the noise. You had to go and beat your sister." They didn't speak to me for six months.

I worked the Bedford Theater Amateur Night, on Bedford Avenue and Bergen Street. Joey Adams was the MC. Sometimes they gave me a dollar, three dollars. My sister quit. "I'm not gonna work with him no more."

Like James Cagney, I said, "Cause you can't touch me."

My father said, "Go to confession. Tell God what a skunk you are."

I go into the confessional booth. The priest said, "Yes?" Like James Cagney I said, "I ain't tellin' you nuttin'. I don't squeal on nobody. Who do you think I am, you dirty rat?"

MAX WECHSLER: Every year Junior High School 50 put on a big talent show that gave the kids in the neighborhood a chance to show off their performing ability. My friend Benjamin Gordon was constantly frustrated. For years, he had tried to get a big part in the show, but to no avail. Benjamin was into everything. He collected war memorabilia, stamps, and soda bottles. He raised gerbils and kept a flock of pigeons in a coop on his roof. But even though he took piano, drum, and tap-dancing lessons for years and walked around with a book on his head to perfect his posture, "those teachers," as he told me, "never give me a tumble when it comes to show business."

Now, Fidgety-Ben, as we called him because he couldn't stand still, was one of the most persistent kids I ever met, and finally, in eighth grade, he pushed his way into a starring role in the show. "Maxie," he said, "it took a lot of effort, but they finally recognized talent. I'm going to show them everything I have."

Although I had no talent, even I got a part in this show. For the big Indian dance number, I got to wear a costume and stand on the stage with a long spear and look out at the audience.

Opening night was packed with students, parents, relatives, and friends of the cast. The teachers who directed the show and the performers felt the pressure. I had nothing to worry about. All I had to do was stand on the side of the stage holding my spear.

Benjamin's time came about thirty minutes into the show. And he was ready. I caught a glimpse of him backstage with a book on his head practicing his balance. He was wearing a colorful Indian outfit: a blue fringed shirt, a yellow loincloth, and a feathered headdress. Then there was a big drumbeat. The lights dimmed, a single spot came on, and Benjamin bounded out to the middle of the stage. They didn't call him Fidgety-Ben for nothing. He was loose out there, bouncing up and down. It took a few seconds before everyone realized he was wearing nothing under his loincloth.

The teachers went berserk. I heard them screaming in the back, "Drop the curtain, drop the curtain!" The audience was *ooh*ing and *aah*ing. But Benjamin was having a ball. It was his moment in the spotlight, and before they dropped the curtain, true to his word, he got to show off everything he had.

CHAPTER 4

One Big Happy Family

FUDGE, FUDGE, CALL THE JUDGE.
MAMA'S GOT A NEWBORN BABY.
WRAP IT UP IN TISSUE PAPER,
THROW IT DOWN THE ELEVATOR . . .
—Jump-rope rhyme

STAN GOLDBERG: My brother Gary came back from visiting a friend who had moved out to Long Island. "It's terrible there," he said. "They have to sleep in their own room. They don't share with the brother."

NEIL SEDAKA: I shared a room with my sister, Ronnie. I used to put on shows, make up radio programs, keep her up to all hours entertaining her. When she left to get married, I cried bitterly.

We lived in a two-bedroom apartment on the second floor of a building in Brighton. At one time, it was my parents, Ronnie, me, my father's parents, and his five sisters. As each of my aunts got married, they moved out. My grandfather died when I was little, but my *nonni* (Spanish for grandmother) lived with us till she died when I was thirteen.

We were the only Sephardic people in the building. We had different foods, different customs, a different language—Ladino. My mother was Ashkenazi, but she learned how to speak Ladino because she wanted to understand what her in-laws were saying about her.

JOAN RIBAUDO: My parents, two brothers, and I lived in a three-room apartment. But other people always lived with us: an aunt and uncle, my grandmother, another aunt. When relatives came from Pennsylvania, we put a drawer on top of the dresser, put some towels in it, and the baby slept there. Another child slept in a drawer on the floor. One time, my brother was sleeping in the kitchen across two chairs. He slid off the chairs onto the floor under the telephone table and slept right through it.

TOBY SCHOM GROSSMAN: When we first came to this country, we lived with my aunt and uncle and their two sons in their little two-room apartment, although sometimes neighbors took us in for a night or so because it was so crowded. But after a while, we got our own apartment in the building.

My parents were Holocaust survivors. My father was in the ghetto on the way to the camp, and my mother was able to get him out. They hid in the woods in Poland for two years. Their little son died. My father was the only one of ten brothers and sisters who survived. My mother lost everyone but two sisters. They tried not to talk about the war too much. Still, I remember my father waking up screaming, howling in the middle of the night.

Being an only child and the child of survivors, I was very protected. I never learned to roller-skate or ice-skate, to swim or ride a bike. I guess they were afraid. Once I went to Washington Baths with my friends, and they all jumped into the pool, so I jumped in, too. I almost drowned.

My mother was from the old school. She set basins out on the fire escape to collect rainwater that we used to wash our hair. On Fridays, she'd bake challah, and the apartment would be fragrant with its aroma. She was an excellent seamstress. At one time, she wanted to get a job, but I said, "You can't. I don't want to come home from school and not find you here." She listened to me. They wanted to move to a bigger apartment. I said, "I can't leave this building. All my friends are here." They didn't move.

PAT COOPER: I lived with my parents and three sisters in a five-family building in Red Hook. The luckier families were on the floor with the one bathroom in the whole building. I was a bed wetter. I felt terrible about it. Instead of helping me, they beat the daylights out of me. There was never "I love you" in that family. The only time you got a smile was when you brought in money. Everybody grabbed theirs.

I was considered the rebel because I had imagination. My father loved opera. But if you had humor, he thought that there was something wrong with you. He was a cold but very bright and handsome man. I don't think he thought I listened, but I picked up on things. He was a bricklayer and worked on the first housing project in the country. They used him to do the foundation so the rest of the building was straight. He had such a sense of balance that if he wore a hat on top of a brick wall on a windy day, the hat wouldn't blow off.

JOAN RIBAUDO: The whole neighborhood thought my father was Italian, including me. It wasn't until after he passed away that we looked through his papers and discovered he was really Portuguese. The immigration people had taken the *dos* out of his name, Ventura dos Santos.

Everyone called him Sam. He was a plumber and the super of our building on West Eighth Street. At four in the morning, he was up putting coal in the furnace. He dragged the heavy pails of ashes out to the curb for the garbage pickup and carried cast-iron sinks and bathtubs on his back. He worked until he was eighty-two years old.

In their wedding picture, both my parents are the same height. But my mother was only fifteen then, and she continued to grow to be five-eight, while my father remained five-three. He had to get on a chair to be eye-to-eye with her. When they had a heated discussion, he'd look up at her and say, "If I knew you'd be this big, I wouldn't have married you."

HERBY GREISSMAN: I came home from school one day, and it was snowing. I said to my father, "I'm not going to work." He said, "You've got an obligation. You've got to go." I peddled the bike through the snow to deliver the grocery orders. You couldn't dodge the bullet with my father.

He was a fruit-and-vegetable broker. In 1951, when things began to pick up for him, he bought a two-door black Dodge. One afternoon that summer, he drove onto the block, and the car was filled with watermelons: the back seat, the passenger seat, the trunk couldn't close. He brought enough watermelons for almost all the people in the building.

HOWARD JONES: We were playing stickball on the street one afternoon when one of the fellows hit the ball into a neighbor's window and it broke. Everyone ran except for my brother Basil and me.

Mr. Baptiste came out and accused us of breaking his window. One thing led to another, and my father came down. "I *saw* your son break the window," Mr. Baptiste told him.

"You're a liar," my brother shouted.

At that, my father hit my brother. "I'll pay for the window," he said to Mr. Baptiste.

"I don't doubt that you were telling the truth," he later told Basil, "but you spoke back to an older person, you called an adult a liar. I cannot allow my son to be disrespectful."

My father, Lynton Mac Jones, came from Jamaica, and he never lost the British influence of his youth. He was a formal man, a meticulous dresser. He bowled in a cricket league and played tennis on

More than trees grew in
Brooklyn. This brownstone
backyard was a verdant
vegetable garden.

the grass in Prospect Park dressed in white flannel. In the back of
our brownstone, he kept a garden where he grew lettuce, green pep-
pers, tomatoes, and calilou, which is a stringy, spinach-type plant.

My father was a baker for Ebinger's, and the smell of cloves and
cinnamon always seemed to cling to him. The summer I was fifteen
and Basil was eighteen, we heard Ebinger's was hiring kids. We asked
our father if he could get us jobs. "Yes, I can," he said, "but I won't."

We were so surprised. He knew how much we needed to work.
"Why not?" we asked.

"Years ago, when I began my job, the foreman told me that not
only would I be there for the rest of my life, but my sons would come
on and do the same thing," he said. "I may still be there, but I will
keep the promise I made to myself that day: no matter what, my sons
will never work at Ebinger's."

NEIL SEDAKA: My father drove a cab for the Rio Taxi Company
in Manhattan. Even though it was cheap back then, he never wanted
to own his own medallion. "I don't want no headaches, Skinny," he'd
say to my mother (he called her Skinny because she was so thin). "I
want to be able to sleep at night."

In the sixth grade, my friend Freddie Gershon moved. His father
was an insurance man and could afford a twelve-thousand-dollar home
in Bayside, Queens. My mother cried to my father. He said, "No,
Skinny, no headaches. I can't afford twelve thousand dollars for a
house." He was from poor people and held on to a buck.

STAN GOLDBERG: My father would come home after working nights, pop in, give us the hugs and kisses, be very warm. He gave us values too. But he had another job. Our family was female-oriented; my mother and grandmother directed what was going on.

The phone was in Grandma's apartment. Once I was going with a girl Grandma did not approve of, because she wasn't Jewish. She telephoned, and Grandma told her, "Stanley moved."

My mother was one of the first women in the neighborhood to drive. She took us to the JCH [Jewish Community House], to Lafayette, to the Mapleton Park library in her '47 Nash. She knew if I was doing a project in science or social studies. While I was out playing ball, she'd go to the library. I'd come home, all the books would be lined up and ready. "Took charge" is an understatement.

LARRY STRICKLER: My mother did not look at the thermometer. She looked at the calendar. Come Labor Day, out came the winter coats. One Veterans Day it was unseasonably mild. A friend and I went out of Brighton Baths across the sand and into the ocean. The water was warm, and I was feeling really good. Here I was, seventeen years old, swimming in November. Walking back across the beach— it must have been about 70 degrees—I hear a great shriek followed by cries about influenza, pneumonia, polio. I look up to see who's screaming. There on the boardwalk is a figure bundled up in a winter coat. It's my mother.

STAN GOLDBERG: I think Brooklyn neighborhoods in the fifties were run by women. They went to the PTA meetings. They went up to school. Very few of them worked.

STARR FROST GOLDBERG: There was so much house-work. My mother shopped for food every single day. And she always was there when I came home for lunch. There were no wash-and-wear fabrics. She would stand over the ironing board for hours.

JOYCE SHAPIRO FEIGENBAUM: My mother washed clothes with a washboard on the deep side of the kitchen sink and hung them out to dry on a clothesline. Later, they installed a washing machine in the basement of our building, and she would lug the heavy bags of laundry up and down two flights of stairs, like she had dragged the baby carriage when we were little. We were so crowded in our little apartment, there was so much stuff.

MORRIS FRIEDMAN: We never ate out in a restaurant, never bought cake in the bakery. My mother prepared every meal and baked every cake we had. She made her own kreplach, all the specialties. She knew how to stretch a dollar.

CAROLINE KATZ MOUNT: In addition to all the housework, the cooking and cleaning, my mother did a lot of handiwork. She took knitting instructions from a store on Bay Parkway. From that, the word *instructions* became associated in my mind with knitting. When the Catholic children got out early from school for religious instructions, I thought they were going for knitting lessons.

My mother had grown up in a rural area in the Ukraine, and although she had been here since she was a teenager, she never got used to city life, to living in an apartment that looked out on a concrete backyard. She talked about how she would bring the ducks down to the water as a little girl and see the frogs jumping about, how it felt to run around on the grass in bare feet, how beautiful the changing seasons were. It bothered her that we were missing the pleasures of a bucolic childhood. Our neighborhood was not particularly beautiful. But on Saturday and Sunday afternoons, we would walk down to Ocean Parkway, and she would point out the trees, the flowers in the little gardens. In the summer, she would pick wild daisies that grew in the empty lots and twine them into a crown for my hair.

My mother was different from the other women in the building. She didn't play mah-jongg and kept mostly to herself. She had this elegant, erect carriage, which made people think she was snobby. But actually, she was very modest and shy, comfortable only with her own family. Her mother, sisters, and brothers and their families all lived in the neighborhood, and her whole life was bound up in the family.

The nation got to know Gary David Goldberg's grandparents in the TV series *Brooklyn Bridge*. Here they are with Gary at his bar mitzvah.

STAN GOLDBERG: We lived in the upstairs apartment of a four-family semiattached house in Bensonhurst, and my mother's parents lived downstairs. My father's parents lived two blocks away, and aunts and uncles lived nearby. The whole extended family made a big deal out of the children. They made me feel I was special. I'd be in the schoolyard and Joe Feiffer, an elderly man and a cousin of my grandfather's, would pass by. "You have money?" he'd ask, and give me a quarter for a soda.

My mother's father had a great effect on my life. He was into the humanistic things: taking care of an animal, noticing how beautiful nature is. My grandfather didn't like that I played ball a lot. He wanted me to go to yeshiva, but it ended too late to play sports, and there weren't any girls; sports and girls, the two most important elements.

CHARLES HYNES: My grandfather Charles Drew was the replacement for my father in every sense of the word. He was very tall, an imposing kind of guy who was still jumping horses at the age of seventy-five. He had come to Boston from Ireland. But after he made some money, he moved to Brooklyn and opened up a riding academy off Ocean Parkway. It catered to an elite clientele who dressed in beautiful riding clothes and drove up in luxurious cars. Irene Dunne was one of them. My grandfather gave me a pet pony, which I walked more than rode. People kidded me about that. But I looked at the pony as a large pet and didn't want to hurt it by riding it.

CLIFF HESSE: We lived on Ridgewood Avenue near Cyprus Hills cemetery, about midway between my father's parents and my mother's mother. Having all that extended family about was a very comforting part of my childhood.

Every Saturday night, we'd pick up crumb cake from the local bakery for Sunday morning breakfasts before church. To this day, crumb cake is my version of Proust's madeleine. I take a bite, and the whole experience comes flooding back: Sundays after church, walking up New Jersey Avenue, crossing Liberty onto Atlantic Avenue (being very careful of the traffic) and heading for my grandfather's drugstore. Sunday dinner was in the large kitchen–dining room of my grandparents' apartment upstairs. It was big and warm, the old stove was there.

My father's mother was English-Scotch—the only one in the family who wasn't German—very much a turn-of-the-century Victorian lady, quite tall, statuesque. She had a proud, noble look, could have been royalty. But how she loved to throw parties for crowds of people. My father's two brothers were musicians who played with the big bands in the forties. All their musician friends would come over, and they'd jam way into the night. You'd go down into the dark drugstore below and the ceiling would be shaking from the music.

MAX WECHSLER: My grandfather Jacob came here from Austria and made enough money as a roofer to buy a three-story brownstone on Vernon Avenue off Willoughby, in Bedford-Stuyvesant. He was short and wiry but incredibly strong. Once I saw him bend a penny between his fingers. The years of working as a roofer had hardened his body and developed his agility. Also, it had given him the opportunity to collect all sorts of things, which ended up in the deep, narrow yard behind his house.

Whenever we visited him and his wife, I would spend the time out in the backyard, exploring the collection of objects along the walks, in the shed and the greenhouse. Years later, when I read *Look Homeward, Angel*, it evoked those times. There were stone lion heads that were incredibly heavy; I wondered how he had the strength to carry them home. There were dozens of plants and shrubs, some planted in plain clay pots, others in elaborate copper and concrete urns. There were bottles of all different colors, pottery pitchers and figurines, watering cans, windowpanes, and copper and brass spheres that may have been plumbing fixtures. There were tin boxes within tin boxes, like matryoshka dolls. There were ladders of various sizes and kinds and big spools of rope, and a lot of tools. Every once in a while, I'd find a Spalding ball or some colored marbles, which I'd bring home.

My father looked upon all this as junk. My grandfather never took the time to explain or show off any of his things to me. He was a cold and silent kind of man. Although I wanted to, I never had much of a relationship with him. Maybe that explains why I spent so much time with the objects he collected, content to be by myself, wandering down the slate paths, picking up and putting down all the different things. My grandfather's yard was a private universe for me.

JUDITH KURIANSKY: Sunday was Grandma's day. Everybody came to her Bensonhurst apartment: her nine children and all their kids. Sitting in the kitchen, sitting on the stoop, playing jump rope. All the generations just hanging out on the corner of a Brooklyn street, the nieces and nephews, the aunts and uncles, the older people, the rows of houses all looking alike, just a few trees and some small gardens.

JOEL MARTIN: When the weather was nice, my father and aunts and uncles would sit on the benches in front of the house and listen to the Dodger game on an old Philco portable. They called anything that had a handle a portable. Like my old Webcor tape recorder, which weighed more than I did. But it had a handle, so it was a portable.

We lived in a four-family house owned by my uncle. One apartment was for transients, the rest were for family. My grandmother, the matriarch of the family, lived downstairs. They called her Tanta Chai, which meant Aunt Ida. She was a beautiful, beautiful woman. I loved her like crazy.

My father was one of six children, four boys and two girls, and they all had families. Every Sunday everyone came over. If one of them didn't, it was noted. They kept track. There must have been a book hidden in a secret room that documented the Sunday attendance: "You know it's been three weeks since Uncle Izzy was here." "You know it's been four weeks since we saw Aunt Rose."

But if Uncle Lester didn't make the Sunday gatherings, he was excused, because he was the youngest and the busiest. He looked exactly like Jack Lemmon and was a big practical joker. In those years, the men wore big overcoats. We'd go to Garfield's Cafeteria, and Uncle Lester would fill my father's pockets with silverware. My father would walk out, and the silverware would start clanging. I never decided whether he wanted to get my father arrested, make me laugh, or both. Sometimes Uncle Lester would go into a restaurant, flash his wallet, and say he was a reviewer. He ate for free at lots of places. Later on he moved to Westchester, which I thought was a place somewhere between Asia and Siberia.

RICHARD KEHOE: Great-Aunt Del lived somewhere in Flatbush in a huge two-family house with six rooms on each floor. She was what we called lace curtain Irish, had more money than my grandmother. We never liked going there for our once-a-year visits. I found out later my father didn't either, because you had to sit there with your hands on your lap so you wouldn't scratch the furniture. My father would take us out for a walk and an ice-cream cone, and that would make the trip bearable.

KARL BERNSTEIN: We often went to Great-Aunt Freida's on Sundays. It was a lot of bodies and legs, a lot of children who were my second cousins. The kitchen table was crammed with people. There was hot tea and wonderful cinnamon cookies that Aunt Freida baked. After she died and I discovered she never learned to speak English, I was so surprised. I always understood everything she said.

FRANCES BLUM: People came and went to Bubbe Freida's all afternoon. The kids would read joke books or play Monopoly in the bedrooms, play in the street or on the stoop, run in and out of the house, up and down the steps. The women would sit in the kitchen, sipping glasses of tea through sugar lumps they held between their teeth, reading out loud the letters they received from the family in Israel. The men would play pinochle in the living room. Uncle Abie, my grandmother's youngest brother who married her oldest daughter, arranged the Sunday games.

MARNIE BERNSTEIN: I used to wonder what Uncle Abie was doing in our otherwise sober and serious family. He worked in the china trade, and his little apartment was cluttered with useless objects ("tchotchkes" my parents called them) that he accumulated for no other reason than that he liked them. He had a small white piano, which he played by ear. His favorite song was "*H-A*-double-*R-I-G-A-N* spells Harrigan" which he rewrote as "*S-U-S-S-M-A-N* spells Sussman." He did magic tricks for the kids, like pulling nickels out of his sleeve or from behind our ears. He played practical jokes; spent money freely on things the others considered frivolous, like magazines; had sweet cream instead of milk in his cereal; and was often in debt. When people asked him what he had put away for a rainy day, he'd say, "I got a big umbrella." My father disapproved of him, I know. But he was a lover of life, and somehow it seemed like a good thing.

MARCO CARCICH: I lived in Queens. But every summer, instead of playing stickball with my friends or hanging around in the streets, I went to stay with my grandparents in Brooklyn. I never brought any of my friends along. Family life was very important, and I wanted to keep it private. I wanted to relish it all by myself.

I would take the subway to Hoyt-Schermerhorn, change to the Brooklyn line, and get off at Avenue J. My grandparents lived in a six-story building near the elevated train, in a high-ceilinged apartment that seemed massive to me. I would lie in bed, staring for hours at the ornate plasterwork on the ceiling-light fixture—it was an old one that had been converted from gas to electricity.

My mother's father, Marjain Sarunich, was born in what would become Yugoslavia. He was about five-six and very stocky. His head was bald as a cue ball. There was no hair even on the sides of his ears. The story was that he walked into a barn when he was about fifteen and saw his aunt in a sexual embrace with the devil. As he turned away, the devil reached out and ripped his hair off.

The gathering of the generations. It was a lot of bodies and legs.

The men who played pinochle "would argue and fight back and forth for pennies."

He came to this country with no papers. Along with Manny, a Russian Jew he met on board, he jumped ship in the Ambrose Channel, where the big ships and tankers enter New York harbor. They swam a mile and a half, maybe two miles, all the way to Coney Island. They were lucky; it had to have been between tide changes. Both ended up working in Coney Island. Manny opened up a knish place, and Matteo (as they called my grandfather) became a masseur at Bushman's Baths.

He got up at 5:30 every morning. If I was still sleeping, he'd splash a glass of cold water on my face. For breakfast, he would have a shot of J&B and a raw egg—to get him going. He brushed his teeth with Clorox. They were gleaming white against his deep tan, which he had twelve months a year. He was a member of the Polar Bear Club—about fifteen men and women, mainly from Eastern Europe, who went for a swim out beyond the breakers every day or every other day, no matter how cold it was.

When the family would gather for dinner at Uncle Georgie's house on Shore Boulevard, we couldn't sit down and eat until my grandfather arrived. Sometimes he was late coming back in the middle of the winter from his swim. He had a favorite fork and would not eat dinner without it. Wherever he ate, he brought that fork along.

After dinner, Matteo, my father, and my mother's brother Georgie would play pinochle in the kitchen. The women sat in the living room, listening to the radio or watching the test patterns on the eight-inch television screen. The men would argue and fight back and forth for pennies. The next time we got together, they might not be talking to each other, because they were still angry over something that happened in last week's game.

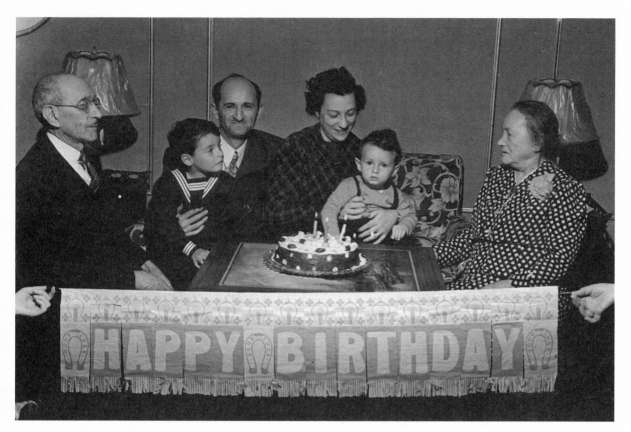

I must have been about nine years old when they sent me to the bar to get beer. "Take the stick," they said. I got this long stick and two buckets, went to the bar, and got the buckets filled with beer. Nobody told me I was supposed to carry the stick like an ox across the back of my neck and over both shoulders. I put it across one shoulder, and of course, I spilled most of the beer.

Matteo did not drive. He did not trust cars, never owned one. He did not trust telephones, never spoke on one. He thought the witches listened to his conversations. About six months after my grandmother died, a giant mosquito—the biggest one I've ever seen—flew into the window. I went to roll up a newspaper to hit it. "Don't," my grandfather said. "It may be Grandma." And with that, the mosquito disappeared.

PART TWO

Living Together

EVERY CUSTOMER WAS
A HALF-HOUR

EVERYBODY KNEW EVERYBODY
ELSE'S BUSINESS

FROM SWELTERING STOOP TO
SHIMMERING SHORE

CONEY ISLAND

ONE NATION—UNDER GOD

AMERICANS ALL

CHAPTER 5

Every Customer Was a Half-Hour

B MY NAME IS BARBARA
AND MY HUSBAND'S NAME IS BOB.
WE COME FROM BROOKLYN,
AND WE SELL BANANAS.
—Bouncing-ball rhyme

MARNIE BERNSTEIN: Summer mornings were very quiet on our block. Hardly any cars were parked along the curb, hardly any people were around. Then, from out of nowhere, this big truck would come down the middle of Twenty-fourth Avenue. It would send out great noisy jets of water on both sides, soaking the whole gutter. After, the asphalt would sparkle, and all along the curbs would be puddles edged with rainbows big enough to jump into and make a big splash.

JOAN RIBAUDO: The street cleaner, dressed in a brown uniform, came down the block wheeling a garbage pail in front of him. With a broom and shovel, he'd sweep up any bit of debris.

   The policeman on the beat walked down the block. He knew every kid who lived there. If he found you on the street when you were supposed to be in school, he'd take you by the hand back to your house. We called him Tarzan, because he was so tall and muscular.

MARTIN SPITZER: The pony ride would come up and down the streets. People dressed up their kids in cowboy vests and hats and spats and took photos of them sitting on the ponies.

   All kinds of peddlers came around selling clothes, small appliances. You'd give one an order. And he'd say, "Okay, I'll bring it to you next Tuesday."

JOAN RIBAUDO: A man used to come around to sharpen knives and fix umbrellas. He rang a bell: two rings meant knives, one ring meant umbrellas. And people would yell out of their windows: "I have an umbrella." "I have a knife." A man with a pushcart sold roasted chestnuts and baked sweet potatoes for a nickel. You could smell them up and down the street.

MARTIN SPITZER: A little peddler wheeled a little cart up the block. Inside were round hot knishes, potato or kashe with onions, seven cents apiece. Another came around selling hot chick-peas in little brown bags for a nickel or a dime. He'd salt-and-pepper them, and I'd devour them.

MARVIN KAPLAN: The lady with the orange pushcart sold "shoe-leather"—dried apricot that was tough and sour.

ROZ STARR: Joe came around the school pushing a wagon with a big copper pot. He dipped apples, marshmallows, and shoe leather into the hot jelly in the pot. Oh those jelly apples! In the summer he switched to Italian ices.

A Brooklyn version of Orchard Street: pushcarts, peddlers, and stores.

ROBERT MERRILL: The iceman came up the six floors every day with the ice on his back.

KARL BERNSTEIN: Just one family on the block, the Laudeuchers, still had an icebox. When the iceman came, he would busy himself chopping a slab off a block of ice, and we would hang around waiting for a piece to fall so we could suck on it.

Blue Coal was the sponsor of my favorite radio show, *The Shadow*, but our coal man delivered black coal in a big truck. He wheeled barrels of coal onto the sidewalk, opened up the chute, and poured the coal down into the basement into the bin. I would beg my father to get the big coal instead of the little coal, not realizing big coal was for industry.

JOEL BERGER: If you didn't want to walk to the store and carry the packages back, you could just sit on your stoop and everyone would come to you: the milkman, the bread man, the fruit-and-vegetable man, the fish man.

ELIZABETH RONCKETTI: The pie man in his open-back truck clanged his bell so loud you knew he was coming. How we waited for his fresh-baked fruit pies and the hot chestnuts in the wintertime.

BILL FEIGENBAUM: The Dugan's Bakery Man, a cool guy with a mustache in a white uniform, drove up in a shiny white step-in truck. He was always very friendly with the women.

JOAN RIBAUDO: The fruit man rang his bell, and the people looked out their windows. They knew him by name, and they'd yell, "What do you have today?" "How much are the stringbeans?" If he had what they wanted and they agreed on the price, they came down to buy. While this was going on, a neighborhood man hung around near the wagon. When the horse made a deposit, he'd shovel it up for his garden.

WILLIAM THOMPSON: My friends and I made some extra money peddling. We'd buy fruits and vegetables and rent horses from one of the stables on Dean Street.

KARL BERNSTEIN: Abie the fish man sold fish off his dilapidated truck with the dropleaf—but only on Fridays. He hollered, "Fish man!" and everybody on the block came out. He would clean the fish, scale it open, throw out the guts.

The rest of the week, he was Abie the fruit man. I saw red bananas on his truck. "Why don't you buy some?" I asked my mother. "Only the Italians buy red bananas," she told me.

"You could just sit on your stoop and everyone would come to you" — even the man who sold pots and pans.

ROBERT MERRILL: The banana man was a heavyset Italian guy with a huge voice who sold them off his truck, a penny apiece. He would yell out, "Banan-yol, banan-yol" in an operatic voice. You could hear him all the way up the six floors and around the block. People waited for him; they'd run down and buy as many bananas as they could, because they didn't last long. And if you bought more than five, he'd give you an extra one for free.

NEIL SEDAKA: In the courtyard, there were these street singers —they were so wonderful. There was a black lady who sang for years and years. She had a gorgeous voice. I would wrap a nickel in a tissue or a piece of newspaper and throw it down from the second-floor window.

JOEL BERGER: Early in the morning, I'd be wakened by the songs of the old-clothes men. They walked up and down the alleyways with packs on their backs, singing in two different cadences: "Clothes-old, clothes-old, I cash, I cash" or "Cash-clothes, cash-clothes, cash-clothes." What do they do with their packs, I wondered? Where do they go?

The elevated train would rumble overhead as you went from store to store.

LUIS COLMENARES: You'd hear the song "Fuller Brush man, Fuller Brush man," and you opened up the door. There was this guy in a short-sleeved striped shirt who had climbed up the six stories of the building. On his back, he carried maybe twenty sweep brooms and a bucket, and in a cardboard box every kind of brush and mop you could imagine.

CHARLES HYNES: The Hegeman man sang a lyrical song: "Hegeman man, Hegeman man." And the responses were like part of the song: "I want three bottles, bring me Fox's U-Bet."

RICHARD GOLDSTEIN: The seltzer trucks all seemed to come from East New York. Everyone took it by the case, a dozen blue or clear bottles in a long slotted wooden crate.

ELIZABETH RONCKETTI: A guy came around with bleach in glass jugs, the strongest in the world. One drop could burn a hole in any piece of material. Talk about recycling. He'd come back and pick up the empty jugs.

JACK EAGLE: For those who preferred going out to shop, Brooklyn had its own version of Orchard Street: Thirteenth Avenue, in Borough Park. It used to be filled with pushcarts and peddlers. Guys sold sweet potatoes and *hasha arbus*—hot chick-peas—from little carts. My poor aunt had a little stand and stood out in the freezing cold. There was a pickle man on the corner of Fortieth Street. He'd sell sour and half-sour pickles, sour tomatoes, fresh horseradish. You'd ask for a pickle, and he'd dig his hand right down to the bottom of the barrel and pull one out. And if you didn't like that pickle, he'd dig his hand down again and schlepp out another one. He was as sour as his pickles. All of that ended when the public market was built on Thirty-ninth Street and the stands went into the market.

Thirteenth Avenue also had a lot of famous stores, like the Majestic Chicken Market and Rothstein's, a department store that attracted fancy ladies who would come with their limousines and chauffeurs to shop for pricey items at bargain prices. Old man Rothstein, the grandfather with a torn sweater, would come out and chase the kids: "Bastards, get away from the store."

BOB ARNESEN: Eighth Avenue in Bay Ridge was called Lopskaus Boulevard, after the Scandinavian stew into which all the leftovers are thrown. It was the shopping area for Finntown, which was on Eighth Avenue around the Forties, and the Scandinavian community.

The stores were reminiscent of Europe. People shopped every day for fresh food. Bay Ridge was a mixed neighborhood. There were Scandinavian bakeries, delicatessens, and fish stores, but the candy stores were mostly owned by Jews, the ice-cream parlors by Germans, the fruit stores by Italians, the bars and grills by Irish. It was an island of small stores.

Behind our house was the Denyse nursery, which went back to the original Dutch settlers. From my bedroom window, I could see acres of plants, flowers, and trees. There was a barn, horses and wagons, even chickens.

My father managed the A & P in Bay Ridge, which was one of the biggest at the time, employing about thirty people. I worked there for forty-five cents an hour, packing the shelves, running the cash register. I knew every price in the store.

HERBY GREISSMAN: My father supplied the produce stores on Eighty-sixth Street between Twenty-third Avenue and Bay Parkway, in Bensonhurst. Every other store was a fruit market. They had no cash registers. The storekeeper would put the produce in a paper bag and add up on the bag. The pencil was always behind the ear. Forty-nine cents, thirty-nine cents. These guys who had no education, they knew more math.

BOB LIFF: My father had a grocery store on the ground floor of a four-floor walk-up on the corner of Union Street and Albany Avenue, in Crown Heights. The cans and boxes were on shelves that went up the ceiling. He got stuff out of reach with a long pole that had a grip on one end and grabbers on the other. He'd grab a can off the top shelf, flip it off, catch it, stick it into a brown bag, write the prices on the side of the bag, and swiftly add the order up.

Years before, my grandfather had a tailor's shop next door to the grocery. But in my time, it was a telephone operators' store, where women sat and plugged in your calls.

AL LEWIS: Pitkin Avenue was a major shopping area in Browns-ville, which had been the largest Jewish ghetto in the world. The delis served the best corned beef and pastrami anywhere. A guy who called himself the Kishke King did a thriving business.

At one time the circus paraded down Pitkin Avenue to the railroad yards in East New York. It was a tremendous event; school was let out. There were all the circus wagons, the elephants, the clowns and acrobats—just like they used to do it in the small towns.

"The stores were
reminiscent of Europe.
People shopped every day
for fresh food."

DAN LURIE: On Saturdays, I'd put on a nice shirt and tie and stroll up and down Pitkin Avenue. It was the Fifth Avenue of Brooklyn, with stores like Abe Stark's men's clothing, Fisher Brothers' ladies' coats and suits, Dubrow's or Diamond and Cooperberg furniture.

PEARL GASARCH: My mother had her furniture custom-made in Pitkin Avenue shops: the sectional sofa; the wing and club chairs all upholstered in damask; the massive mahogany-veneered Philco console that held a television set, high-fi, and bar; the bulky credenza she filled with china and collectibles. Our house in Sea Gate was furnished with Pitkin Avenue's best.

DAN LURIE: Mayrock's, which was the fancy store of the Fortunoff family, was on Pitkin Avenue. Fortunoff's, which catered to the poorer customers, was on Livonia Avenue under the el near Firkey's gym. A little guy named Max was the manager. He knew the price and location of any item in the store.

PHIL FAGIN: Fortunoff's was spread out over maybe a dozen stores. The elevated train would rumble overhead as you went from one to the other along the darkened street, shopping for dishes, glasses, linens, toasters, irons, pots and pans. The stores stretched from the end of Brownsville to the beginning of East New York.

CLIFF HESSE: The drugstores of East New York were scattered up and down Atlantic Avenue. My grandfather's, Hesse's Pharmacy, which he opened in 1904, was right near Pennsylvania Avenue. If my grandfather didn't have something, he'd send me down three blocks to the next store, and the owner would say, "Sure, take it." They exchanged things all the time.

Hesse's Pharmacy was a small place, about the standard city lot of twenty-by-one-hundred. It had wooden floors (which my grandfather liked scrubbed very clean), slanted glass cases with candy for the kids, two wooden phone booths, and a counter with the old crank cash register. Behind it was a higher counter, where he made up prescriptions with the mortar and pestle, the pill boards with tiny holes. He'd pour the medicine on the board, push it into the holes, knock it out —and that would be the tablets. Like making pancakes.

In back was a little yard trapped between two buildings. You couldn't see out of it at all. At the beginning of the summer, I'd go out with a scythe and hack down the grass, which had grown to a foot and a half high. My grandfather had put in a little trellis for a rose bush, and it was filled with roses all the summers I was there.

There was a little electrical repair shop on Liberty Avenue, a nondescript kind of place. I don't remember ever buying anything there. But every Christmas, the owner put an electric train set in the window and surrounded it with little lights. It was O-gauge—the very big old trains, like the British model trains. The engine and cars were about a foot long and six inches high. The rails were two inches apart, and the train ran around a circle that was maybe four feet wide. How I loved standing outside the window watching the train go around and around.

I also loved the smells in the neighborhood: the pungent odor of ozone from the electric generating plant that served the local area and the aromas from all the Italian and German bakeries.

ANGELO BADALAMENTI: Every Sunday morning, my father went to the Danish Bakery on Tenth Street and Kings Highway to buy the most delicious confections. My favorite was the "cake with pimples"—crumb cake filled with rich custard cream. Lovely ladies with pale, pure skin and flaxen hair in nets waited on you. Everything was so fresh and good. It was better than Ebinger's.

DORIS MODELL TIPOGRAPH: Throughout the Bedford and Snyder Avenue area, the aromas from Ebinger's baking plant filled the air. It supplied all the Ebinger bakeries in Brooklyn with daily deliveries of breads and cakes. My favorite were Othellos: little mounds of buttercream-filled white cake smothered with chocolate.

TERRY PERNA ARNESEN: Ebinger's goods were so nicely presented, with extreme cleanliness and fine taste. By two o'clock in the afternoon, the Eighteenth Avenue store would not have anything left to sell.

JUDY BERGER: Getting an invitation to relatives who moved to Long Island depended on the supply of Ebinger's in their freezer. Each of us would walk out of the bakery carrying cakes, one piled on another to the top of our heads.

JOEL BERGER: I did Ebinger's for my mother's Saturday night get-togethers. Early Saturday morning, I'd walk down Kings Highway and try the Ebinger's near Coney Island Avenue. If it was too crowded or out of what I wanted, I'd go on to the Ebinger's on East Seventeenth Street; from there, to the one on Avenue M; and then on to the one on Avenue J. If need be, I'd go to all four in order to get the "blackout cake."

Doc Hesse with the tools of his trade in his Atlantic Avenue pharmacy.

During the war, there were rumors that Ebinger's was run by Nazis, but we managed to put them aside. The saleswomen didn't look like Nazis. They were nice old ladies with blue hair pulled back into hairnets.

MARNIE BERNSTEIN: The woman in Block's ice-cream parlor wore her blue hair in a bun. Her skin was ashy white; she wore no makeup, was always in a white apron. Her ice-cream parlor, on the corner of Bay Parkway and Sixty-third Street, was a long and dark and very cool place with a turn-of-the-century feeling. The floor was black-and-white tile. The tabletops and counter were black marble, and the wall behind the counter was lined with mirrors and inserts of stained glass. You'd sit on a high stool and stare at the panels of flowers and fruit trees or watch yourself sipping a cherry soda that was so foamy it ran over the sides of the glass, and so full of fizz the bubbles went up your nose.

POLLY BERNSTEIN: Mrs. Block had a son who became a dentist on Bay Parkway. He died young. After that, Mrs. Block was inconsolable. She'd serve you an ice-cream soda, and the tears would be running down her face.

SAM BERNSTEIN: New stores opened up on Bay Parkway after the war, on Sixty-fifth Street too. Bensonhurst got more crowded. People had more money. Some groceries became what we called self-service; they were our first supermarkets.

HERBY GREISSMAN: The grocery store on Sixty-fifth Street was so active it required four delivery boys over and above the full-time help: me and my three friends. Every afternoon, we would race home from school to take out the orders. We walked up four flights of stairs

An active Bensonhurst shopping street after the war.

with two boxes of groceries, one on top of the other, so we wouldn't have to make the same trip twice and would be able to get back to the store quicker for the next order. We hustled for tips.

One day my friend delivers to this woman on Avenue P. She's not home. He's pissed because she's never home when he delivers so she doesn't have to tip him. He picks up a milk bottle and breaks it on the threshold of her apartment. When the woman came in to complain the next day, the owner said, "Well, if you would be home, this kind of thing wouldn't happen."

There was someone on Sixty-third Street who was cheaper than free lunch, and that's pretty cheap. He'd make believe he didn't hear the doorbell ring. One day, he asked for a delivery and the owner said, "No." He said, "Why not?" "Because you don't tip." The owner was on our side.

A dime tip was fair. Somebody gave you a quarter tip, it made your day. Mr. Katz, who lived in our building with his lovely wife and two daughters, was a quarter tipper. Strange as it may seem, everyone, no matter what age they were, called him Mr. Katz, including my father. For Passover, Mrs. Katz would come into the store and shop for her order, whatever that might be. Everyone's Passover order was more than one box in those days, so you had to schlepp pretty good. But we literally fought over who would deliver the Katz order, because Mr. Katz would give us a one-dollar tip. I guess it was in the spirit of the holiday. Nobody else did that. A dollar was a lotta, lotta money.

STARR FROST GOLDBERG: Morris-the-sweater-man was a refugee who peddled sweaters from a stand on Sixty-fifth Street. When it rained, he'd open a pair of iron cellar doors on the sidewalk and take his sweaters down the steps to the basement under one of the stores. That's where he stored his stock. He liked the girls, and he'd always want you to come down to the basement where he said he kept his special sweaters. The "busty" look was in then. We all wanted to look like Marilyn Monroe or Jane Russell, and Morris was only too glad to oblige. He did so well that after a while the cellar became like a regular store. Then he rented the space above it, and it became Morris' Boutique.

HELEN FRIED GOLDSTEIN: In those days, everyone wore hats. Men wore the fedoras and Stetsons. Women did not consider themselves dressed without a hat and a pair of gloves. So Jonas Millinery on Fifth Avenue in Bay Ridge was a thriving business. I was still in school when my grandfather got me a part-time job there. They used to call me "the kid." There was such a thing in sales known as the p.m., for *postmortem*, which referred to a hat that had been lying around since last year or the year before. If someone sold a postmortem, they earned another fifty cents. The experienced salespeople didn't want to be annoyed with the p.m.s, so they became my baby. If a woman walked in who didn't look very sophisticated, the others would say, "Let the kid take that one." I would take the hat, retrim it with a feather or flower, and make the sale.

DORIS MODELL TIPOGRAPH: The original off-price boutique was opened by Frieda Loehmann in Brooklyn in 1921, on the site of a former plumbing store. She haunted the wholesale houses, picking up high-fashion samples and overstock, paid cash, and passed the savings on to her customers. Like the ones that followed, the first Loehmann's, on Bedford Avenue and St. John's Place, attracted smart shoppers—very elegant women who had salesgirls call them when a special shipment was due. Then the news would spread like wildfire. Once I got a Pauline Trigère with the label cut out, but I recognized it.

GAIL EISEMAN BERNSTEIN: Loehmann's on Bedford Avenue was ornate, rococo, with banquettes done up in striped zebra material, like the ones in El Morocco. Frieda Loehmann held court on the second-floor landing. Unapproachable, she sat in a thronelike chair observing everything that went on. She wore a black dress, black stockings, black shoes. She had one pat of rouge on each cheek— two absolutely perfect round circles. Her hair was red in the style of Jane Avril, the model for Toulouse-Lautrec. Her money was in her garter. Everybody knew that she had hundreds of dollars there.

The imperious queen of off-price high fashion: Frieda Loehmann.

DORIS MODELL TIPOGRAPH: There were no dressing rooms. You tried on clothes right there on the floor. Men sat on gold thrones on the landing between the stairs. They couldn't walk around where the women undressed.

NORMAN TIPOGRAPH: Some tried.

KARL BERNSTEIN: As kids, it was a treat for us to sit there and watch all the women in their underwear.

GAIL EISEMAN BERNSTEIN: The fancy part of Loehmann's was the upstairs room. The downstairs was for the hoi polloi. You hung your clothes over your pocketbook over the rack and hoped nobody stole anything. And you ran around in your undies.

ELIZABETH RONCKETTI: Schroeder's Butcher Shop, in Greenpoint, was not for bargain customers. But if you didn't have the money, they would trust you. Come back tomorrow, come back when you can, they would say, letting you take all the goulash, pork chops, chicken fricassee that you wanted.

TOBY SCHOM GROSSMAN: I'd go with my mother to buy a chicken from one of the kosher butchers on Sixty-fifth Street. She'd pick one out, and we'd go in the back to the little chicken-flicking room, where she'd flick the chicken. Then they'd cut it up and give her the insides. Later on, I found out I was allergic to chicken feathers.

FRANK BARBARO: My father's butcher shop, the Majestic Meat Market, on Hamilton Avenue and Nelson Street in Red Hook, was sort of a community center, a social center—like the general store with the cracker barrel in New Hampshire. When La Guardia was running for mayor, the Italians were on a mission. The night of the election, everyone had gathered in my father's butcher shop, listening to the radio on the butcher block. They were ecstatic when he won.

On the sawdust-covered floor were maybe ten metal chairs where the women would sit, waiting their turn to buy meat. It was cut to order like a new suit, a little thicker, a little thinner. My father, in his apron and straw hat, would talk to the customers in Italian. Every customer was a half-hour.

"Before everyone had TVs, the barber shops and beauty parlors gave people a place to go where they could talk with other folk."

Because my father could speak English, he was a kind of a community service person to the Italian immigrants. When they had problems, he could direct them here and there. People like him were the conduits to the Anglo-Saxon community. The real estate broker around the corner, who could read and could notarize something, was called the Professor.

JOAN MAYNARD: Barber shops were in their flower during my childhood. They were centers of communication, places where men exchanged ideas. Younger men were in company with older men, where they could learn the mores of the community. Beauty parlors served the same role for women. We went to a sparkling pink-and-while salon on Ralph and Marion streets, in Bedford-Stuyvesant, to have our hair washed, pressed with an iron, and curled. That was standard procedure. Thelma, the owner, came from North Carolina. Holiday time, her family down south would send her country ham that was prepared in a special kind of way. She gave out slices to all the customers. Before everyone had TVs, the barber shops and beauty parlors gave people a place to go where they could talk with other folk.

RICHARD GOLDSTEIN: In 1951, someone offered Abie, the neighborhood barber, a year's use of a television set in exchange for a year's free shaves and haircuts. In that way, Abie's Barber Shop, on Howard Avenue in Crown Heights, became a neighborhood gathering place. He drew quite a crowd.

KARL BERNSTEIN: People got together outside of stores that sold TVs and watched them through the windows. The first TV I ever saw was at Rugby Radio on Linden Boulevard, just above Utica Avenue. It was the time of the World Series, and they had a Philco projection TV which projected the image onto a screen.

BOB ARNESEN: When my grandfather came to live with us, he spent his days in the bars and grills of Bay Ridge, where he drank his schnapps and enjoyed the camaraderie. The bars were something like the English pubs, gathering places for primarily the Irish and Scandinavian men.

MARNIE BERNSTEIN: Sam Germaine's candy store, on Twenty-fourth Avenue, was the gathering place for the men in the neighborhood. Once it had been a garage, and inside it was small, dark, and dusty. There was only enough room for a little soda fountain; a big red ice chest you would open from the top, stick your hand in, and come up with a wet, cold bottle of Coke; and shelves filled with cheap toys, comics, and coloring books. All the kids bought their daily ice-cream cone or Melloroll at Sam's for seven cents. Sam was a gruff but good-natured guy who spoke in a raspy voice through a big fat cigar clamped between his teeth. His assistant was a silver-haired old gentleman named Harris who came from England, the only Englishman any of us knew. Once he was crossing Twenty-fourth Avenue, and a gust of wind blew his hat right off his head. He took off after it, ran like a sprinter, and caught it.

Because the inside of Sam's was too small to hold more than three or four people, all the action took place on the driveway out front. There was a newsstand, penny machines for Indian nuts and Chiclets chewing gum, and a rickety bench along the apartment house wall next door. The men would come out on a Saturday morning, pick up a newspaper from the stand, buy a pack of Chesterfields or Camels, and hang around, kibitzing till lunchtime. Or at night, after dinner— especially before everyone had television sets—they'd get together outside of Sam's, even in the wintertime.

JUDY BERGER: The radio was always on in the small candy store on Avenue M, and people sat at the fountain listening to the event of the day or the baseball game. The penny candy was behind a sliding glass case. You stood there forever with your two cents or nickel, deciding between the red licorice whips and the dots stuck to strips of paper, or leafed through the comic books that cost ten cents apiece. My favorite was *Superman*.

JOEL BERGER: My favorites were Classic Comics. The first one was *The Three Musketeers*, then *A Tale of Two Cities*, then the one I remember best, *Les Misérables*.

ELLIOT GUNTY: Saturday nights we hung out at the candy store on East Ninth Street and Avenue H until the news truck came. The guy would yell, "Yo!" The candy-store owner would give me two dollars, I'd pick up maybe fifty papers and bring them to the store. In no time, we'd be cleaned out.

JOEL BERGER: Schechter's candy store, on Avenue P, was filled with a jumble of pens and pencils and pads and all kinds of different little toys and games, plus an ice-cream fountain where the ice cream was sold hand-packed into little cartons that looked like the kind you get for Chinese take-out food.

cream that looked like the crown of a king. I swept the Indian nut shells off the floor.

As in all candy stores, people hung around. Some of them were Mafia guys. I've played these tough-guy roles, like the one in *Godfather III*, and based my characterizations on the people I used to see hanging around Bertha's.

ALAN LELCHUK: We all knew the history of gangsters in Brooklyn, people like Bugsy Siegel, Dutch Schultz. The lore about the local barber shop was that Bugsy used to slice up troublemakers while they were taking a shave there.

AL LEWIS: Brownsville was the home of Murder, Inc. I knew guys who were for hire to kill. I used to see them in the street—no big deal.

Abe Reles, allegedly a member of Murder, Inc., used to go to the Loew's Pitkin. Henrietta Kamern, who was the organist for the Dodgers before Gladys Gooding, played the organ while the people were walking in and out. Reles used to request his favorite song: "Be Sure It's True When You Say I Love You, It's a Sin to Tell a Lie." Every time she played it, he sent her a twenty-dollar bill.

NORMAN SPIZZ: There was a Mafia presence in the Brooklyn nightclubs in the fifties, although I didn't know it back when I got out of high school and was playing in nightclub bands for Pat Cooper, who was still a part-time bricklayer, and a whole bunch of singers: Al Hibler, Jerry Vale, the DeCastro sisters, the DeJohn sisters.

ROZ STARR: When I began my singing career at a small club, an elegant gentleman came in wearing a suit that in those days must have cost close to a thousand dollars. He asked me to sing "Melancholy Baby," which is the song every singer hates, because they're always asked to sing it. This was the kind of place where people were always talking, but while I sang "Melancholy Baby," no one made a sound. The guy tipped me ten dollars; I was getting twenty-five dollars for the whole evening. The next day, I open the paper and his picture is in it; he's dead. It was Albert Anastasia. Me and gangsters—they love me.

WADE SILER: The Krulick brothers, owners of the Baby Grand in Harlem, also owned the Brooklyn Baby Grand, at Nostrand and Fulton. The audience was mostly black. They drank straight whiskey in a shot glass or scotch and milk, which was supposed to put a lining in your stomach.

JOAN MAYNARD: It was the kind of nightclub where ladies felt comfortable.

Dressing up and going out: the Oriental Beach employees in Tappan's Restaurant at Sheepshead Bay.

WADE SILER: A lot of big celebrities started out there, on the bandstand above the bar. My song was always "Body and Soul." They called me another Billy Eckstine.

HERB BERNSTEIN: Brooklyn had major places for live entertainment then. Shows ran all week. The whole thing was the going out, the dressing up. People drove up in terrific cars that cost three or four thousand dollars and gave the keys over to valet parking. The four-hundred-seat Elegante on Ocean Parkway, right next to the Washington Cemetery, had performers like Patti Page, Mel Tormé, Joni James.

BARRY FRANK: The Suburban Supper Club, across the cemetery from the Elegante, was chic and intimate, with a candlelit dining room. I sang "Zing Went the Strings of My Heart" and "Unchained Melody" and thought I was doing great making about $150 a weekend. Ben Maksik's Town and Country was the Copacabana of Brooklyn. It had the Copa attitude. Tony Bennett, Judy Garland, Milton Berle worked there.

HERB BERNSTEIN: It was a Las Vegas–type operation on Flatbush Avenue. With about twelve hundred seats to fill, it was so large that it started to lose business. They couldn't afford the big acts, and the people wouldn't come to see the lesser acts. So, as a kind of lark, Town and Country put a group in called the Jewel Box Revue. They were a bunch of transvestites, gorgeous. It was unusual for those days, especially for Brooklyn. People came out of curiosity, and it kept the club going for a while.

STEWIE STONE: When I MC'd at the Airport, I dreamed I'd be lucky enough one day to cross Flatbush Avenue and work at Town and Country. But I never did. It closed down.

I used to go to a coffeehouse in Sheepshead Bay called Pips to watch guys work. It was the forerunner of the comedy clubs. David Brenner got his start there. All the stars would come out to practice before they did the *Ed Sullivan Show* Sunday night. You could sell your late Saturday night spot to whoever was doing Sullivan the next night. Like Joan Rivers would pay you to let her try out before that live audience. Every performer worked at Pip's.

"At Sheepshead Bay, you could eat at one of the restaurants, buy fish fresh off the boats, or throw a line off the wooden bridge connecting Sheepshead Bay and Manhattan Beach."

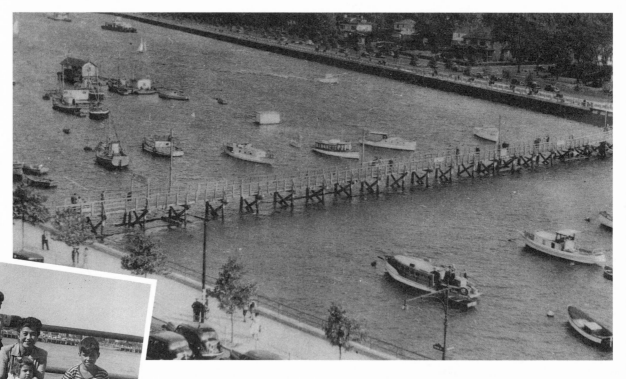

MARTIN SPITZER: Eating out was a Sunday ritual. My father came back from playing handball at Brighton Beach about 12:30, and we'd all go out for lunch. If friends were there, we took them along. Out of a month, three weekends we would go Chinese, and the fourth weekend we would go Italian.

There was a good Chinese place on Eighty-sixth Street upstairs, right near the elevated trains, and also the New Deal, on Bay Parkway and Sixty-fifth Street; later, it changed its name to Tang Fong. There were always lines outside and people we knew from the neighborhood inside. They didn't have all the fancy dishes they have today, just chow mein and chop suey, wonton soup, spareribs, egg rolls, and fried rice.

For Italian, we went to one of the restaurants in Coney Island. Stella's was a little family-owned storefront. You walked in and sat yourself down. They'd come over with their menu—not a big folded thing, but a paper sheet. I don't even think they had tablecloths. There was a big potbellied stove in the kitchen that you could see from the dining room, and you could overhear the family arguing in there. It made you feel like you were one of them.

KARL BERNSTEIN: Gargiulo's was and is the fanciest of the Coney Island Italian restaurants, with high ceilings, ornate decorations, and tile floors.

The Carolina used to have a little garden that was an outdoor dining room in the warm weather. You had to walk through the kitchen to get to it. After they paved the garden over, you still had to walk through the kitchen to get to the dining room.

MARTIN SPITZER: For pizza, there's no place like Tortone's, on Neptune and Fifteenth, just a little storefront with no signs. They use a little brick oven, all fresh ingredients, and make just so much dough. When the dough is gone, they close for the night; so if you're not there early enough, forget it. If you take a pizza out, they put it on a round cardboard and wrap it in brown paper. The aroma was unbelievable. People would come from all over; they still do.

LARRY STRICKLER: For seafood, everyone went to Sheepshead Bay. There was Pappas and there was Tappan's, but Lundy's was the tops, the apex. It was a beige stucco, two-story Spanish-style building with a red tile roof and green shutters on the windows that took up a whole block. The gigantic parking lot went all the way back to the Belt Parkway.

MARTIN SPITZER: They'd open up the cherrystones and littlenecks and sell them a half-dozen or a dozen. You could put your hand in this jar and take out crackers—they weren't wrapped up, just loose—and eat them while you watched the fishing boats in the bay.

SHELLY STRICKLER: There were so many entrances to Lundy's, and it was mobbed, especially on Sundays. There was no such thing

Lundy's was the tops, the apex of Sheepshead Bay dining.

as a line. You looked for a table that was finishing, where they were having dessert, and stood behind it, waiting, ravenous.

NORMAN TIPOGRAPH: Patsy, a head waiter, was a handsome black man, very dignified looking in his black jacket and pants, black bow tie with a white shirt. He had been at Lundy's for many years. Henry, my father-in-law, would walk up to him: "I'm here with the family."

"All right, Mr. Modell."

And as soon as a table cleared, we got it.

DORIS MODELL TIPOGRAPH: We had the shore dinner for about six bucks. This was what you got: a shrimp cocktail, a cup of clam chowder, the little round biscuits (which were heaven), and the hardtack like a soda cracker; then a salad of sliced tomatoes and onions, half a cold lobster, half a broiled chicken, french fries, home fries, or corn; and then the best blueberry pie or apple pie, with Breyers ice cream.

LARRY STRICKLER: The waiters all seemed to have Caribbean lilts. They were so abrupt you had to know exactly what you wanted when they came over, or else they'd be gone and you'd wait an eternity. They looked like they were moving fast, but the food never came out.

NORMAN TIPOGRAPH: They were brusque because they had to serve a lot of meals and wanted the turnover. It was hard work, and they worked for very low wages.

ELLIOT GUNTY: After they finally took your order, you'd sit there twenty minutes. The kitchen was so far away. And then it all came.

LARRY STRICKLER: You'd put some butter on the hot biscuits and it would melt. My mother would be screaming I should stop eating them. I'd be whispering to my father to ask for more.

JOE SIGLER: When a relative came to town, we'd take him to Lundy's for breakfast: clams on the half-shell. We'd bring back one of their pies, leaving a deposit for the tin plate.

But Sheepshead Bay was more than Lundy's to me. I remember watching the sun rise over the water hours before Lundy's opened. I'd go down there with Sherwood Levine, who lived in the apartment underneath me. We had this system of knocking on the radiators to wake each other up at 4:00 A.M. We'd get dressed, grab our fishing poles, and take the subway at the Parkside Avenue station. It would still be dark out, but there we'd be, fishing off the docks at Sheepshead Bay.

TERRY PERNA ARNESEN: When my father went to Sheepshead Bay, it wasn't to eat at Lundy's or Tappan's, but to buy fresh fish off the boats. He and my mother came from a small island between Rome and Naples, and fish was a staple in their diet. Every Sunday morning, he'd go down and wait for the ships that came in about noon. He'd buy eight flounder or bluefish for a dollar, bring them home, clean them, and we'd have fried fish, fish stew—you name it.

NORMAN TIPOGRAPH: A ferry used to run among all the fishing and excursion boats in Sheepshead Bay. It left the pier at Ocean and Emmons and crossed the Rockaway Inlet to Lois's Pier at Breezy Point, the western tip of the Rockaway peninsula. It cost twenty-five cents for a forty-minute ride. That's where I took Doris on our first date.

Sometimes late in the evening, after taking Doris back to her home in Manhattan Beach, I'd walk the distance to Sheepshead Bay. It would be the middle of the night, but there'd always be people fishing off the wooden bridge. I'd ask a fellow to give me a line, and I'd fish or crab until the sun came up. Then I'd grab the Ocean Avenue trolley and take it back to Flatbush, where I lived.

CHAPTER 6

Everybody Knew Everybody Else's Business

YOUR MOTHER AND MY MOTHER
WERE HANGING OUT CLOTHES,
YOUR MOTHER GAVE MY MOTHER
A PUNCH IN THE NOSE.
WHAT COLOR WAS THE BLOOD?
—Choosing rhyme

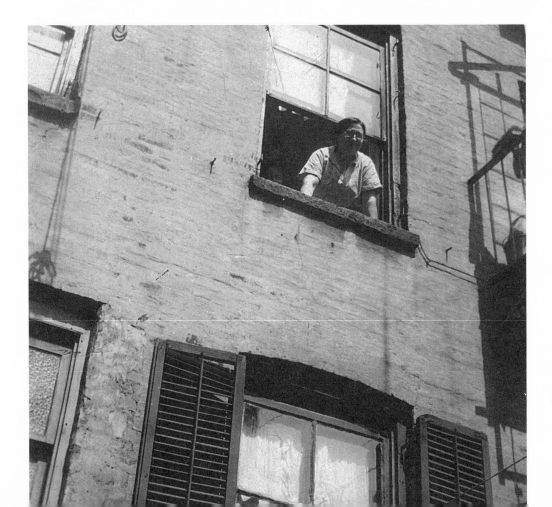

DONNA GEFFNER: Our windows of our apartment faced the court-yard. If a light was on at one o'clock in the morning, a neighbor would telephone, "Is everything OK?"

JOAN RIBAUDO: When someone was sick, the news went through the building like lightning. Within minutes, everybody knew, and people would be knocking on your door to find out if you needed something.

JOYCE SHAPIRO FEIGENBAUM: My father was an auditor for the IRS. On the way to work, people would waylay him and try to turn one of the other neighbors in. My father would take out a little pad, write something down, and say, "Thank you for letting me know." But he never did anything about it.

MIRIAM KITTRELL: Everybody knew everybody else's business: what they did for a living, who was making money and who was laid off, what was going on with the children. From their windows, the women would call to each other across the courtyard: "John—the super—was drunk last night."

"Well, he's not Jewish, so he can be an alcoholic."

MARCO CARCICH: Whenever I walked through the entrance courtyard of my grandparents' apartment house on Avenue J, I'd be aware of all these conversations going on over my head. People were shouting back and forth, from window to window: "Where are you going?" "Are you going shopping?" "Where's the game tonight?"

CAROLINE KATZ MOUNT: Notions of privacy were very differ-ent living in those apartment houses. You'd overhear another family's life: the arguments, the scraping of chairs, the creaking of furniture, the footsteps on the wooden and linoleum-covered floors, the doors slamming as people went in and out.

MAX WECHSLER: My bedroom up on the third floor faced out onto the courtyard. I could smell food cooking, hear fights, different kinds of music and ball games on the radio. And at night, if a light was on and a shade was up, I could see whatever was going on. The guy who lived in the apartment directly across from my window had married a German girl and brought her and her sister over. They were tall, blonde, and shapely—and into calisthenics, which they performed without any clothes.

What I liked best was when they lay side-by-side on the bed and did leg-lifts. Benjamin Gordon—Fidgety-Ben—would come over with the telescope he bought for stargazing; he liked the arm rotations best. Once the girls noticed us watching. But they didn't lower the shade or stop exercising. It got so that my friends were dropping by every evening for a private showing.

TOBY SCHOM GROSSMAN: Neighbors were always dropping in unannounced, but my father loved people, and having company made him very happy. I never knew my own grandmothers, but Mrs. Epstein, who lived on our floor, was like a grandmother to me. She was a tiny old lady, always beautifully dressed, with silvery tinkly jewelry and big glasses that magnified her eyes. I never had any sisters or brothers, but there were so many children in the building or children visiting family in the building that it seemed like I had a big family.

HERBY GREISSMAN: In 1948 or '49, a family named Unger purchased the first television in our building. At eight o'clock on Tuesday night, the whole apartment house went into the Unger living room. They had more people in that one room watching Milton Berle.

GAIL EISEMAN BERNSTEIN: One day when I was in the fourth grade, I came home for lunch (my mother made me a tuna-fish sandwich for lunch every day), and some men were there delivering our first television set, a Shaw Video TV. It took all day. They put our antenna up on the roof on top of the elevator shaft, so we would get the best reception.

From then on, we didn't have to go to Eleanor Schaeffer's anymore to watch TV. Everyone in our forty-two-family building used to go to Eleanor's apartment, E-1, on the fifth floor. The set was in the foyer. It was wall-to-wall chairs for the grown-ups; the children sat on the floor. No food was ever served. We were there to watch television: Milton Berle, *I Love Lucy*, *Man Against Crime*.

FREDDIE GERSHON: A couple of hundred people lived in my apartment house, and everyone socialized with everyone else. If two women had a fight over a mah-jongg game, the building lined up in two camps.

STAN GOLDBERG: Mah-jongg was the social thing for the women in the neighborhood, the status symbol. My mother's game was Class A. Class B was another game hoping to develop into Class A. You had to be sharp to be seated in my mother's game—you had to be fast, a first-rate player. Pat Meyers, the epitome of the all-American

In time, the television set replaced the radio in the honored spot of the living room.

girl, was the daughter of the number-one per-diem player in my mother's game, on call when someone backed out. That was a big deal.

Pineapple was a must. It was served at every game, sliced and spiked with fancy plastic toothpicks that looked like little swords. Sometimes my grandmother sent sponge cake up on the conveyor belt—that is, the bannister—from her apartment downstairs.

My room was about three feet from the living room where the games were played so I overheard all the conversations. Once one of the ladies said, "When my Irving wants something special, he puts his arm around me." Just then I called out, "Ma, can I have some water?" They all screamed. "Oh my God, he heard me," the lady said. "I thought he was sleeping."

The Class A mah-jongg group and spouses celebrate at a bar mitzvah.

My mother introduced me to a new player. She took a look at me and said, "This one has bedroom eyes." Later I said, "Ma, did I look that tired?" I didn't get everything right away. But as time went on, I'd realize, "Oh, that's what they meant."

The mah-jongg games were very provocative. One woman was caught planting tiles in her bosom. They were talking grand jury, but she got off. She had a good attorney.

These were bright, upbeat women who talked about world events, McCarthyism, race relations during the games. They were active in neighborhood things, formed an organization named after a local boy who was killed in the war that helped the veterans' hospital, and had

Memorial Day and Veterans Day services every year. They were well-groomed and attractive women, not yentas in housecoats with rollers in their hair.

KARL BERNSTEIN: My mother and a group of ladies on the block formed a group they called the Musicale. Each month they met at someone's home, where each woman would perform a piece on the piano, and then they would have coffee and cake. Over the years, there was less and less playing, more and more eating. After a while we started calling it the Musicalorie.

HERBY GREISSMAN: On our small block on Twenty-fourth Avenue between Sixty-fourth and Sixty-fifth streets, there were three walk-up apartment houses—about forty apartments in each building, most of them filled with families. We were war and postwar babies, kids my age, a couple of years older, a couple of years younger.

JOAN RIBAUDO: There was always a series of youngsters, like a stepladder—we grew up together. We played in the streets, and the grown-ups sat along the sidewalk and watched.

Once a father commented, "You boys don't know how to play punchball. In my day, we could have beat you." Of course, it was a challenge. This they couldn't do in the street, because it had to be properly witnessed. They went to Seth Low Park. All these men with nice upright posture walked the four blocks to the game. But coming back, they were the dregs of the earth, and in the following days we saw legs in casts, arms in slings.

HERBY GREISSMAN: The building across the street had two glass doors in front. One was always closed, and the other you opened to go in and out. The glass on the closed door broke, and for a long time it stayed that way—just the iron frame without any window pane inside. There was one kid in the building who would come down and take a running jump through the iron frame of that stationary door. He did it every day, every time he went out, every time he came in. Finally they get around to replacing the glass. Only nobody tells him. Next day, he comes down, takes a running jump, and *crash!*

He got scratched up pretty good, but we were always getting scratched and bruised from playing and fighting with each other. My mother, however, never got involved in any of her children's battles. "The children fight and make up, and the parents stay mad forever," she'd say.

JOYCE SHAPIRO FEIGENBAUM: When Carolyn Cantor got into a fight, she'd not only slap and scratch, she'd bite. One day she bit Judy Levine in the hallway outside of the Levine apartment. Judy's mother was in the shower at the time, but that didn't prevent her from hearing her daughter scream. She ran out soaking wet, with just a towel wrapped around her, grabbed Carolyn and started shaking her, yelling how she was fed up with her biting all the kids. Mrs. Cantor appeared. "Leave my daughter alone," she cried, pulling Mrs. Levine off Carolyn. The two women began wrestling on the ground. In a flash, the whole building was at the scene. My mother picked up the towel, which naturally had fallen off Mrs. Levine, and ran around the pair holding the towel over them. That was one argument that took a long time to heal.

CAROLINE KATZ MOUNT: None of the kids in our building could get into a fight when Nick, the super, was around. He'd always get in the middle, stop the battle, make us shake hands and make up. Every kid in the building loved Nick. No matter how busy he was, he always paid attention to us.

TOBY SCHOM GROSSMAN: The first time I saw Nick, I was three years old. It was a January afternoon, the day I arrived in this country. I was born in a displaced-person camp in Germany. My aunt and uncle sponsored my parents and me. They met us at the ship and brought us to their building. When we got there, it was snowing lightly and just starting to get dark. A man was standing outside, all by himself. It was Nick. I thought he was waiting for us. He took me by the hand and brought me to my aunt's apartment, which was next door to his own. I didn't understand a word he said because I spoke only Yiddish.

MARNIE BERNSTEIN: Nick was short and squat, tough-looking like a wrestler, but actually he was a very gentle and warm man who loved children. He had maybe five or six of his own, but only one son lived with him. The rest were in foster homes because his wife was unstable, in and out of hospitals. One Christmas she came home for a few days. She went into the lobby in the middle of the night, dressed in a nightgown, her hair long and wild, and rang all the bells. It was terrible. Nick's favorite child was the baby, Rosemarie. He always talked about her, showed off her picture. She stayed with him for a little while, and we all thought she was just beautiful, like a pink doll.

HERBY GREISSMAN: Nick had so much work to do. He collected the garbage from every apartment using dumbwaiters that operated through open shafts in the building. The furnace was fired by coal, so he had to stoke it every day and bring out the ash barrels.

CAROLINE KATZ MOUNT: There were so many babies in those postwar years, and the carriages for all the babies in the building were kept in the cellar. Every morning, Nick would wheel them up onto the street. They'd be standing there in a row waiting for the mothers when they came out with their babies. And in the late afternoon, he'd push them back down, making a long line of carriages, one behind the other, wheeling them around the corner, down the sloped alleyway, and into the cellar.

MARNIE BERNSTEIN: Nick had been in vaudeville with his four brothers in an act called the Shanghai Five. He let us look through his big album at the old programs, newspaper reviews, and photos of the group taken with Eddie Cantor and Jimmy Durante. They were dressed in Chinese pajamas and made up to look like Charlie Chan. The Shanghai Five played at Coney Island saloons and at theaters all over the country, even the Palace, until vaudeville ended.

Nick still had a great voice. On rainy summer nights, everyone would bring their folding chairs into the lobby, and Nick would entertain. His favorite song was the Neapolitan ballad: "Oi Marie, oi Marie, quanto notti aggio perso per te. . . ." His tenor voice was so strong, neighbors in the buildings across the street and next door heard him. They would come over, crowding into our lobby.

Nick wasn't the only singer in the building. There was also Mrs.

"There were so many babies in those postwar years."

Parker, who lived in a top-floor apartment with her husband, a cordial and elegant bookie who dressed impeccably in well-cut suits and silk shirts and ties, and their beautiful redheaded daughter. Mrs. Parker mostly kept to herself. The other women referred to her as the Nightingale, I guess because she would sit by the open window of her bedroom overlooking the courtyard, her plump arms crossed on a pillow, and sing Jerome Kern and Sigmund Romberg songs. In warm weather, when the doors to the courtyard were open into the lobby, you'd walk through and "You are the promised kiss of springtime" would be echoing through the halls.

TERRY PERNA ARNESEN: My mother sang all the Neapolitan love songs around the house while she dusted and cleaned. We always listened to records, to opera on the radio. Part of being Italian was knowing all the different Italian operas. Our neighborhood was a mixture of Italian and Jews. But when you passed by and heard the music, or saw the backyard with the tomato plants and the sweet basil and the fig tree with the little pink blossoms, you knew it was an Italian family.

ANGELO BADALAMENTI: The Italians always bought little houses, because they needed a place to have tomatoes, basil, and some flowers. That all came from the old country, along with the love of music.

When I was very young, we lived on Harway Avenue, an exclusively Italian neighborhood. Every weekend in the summer, they had shows in tents on the empty lots that were all over the area. They were mostly Italian dramas. The audience would be very quiet. Except every once in a while, you would hear somebody snore.

KARL BERNSTEIN: Mrs. Capricilli, who lived across the street from us, kept a beautiful and immaculate garden in the back and poplar trees in the front. I guess they reminded her of Italy. When Mr. Capricilli died, my mother and Aunt Sally paid a condolence call, and my cousin Billy and I went along. It was the only time I was in that house. The walls were painted purple and black. Beautiful paintings hung on the walls. She was an elegant lady, but still she used to scrub her stoop and the driveway from back to front every morning, on her hands and knees with a bucket and brush. Then she would sweep the debris in the gutter from her side to ours.

Bugsy Goldstein, who lived across the alley from us, was a hit man for the mob. He was tough. When he spoke to you, it was like hearing James Cagney. He was away a lot of the time; I guess in jail.

His daughter Joannie was my closest friend in first grade. My cousin Billy and I were invited to her birthday party, and my Aunt Sally and my mother were so excited because all the "gun molls" would be there. They wondered what they would talk about. The "gun molls" talked about what other mothers talked about: diapers, formula, babies. But at that party, Bugsy went out to get ice cream and was picked up by the police. When finally he was electrocuted, his mother and father were screaming outside in the street. Then they moved away.

MAX WECHSLER: Everyone in the neighborhood knew that Marvin's father was a big-time gangster. His family lived on Roebling Street, in a duplex apartment on the top floors of the best building in all of Williamsburg. It had a doorman, furniture in the lobby, and an elevator. Two guys dressed in dark suits always sat right outside the elevator, reading the newspapers and smoking Lucky Strike cigarettes. They were bodyguards for Marvin's father, screening all the people coming on the floor, and sometimes were runners for the numbers game.

In junior high, Marvin and I became friends. We used to play cards in his apartment after school. Once, we had finished a game of poker and were walking out to the elevator when one of the guys, a big, heavyset man, put up his fists like Rocky Marciano. "Come on, kid, let's go a round or two," he said, giving me a playful but hard slap in the face.

For the moment, I forgot where I was and lashed out at him, landing a closed fist right on his nose with all the force I could muster. He went back against the wall, and at the same instant, reached inside his suit jacket and pulled out a gun. Lucky for me, his partner jumped in front of him. "For Chrissake," he said, "he's just a kid."

The next day Marvin told me his father really gave it to the guy. Still, I stayed away from the apartment for a while. When I finally went back after a couple of weeks, the guy greeted me at the elevator. "You gotta learn to take a joke, kid," he said sheepishly. "I woulda never hurt you."

LUIS COLMENARES: Trina and Johnny Castros lived next door to us in a seven-room apartment, two of which they rented to boarders. Maybe because they had no kids of their own, they always invited us in to listen to the radio or to stories Johnny told about Puerto Rico, where he was born. Trina was very tall and thin, a Miss Brooks–type personality. Johnny was very short, with a lot of white hair; we thought he looked like Albert Einstein. He made cigars in a place on Fulton

Street, and there was always a sweet aroma in the room he kept for himself in the back of the apartment.

CHARLES HYNES: Mr. Helman spent the nice days sitting in the large open courtyard of our building, wearing very dark glasses. Once he had been an executive in the garment business, but he lost his sight when he was in his early forties. The kids used to greet him. He got to know all of us by our voices. He would say things like, "If you point one finger, three point back" and "It never hurts to talk" and "Never answer a speculative question."

AL LEWIS: We lived in four different buildings on Douglas Street, which later became Strauss Street, in Brownsville. They were tenements, six-by-eight rooms, railroad flats. People joked about putting the key in the front door and breaking the window.

DORIS MODELL TIPOGRAPH: When we moved to the brand-new Nathan Hale, on Avenue K, I thought we were so rich, because the building had an elevator and an incinerator.

DONNA GEFFNER: Our building on Twenty-third Avenue had an elevator and an incinerator, and also our very own doctor. Dr. Smilensky's office, on the ground floor right, was always filled.

The sectional couch defined the elegant apartment-house living room and was the favored spot for entertaining.

Everyone in the building used him. He knew about the head, about the ears. He knew when it was emotional; he knew when it was physical. If you were sick, he'd come up to see you in your apartment, and as soon as he walked in, you had that feeling of *refia*—that you're going to get better.

ALAN BLANKSTEIN: When I was a kid, doctors had much more of a personal relationship with the patients. They all made house calls. But even in those days, Dr. Matthew Brunner was in a class by himself. I was asthmatic, and my parents used Dr. Brunner because he was such a big specialist. His office was on Eastern Parkway, which was quite a distance from our Flatbush house, but when I had an asthma attack, he'd come to the house, and he wouldn't leave until he was sure I'd be all right. Sometimes he stayed all night. He would sit around the table talking to my parents and play the piano to keep himself occupied.

MARNIE BERNSTEIN: A blast on the outside bell announced the arrival of Dr. Kaufman. He reminded me of Groucho Marx: the bright black eyes, the wide grin, the fast, long stride. He'd storm into the apartment, examine the patient one-two-three, make a quick diagnosis, write out the prescription, get his five dollars, and be gone. The only time he hung around was during the Rosenberg trial. His brother was the judge who sentenced them to the electric chair. "Guilty, guilty, no question about it," he'd tell my father.

PAT COOPER: Dr. Rini's office was on First Place and Clinton, but if you were sick, he'd come to your house, sit down, have a dish of macaroni. He never got paid. I was about twelve when my father took me to Dr. Rini. "My son has an appendix," he said. "I tell you right now, you don't make the scar more than one inch and a half or I'll kill you. Because my son has to be a man. And when he takes his clothes off with a woman, I don't want my son to scare her with the scar."

I'm looking at my father. This guy's crazy. He has me taking my clothes off with three girls in the room, I'm dropping dead from the pain, and he's worrying about my scar. But if I showed you my belly now, you'd never find it.

HOWARD RAPP: For years and years we went to Dr. Grodzicker, whose office was on the ground floor of a brownstone in Williamsburg. He drove a new Oldsmobile and handled every ailment. My mother was afraid my brother was going to be short, so Dr. G. gave him a

The family doctor was
hard to spot in the crowd
assembled for this *Brith*
(ritual circumcision).

series of shots to make him grow. I got away without taking them. We both wound up the same height—on the short side.

KARL BERNSTEIN: Dr. Feller was my grandmother's and my great-grandmother's doctor. He did surgery, he delivered babies. We still have his instructions in the baby books.

His full name was A. Archibald Feller, but everyone called him Dr. Feller, except for my cousin Helene, who called him Doc Archie. She was part of the family that still lived in Williamsburg, where his office was.

POLLY BERNSTEIN: After we moved to Bensonhurst, we would go by train to visit him. Once he got sick and he said, "Polly, you'll have to get yourself another doctor." And I said, "What's another doctor? I don't know another doctor."

He was a very temperamental man. You had to watch out not to annoy him. I was in the waiting room when a religious couple came in with a little boy. All of a sudden, I heard him yelling, and when he yelled, it was really frightening. "Your child is dying, and it's all because of you. Last week you were here, and I told you to take him to the hospital. Now you're coming back here, and there's nothing I can do."

MAX WECHSLER: Cuffs on the side of the head, two meat-hook–type hands grabbing my shoulders, and a physical presence that was like a football fullback—that was Dr. Feller.

There were the times I would be pulling my pants down, and I wasn't fast enough for him. He'd help out, yanking on my belt the way somebody would pull on a window shade. Then I'd be on the table belly-down and get a needle in the behind. His famous B-12 shots. He believed in that stuff.

KARL BERNSTEIN: Dr. Feller was a massive man, six-two or six-three. He was gruff, he had a raspy voice and a bald head always covered with sweat, and he smelled of chopped liver and onions. In hot weather, he wore a cutout undershirt with his white coat over it. He came all the way to our house in Flatbush in his great big Buick. Once he had indigestion and asked my grandmother, "What do you have for heartburn?" She gave him Pepto-bismol, which he always liked.

Most of the time, though, we went to his office. During the war, when my father's car was up on blocks in the garage, we went by trolleys: the Coney Island Avenue trolley to Park Circle and the Franklin Avenue trolley to Williamsburg.

His office was the bottom level of his house, a converted brownstone on Bedford Avenue and Wilson Street. The waiting room had a fireplace and a set of children's furniture: a table with folded leaves and two little chairs. The kids would wait in line to sit on those chairs. The wait, of course, was interminable. And then you got called into an examining room, and he fluoroscoped you.

MAX WECHSLER: It had a white scale for babies that looked like it was designed for fruits and vegetables, a scale for adults with a vertical strip to measure height, about five different clocks, and glass-fronted cabinets with all kinds of bottles behind them. Everything was immaculate.

After he examined you, Dr. Feller called you into his office in the back with the huge desk and built-in bookcases. Military certificates hung on the wall along with his doctor's diplomas. They seemed like testaments to his valor. There were medals and a little statue of a soldier—memorabilia from his World War I time. The word was that he had been a major. He was always rough and ready, caring, and in perfect control of any medical and family situation. He was the kind of man that you would want to follow into battle.

MARTY ADLER: Prior to going off to battle in Cuba, Teddy Roosevelt took his troops down to Brighton, in the area that now is the very end of Ocean Parkway, and they practiced landing on the sand. A twenty-by-forty-foot area called San Juan Park marks that event. It has a plaque with part of the hull of the battleship *Maine*. For our generation, that part of Brighton was famous for its own kind of battles: the handball games.

LOUIS COHEN: I played all over Brooklyn, but especially in Brighton. I loved it. I never got tired. Every Saturday morning, every Sunday morning, no matter how cold it was, I was out there in shorts, no undershirt.

I began playing handball in the 1930s, during the Depression, when no one had money for baseball gloves and bats. All you needed for handball was a small black ball and gloves. You played anybody who came along; you needed only one or two guys to get a game going. Guys in their fifties, sixties played. I saw fellows play who were in their eighties. It was amazing how much stamina they had, but that was because they played all the time. They never stopped.

MARTIN SPITZER: Handball players were guys who worked in the shipyards and in factories; they were blue-collar workers predominantly—men used to using their hands, which were strong and callused. They showed off their strength and power on the handball court hitting that little black ball. Handball was their way of letting off steam from working all week long.

FREDDIE GERSHON: All the men were expected to play handball, and it was a rough sport. My father tore a ligament in his knee and had to wear a cast for a month. My uncle Jack Zirn got so good he went on the circuit and became a champion. He got a heart attack while playing and actually died on the handball court.

MARTIN SPITZER: The matches were very intense. You knew if you watched that you'd have to be quiet. Even if a great shot was made, there was no applause. It was not an exhibitionist era. There were no official umpires. Crowds of about two dozen people hung around at the different courts. Most were other players waiting for the next challenge. To get on the court, you had to wait for a loser.

World-class then was just the guy next door, without the big money that people make today. Even players like Jimmy Jacobs and Victor Hershkowitz would come down on Sunday in between their tournaments and play on court number one.

LOUIS COHEN: Handball was my life. My wife would say, "Lou, will you ever stop?" I said, "I'll never stop." But I got hit by a van. My back is bad. I can't bend. It kills me whenever I go out to Brighton and look at the handball courts. I want to play.

From Sweltering Stoop to Shimmering Shore

(TO THE TUNE OF "HOME ON THE RANGE")

WHERE THE SWEET BREEZES DESCEND,
FROM THE SHORES OF GRAVESEND,
AS WE SINK SLOWLY INTO THE BAY.

—Lafayette High School Senior Sing, 1954

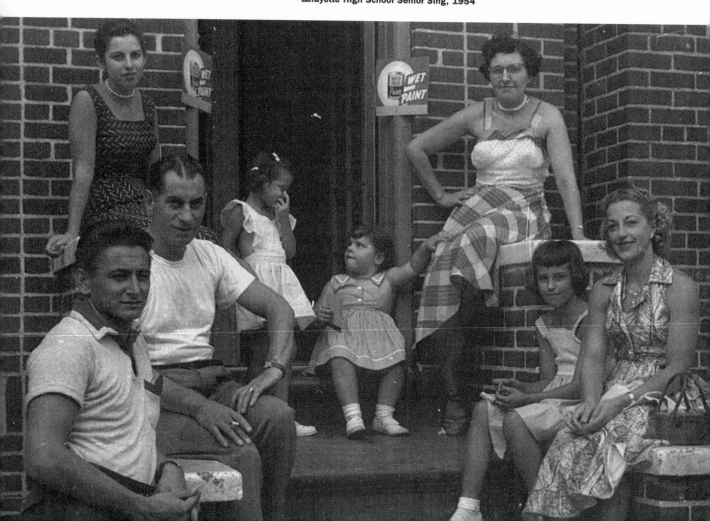

CAROLINE KATZ MOUNT: In the summers, the courtyard of our building became our patio, playground, even wading pool. When it got very hot, Nick—the super—would sweep it out, run up a hose, and hang it like a shower. We would run under the water. It was a wonderful treat.

JOAN RIBAUDO: My father attached a hose to a series of connected pipes in the courtyard. He'd have the kids tell their mothers. They'd come down in their bathing suits with chairs, bring lunch, and sit out in the courtyard all afternoon, going under the spray to keep cool. It was like our own private pool club.

HERBY GREISSMAN: On Sundays, my father and his friends would set out a bridge table and chairs in the courtyard and play pinochle. The laundry hanging on the lines gave them some shade. They'd send me across the street to the candy store for sodas, and I'd get a tip.

Our living-room windows with the fire escape were right over the front entrance to the building. One summer, somebody gave me a toy bugle. When my mother said, "It's time to go to sleep," I would go out on the fire escape and blow my bugle. That became a nightly routine.

I always had an audience because on summer nights, the whole block would be lined with people sitting on bridge chairs, a row with their backs to the building, and a row facing them with their backs to the street. When Rabbi Gartenhouse, who was very Orthodox, passed by, he'd walk in the gutter because he was afraid of brushing against a woman—that's how crowded the streets were.

CAROLINE KATZ MOUNT: The sidewalk became a narrow path. When we came home with boyfriends, it was like walking a gauntlet, having to say hello to all the neighbors and knowing they were giving you and your date the once-over.

The women did their handiwork while they sat outside. They'd be knitting sweaters, crocheting blankets, embroidering tablecloths and napkins in a cross-stitch pattern. The summer of 1949, there was a craze for basket bags—crocheted drawstring pocketbooks with little straw baskets forming the base. Everyone was making them.

ALAN BLANKSTEIN: The summertime scene on East Twenty-seventh Street was like a big hotel. About a hundred people would be out sitting on the little stoops of the semidetached houses, or on beach chairs. They'd walk over, sit on our stoop for a while, then we'd go

Tar beach: the apartment-house roof was a great spot for sunbathing.

over to them. Every woman on the block I called aunt, every man uncle. It was Aunt Miriam, Aunt Evelyn, Uncle Julius, Uncle Sheldon.

JOEL BERGER: If a night Dodger game was on, you could walk down the streets, go past house after house, and hear the southern voice of Red Barber on the radio without missing a single play.

KARL BERNSTEIN: People sat outside as long as they could to avoid the oppressive heat in the apartments. They'd bring out a torch lamp with an extension cord and a bridge table and play mah-jongg or cards till eleven, twelve o'clock.

TOBY SCHOM GROSSMAN: Not only were front doors never locked, people kept them open in the summer for cross-ventilation. Sometimes on hot nights, my father slept on the roof. On Tuesday nights, we all went up there to watch the Schaeffer fireworks from Coney Island.

CHARLES HYNES: Sometimes my mother would get me up in the middle of the night and say, "It's so hot. Let's go down to Coney Island." During the war, when gasoline was difficult to get, the car ran on naphtha, and we had all these cans of naphtha in the trunk. It's a wonder we weren't blown up. But we'd make it to the beach, put our blankets on the sand, and go to sleep. How safe it was, sleeping on the beach a summer night.

MAX WECHSLER: We would wake up with sand in our ears and hair and nose. Still, it was worth it. As bad as those summers could be in Brooklyn in those years before air conditioning, there was always relief at the beach and along the water.

FREDDIE GERSHON: My parents paid around sixty dollars a month for our three-room apartment on Coney Island Avenue across the street from the Brighton Beach Baths. We used to scornfully watch "the outsiders"—those people who had to travel to the beach—get off the train at Brighton Beach Avenue, at the site of Mrs. Stahl's knishes.

We did not go to the public beach. We belonged to Brighton Beach Baths, our select private club, which cost thirty to forty dollars a season for a locker, which we shared with three or four other families. Many members were European-born and very aware that they had their picture laminated in the back of a pass that enabled them to get in and out of the Baths. But it was their passport to a private and wonderful world.

LARRY STRICKLER: There were no real baths at Brighton Baths, just cold showers. Still, it was a great playground, with the ocean being only one of the amenities. If you exited onto the beach, you got the back of your hand stamped so you could get back in. There were always a gang of kids waiting under the boardwalk who did not have a ticket and would beg you to blot the still-wet ink from your hand onto theirs.

Inside was a kiddy pool, a gigantic swimming pool, a diving pool, handball and paddle-tennis courts. In the early days, there were hand-tennis courts; people played with their hands. It was not until the mid-fifties that it became fashionable to play with a paddle and a dead tennis ball.

There was a big round building with a cafeteria and picnic-style benches and a beautiful bandshell where a live band with two vocalists played for nine weeks in the summer, Tuesday through Sunday, two hours a day. People would get there early to get a good seat, or they reserved one by tossing an extra bathing suit or a towel on one of the multicolored Adirondack-style chairs. We danced on the sand in the hot summer afternoons to "I'm Going to Get You on a Slow Boat to China," medleys from Broadway shows like *Oklahoma* and *South Pacific*, or mambo music like "Sweet and Gentle," "Cherry Pink and Apple Blossom White," and "Mambo Number 5."

FREDDIE GERSHON: Everyone was taking dancing lessons, learning the rumba box step, which was very big. My grandmother, Grandma Becky, loved to sing in a heavy Rumanian accent and dance to "The Miami Beach Rumba," her platform shoes and clunky jewelry adding to the rhythm. She claimed to be a gypsy, and watching her sing and dance, you could believe her.

Brighton Baths had nude sunbathing facilities, separate sections for men and women. Everyone believed the sun was healthy. The more you exposed yourself, the better. They smeared themselves with baby oil and iodine and used sun reflectors to enhance their tans. Even in the wintertime, Grandma Becky and her girlfriends would go on the tar roof of our six-story apartment house, where they'd sit with their reflectors in beach chairs and take in the sun.

RALPH GASARCH: Brighton had all these big apartment houses, and some, like the Shelbourne on Ocean Parkway that took up a complete block, were quite luxurious. They had their own lockers and saltwater as well as freshwater showers, so you wouldn't bring sand up to your apartments. The roofs had separate men's and women's solariums for nude sunbathing. There was a European feeling in Brighton that something healthful was to be gained from the beach air, the salt and minerals in the water.

We lived in the eastern part of Coney Island, but we called our neighborhood West Brighton. I guess we didn't want to be identified with Coney Island. Both Brighton and Coney had bathhouses, but those in Coney Island, like Raven Hall and Washington Baths, were less upscale. Coney Island was transient. Brighton had a sense of permanence.

POLLY BERNSTEIN: One summer we took a locker at Coney Island. I hated it like poison. My brother-in-law and his wife rented an apartment in Coney Island after they got married, and I couldn't understand it. I didn't like all the common people, the yentas, the fat ladies. I'm not exactly a snob, but I don't like schleppers.

MARTIN SPITZER: We lived in Coney Island in a house owned by my grandparents, about half a block from the beach. They fixed up the basement as an apartment for themselves. My family lived on the first floor with the porch. Upstairs were four bedrooms and a bathroom. People came from Canada to stay in the summer. It was like a boardinghouse. What a fabulous place to live in, especially during the summer.

When I went away to college in Virginia and told people where I came from, they couldn't believe it. They thought Coney Island was all rides and amusements.

BILL FEIGENBAUM: We lived in Coney Island until I was a teenager. Then my father started to do better, and we moved to more-prosperous Flatbush. But to tell the truth, I liked it better in Coney. The resident population was working-class, bright and well-read, but dissatisfied, angry, being fed that propaganda that it was paradise in Russia.

Communist party rallies used to be held at different community centers in Coney Island, and my parents, who were politically left, brought me along with them. The entertainment was great. Usually it was supplied by a local beach bum, a slim, red-headed guy with a lively sense of humor who used to sit on the beach wearing a cowboy hat, strumming his guitar. It was Woody Guthrie. He came from

Three bathing beauties making plans.

Oklahoma or Texas, but he lived in Coney Island with his wife and two kids. His landlady, Anna Lomoff, owned a left-wing bookstore on Thirty-third near Mermaid Avenue. "That Voody, that Voody," she used to complain. He never paid his rent. But boy, he put on a terrific show. At one of the rallies, he brought a whole stack of his records along and sold them for a dollar apiece. People took them home and found they were all warped from the sun. He was on everyone's shit list.

KARL BERNSTEIN: From the heart of Coney Island, you could take the Norton's Point trolley just a short distance into another world. It started up in the air at the Stillwell Avenue subway station, crossed Stillwell Avenue on an elevated structure, dropped down to ground level on a right-of-way between Surf and Mermaid avenues, and ran to the western tip of the peninsula: Sea Gate.

PEARL GASARCH: People who lived in Sea Gate never thought of themselves as having a Coney Island address. Theirs was an exclusive enclave, only about a mile long and less than a half-a-mile wide, set off from the rest of the world by a guarded gate. It had its own garbage collection, security, and block of stores. Huge turn-of-the-century Victorian houses lined the waterfront. But by our time, they had been converted into rooming houses. When we were still living in Williamsburg, we rented an apartment in one of those old houses for the summer. It was a big dark place with varnished wood floors and stairs and bannisters. I'd climb the stairs and there would always be the smell of wood polish.

Later, my parents bought a home in Sea Gate, and we lived there year-round. Many of the people in the community were in the *shmata* business—that is, the garment trade—and during the war there was a lot of black-market money around from the goods they smuggled in from Canada. Also, for some reason a lot of bookies made their homes in Sea Gate, so there were always these big card games: pinochle for the men, canasta for the women. My father used to tell me that as the war progressed, the betting became bigger and bigger.

But to me, Sea Gate had nothing to do with playing cards. Living there felt like being in a seacoast town in Italy, far away from Brooklyn. It was a safe, gated world.

DORIS MODELL TIPOGRAPH: When we moved from Flatbush to Manhattan Beach, I thought it was like living in a resort area year-round. Our house on Dover Street had a lovely yard, and in the summertime we'd be engulfed by the aroma of honeysuckle; it was all over, so strong it was intoxicating.

I used to say that Brighton Beach, to the west, was for our grandparents; Oriental Beach, to the east (where Kingsborough Community College is today), was for the rich; but Manhattan Beach was for us.

Overchoice of summer pleasures at Manhattan Beach.

NORMAN TIPOGRAPH: Manhattan Beach was a glamorous summer place. Bands played for dancing, there were aquacades, you met lovely girls. Enclosed by Sheepshead Bay to the north and east and a magnificent beach to the south, it was a beautiful neighborhood. The streets were lined with substantial private homes. People like Judge Samuel Leibowitz, who defended the Scottsboro boys, and the wealthy Williamsburg Steel family lived there.

DORIS MODELL TIPOGRAPH: Instead of a boardwalk, Manhattan Beach had an esplanade that we walked along, trying to pick up guys. At night we'd ride our bikes along Shore Boulevard and watch the fishing boats on Sheepshead Bay.

ELIZABETH RONCKETTI: In the summers, people in Greenpoint always would go down to the East River piers. They'd sit there and dream, they'd fish. Newton Creek runs through the neighborhood. There used to be Whale's Creek also, but that was filled in. Boys have always swum in the East River. Some haven't quite made it and had to be fished out by the Fire Department.

BARRY FRANK: The thing about Brooklyn was that you always had a sense of the water. There was always that escape from the heat. But for me, it was something else as well. I was always drawn to the water. I'd get on my bike and head south, knowing I'd reach the end: the ocean or Jamaica Bay or Sheepshead Bay or Gravesend Bay. I could stand and look out at the horizon for hours.

TERRY PERNA ARNESEN: I loved to ride my bike from Borough Park down to Shore Road, to watch the ships in the Narrows coming up into New York harbor. Later on, when I taught at Curtis High School in Staten Island, I would take the ferry across the Narrows. That was before the Verrazano Bridge was built. I used to stand on the deck on foggy mornings and listen to the gulls and the foghorns. The Brooklyn docks were so busy back then. As many as twenty ships could be standing in a row, waiting their turn to get into port.

IRWIN POLISHOOK: From my home in Williamsburg, I could walk over to the Williamsburg Bridge and to the Lower East Side, in Manhattan. I would lean over the sides and look at the East River wind southward under the Manhattan Bridge and the Brooklyn Bridge till it flowed into the harbor. Or I'd look northward, follow the river along uptown Manhattan and wonder where Brooklyn ended and Queens began.

SYLVIA COLE: My first husband was a great romantic. He liked to stride along the boardwalk and the sand in Brighton, reciting Goethe. The ocean gave him that impetus to shout into the wind and the waves. That rotund German came out so big and round and dramatic.

NEIL SEDAKA: During a hurricane, I'd get dressed up in my galoshes and rain gear and walk the boardwalk. The wind would be blowing fifty miles an hour, and I'd hold onto the railing and breathe in the storm. I loved the ocean.

JUDY BERGER: Sometimes we rented horses from a stable at Bergen Beach and rode along the shore of Jamaica Bay. It gave us such a feeling of freedom and adventure. But it was also a little scary because we were so far from any kind of civilization.

Bergen Beach, Marine Park, Mill Basin, Canarsie—these were wild waterfront areas when I was a kid, so different from the crowded neighborhoods where we lived. I remember the big expanses, the fields of tall horse grass with only a lone house here and there. It seemed like the end of the world.

DAN LURIE: Our little house in Canarsie was about a quarter of a mile from Jamaica Bay. Around us were big, flat fields cut through with canals of water maybe a foot wide. We jumped across them when we played. We swam what we used to call BA (with no bathing suits) in a channel near where Starrett City is today, smearing its black mud all over our bodies. We rubbed it in good, jumped in the water, and got all cleaned off.

"Manhattan Beach was a glamorous summer place. . . . You met lovely girls." A favorite place for meeting: the Manhattan Beach casino.

Some of the houses were built on stilts because the water table was so high. Most of the roads were paved with dirt. A trolley ran from the end of the BMT line on Farragut Road and Rockaway Parkway, two miles down to the water. The tracks went along a right-of-way that was a narrow path cutting through the middle of East Ninety-fifth and East Ninety-sixth streets between the backyards of the houses. It went all the way down to Seaview Avenue, crossing Avenue L, Avenue M, Avenue N. . . . At the shore was an amusement park like a miniature Coney Island, and the Golden Gate arena, where they had boxing and wrestling bouts.

When I was a little boy, I used to have the same dream over and over: I dive off the Canarsie pier and swim to the bottom of the bay. It's blue and beautiful. Then I see this big chest. I open it up, and it's filled with pearls and jewelry and money.

Once I went fishing off the pier. It was at night, so I had a little kerosene lantern with me. When I caught a fish, I got so excited, I dropped the lantern into the water, and in pulling up the rod, the fish got off the hook. I lost everything. The following year, fishing in the same area in the daytime, I threw the line in and caught the lantern. My big fish story is that the lantern was still lit.

TOM BOORAS: My grandfather's hardware store, on Atlantic Avenue just below Hicks Street, was close by the waterfront. There were berths from the foot of the Brooklyn Bridge to Thirtieth Street and the Bush Terminal area. The Navy Yard came around the other end. Right under the Brooklyn Bridge was where Brillo manufactured the soap pads. All the raw materials came in on ocean vessels and were loaded into what they called boat warehouses.

My grandfather serviced pretty much that whole waterfront area in the lower end of Brooklyn. All these big, hulking longshoremen would buy their grappling hooks from him. They would either lose them or misplace them or get drunk and leave them behind. So they'd always need new ones. My grandfather sold them by the thousands.

LONNY IRGENS: My grandfather came to Bay Ridge from Norway and worked as a shipping master. Only recently did I learn what that job entails: a shipping master finds drunkards or tramps, knocks them out, picks them up, and shanghais them. When they wake up, they're out at sea. My grandfather accomplished this with the use of one arm. The other arm he lost when a train ran over it. He was one tough guy.

BOB ARNESEN: From Sixty-ninth Street up, the Brooklyn waterfront was lined with docks, which probably is why so many Scandinavians settled in Bay Ridge. They were seafaring people, and many worked on the ships.

Crossing the Narrows from Brooklyn to Staten Island, ferry-goers never tired of gazing at Lady Liberty.

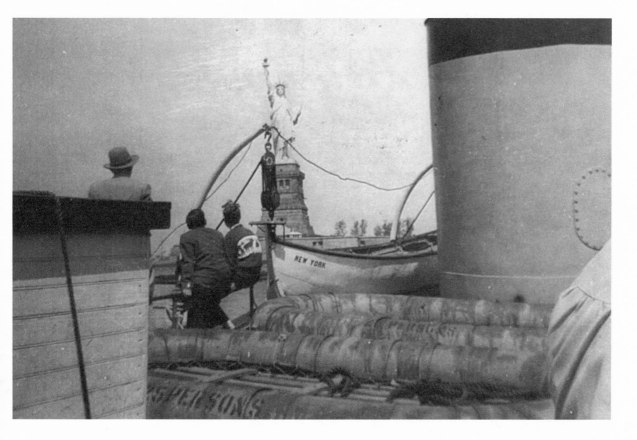

TOM BOORAS: From the time I was a kid, I was fascinated by the docks, the ships, and the water. Our house in Brooklyn Heights was right near the East River. When we were dating, my wife and I had this routine, it was like a ritual: I'd walk from my house on Sydney Place to her house on Hoyt and Warren. Then we would walk back on the Promenade, looking at that magnificent view of the New York City skyline across the river. Before the Promenade was built, around 1954, we used to walk across what they called the Penny Bridge that went from the end of Montague Street across to the St. George Hotel. We'd go up to the balcony above the hotel's saltwater pool and watch the swimmers below.

LUIS COLMENARES: The St. George had the only saltwater pool in Brooklyn. It was enormous and had a waterfall at one end. The walls, the ceiling, and the hallways leading to the pool were of a kind of golden, bluish glass carved with mermaids, mermen, and beautiful fish. If you sprang up off the high diving board, you could almost touch the glass ceiling.

TOM BOORAS: As I was a water rat, I could watch the swimmers at the St. George for hours. My father was the swimming coach at St. Francis Prep, and I had been swimming there from the time I was eight. From my earliest days, I've had this connection to the water. That's my connection to Brooklyn.

MARCO CARCICH: Out in Gravesend Bay you can see small lobsters, abundant fish. The whole coast along Coney Island is still one of the clearest sections for diving in the region. At every tide change, there's a complete change of water. The sweep of the Atlantic current drains the East River, the Hudson River, all the inlets. And that makes Brooklyn's shorefront the cleanest water in the New York area.

ELI WALLACH: Wherever you are in Brooklyn, you have a sense of the sea. From Coney Island, to the shorefront communities of Sea Gate and Manhattan Beach, to all the bridges that link the borough to other shores, to the boats coming into port, to the avenues and parkways named after the ocean and shore—there's water, water everywhere.

Coney Island

THERE STANDS ME WIFE,
THE IDOL OF ME LIFE,
SINGING ROLL OR BOWL A BALL,
A PENNY A PITCH.

—Barker's song

HENRY GERSHON: The subway doors opened up at the Stillwell Avenue station of the BMT, and I stepped out onto the elevated platform. There was brilliant sunshine, a breeze coming off the ocean, a taste of salt air. The masses of people swept me along onto Surf Avenue. I had only been in this country for a year, and I didn't know where to look first. I heard the organ-grinding music from the carousels, and that reminded me of the fairs in Europe. But they were nothing like Coney Island.

ELI WALLACH: I was entranced by the life-sized puppets enacting battle scenes. There were the freak shows, the bearded lady, the fat lady, the barkers, the whole carnival atmosphere of Coney Island. They influenced my decision to become a performer.

MARTIN SPITZER: Aromas came from all the little shops on the boardwalk: the melted butter on popcorn and hot corn on the cob, the sharp mustard, the burnt sugar from spinning swirls of cotton candy.

BILL FEIGENBAUM: You looked up and saw little wonder-wheel cars swaying in the blue sky, the parachutes opening up like big clouds before they dropped to the boardwalk. You heard the cries of barkers over loudspeakers, trying to lure the crowds, the roar of the roller coaster plunging down the wooden tracks and the screams of the riders.

NEIL SEDAKA: I knew every roller coaster in Coney Island. The Cyclone was the biggest; second was the Thunderbolt, across from Steeplechase. Down was the Tornado, the LA Thompson, the Bobsled, then the Virginia Reel, which was a round car that went up and down hills. Once in the wintertime, I had to walk up and down the tracks of the LA Thompson when it was closed. I don't know what it was about roller coasters; I was a bit freaky about that.

MARCO CARCICH: My first time on the parachute ride was a beautiful clear day. Before me was all of Coney Island, the whole beach crowded with people, the sparkling sea. I had never been up so high before. In those few seconds before the canopy of the parachute opened, sitting there with the straps dangling, I was as frightened as I've ever been.

KARL BERNSTEIN: We were on the Whip on a Friday night, all the guys from APO, the service fraternity at Brooklyn College. You sat two in a car and it went along smoothly till you turned the corner where it would whip around. We kept staying on. A crowd was waiting. They kept screaming, "Get off, get off." When we finally did, we pooled all our money, maybe twenty dollars and told the operator to keep the crowd that got on going till the money ran out. Those guys were screaming. When they finally got off, they were limp, wet rags.

Our favorite ride was the Tornado, because just as you got to the top, you overlooked one of the ladies' bathhouses, and it was always filled with nude women. But just as you got a good look, *whoosh!* you went down.

MARCO CARCICH: The people who worked in Coney Island formed a clique. Any kid of a member of the clique could go on all the rides for free. Since my grandfather worked at Bushman's Baths, when I'd come up to a ride, they'd say, "That's Matty's kid. Let him on."

Bushman's Baths was right on the boardwalk next to Manny's Knishes, which my grandfather's friend owned. Sometimes I'd go into the steambath. What struck me most about it was the strong odor of soap. I'd inhale and feel that the whole inside as well as the outside of my body was clean, 100 percent clean. The first time I went in there, I had a towel wrapped around my waist, but my grandfather pulled it off. "There's nothing to be ashamed of. The human body is something beautiful," he said.

Most of the time, though, I just liked to wander around on the boardwalk, which went on for miles. It was made of beveled planks, cut at probably a 30-degree angle, which gave it a herringbone effect and made it look wider than it actually was. All over the boardwalk were food concessions; penny arcades; rides and games like the poker game Fascination and the guessing games Guess Your Weight and Guess Your Age; shooting and throwing arcades; scooter ball, where you tossed a ball into a series of concentric rings and if you won, you got these coupons that you collected and saved in a big bag. At the end of the summer, I'd trade in five pounds of coupons and walk away with a whistle or a key ring. The most common prize was the Kewpie doll, which was made of hollow plaster, painted with gaudy colors, and decorated with gilt or sequins that got all over your hands and clothes. The Kewpie dolls were made by one manufacturer, so they all looked the same, although some had feathers stuck on their heads or were attached to long sticks. There were also piggy banks, teddy bears, and big cuddly dolls up on the shelves behind the games. But you didn't have a choice. They gave you what they wanted, usually the key rings or the Kewpie dolls.

The whole place was so confusing. You'd go off the boardwalk down one block, and there'd be rides and a new area to explore. For years, I couldn't map out in my mind where I was, where all the rides, the concession stands were. I would try to look for a focal point to get back to the boardwalk: a billboard, a flagpole.

I guess I never got over that early childhood experience of getting lost at Coney Island. I was about four or five, and my father and I had walked from the beach down to Nathan's for hot dogs. On the way back, we got separated in the huge crowd. I watched my father disappearing into the mob of people that was moving toward the boardwalk. He was holding up five franks in each hand and calling out my name. Soon all I could see were two plates of franks above the crowd. There was so much noise, I couldn't yell loud enough for him to hear me. I panicked. My next recollection is being held up in the air by some cop blowing a whistle and crying, "Whose kid is this?"

But by the time I was a teenager, I had developed a pretty good sense of the area. By then, one of my favorite occupations was sitting with a friend under the boardwalk and sifting through the sand for change. Also, we'd look up through the cracks and air spaces and watch people walking overhead. We could spend hours looking up the ladies' dresses. I'd catch a glimpse of something, and my imagination would run wild.

ROBERT MERRILL: I liked to sit under the boardwalk, strum on my ukulele, and sing along, imitating Bing Crosby. I didn't bother taking the train, I would walk to Coney Island all the way from Bensonhurst.

IRVING FIELDS: I played the piano in dozens of saloons on the Bowery, the pedestrian street running parallel to the boardwalk. I was about twelve or thirteen at the time, and I used to get paid off in hot dogs and sodas.

SHELLY STRICKLER: Late at night, people gathered in the little open-air gazebos on the boardwalk and made their own music, singing along to accordions, concertinas, balalaikas.

RALPH GASARCH: There was an entire week of big parades down Surf Avenue. The firemen from all over the city came on Fireman's Night, their red fire trucks polished and shining. There was Policeman's Night, baby parades on Saturday afternoons, floats and clowns and music.

MARTIN SPITZER: The Mardi Gras was on Labor Day. It was like New Orleans, with all the floats on Surf Avenue. I helped my uncles make confetti in the basement of my grandmother's house and sell little bags full for five cents apiece.

MURRAY HANDWERKER: One time, we had the Brooklyn Dodgers in the Mardi Gras parade. I remember Jackie Robinson sitting on the back of a car, waving to the people. The year the Brooklyn Dodgers won their only world championship, they came through Coney Island in a car caravan.

PAT AULETTA: I had a sporting-goods store on Stillwell Avenue, but I also sold a lot of beach stuff: Coppertone, bathing suits and caps, pails and shovels, sun reflectors. Did I sell them? I had a waiting line. There weren't many amusement parks, unlike today. Coney Island was a poor man's paradise.

MURRAY HANDWERKER: Coney Island was open twenty-four hours a day, and there was always a police presence. From Decoration Day to Labor Day, each precinct had to give up a certain number of officers to work in Coney Island. There were millions of people and very little crime.

Nelson Rockefeller (second from right) enjoying a Nathan's hot dog.

Steeplechase was in its heyday. There was no more Luna Park; it had burned down. Feltman's still had its shore dinner crowd and the oompah band used to play where Astroland is now. The rolling-strolling chairs would go up and down the boardwalk. And in the midst of it all was Nathan's.

Back in 1916, Eddie Cantor and Jimmy Durante talked my father into opening up his own frankfurter stand to compete with Feltman's.

They told him to sell his franks for a nickel, as Feltman's charged a dime. He started with a corner stand on property he rented (and later bought) from George Tilyou, the owner of Steeplechase. And then the subway opened up—the terminal at Stillwell Avenue—pouring the people out to the beach. That made Coney Island and Nathan's.

He was there, but without a name. People used to say, "Nathan, why don't you put up a name? I tell people to go down there, and I can't tell them what name." So in 1925, he incorporated. The word *famous* was being used a lot then. He put the sign up: Nathan's Famous.

BILL HANDWERKER: As a kid, I had no concept of what Nathan's meant. I just knew my father and my grandfather worked together in this big restaurant. As I got older, I began to realize the importance of it—how much people enjoyed eating at Nathan's and Coney Island amusements in general.

DOROTHY HANDWERKER: Sundays at Nathan's, there was such excitement. Murray was so enthusiastic, always full of ideas. He had lobster in New England and got the idea to bring lobster roll to Nathan's.

MURRAY HANDWERKER: On a Sunday morning, I'd get to Nathan's at 6:30. We had to blanch the potatoes. That means we half-cooked them and stored them in hundreds of wire baskets. When you had 90, 100 degrees before there was air conditioning, people who lived in New York streamed out of that subway terminal—great masses, crowds of people. On the way to the beach, people would stop for a drink or a hot dog. Then by two, three o'clock in the afternoon, it was the peak period, and it was crazy. The interesting thing, though, was the hotter it was, the less business we did. It was too hot to eat. Not that we didn't make money on the soft drinks— they ran off the beach to get sodas, sodas, sodas.

BILL HANDWERKER: If it was hot and the weather changed to rain in the late afternoon, the number of people coming off the beaches would be so astronomical that I could not raise my head from serving the french fries and collecting the money for, like, an hour straight. Everyone had to pass us on the way to the subway.

MURRAY HANDWERKER: When I first started working, Danny Fariello used to deliver the blocks of ice. One day we were short, and my father hired him to help out. That was it: Danny became our fastest handler. People came around just to watch him. You'd say, "Give me five franks," reach for your money, and when you looked up, the five franks were there. He served a frank a second.

My job was to see that everything was being run properly. Everyone handled cash. To ring up money held up service. So I designed a box with a chute and a fan to suck the money down. At the end of the day, we smoothed out the salty, greasy bills and counted them by hand.

During the summer, managers worked seven days. I told my father, "You gotta give them a day off." The first week that I gave these old-timers a day off, every one of them got burned to a crisp after hitting the beach. They couldn't come to work the next day. My father gave me hell. As for myself, I never went on the beach in the summertime. I was too busy. If I had a day or half-a-day off, we'd walk on the boardwalk, go to Steeplechase, the Aquarium.

The winter of 1947 there was the big blizzard. I walked to work all the way from East Twenty-third and Avenue M. The plow had

Steeplechase Park: "It didn't have the technology of a Disneyland, but it had an innocence that was so appealing."

pushed the snow against the store. The shutters were closed because it was so cold. But the workers were there from the night before; they had been snowed in and slept in the warehouse. So we opened for business. That day we sold twelve hundred franks. People drove up on the sidewalk to the opened windows and bought their franks and french fries. My father called from Florida. "What are you doing there? The place is closed, isn't it?" I said, "Dad, the place is open."

In 1954, Feltman's closed down. That summer we sold fifty-five thousand frankfurters in one day. But another year in the early fifties, we didn't do business. It was a magnificent summer. Beautiful weather—I don't think it rained one Sunday. But it was the year of the polio scare. The beach was empty. People wouldn't sit near each other, wouldn't go to crowded places. It was a rough season.

We were the original fast-food operation. We called it finger food; you didn't need a knife and fork. But it was always quality. My father insisted on that. Our potatoes came mostly from Maine. My father would go there to buy them. Originally, the french fries were put in a glassine bag—waxed paper. You had to open them up and put the scoop in the bag. Then we designed the cone, because you didn't have to open it. Corn was always a favorite. It came from Idaho, and we stored it in a freezer. The hot dogs were my mother's recipe, her spice formula, but they were made by Hygrade, which used to be a half-a-block away from Peter Luger's. We supplied the spices. All beef, less fat than the government allowed. I took over an old bathhouse to store all the food.

BILL HANDWERKER: I grew up in Lawrence, Long Island, where a typical birthday party was going bowling or roller skating. But every one of my birthdays for the basic years of my childhood were spent at Coney Island. My mother would bring me and about six of my friends to Nathan's. We could order whatever we wanted. The hot dogs were the favorite, of course, and then the lobster rolls. We'd go on the rides, walk along the Bowery, and from there enter Steeplechase Amusement Park. I loved their horse ride. I was less than thin, and the principle of the Steeplechase ride was the heavier you are, the faster you go. I won every time.

BILL FEIGENBAUM: It's amazing that nobody got hurt on those Steeplechase horses. Nobody got strapped in. Two people sat on a horse one behind the other. The ride went on sheer gravity. It was great for the boy-girl stuff; you'd go on with a girl, she'd be in the front, and you'd have to hug her tight to hold on.

The whole idea of Steeplechase was fun and sex. Everything was based on guys and girls making close contact. When you came in the main entrance on Stillwell Avenue, you had to go through a huge revolving barrel. Everybody would fall down and turn over, bump into each other trying to get up, fall down again, one on top of another. The Steeplechase horse ride exited onto a stage where wind tunnels blew up the girls' skirts, and clowns ran around giving people little electric shocks. When I worked at Steeplechase, I used to spend my whole lunch hour sitting in the audience watching the parade of people coming off the horse ride. And I was surprised to discover so many girls didn't wear panties. I remember one woman—she must have been 250 pounds—who did a little belly dance and had nothing on under her skirt.

MARCO CARCICH: You went down this enormous slide that landed you on one of maybe ten or fifteen large metal discs spinning in different directions. You'd slide onto one and spin left, then roll onto another one and spin right. You couldn't stand up on the discs. They kept you rolling over and spinning you around.

BARRY FRANK: My uncle, who was on the police force and looked as Irish as could be, would always get passes to Steeplechase. My favorite thing was sliding down into the pool, even though I always got an elbow burn or a knee burn because I couldn't land right.

"Most of the time, though, I just liked to wander around on the boardwalk, which went on for miles."

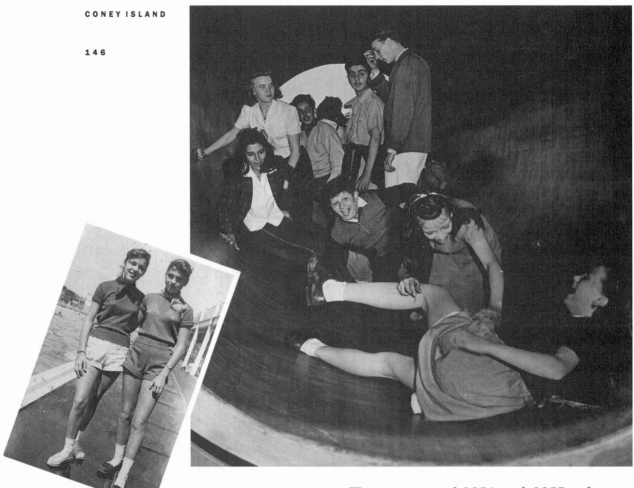

Going through the barrel and posing by the pool. "The whole idea of Steeplechase was fun and sex."

BILL FEIGENBAUM: The summers of 1956 and 1957, after my junior and senior years in high school, I was a Steeplechase scooter boy. I got the job through my friend Jerry Pellegrino, whose Uncle Jimmy was the manager. George Tilyou, the owner, wasn't Italian, but Jimmy was. And everyone who worked there was Italian except for me and two other Jewish guys.

As a scooter boy, my job was to bust up jams. I didn't wear a uniform like Jimmy, who worked the barrel, because the scooter work was so dirty. And there was always that smell of grease combined with the cotton candy and the salt of the ocean. But I loved every minute of it.

On Saturday night, the ride was jam-packed. Each scooter held only two people. People waited for as long as an hour and a half on a line that went all around the ride. There were a lot of single girls waiting, and you could attract their attention by showing off your athletic prowess, like flipping over the carts or running in between them to bust up the jams. I practiced a lot and could go from one end of the ride to the other without touching the floor, just by car-hopping on the little running boards around the cars. While the cars were emptying out and other people were getting in, I had the chance to pick up a lot of girls.

Once there was this southern guy waiting on the line who was bragging he was Elvis Presley's cousin. I bet him ten dollars to prove it. He takes out his wallet, and he's got this long series of pictures of him and the King hugging. He *was* Elvis Presley's cousin. The money this guy made doing that!

A camaraderie existed among Coney Island scooter boys. We all knew one another. We had our special heroes. One was a guy called the Cockaroach. He would spend every summer going cross-country from California to New York, from scooter ride to scooter ride, doing cartwheels and acrobatics across the ride. All summer the rumor kept going: "The Cockaroach is gonna be here by Labor Day." I thought they were making this up, like it was some kind of joke. But sure enough, Labor Day, the Cockaroach showed up. He must have been about thirty-five years old and looked like an aging Hell's Angel. And he did unbelievable acrobatics across the whole scooter ride, busting up these jams. He only got paid the standard seventy-five cents an hour, the same we all made. He did it because it was his thing.

Steeplechase was my thing. Everything was based on having a good time, on innocent sex. There was all that touching, hugging, falling down, bumping into each other, air ducts everywhere, stupid jokes everywhere. Music blared over loudspeakers: "Bye-Bye Love" or "Sha-boom by ay, ya-da-da-da-da. . . ." The art direction was great. It was such a beautifully designed place: blazing hot carnival colors, art deco motifs, the logo of the smiling man with all the teeth, the gorgeous imported merry-go-round. It didn't have the technology of a Disneyland, but it had an innocence that was so appealing. It was the best thing in Coney Island.

MARCO CARCICH: Almost every day of every summer I spent with my grandparents in Brooklyn, I would go to Coney Island. I had such a great time. I never wanted the summer to end.

But one day I was taking the trolley back to my grandparents' apartment when it suddenly came to a halt. All the passengers were surprised. It wasn't a regular stop. Nobody was waiting to get on, nobody was getting off. Then the conductor got up. He walked down the length of the trolley car and solemnly shook everybody's hand. "This is our last trip," he said. "The trolley won't be running to Coney Island anymore."

One Nation—Under God

FIRST COMES THE CHURCH,
THEN COMES THE STEEPLE,
OPEN THE DOORS,
AND OUT COME THE PEOPLE.
—Finger game

CLIFF HESSE: We belonged to a Lutheran church. A block away was the Russian Orthodox. Down the block was a synagogue and a small Catholic church. Nearby was an Episcopalian church and some Baptist churches and another kind of Lutheran church. They don't call Brooklyn the borough of churches for nothing.

BOB ARNESEN: My mother belonged to the Norwegian Methodist Church in Bay Ridge. I joined the Scotch Presbyterian on Seventy-fifth and Sixth. The parishioners spoke with burrs, and the minister was named Ian Scott, but the organist was Norwegian. Bay Ridge was filled with churches.

CHARLES HYNES: It was one of the wealthiest parishes in Brooklyn. For midnight mass, people like the Trumps, the McAllisters drove up to Holy Innocents on Fort Hamilton Parkway in horsedrawn carriages.

PAT COOPER: Sacred Heart in Red Hook was one of the poorer parishes in Brooklyn. In the winter, the priests would collect coal from between the tracks in the train yards and bring it to families who didn't have enough fuel to heat their houses. The younger priests would go around and bang on the doors: "Mrs. Esposito down the street, her husband lost his job. We have an obligation here." And people would give twenty cents, send a piece of meat, some vegetables over.

TERRY PERNA ARNESEN: The church on Fourteenth Avenue and Sixty-fourth Street was referred to as the Italian church. We lived closer to the one on Seventeenth Avenue and Forty-sixth Street that had mainly Irish parishioners. But they acted as if we were invading their territory. "This isn't your church. You really belong to the one on Fourteenth Avenue," they said. This enraged my father. Like many of the Italian immigrants, he was anticlerical, always angry at the Church. But the children reversed, became ardent Catholics.

TOM BOORAS: There was so much ritual in Catholic life, it spilled over into your social life. When I was a kid, Catholics weren't allowed to eat meat on Friday, and so we developed a ritual for Friday night, which was our date night: a whole crowd of guys and gals would jump into cars and drive from downtown Brooklyn to Coney Island. We had it timed so that we got there as close to midnight as possible. At the stroke of midnight, we'd be standing at Nathan's hot dog counter. A minute later, meatless Friday was over, and we'd be devouring franks.

In order to receive holy communion, you had to fast from midnight Saturday until you went to mass Sunday morning. We found a church that had mass at 1:15 A.M.: St. James Procathedral, on Jay Street. That made for another ritual: Saturday night, my buddies and I would hang out at a corner tavern on Jay Street, drinking beer till midnight. A quarter to one Sunday morning, we'd cross over into St. James Pro and sit down like the little holy boys that we were. A half-hour later, we'd get up and walk down the aisle for communion. We'd be kneeling at the rail, and the priest passing before us would always stiffen as the smell of the beer hit him.

RICHARD KEHOE: A Roman Catholic population surrounded St. John the Baptist Church in Bedford-Stuyvesant. You could go from kindergarten to university without leaving the area. The grammar school was for boys and girls from the parish; but St. John's Prep, the high school, drew from the whole city and was all boys. The buildings were clustered around Lewis Avenue between Willoughby and Park. On one side you had the old brownish-stone college building, the seminary, the residence for the priests. The prep was across the street from these buildings; next to it was the grammar school. The church, a large neo-Gothic structure built some time around the first decade of the twentieth century, was behind the college building. Beyond it was the athletic field, which didn't have a blade of grass. We called it the dust bowl.

A familiar scene in the borough of churches: receiving communion — here at the Holy Trinity Episcopal Church.

ROGER GREEN: St. John's, Concord Baptist, and Cornerstone Baptist were anchors in the Bedford-Stuyvesant community. The pastors of both Concord and Cornerstone graduated from Morehouse College in Atlanta, the same school Martin Luther King, Jr., attended. Everybody who goes to Morehouse comes away with the same kind of preaching style. The Baptist religion was very strong in central Brooklyn, and these two churches were the most renowned.

Concord Baptist, the largest African-American Baptist church in Brooklyn, had originally been in the Fort Greene area. When it burned down, there was a major fund-raising effort to build the new church in Bed-Stuy, a project in which my grandmother Alice Dedham was very involved.

Every Friday, my father would pick up my two girl cousins from Brownsville and bring them to Madison Street to stay with us. Early Sunday mornings, my grandmother would cook breakfast for us, and then we'd all go to church.

Our family had come to New York to escape the racial conditions that existed in the South. But nonetheless, we were definitely rooted in the southern traditions. Our church had various clubs reflecting the different places people came from: a North Carolina club, a South Carolina club, a Virginia club. My grandmother was head of the North Carolina club. She was also the head of a group called the Dixie Belles and the Gospel Chorus. Furthermore, she was part of the building committee and deaconess at the church. With all those activities, there was always an event. Sundays I was not at home.

HOWARD JONES: I began playing basketball at Concord. My brother was a Boy Scout and I was a Cub Scout there. All the churches in Bed-Stuy had Boy Scout troops.

ALBERT VANN: Our troop, Number 199, met at Brown's Memorial Baptist Church. On Brooklyn Day, when entire congregations from the Baptist and Methodist churches would turn out in all their finery, they were always led by the Boy Scouts. Those were magnificent days.

CLIFF HESSE: There was a special route we'd follow for the Brooklyn Day Parade. All the churches took part. There were so many different sects, and you got to know all of them.

JOAN MAYNARD: Brooklyn Day was originally a Protestant holiday. As a Catholic child, I couldn't participate. I was going to Holy Rosary School, and the nuns would never let us out of school early. So I'd run like heck to get home, get out my clothes, and go out on Stuyvesant Avenue to watch my friends marching in the parade. After, they all went to their individual churches for ice cream and cake. Today, all the public schools are closed for Brooklyn Day. But I can still remember how it felt to see that wonderful parade, with all the varieties of Protestant observance, from the sidelines and be excluded from the celebrations.

SOLOMON AIDELSON: Every shape and form of Jewish life I knew in Europe before the war existed in Brooklyn in the 1950s: the Bund, the leftists, the nonaligned, the observant, the Hasidic. Brooklyn was an area rich in Jewish cultures.

DICK KITTRELL: My family was what one might call sentimental Orthodox. Neither my grandparents nor my mother were particularly learned or observant. But there was the celebration of the Jewish holidays and the support for Jewish causes. My grandmother was always shipping clothes to Palestine. And we were always putting coins in the blue *keren ami* box that stood on a shelf in our kitchen. I actually collected more money two years in a row in my box than any other kid in my Hebrew school. I would sneak onto the subway at the Brighton Beach station and go back and forth to Times Square, going among the passengers and getting contributions.

Grandpa reading the Haggadah at a Passover seder.

On Friday afternoons, I would come home from school and find Grandma preparing for Shabbos. The floors were scrubbed and shining and covered with the previous Sunday's Jewish newspaper. On a white tablecloth on the kitchen table, she'd be making a strudel, the dessert for our Shabbos dinner. After preparing the dough, she'd roll it out and stretch it paper-thin until it covered the entire table. Then she'd add the filling of apples, raisins, and nuts and roll the strudel into its traditional shape.

Grandma was also a moonshiner. Before Passover, she'd prepare raisin wine. It was sweet, felt good going down, and packed a terrific kick. Passover was the one time Grandma allowed me to have coffee. For breakfast I'd get a tall glass filled half with coffee and half with milk. I'd stir in four spoonfuls of sugar and place some pieces of matzoh in the glass. I'd spoon it out and eat the soft, sweet pieces.

DONNA GEFFNER: Around the time of the Jewish holidays, our apartment house would have an aroma, a *shmeck*. You'd walk through the halls and smell the soup simmering and the breads baking. Goldie on the third floor, God bless her, would bake the honey cake, Mrs. Levine in the apartment beneath ours would make the challah, and my mother would make the stuffed cabbage. My job was to bring Goldie and Mrs. Levine the stuffed cabbage and get the cake and the challah from them.

IRWIN POLISHOOK: In the fall of the year, Brooklyn always has a particular smell of damp leaves, of something smoky in the air. The leaves fall from the trees. Acorns litter the ground. And I am always reminded of going to shul on the High Holy Days.

DONNA GEFFNER: All the people would come out. And they'd be well-dressed. You'd stand on the corner, walk on Bay Parkway, Ocean Parkway. It was the time to see people, flirt with the boy you had a crush on. Maybe he'd show up at Temple. It was the time to wear your new outfit: the gray felt skirt with the white poodle and the chain, the cardigan sweater and the bobby sox.

MORRIS FRIEDMAN: Before the High Holy Days, we would be outfitted with new suits. As my mother was ill, my father did most of the shopping. Often he would buy things without our being present. Sometimes the shoes were a little too big or a little too small, but we managed. During the rest of the year, we could go for months without him buying us clothes, but come the holiday, everything had to be new.

BOB LEVY: Being all dressed up and walking down the boulevards of Brooklyn, you stood out from the non-Jewish world. Everyone looked so good. It made you feel set apart, special.

HELEN FRIED GOLDSTEIN: There was an austere yet heart-warming atmosphere at B'nai Israel of Bay Ridge during the High Holy Days that made me want to sit with my family rather than run around outside with my friends. Everyone was orderly and composed. It was a serious occasion. My grandfather Isaac Boehm, who was an important man in the synagogue, would be up there on the *bima*— the platform. The silver threads on the neck of his *tallit* glittered as he stood before the Torah scrolls that were enclosed in gleaming silver cases. When they were lifted, the little ornaments on top would tinkle. It was like a fantasy world to me.

MARTY ADLER: For Simchath Torah, we got a little flag with an apple stuck into the tip of the flagpole and a candle stuck into the apple. All the kids would march around the neighborhood with their flags. We belonged to an Orthodox shul. It seemed to me that everybody was Orthodox then.

MORRIS FRIEDMAN: Many people who attended Orthodox synagogues were not Sabbath observers. They came from European backgrounds. They were more comfortable with Orthodox ritual, to men and women being separated. A Conservative synagogue would be foreign to them.

HERBY GREISSMAN: My father wanted me to go to the little shul he belonged to. It was one long room with a doorway in the front and the back, no windows on the sides, and a long aisle down the middle with wooden benches on each side. I told him, "I don't understand Yiddish. If you want me to go, you gotta send me where I can understand it." So we shifted to the newer, more modern synagogue on Twenty-third Avenue. But my father never forgot Rabbi Gartenhouse and the little shul. On Succoth, when they needed fruits to decorate the succus, or on Simchath Torah, when they needed apples, he kept him supplied.

DICK KITTRELL: My grandfather was an itinerant shul-mensch. Each year he went someplace else. Once he found a storefront synagogue on the boardwalk in Brighton.

MORRIS FRIEDMAN: Most of Brooklyn's big synagogues were built in the 1920s. They were regal, impressive structures with the Ark as the focal point and a balcony area for the women. The Brooklyn Jewish Center on Eastern Parkway, which today is a Lubavitcher facility, was once a cathedral of Conservative Judaism. People would walk miles to listen to Rabbi Israel Levanthal, one of the giants of that period.

Borough Park was more upscale than Crown Heights or Williamsburg, which also had big Jewish communities. It had a number of distinguished Orthodox congregations, such as Temple Beth El, on Forty-eighth Street and Fifteenth Avenue, and one major Conservative synagogue: Temple Emanuel, on Forty-ninth Street and Fourteenth Avenue. Kuzavitsky, the greatest of all the cantors, was in that congregation.

When you saw a Jew walking down a Borough Park street on a Saturday morning, you never knew which synagogue he was going to. It had nothing to do with membership. It had to do with where a particular guest cantor was dovaning. The great cantors went around to different synagogues, and people would go to hear them. It was the golden age of cantors.

SOLOMON AIDELSON: When I came to this country in 1953 and saw the remnants of the great Hasidic dynasties in Brooklyn, it made me feel like nothing had changed. The Hasidic communities grew and flourished in Brooklyn in the years after the war. Very few rebbes had survived the Holocaust. But those that did developed a following, because people wanted to hang onto something that was familiar to them.

PRECEDING PAGE
The High Holy Days and *simchas* (celebrations) were times to dress up in your very best.

For a while I lived with my great-uncle Sholem Kalish, the Amshinover rebbe—a group named for a city in Poland where this Hasidic dynasty originated. He spent the years of the war in Japan, where he and other Jews were treated very civilly. By this time, he was in his seventies and living in an old-fashioned three-story stucco house in Borough Park. It was an open house. Anyone could come in for a meal or for a place to sleep—and of course, for advice. He was the most generous man I ever knew. Someone would give him a donation. The money would be lying on the table. If the next person to come in was in need, he'd give the money to him.

ISAAC ABRAHAM: My parents were survivors of Auschwitz. After the war, they came to Williamsburg, and my father became a Satmar—a Hasidic group named after an old town in Russia. It is basically a congregation and a school system with a rebbe at the hub of the wheel. We lived just a block and a half away from the old grand rebbe Joel Teitelbaum. I used to walk over with my father and brothers to see him. In my younger years we lived in a two-bedroom, top-floor

The whole *mishpachah* (extended family) assembled for a Brooklyn bar mitzvah.

unit on Taylor Street next to a chicken market. We learned how the kosher slaughtering and salting of chickens was done.

BOB LIFF: Every year around Succoth, people in black coats and hats would go walking down the street carrying a *lulav* and an *esrog*: the palm leaves and a citron, which is a lemonlike fruit. They'd come up to you and say, "You Jewish?" You'd say, "Yeah." They'd interrupt the punchball game, stick a yarmulke on your head, stick those things in your hands, and make you say the *broche*—the blessing. Years later, as a reporter covering the Lubavitch, I realized that's who those guys were.

CLARENCE NORMAN, SR.: My friends and I were hanging out on the stoop one Friday night in August when this very simple couple walked by and said, "Come and be with us." We had nothing better to do, so we ambled over to this little storefront church on Flushing Avenue.

Mr. Kendrick, a former nightclub performer, was the self-ordained

CONFIRMATION DINNER & RECEPTION
TENDERED BY
MR. & MRS. NAT KOEPPEL
IN HONOR OF THEIR SON
JEROME
ELITE CLUB   NOV. 30, 1940

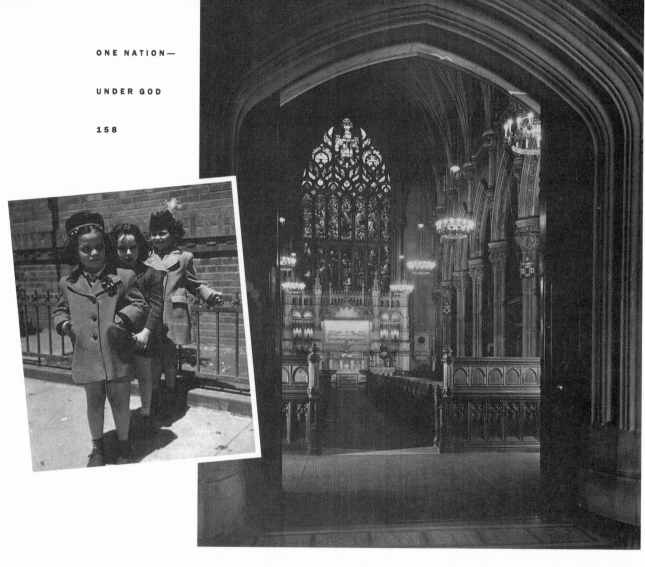

minister. Mother Kendrick was a gray-haired grandmotherly type, wearing the long black dress typical of the Pentecostal church. Their whole thing was to save souls, and I was a lost soul. At that time, I did not know where I was going, but they told me, "This is what the Lord wants you to do."

I started going to Bible classes and revival meetings where you shout and have a good time, singing along to the piano and tambourine. I'd stay till two or three o'clock in the morning and walk home, never fearing anyone. I began teaching Bible class and became a deacon in this small church. After a while, I decided I wanted to become a minister and enrolled in Howard University.

When I came home for Christmas, my wife and I went over to the Little Zion Baptist Church in Williamsburg. They were in the midst of a controversy. Since I was a young man home from college, I was asked to help organize a church. We started with ten men and their families in a storefront at 122 Throop Avenue. They ordained me minister of that church, and I organized them into a Baptist mission. I intended to stay for a year and then go back to college. I stayed two years. I stayed three years. In 1962, we moved out of Williamsburg and bought a Presbyterian church on Monroe Street. In 1967, we moved into a former catering hall in Crown Heights.

During the fifties and early sixties, the emphasis was placed on living, dying, going to heaven—not the social ills of the community. Most of us in the clergy supported the civil-rights protests morally and financially, but we did not get personally involved. But after the march on Washington in 1963, as we moved through the black power era, the black theology period, I became conscious of the fact that the church had a role to play socially. It was then that I became involved in the struggle. Today I am pastor of the largest Baptist congregation in Crown Heights. That little storefront church on Flushing Avenue was the doorway to my salvation.

**A Brooklyn Heights family in
their Easter Sunday finery.**

CHAPTER 10

Americans All

IF YOU PLEASE AND THANK YOU,
SAYS THE AMERICAN CHILD.
AND EVERY TIME SHE SAYS IT,
SHE SMILES AND SMILES AND SMILES.

—Kindergarten song, P.S. 177

FRANK BARBARO: When I was growing up, you had an ethnic mix across the borough. You had Jews, you had Italians, you had Poles, you had Irish, you had blacks. Predominantly it was working class, and people were struggling. I'm not suggesting racism, anti-Semitism didn't exist. But people more or less stayed in their neighborhoods, and if someone ventured out, he was looked upon as an oddity, not someone to be attacked.

ALAN LELCHUK: At the handball and basketball courts at Lincoln Terrace Park, I saw camaraderie and rivalry, but never violence. That was remarkable because of the mixtures, the rivalry of neighborhoods. When you played teams from another area, you were playing against that different culture. But it was always within strong boundaries of gamesmanship and decent behavior.

BOB ARNESEN: For the longest time, Bay Ridge had the largest Scandinavian community in the United States outside of Minnesota. On my block, though, we were the only ones. Salami, a Syrian boy who ate the big flat breads, was a good friend of mine, along with Jackie Woods, who was Irish, and Arnold Kahn, who was Jewish. My father's friends were the men in his poker game: Italians, Jews, Irish. We associated freely, did not divide up into ethnic enclaves. It seemed most immigrants then did not dwell on their ethnicity. They tried to become fully assimilated Americans.

TOBY SCHOM GROSSMAN: I helped my mother study to become a citizen, tested her on the questions in the book—who was president, etc. She came home from the test with a big smile. "I think everything's OK."
   "How do you know?"
   "I told the judge I love the United States of America."

POLLY BERNSTEIN: How much I wanted to become a citizen! When my family emigrated, we couldn't come into the United States, so we settled in Canada. In 1940, I married an American, crossed the border illegally, and moved here. Lots of people did that then. A man on our block worked for the Immigration Department. I knew if he went through my papers, he could get me deported. Every time I saw him, I would take a walk somewhere. Years later, after I became a citizen, I told him. He said, "For crying out loud, you should have let me know. You could have been a citizen in three months."

TERRY PERNA ARNESEN: My sister began P.S. 180 speaking Italian, which was her first language. After a few days, she told my father that she never wanted to speak Italian again. He agreed: "We speak English, we speak English in the house." He went with my mother to the local junior high school two nights a week to take English for foreigners. My mother used to sit around the dining-room table with us and follow our homework in English. She was reading *The New York Times* and *The Wall Street Journal*.

My father wanted us to be part of everything in his new country. When the priest paid us a call to find out why we weren't going to parochial school, my father said, "I didn't come to this country so that my children can go to Catholic school." Everyone wanted to be American. Typically, the Italian boys of my age would marry Irish girls, to make sure they melted into the English-speaking scene.

KARL BERNSTEIN: Mrs. Montana, who lived down the block, was very Americanized and only spoke English—until her daughter had a big fight with her husband, and it spilled into the street. Then I heard Mrs. Montana yell in Italian. She was too much of a lady to say what she had to say in English in front of the neighbors.

DONNA GEFFNER: We were tested for speech in my English class at Lafayette High School. As I was in the drama club and very enthusiastic over speech, I probably gave an affected reading, which the teacher interpreted as a foreign accent. She gave me a letter to take home to my parents stating that I was going into a special speech class.

My father, who had come to this country as a small boy and was very proud of being an American, took great offense. "What does this letter mean?" he shouted. "They think you come from European parents? You're an American!" The next day he went into school and stormed into the speech chairman's office. "My daughter is not going into speech class," he told Miss Curran. "She is not foreign-born. I'll have you know my grandfather fought in the Civil War."

FRANCES BLUM: Growing up in Bensonhurst, I knew Jews and Italians. That's how the world was divided up for me. Until one day, a friend and I went for a long walk and ended up in Sunset Park. I couldn't believe what I saw. Here there were all these Scandinavians, so many handsome blondes. It was like going into another world in Brooklyn.

BOB ARNESEN: Among the people I knew, there was a great deal of intermarriage. My mother was the only one from her family who

I pledge allegiance to the flag of the United States of America and to the Republic for which it stands, one nation indivisible, with liberty and justice for all.

married a Norwegian. My wife is Italian; my children are married to people from different backgrounds.

TERRY PERNA ARNESEN: Marrying Bob gave me the chance to learn about a whole different culture. I would go out to watch the big parade and join the festivities at Leif Erikson Park every May 17 to commemorate Norwegian independence from Sweden. Many Scandinavians were in the home construction field, and one of the customs I found so appealing was the way they placed a branch from a tree on the top of a house before putting on the roof. I was told that was their way of saying we're almost finished. But to me, it was also a symbol of something God has made, a reaching to the top.

BOB ARNESEN: We are living proof of the melting pot that Brooklyn used to be. We combined our heritages. Christmastime, we'd have a Scandinavian kind of rice pudding, crepes filled with jelly and dried fruit with cinnamon thickened with tapioca, and all kinds of Italian fish dishes.

MATT KENNEDY: If the lady next door cooked gefilte fish, she'd pass it over the back fence; if my mother made corned beef and cabbage, she'd give to her. We used to boast and brag about the variety of ethnic groups who lived together in Coney Island. I wish I had a nickel for every time I was in the shul. If the Catholics had a bazaar, it was patronized by the shul, the Lutheran church, the whole community.

ELLIOT GUNTY: My grandfather lived with us in our one-family house in a mixed Flatbush neighborhood. He was a little man who came from Austria, very Orthodox. On Saturdays, he would walk down the street on his way to Temple, and all the gentile neighbors would clear a path for him. "Mr. Harris, good morning." "Mr. Harris, how are you?" They showed him the highest respect.

MORRIS FRIEDMAN: When my father was out in the backyard of our Borough Park house doing carpentry work, our Italian neighbor would come over. On Friday nights, he would come in to turn out the lights for us. It was that kind of a relationship. We could ask one another for things. Our neighbors became very familiar with Jewish customs. We'd put up the succus, and they'd come in, have a drink, something to eat.

"Our neighbors became very familiar with Jewish customs." Manischewitz Wine owner Meyer Robinson (far right) treats the Dodgers to dinner and ample samples of his kosher wine.

ANGELO BADALAMENTI: Since my family was the only goyisha one on the block, I became the Shabbos goy at the synagogue on West Seventh Street and Avenue P. After I shut the lights, the rabbi would show me the bowl filled with change—he couldn't touch the money

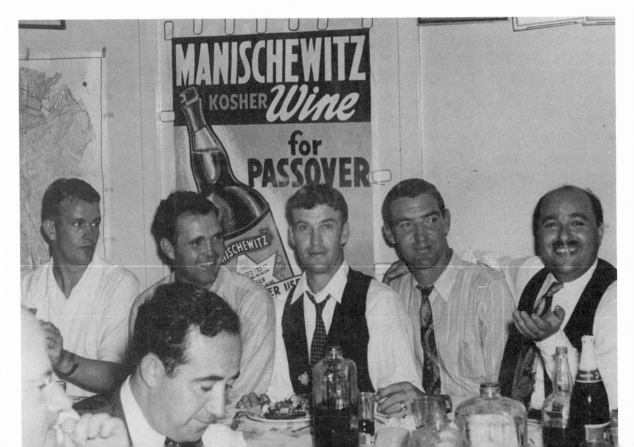

because it was the Sabbath. I would go in whole hog. "Wait, Angelo," he would say. "Take one." I would dip in and hope it was a quarter.

CHARLES HYNES: I lived at 224 Hinckley Place, in an eighty-four-family apartment house with two goyisha families: the super's and mine. I learned a lot of Yiddish expressions living there.

TERRY PERNA ARNESEN: On Sundays, all my brother's Jewish friends went to the Workmen's Circle for Yiddish lessons. He was left with nothing to do. My mother gave him the fifty cents so he could go along. Later on, when he was delivering groceries, the old Jewish ladies just loved this little Italian kid who talked to them in Yiddish.

FRANK BARBARO: My aunt lived at 1926 Seventy-second Street. She was from Italy and could not speak one word of English. Her neighbor in number 1924 was a Jewish lady who also did not speak one word of English. They sat on the bench in front of their houses and talked for hours. Nobody could ever figure out how they communicated.

JOEL MARTIN: The neighborhood I grew up in, on the border of Flatbush and Borough Park, was largely Jewish and Italian. We didn't know of things like racism and prejudice. But one day, I overheard the adults talking: "The neighborhood is becoming mixed." What happened? An Irish family had moved onto the block. You could be Jewish, you could be Italian. There was kreplach, there was ravioli. But from Irish, they didn't know.

We spent days walking our way up the cellar doors in back of their house and peeking in the windows. We wanted to discover what made that family different. They were blonde, fair-skinned—but other than that, they seemed like us. We couldn't figure out what the big commotion was all about.

In some ways Brooklyn seemed to be more of a beef stew than a melting pot. The carrots and the celery were all in the same pot, but they never got to really know each other.

HERB BERNSTEIN: When I was twenty-two, I began teaching in a junior high in Ridgewood, on the Brooklyn-Queens borderline. It was a blue-collar, Polish-Irish-Italian-German neighborhood, the type of place that if you hit a kid, the parents said, "You're right."

Once two girls had a fight, and one said to the other, "You no-good Jew bitch!"

I said, "Elizabeth, why did you say that? Rosemary isn't even Jewish."

She said, "I know, but my father always says that when he gets mad at somebody."

I said, "Do you know that I'm Jewish?"

She started to cry. "You have blue eyes, you're handsome and nice."

The word got out. The kids said, "We thought you were German, we thought you were Polish."

I said, "Does it have any effect, does it make a difference?"

They said, "No, but we didn't expect."

MARNIE BERNSTEIN: At some point I learned that Jesus was Jewish. I passed that along to my Italian friend, Mary Quintero. "He may have been once," she said, "but he isn't anymore."

JOE SIGLER: We knew the Knickerbocker Club on Tennis Court was restricted, but we didn't care. Our neighborhood was predominantly Jewish, but I had Irish friends, Italian friends, a Greek friend, a black friend who lived down Ocean Avenue. There was no black-white-Hispanic issue.

DICK KITTRELL: As a teenager, I was involved in the B'nai B'rith Youth Project, collecting canned food for Brooklyn Jewish Hospital. We divided up Crown Heights and Brownsville, and I got the blocks around Carroll Street and New York Avenue, an area with a lot of brownstones. It turned out to be a black neighborhood right in the midst of a white neighborhood. People were very nice and gave me lots of canned food. It was my first contact with a black community, but they had been there for years.

WILLIAM THOMPSON: Brooklyn started with a small black population, just Bed-Stuy and the poor who lived in Brownsville. Harlem had the name—the action was in Harlem. But after a while, in terms of numbers, we ate them up.

HOWARD JONES: When I was a kid, Bedford-Stuyvesant was an integrated neighborhood, and I was oblivious to prejudice. I knew I was a different color than white kids, but there never was a question of race. Maybe that's because I lived in a vacuum of sports. We all played ball together.

ROGER GREEN: My parents were part of the in-migration of Af-
rican-Americans from the South just before the war. We lived in
Bedford-Stuyvesant, which was essentially a working-poor and working-class neighborhood during the 1950s and 1960s. We did have
some families from the West Indies, though, and they tended to come
here with some disposable income, so they could purchase property.

WILLIAM THOMPSON: When the West Indians hit Brooklyn,
property was their thing. They're the ones who bought the brownstones.
Relatives would come into our house. My mother would get them a
job working in service, as they called it—as a domestic, a cook—
until they saved enough money. My father would find them a house.
Boom! They'd start.

ROGER GREEN: We were first-generation New Yorkers, and we
were mindful of that. I had a healthy childhood. Still, it was inevitable
there'd be times when I'd be confronted with racism. When we moved
from Bed-Stuy to Carroll Street in Crown Heights, we were one of the
first black families in that neighborhood. Everybody was very civil.
The only incident I recall happened at P.S. 222, where a white student
once called my friend and me "nigger," and nobody said anything.

Children of immigrants and in-migrants on the steps of Brooklyn College.

But when we were bused into Winthrop Junior High, which was near the Rugby section of Brooklyn, we made sure not to wear our better clothes on Fridays, because we knew we would have to fight our way home. The white kids from Pigtown, as they used to call it—because people used to raise pigs in their backyards—would waylay us.

JOAN MAYNARD: Of about thirty-two kids in my graduating class at Holy Rosary High School in 1946, there were six blacks—one boy and five girls. Rita, an Irish girl, had a graduation party. She invited the black boy because the white boys told her if she didn't, they weren't coming. But she didn't invite any of the black girls. I had no illusions.

JOYCE SHAPIRO FEIGENBAUM: The granddaughter of the black janitor in our building came to live with him, and Helen and I became friends. This caused a controversy in my home. My mother was afraid for me to play with her. This one time, my father, who was always a kind of retiring figure in my upbringing, came forward. "Leave her alone, let her play with the child." Imagine, we deigned to do

Two heroes of the time of growing social consciousness: Jackie Robinson and Dr. Martin Luther King, Jr.

this child a big favor. Helen and I were good friends until the sixth grade, when she made the SP, a class where you skipped a grade, and dumped me for Lila Dansky.

ROGER GREEN: My father came here from North Carolina when he was thirteen years old because of a racial incident. He was always a fighter. His greatest hero was Paul Robeson.

WADE SILER: I came to Brooklyn from North Carolina. I had been a Yankee fan, a DiMaggio fan. But being in Brooklyn when Jackie Robinson came up, I was transformed into a Dodger fan. As a black man, it was so exciting for me to see him.

RACHEL ROBINSON: The one thing that concerned Jack was the possibility of an overenthusiastic black response. We saw it more in the South than in Brooklyn, but every time he came up to bat early on, even if he hit a pop-up, there would be a tremendous reaction. We worried this overresponse would lead to fights in the ballpark, but it didn't happen.

BILL FEIGENBAUM: We used to go to Ebbets Field—local synagogue groups, left-wing groups. All the left-wingers, who were mostly Jews, were great champions of liberal causes at that time. It was a big victory for them when Robinson got into the major leagues. We'd sit in the bleachers and watch Jackie Robinson and cheer more for him than anyone else. He was red hot.

JOEL BERGER: There was a social consciousness among many people. There were teachers who were committed to civil rights, and they passed it along to their students. Some belonged to world peace movements. At Lincoln High School, one teacher brought in Earl Robinson's "Ballad of Americans" to study and sing; another had us read Richard Wright. More than a few ended up being named communists or sympathizers, railroaded by an investigation, and made to retire or resign. Their civil rights were violated—they did not have due process. It was part of the climate of the time.

LARRY STRICKLER: Morris Lipshutz was my friend's teacher in P.S. 253. One day in 1952, he disappeared. There was no explanation; it was as if the earth opened up, and he was gone. Parents were up in arms. This was a great teacher, a man of principles. They staged a rally for his reinstatement. But he was branded a communist and became a victim of the McCarthy witch-hunt.

Henry Modell gets Jackie Robinson's autograph. Jackie was "red hot."

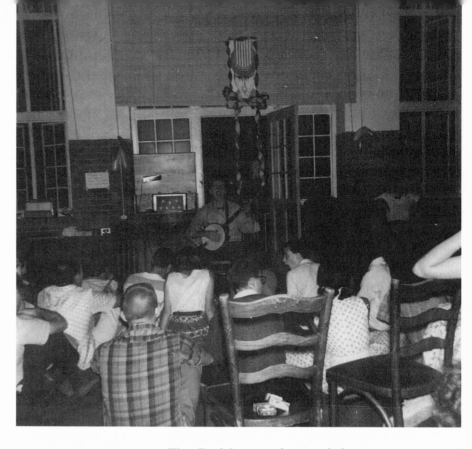

"My universe was opening up. . . . I was meeting kids from all kinds of backgrounds."

FRANK BARBARO: The Red hunts, the witch-hunts were part of the attempt to kill the militant, progressive trade-union movement. The ruling financial circles of our society were very frightened of that movement and had to stifle it. The Communist party never was a big party in this country. At its highest point, it had twenty thousand members, most of whom were in New York City. Nevertheless, unions in the fifties made tremendous advances because the economy was growing.

JUDY BERGER: There were reactionary forces around that tried to link the civil-rights movement to communism. But there were teachers, community leaders, rabbis, priests, and ministers all over Brooklyn who worked hard to promote ideals of brotherhood and integration. If you were active in student government, you got caught up in it.

CAROLINE KATZ MOUNT: The National Conference of Christians and Jews began working with high schools, promoting interfaith activities, civil rights. They had summer camps in upstate New York, and all the high schools sent delegates. This was the time the boycotts and sit-ins were starting in the South. I came back all fired up, full of youthful self-righteousness. When my father asked me how many black girls were in my bunk, I said, "I don't know. I didn't notice."

He became exasperated. "How could you not notice such a thing?"

I ran into the bathroom crying at the intolerance I was experiencing in my own home and reminding myself what they told us at camp: when we came home we wouldn't find as perfect a world as there was at NCCJ.

But my universe was opening up. For the first time, I was meeting kids from all kinds of backgrounds, from all over the city, who were interested in broader social issues. I started attending meetings in downtown Brooklyn, which for me was a big trip. "Black and white together, we shall not be moved"—that was our credo.

ROGER GREEN: I was always aware that there were white folks who were supportive of the movement, because of the way my father presented things to me. He was active in the NAACP and CORE. He was on the front lines, marching, picketing. On Fridays, he'd come home with oak tag and have us write up slogans. Saturdays we'd go out and boycott Woolworth's, because it was segregated in the South. The demonstrations were educational experiences. My vocabulary started building. I learned words like *discrimination* and *segregation*. My father would take me when Dr. King was in town, and hearing him speak was so moving. Those kinds of experiences saved me. I started believing in something.

CAROLINE KATZ MOUNT: By the late 1950s, we were starting to get a sense of changing times. We knew about *Brown* v. *Board of Education*, and many of us were imbued with idealism and a desire to make things fairer for everyone. It seemed so right and also so easy, so within reach. There was this poster you'd see on billboards, in buses, and on trains. It showed a frowning white woman, a couple of white kids with baseball equipment, and a black kid on the sidelines. And one of the white boys is saying to the woman, "What's his race or religion got to do with it? He can pitch."

PART THREE

The Days
of Our Glory

WHAT HIGH SCHOOL DID YOU GO TO?

HANGING OUT AND MAKING IT

CHAPTER 11

What High School Did You Go To?

OH, TALK NOT TO ME OF A
NAME GREAT IN STORY;
THE DAYS OF OUR YOUTH ARE THE
DAYS OF OUR GLORY.
—GEORGE GORDON, LORD BYRON
—Epigraph in the 1960 Lafayette High School Yearbook

JOEL BERGER: Even now after all these years, whenever I meet somebody and it comes out he came from Brooklyn, I ask, "What high school did you go to?" If a person of a certain age tells me he went to Brooklyn Tech, I know he had to have done well scholastically. If he went to Lincoln or Midwood, Madison or Erasmus, Lafayette or New Utrecht, we were similar: middle-class kids with aspirations of upward mobility. We grew up in the same kind of neighborhoods, we were part of the rivalry between the schools, we attended the same basketball and football games. If he went to Boys High or Eastern District, we were different. He was tougher, hustled a buck more, had a special lingo.

There was a high school with thousands of students in every Brooklyn neighborhood. In some ways they were alike, yet each had its own identity. It was like all the Brooklyn high schools were part of a league, and yours was the best.

HOWARD JONES: You had so much school spirit. You knew the words to the school songs, which were often original compositions written by the music teachers. You would sing, and you would cheer, and you would cry. You went to the games, took part in school activities. White and black, there was a spirit of support.

When I was at Boys High, from '44 to '48, our rivals were Brooklyn Tech, Manual Training, and Thomas Jefferson. When we lost a football or basketball game to them, we couldn't go back into the neighborhood.

BOB ERTEL: Everyone at Midwood seemed to be on some kind of team or a cheerleader, even though we hardly won any games. For three or four years, Midwood lost every football game. When they tied Manual Training at last, it set off a tremendous celebration.

ALAN LELCHUK: In 1955 the Jefferson basketball team won the city championship, a feat tantamount to being one of the top thirty college teams in America. Bernie Tiebout, my best friend and a great black player, was on that team. That was the year the Dodgers won the World Series, and there was a feeling in Brooklyn that we could conquer the world.

HOWARD RAPP: The kids who lived on my side of Rockaway Parkway went to Jefferson; the kids who lived on the other side went to Tilden. All of us had played on the street together, had gone to elementary school and junior high together. Now we were the biggest rivals because our loyalty was to our high school. We faced off at what became the major event of the year: the Thanksgiving morning football game at the Boys High field.

"There was a high school with thousands of students in every Brooklyn neighborhood."

EVERETT KERNER: The kids at Tilden had such a love and feeling for the school, you couldn't get them out of the building. It was the focus of their lives, just like in a small town.

ABE LASS: The high school years are the flowering of adolescence. There is never again the same sense of awakening to the world. And here you had first- and second-generation American adolescents, sent to school by parents highly motivated for their kids to succeed, meeting up with great, dedicated teachers. It was a school system you will never see again.

We called it the Fertile Crescent. It started along the shoreline with Lafayette. Then came Lincoln, backed up against the ocean. Then inland was Madison, then Midwood, then Erasmus—a really great school of its time. Tilden was further inland, a good school also. There was a strong intellectual current in the schools and an informed, highly liberal faculty. Everything the school did was right to the parents. They didn't demonstrate against it. The teachers were unquestioned authorities. My friend Sam Levinson, who at one time taught Spanish at Tilden High School, told this story, which was probably apocryphal: "I got a note home from school which I gave to my father. 'Dear Mr. Levinson, your son Samuel shows signs of astigmatism.' My father read it and gave me a smack, crying, 'To a teacher, you show signs of astigmatism?'"

During my tenure as principal, from 1955 to 1971, Lincoln was, in my book, the best academic high school in the city without any specialized examinations. I was there for the glory days. Lincoln drew from a middle- and lower-middle-class neighborhood. A small number of kids came from Manhattan Beach, but mostly they were from Brighton and Coney Island. And there is a very close relationship between what we call socioeconomic standing and intellectual achievement, no question about it. So what was it that made Lincoln so special?

Out of the five thousand students, 80 to 85 percent were Jewish, with what that means in terms of orientation to education, to family, to respect for learning. The whole thing comes into the school. Lincoln, though, had something more. Fully 50 percent of the kids were either children or nieces or nephews of Lincoln graduates. There was that continuity to the 1930s, when it opened. The neighborhood was stable; people stayed. So the students were not just going to high school, they were going where their mother or father, their uncle or aunt had gone.

IRVING FIELDS: Lincoln was white and brand-new when I attended. In the springtime, the cherry trees blossomed on the front lawn. It was so beautiful. Because we were near the ocean, there was always the smell and taste of the sea in the air. I'd come down the broad front staircase, cross over to the pedestrian path along Ocean Parkway, and walk all the way home to Twentieth Avenue and Sixty-second Street.

JOEL BERGER: We had the feeling we were lucky to be going to Lincoln. It was customary to throw pennies, which have Lincoln's head on them, to wish someone good luck or pay him a compliment. In required music, we threw pennies at our teacher, Mr. Goldman, to show our appreciation. Before a big game against Madison, we'd shower the statue of Lincoln with pennies.

ABE LASS: I'd come into Lincoln early in the morning, throw my hat and coat in the office, and start my rounds of the building. I observed a class every day. I didn't come to see a teacher who wasn't doing a job. I just wanted to see what was going on.

Within the first couple of days of my being principal, I was walking around, appraising my real estate, strolling through the halls, and I see a kid standing there. "Do you have a problem?" I asked.

He said, "No, I don't have a problem."

I said, "Who are you?"

He said, "Who are you?"

"I'm the new principal, Abe Lass."

He reached out and shook my hand. "I'm the new student," he said, "Harvey Keitel."

Abe Lass strides across part of his "real estate": the Lincoln High School football field.

RALPH GASARCH: Lincoln had the best cafeteria anywhere. It was run by Florence Green, a plump and happy nurturer, a woman way ahead of her time. She introduced gourmet food. She had a pizza maker come in for the kids before pizza was a household word. She baked rugelas out of the excess butter and sold them on Fridays. People lined up to take home weekend packages.

ABE LASS: Lincoln is the only school in the country that has produced three Nobel Prize winners. An elderly lab assistant named Sophie Wolf, a clucking-hen kind of woman with a maternal interest in the kids, was responsible for that.

JOEL BERGER: Thomas Lawrence, a biology teacher at Erasmus, had the most Westinghouse semifinalists of any school in the country. Ten, twelve, fourteen a year in the late fifties, early sixties. Erasmus Hall was, at one time, the premier of all the schools. The principal, James McNeil, was an English educator of some note and a colonel in the Air Force during World War II. He ran the school like a squadron.

GAIL EISEMAN BERNSTEIN: Dr. McNeil was very strait-laced, unapproachable. He wore white shirts with pointed collars, ties, and vests.

KARL BERNSTEIN: His administrative assistant was Miss Grace L. Corey, who would dock teachers for being a minute late. That's the kind of school they ran. Nobody stepped out of line.

Erasmus was the only high school in Brooklyn that didn't have girl cheerleaders. But these guys got the crowd going.

GAIL EISEMAN BERNSTEIN: Erasmus was the only school in the city that taught classical Greek. They catered to the elite, to the very bright students. But if you were a middle-of-the-road student, it was not the place for you.

JOEL BERGER: Erasmus was the first public high school in the State of New York, with origins in the 1600s, and it retained this sort of English-preparatory-school atmosphere. In every other high school, the kids went to study hall. In Erasmus, they went to "chapel"— which was the auditorium, but it had stained-glass windows. The Erasmus kids who were in student government wore shirts and ties. They were college-bound.

GAIL EISEMAN BERNSTEIN: It was the only high school in Brooklyn that did not have girl cheerleaders. That went back to the olden days, when it wasn't proper for young ladies to show themselves.

JOEL MARTIN: All through junior high, I heard horror stories that Erasmus Hall High School had a tough principal, that you had to take things like math, that you had to study. My friends went to Erasmus, my girlfriend went there. But thank God, I could draw. That's how I escaped. By going to the High School of Art and Design, I avoided Erasmus and was able to major in cartooning—that meant I could legally read comic books all through high school.

BOB LEVY: Erasmus was like a castle. You couldn't find your way around it. I had to come in at six in the morning for detention. There was no elevator, and it was a long, long walk up the stairways to the bell tower.

STEWIE STONE: I never knew how big Erasmus was. I never realized it had seven thousand students. I just walked in a door and stayed inside, going from classroom to classroom. I was a senior before I found out about the quad in the middle of the building, with the original schoolhouse and the statue.

JACK EAGLE: I was a senior before I found out there were streets in the Erasmus district like Tennis Court and Argyle Road. There was a dichotomy at Erasmus between the kids from the poor part of Flatbush, where I lived, and the ones from the rich part.

GAIL EISEMAN BERNSTEIN: The girls who had the clothes lived on Albemarle Road, Rugby Road, Ocean Avenue. They were the wealthier but not necessarily the smarter kids, and they formed a clique. The poorer kids lived on Rogers Avenue, Linden Boulevard, near Holy Cross Cemetery. The Erasmus district went up all the way to Eastern Parkway and Crown Heights. It drew from such a wide variety of neighborhoods.

BOB ERTEL: Midwood was in one of the richest neighborhoods in Brooklyn, on Bedford Avenue, right next door to Brooklyn College. When you went to Midwood, you had the feeling you were on a campus. I came there from Montauk Junior High in Borough Park, which was famous for an enormous amount of lunchtime fights. The whole school came out to watch them. From Montauk, kids fed into Erasmus, New Utrecht, or Midwood. When I arrived at Midwood, when I saw those big pillars out front and the domed roof on top, I thought I was in heaven. Also, I had never seen so many beautiful girls.

There was a distinction at Midwood between the tough kids—guys who wore the DA haircuts and motorcycle jackets and gals who wore the tight skirts with the slingback shoes—and the Ivy League–looking kids who were college-bound. But overall, the school was scholastically elite. Kids from out of the district went there if they had pull—like their father was a judge, their uncle knew somebody. That's how desirable it was.

KARL BERNSTEIN: I lied about my address to go to James Madison High School, a few miles south of Midwood High, along Bedford Avenue near Kings Highway, and a similar kind of school. The kids were mostly children of doctors, teachers, lawyers. Over the front doors was the inscription: "Education is the true foundation of civil liberty." James Madison said that.

RICHARD GOLDSTEIN: The inscription at the front entrance of Thomas Jefferson High School, in Brownsville, was "Let reverence for the laws be the political religion of the land.—Abraham Lincoln." The inscription in the auditorium was "A thing of beauty is a joy forever.—John Keats." Thomas Jefferson didn't make it on the walls, anywhere.

HOWARD RAPP: Jefferson was an integrated school, but there was no black-and-white situation. And God forbid if anyone went after a kid from my school. We always protected our Jeffersonians.

EVERETT KERNER: At Tilden, there was a contrast between the Jewish kids from the private homes in East Flatbush and the less

Fifty-first
Commencement
Exercises

James Madison High School
Brooklyn, New York

June 27th
Nineteen hundred fifty-one

Program

1. PROCESSIONAL—'March of the Peers' from 'Iolanthe' . . . Sullivan

2. 'STAR-SPANGLED BANNER'

3. SALUTE TO THE FLAG

4. CHORAL SPEAKING FROM 'ECCLESIASTES'
   VOICE CHOIR OF SENIOR ENGLISH CLASS

5. SCHOOL HYMN—'Deo Gratias'

6. GREETING—MR. MURRAY DAVIS
   SENIOR CLASS ADVISER

7. HONOR FORUM
   Graduates: DORIS GELLER, JAY HOFFMAN, MARTIN HYMAN, AGNES LEIBOWITZ, EDWARD ORSHAN, ALAN RICHTER, ROBERTA RUBIN

8. OVERTURE—'Egmont' . . . . Beethoven
   JAMES MADISON HIGH SCHOOL BAND
   UNDER THE DIRECTION OF MR. AARON RAPHAEL

9. ADDRESS—MR. MAX NEWFIELD
   PRINCIPAL

10. 'THE GREAT GATE AT KIEV' . Moussorgsky
    BAND

11. PRESENTATION OF AWARDS
    MR. GEORGE B. DOWNING

12. CLASS GIFT TO THE SCHOOL
    JEFFREY BROIDO
    PRESIDENT OF SENIOR CLASS

13. CONFERRING OF DIPLOMAS
    MR. MAX NEWFIELD, PRINCIPAL

14. SONG—'GOING BACK TO MADISON'

15. RECESSIONAL . . . . . Hadley
    'Madison Forever'

Audience will kindly remain seated until after Recessional

affluent Italian youngsters from the Canarsie area. But I don't remember a fight or conflagration between them. Scholastically, it may not have had the reputation of Midwood or Erasmus, but it was an excellent and beautiful school in a lovely residential neighborhood.

A school bus en route to Lafayette. On rainy days, your bus always got stuck in the mud.

FRANCES BLUM: New Utrecht, in Borough Park, was old even when I went there in the early fifties. I think it was built sometime in the 1920s. There was nothing fancy or very pretty about the school or about the West End elevated line it overlooked. There was a rumor that the Mafia had a hand in building it, and that was why everything was so topsy-turvy. The back of the building should have been the front. The gym was behind the stage of the auditorium, separated by a wall that went up and down. When it was down, you had the stage. When you picked it up, you had the gym.

The students were mostly working class but with a middle-class ethic. Many of the girls took a commercial or co-op course, where they worked one week and went to school the next week. We were brought up to finish high school, go to work, get married, and have children. Many of the Jewish boys were going to college, and it seemed to me most of the Italian boys were going into blue-collar work. But we liked them better; they were the heartthrobs, with the black pompadour hair. The Jewish boys were the shorter, pudgier types.

CAROLINE KATZ MOUNT: Lafayette was built in 1939 in a deserted area of Bath Beach. There were rumors that the empty lots

Lafayette High School: "The building looked . . . more like an orange-colored factory than a school."

around the school contained the bodies of Murder, Inc., victims. The building looked like a WPA project—very simple and spare, more like an orange-colored factory than a school. Parts of Benson Avenue were still dirt roads through the 1950s, and on rainy days the school buses always got stuck in the mud.

The district was Bath Beach, Bensonhurst, and parts of Flatbush—a wide range of neighborhoods, from working class to upper middle class. The population was pretty evenly divided between Jewish and Italian kids.

ANGELO BADALAMENTI: There were so many talented people at Lafayette, so many kids interested in classical as well as popular music, theater, art. You were encouraged to be creative. In the afternoon after classes, I could go into the empty auditorium, sit down at the piano, and improvise. I liked to fool around with tunes of the forties and fifties, songs like "These Foolish Things Remind Me of You." At that age, you like to indulge in that kind of reflective mood.

Vito Farinola, who later became Vic Damone, went to Lafayette with my brother. The Italian teacher loved him. She'd say, "Vito, come up here with your beautiful voice and sing something." Vito was happy to oblige. He would get up and sing: "Come back to Sorrento. . . ." All the guys couldn't control themselves. They would roll off their chairs, go *"Uggggh."*

JOYCE SHAPIRO FEIGENBAUM: The most popular boys were the guys on the football team, especially after Lafayette won the public league championship in '54. Several of them had been left back, but that didn't matter. There was this anti-intellectual strain; if you wanted to be popular, you didn't let it get around that you were an A student. So these Super Seniors, as we used to call them, suffered no loss of prestige for being in high school an extra term. They took things like home economics—imagine tough, big football players in aprons! The whole bunch of them were so crazy, so wild. One went on to become a bouncer in the Peppermint Lounge. They represented adventure. You had to fight them off a little harder.

MARTY ADLER: Ft. Hamilton High School didn't have a football team. It was younger than most of the other high schools, and it didn't have the characters or the history. The kids were good students and good citizens, but maybe they had a little less flair than other Brooklyn kids. Still, it was a handsome Greek-style building set on a bluff overlooking the Narrows in an upper-middle-class, safe and beautiful neighborhood.

Since I lived in Borough Park, I expected to go to New Utrecht High School, but my whole graduating class from Pershing Junior High went to Ft. Hamilton. Either New Utrecht was too crowded or they

Lafayette's football heroes: "You had to fight them off a little harder."

wanted to get more Jewish kids into Ft. Hamilton. The school's population was about 2 percent Jewish, 30 percent Greek and Syrian, and the rest Scandinavian.

When I was in high school, they were driving in the piles to build the Verrazano Bridge. We were allowed out for lunch, and we sat on Shore Road and watched.

BOB GERARDI: When I entered Brooklyn Tech, in the early fifties, the enrollment was five thousand boys, from all boroughs. It was a competitive school; you had to score high enough on a test to get in. It was one of the finest high schools anywhere.

The school was built as a WPA project. It had its own radio station. It offered a course in architecture, and every semester a frame of a one-story house would be built in a classroom. There was a power lab that looked like a movie set, with dynamos and pipes running all over—huge pumps, things that you might see in a city power station. There were forges where metal could be bent and changed, wood shops where castings for engine parts were made. Kids learned to handle powerful machinery.

MAX WECHSLER: Boys High looked like a jail out of the Middle Ages. Which is not to deny its magnificence: the ornate towers, the Tiffany glass windows, a massive pipe organ in the auditorium. The building itself took up a whole city block in the heart of Bedford-Stuyvesant, and the little brownstones and small apartment houses that surrounded the school seemed like small pieces on a chess board. Boys High was what controlled the board.

Since the school was unzoned, the students came from everywhere—a mix of black and white, Jewish and Christian. Since it was an all-boys school, there was a rowdiness and roughness that was kept under control by tough teachers and even tougher deans. We were all aware we were at a place of great tradition and history, with many famous and distinguished alumni, some of whom came back to speak at assemblies. The serious athletes and the serious students got what they wanted at Boys High because in the postwar decades, Boys had great teams and wonderful teachers.

TERRY PERNA ARNESEN: Bay Ridge High was an all-girls school that was run like a finishing school. The building was a beautiful Victorian structure with turrets and towers overlooking the park. Inside was a lobby filled with antiques. The young ladies were always properly dressed and very proud to be there. They studied a combined academic and commercial course because the belief was they would have to work and go to school at night. Bay Ridge prepared them for both.

It was the only high school in New York that taught Norwegian. The students were mostly Scandinavian and Irish, although some were Italian. Many had gone to parochial elementary schools, and the parents felt comfortable sending their daughters there.

Three Irish women were principals: McGinniss, Fitzpatrick, Ryan. Miss Fitzpatrick was about five-six, a dignified, handsome woman, subdued in dress and coiffure. She'd walk down the hall with that elegant carriage, and everyone would take notice. But she was also a martinet, very antiunion. She handpicked her faculty, although Charles Cogan, who was president of the UFT—the teachers' union—taught there. Him, she didn't handpick.

RALPH GASARCH: Lincoln's original principal, Gabriel Mason, was the first to handpick the chairmen and faculty. Then he retired to his office to play chess and rehearse his lines (which he would always forget) for the Varsity Show. Since he had to have a starring role every year, all the plays had to have an older man as a lead.

But he trusted the people he brought in. Most of them were inbred, married to teachers or supervisors. They lived in those enormous

"Hermine Bernstein, who taught art, . . . was like a certain type of woman teacher of that time who dressed in bohemian-style clothes and dramatic jewelry."

houses in the fancy areas of Flatbush and owned pieces of summer camps. Overall, though, they had a Depression mentality.

ABE LASS: Coming out of the Depression, teaching was a coveted job. As Sam Levinson used to say, teachers weren't making much, but they were getting salaries when other people were selling apples. Teaching in the city was a pleasure; because it was secure, gifted college students, often the top drawer of their class, became teachers. They lasted through the postwar decades. This was a phenomenon.

JOEL BERGER: High school teachers had to pass very rigorous and competitive exams and earned a higher salary. They were masters.

Hermine Bernstein, who taught art, helped me learn the ropes my first year of teaching at Erasmus. She was striking-looking, with jet-black hair pulled back into a chignon, dark lively eyes, and a bright Ipana-toothpaste smile. Hermine was like a certain type of woman teacher of that time who dressed in bohemian-style clothes and dramatic jewelry. On weekends, I would see them in museums, at concerts and the theater.

GAIL EISEMAN BERNSTEIN: There were also these mean old bitty women at Erasmus: Miss Corey, who had white hair and scrunched up glasses; Miss Carpenter; Miss Genung; Miss Brenner, who spit when she talked and made you stand up to recite your Spanish conjugations; Miss Alberta Crespi, who taught math and gave me a zero when I tried to copy a test and the girl in front covered up her paper with her arm. There was a man who taught biology who was still wearing spats in the late 1950s.

ABE LASS: Typical of the staff at Lincoln was Leon Friend, art chairman and the greatest single art teacher in the whole city. Leon had insomnia. He arrived at school at 6:00 A.M. The gates were locked, but he had the key. Leon had a group of devoted followers: the art squad, kids who scaled the spiked fences at that hour to be with their maestro. They were crazy about him, and for a very good reason: he was crazy about the kids. I can't tell you how many of Leon's students walked from Lincoln right into a job at any one of the big advertising companies.

Lou Gossett was one of the very few blacks in Lincoln when I was principal. His mother was vice-president of the Parents' Association, and Louie was a basketball player with the special condensed programs for athletes: no gym, four or five periods of classes, lunch, and out by 11:00 A.M.

"Mickey Fisher was teacher, coach, friend, and parent to every kid who played basketball for him at Boys High."

During his last year, Louie broke an ankle and was transferred into Gus Blum's class. Gus had wanted to be an actor and a director. But times were bad, so he sublimated his feelings about the stage by teaching drama and directing two student productions a year. Louie had never been in any dramatic class or play before, but Gus spotted his acting potential. Louie bloomed under Blum. Had he not broken his ankle, he might never have become an actor.

LARRY STRICKLER: Gustav Blum was a short, rotund man with a warm heart and great sensitivity. In my senior year he had a heart attack and was rushed to the hospital. After that he couldn't come back. He wasn't a young man. Today you hear you need young teachers because kids can relate to them. You don't relate to young; you relate to good. Blum was good.

HOWARD JONES: Mickey Fisher was teacher, coach, friend, and parent to every kid who played basketball for him at Boys High. He had the respect of everyone in that school. He wasn't a phony.

The first time I saw him was at a Boys High basketball game when I was in the eighth grade. I was on my knees between two guys, watching through the railing of the track that ran above the gym. There was this short guy down on the floor in a red-and-black sweater, coaching the team. I knew who he was. I had heard the older kids who played basketball at the Carlton YMCA talking about him. They said he was fair and had their interests at heart.

The next year, when I came to Boys, I saw Mickey Fisher at work. Each member of the basketball team had to report to him every morning. If you didn't report, you could not practice or play that day. All he wanted was for you to come in and say, "I'm fine. I don't have a problem" or "I'm having trouble in this or that class."

At practice he screamed like a maniac. He was intolerable. He was so frightening, so demanding, you could hate him. But after practice, he would put his arm around you and say, "Son, you know you make me proud of you."

Later on, Mickey got me to do my student teaching at Boys High School, and during that time, Connie Hawkins came along. They called him the Hawk, because of his long hawkish face. He was fourteen years old, undernourished, about six-two. He towered over both of us.

Connie came into the gymnasium, and Mickey called me over. "Howard, I'm telling this young man that he will be an all-American high school and college player if he comes to school. That's how good he is. But he's missed over a hundred days in elementary school." Then Mickey turned to Connie: "Son, if you listen to me and come to school, I'll make something out of you." Connie loved basketball. He came to school every day. He was the best we ever had.

Mickey started building the strong teams in the fifties with the Sihugo Greens, the Vinny Cohens, the Solly Walkers, the Lenny Wilkens. Jefferson, Erasmus, Lincoln had very good teams. But through the fifties and sixties, Boys High dominated basketball. Mickey Fisher did so much for the kids; every one of them graduated. He did so much for the school and the community. People focused on the team. They took pride.

KARL BERNSTEIN: "You're all a bunch of Kings Highway bourgeoisie," Miss Deborah Tannenbaum would tell us. "You hang around in front of Dubrow's getting vicarious thrills out of life." I didn't understand what she was talking about. Miss Tannenbaum was only about five feet tall, but she was dynamite. She taught only the best English classes at Madison, and on such a high level. We read *Portrait of an Artist*, and I became scared to death of going to hell. I hardly ever opened my mouth, I was so afraid of the woman. But I sat down and took the English Regents and got a 96.

I thought Miss Amy Hemsing, who taught Latin at Madison, was

"The afterschool activities meant everything. You made friends, got to know your teachers on a different level. A teacher always had such a great aura for us."

old enough to have been there when Rome burned. On one exam, I forgot everything and got a 50. "This is not the kind of work you do," she said. She ripped up the paper and didn't count the grade.

JUDY BERGER: We were incoming sophomores, waiting outside the room the first day of classes at Lafayette. Our teacher was late. Finally, this very heavy man came along. His sheer size was enough to scare the daylights out of us. We followed him into the room, took our seats, and began filling out the Delaney cards. He took a look at them and shouted in that booming voice: "Sophomores? Sophomores? How dare they give me sophomores? I'm going to see the chairman!" And he stormed out.

That was my introduction to high school and Marvin Feldman. That history class became the first time in school that I felt ill at ease because of my ignorance. Mr. Feldman spouted theories, opinions, dates, and quotes. He appeared to know everything. And of course, later on in life, I learned he really did.

STAN GOLDBERG: Marvin Feldman forced us to think. He would throw questions out, directing them from Stan to Don to Judy and then back to him. He would make provocative statements. Every other teacher told us all the American presidents were great—not Mr. Feldman.

CAROLINE KATZ MOUNT: "Schub-Shostack-and-Shapiro" was a song in one of the Sings that described three literary, intellectual English teachers at Lafayette. Dr. Schub was a Shakespearean scholar, Mr. Shostack wrote the Regents Review and College Prep books, and Joe Shapiro was chairman of the department and also a songwriter. "Round and Round" was his biggest hit. He was born in England and retained that kind of elite Oxfordian manner, but he was also a charming, bon-vivant type. He would get excited about literature and read the dramatic parts in his resonant voice. I thought he sounded like Laurence Olivier. Alice Roth, who also taught English, was a Barnard graduate. She was so composed and witty. She used to say girls who are pretty often rely on their looks and don't bother developing a personality. Those who are not pretty work on their personality, and that's much more important. I didn't know where I fit in. But I knew I wanted to be like her.

DONNA GEFFNER: It was Mrs. Roth who brought Sing to Lafayette. Sing, wonderful Sing! It was all over Brooklyn. Lincoln was doing their Sing, and Midwood was doing theirs, and that made you have a real school spirit in addition to your class spirit, which you had even though you knew the seniors would probably win.

The excitement started in September. It built all through the fall as you wrote the script and cast the show and rehearsed the chorus and solos. And then finally, in December, just before Christmas, the climax—three glorious nights of performance.

Scenes from "Sing, wonderful Sing!"

LARRY STRICKLER: The curtain would open, and there would be this massive immobile chorus on risers, a dazzling display. There were as many as three hundred kids in a chorus, all dressed alike, and when they did their animated hand-motions with sequined gloves or shakers or flags, it was quite a spectacle.

DONNA GEFFNER: Sing gave students a chance to really express themselves. Writers, dancers, singers, actors, musicians, artists, costume and set designers, lighting people—everyone got a chance to show off his or her talent. And if you didn't have a special talent and were just part of the chorus, you were important, too. Each class— sophomores, juniors, seniors, and sometimes even freshmen—put on its own show. You'd start with nothing, just a couple of ideas for a theme. Then you'd decide on one and write a whole show based around it with inside jokes, takeoffs on teachers, and clever, satiric lyrics set to familiar melodies. "I'm the klepto in the G.O." (student government), sung to the melody of "Tip-Toe Through the Tulips," was the big hit of the "psychology" theme one year. In my senior year, our theme was "Camelot." Ironically, that was in 1963, and we went on less than a month after President Kennedy was assassinated.

Sing rehearsals got underway by mid-October, when it was starting to get dark early. We'd begin after classes ended and go on into the late afternoons and evenings. The school building would close. The hallways would be darkened, the classrooms empty. It was magical, theaterlike.

MARNIE BERNSTEIN: The bus would be waiting for us after rehearsal. How unusual it was to be coming home from school in the dark. All the way down Bay Parkway, Christmas lights were strung from one side of the street to the other. The store windows were decorated with tinsel and stars. And we'd be riding home, singing at the top of our lungs: "Mr. Sandman, send me a dream, . . ." even though we had just spent the last three or four hours rehearsing.

DONNA GEFFNER: The afterschool activities meant everything. You made friends, got to know your teachers on a different level. A teacher always had such a great aura for us.

KARL BERNSTEIN: Jack Barnett, the acting chairman of music at Madison, a bald, fat, roly-poly man, produced a five-night run of *Patience*, the entire Gilbert and Sullivan operetta, conducting a full orchestra and directing two casts. He also was one of the conductors of the All-City Orchestra, which had kids from all five boroughs. I

THE MUSIC DEPARTMENT
James Madison High School
MAX NEWFIELD, Principal
presents—

PATIENCE
An OPERETTA by GILBERT and SULLIVAN

Directed and conducted by MR. J. A. BARNETT
Chairman Music Dept.

May 18, 19, 20 • 1949
J. M. H. S. AUDITORIUM

made first stand playing the cello at All-City, which meant having to go to Brooklyn Tech at nine o'clock every Saturday morning for a three-hour rehearsal. The conductors were all teachers who gave up their Saturdays to do this. Twice a year we gave concerts at Carnegie Hall.

NORMAN SPIZZ: It was like a microcosm of the big-band days at the Paramount when Lincoln High School held its annual jazz concert. The dance band was three trumpets, three trombones, five saxes, and three rhythm. We played all the numbers: "One O'Clock Jump," "Sing, Sing, Sing," "Tangerine," a lot of Glenn Miller, Freddy Martin. When we had the solos, we stood up and the lights would shine on us. Kids got up and danced in the aisles till the cops came and stopped them, because it was a fire hazard. Our dance band was the best in the city. Playing in it was like being the captain of the football team. We had dance-band sweaters—white with a big *L* on it. Those sweaters could get you a lot.

MARNIE BERNSTEIN: The annual concert at Lafayette was always on a beautiful night in May. The auditorium would be bathed in a pink glow and crowded with parents and brothers and sisters of performers in the orchestra, the marching band, the jazz band, the glee club, and the cantata.

Our junior year, Terry's parents got there late and had to sit up in the balcony. We were in the middle of Tchaikovsky's "Waltz of the Flowers," when out of the corner of my eye I saw something fly by. Everyone turned for a moment. There was Terry's father hanging over the balcony railing and sailing down paper airplanes. That was just the kind of thing you'd expect from him. He was such a zany guy.

While the first violins of the Lafayette orchestra did the melody to "Waltz of the Flowers," Terry and I played the second violin part: "bum-bum, bum-bum." Before us on the podium, Grace Greenwald, ever true to her name, conducted on her tiptoes. Amazingly, the whole collection of instruments—even the big bass fiddles and kettledrums, the tubas and bassoons—followed the wand of this diminutive silver-haired lady who looked like a tiny ballerina atop a music box. How Mrs. Greenwald, with the manner of an angel and the gentlest of voices, got a bunch of kids to make the finale of Beethoven's Fifth really sound like music is something I will never forget.

ANGELO BADALAMENTI: Mrs. Greenwald was "Mama," and Louis Pierro, chairman of the music department, was "Papa." They were short in size but long on talent—first-rate violinists. In every other way, they were totally different, yet they complemented each other. Mr. Pierro was a formal and elegant man, impeccably dressed, with wavy dark hair and a twirling mustache. If Toscanini had been a school teacher, he would have been Mr. Pierro. He spoke softly, but all he had to do was give us a look, and we got quiet. Mrs. Greenwald, on the other hand, was so warm and soft and sweet and beautiful. I had a terrific crush on her.

NORMAN SPIZZ: Ben Goldman, the music teacher at Lincoln, was a frustrated songwriter and a terrific conductor who really knew his stuff. He was tough. If you didn't do your thing, he threw you out of the band. But if you were serious, he was there for you, got you jobs playing up in the Catskills, at proms, bar mitzvahs.

ANGELO BADALAMENTI: You got fifteen or twenty dollars a night playing at bar mitzvahs and weddings all over Brooklyn, plus all you could eat. At the Italian weddings of that time, there would be literally fifty sandwiches at every table, and they would just keep coming and coming. They used to call them football weddings. Someone would call out, "Pass the provolone," and you'd fling it like Joe Namath across the room. "Ham and cheese." *Boom!* I would bring along my brother's empty trumpet case, and at intermission, when the band would eat, I would stuff the case with sandwiches. Monday mornings I'd be the most popular boy in the Lafayette High School cafeteria. All my friends would sit at this long table and we'd have an encore of the football wedding. Those were known as Angelo's sandwich days.

Actor Paul Sorvino early in his career was captain of the Junior Showboat in the Lafayette High School Sing.

KARL BERNSTEIN: Barry Greenberg was the star tuba player at Madison and brought the house down with his performance of "Tubby the Tuba," with the whole orchestra behind him. He was a skinny kid with blonde curly hair and bright twinkly eyes, and always into some kind of mischief. But he was such a good musician, he managed to get away with everything. We were hanging out in the instrument room one day when Mr. Rattner came in unexpectedly. Barry didn't have a chance to put out his cigarette, so he threw it into the tuba. Mr. Rattner was in the middle of explaining something when he stopped and sniffed. "Barry," he cried, "your tuba, it's on fire!"

ABE LASS: Neil Sedaka was a fantastic piano player, very talented, and also very charming. I used to come down in the afternoons when the school band was rehearsing and sometimes we'd play duets.

"Lincoln was such a creative force in my life."
— Neil Sedaka

NEIL SEDAKA: I was the accompanist in the pit, rarely a performer. But at one Ballyhoo show in the auditorium, I sang and played the piano to a song I wrote called "Mr. Moon." It was in the new doo-wop style, and it caused a riot. Everybody got up, all the toughies were cheering and dancing.

Mr. Lass called me to his office. There was a second show that afternoon and he said, "Neil, I really think that you should sing something other than 'Mr. Moon.' It incites all the kids a little too much. It's very wild music."

The kids got wind of this and passed around a petition insisting I sing "Mr. Moon" again. And, of course, I did. That made me a bit of a hero—so much so that I could go to the sweet shop where the toughies hung out. These were kids from Coney Island who wore the DA haircuts and leather jackets. There was this guy Alfred Abasso and his girlfriend, Frenchie, who piled her hair on top of her head. They said, "There's Mr. Moon. Let him in. Let him in."

Lincoln was such a creative force in my life. Music teachers like Ben Goldman and Alice Eisen, who led the chorale, inspired so many

Celebrities

13. Most Likely to Succeed—Caroline Katz
14. Most Popular Girl—Barbara Ventura
15. Most Popular Boy—Nick Lampariello
16. Class Poet—Louis Nordstrom
17. Class Scientist—Joel Schiff
18. Prettiest Girl—Sue Benedetto
19. Handsomest Boy—Irv Moskowitz
20. Class Artist—Mark Sherman
21. Person Who Did Most For Sing —Jeff Lass
22. Best Dressed Girl—Elsie Tom
23. Best Dressed Boy—Bob Price
24. Miss Co-op—Amelia Marchica

of us. I went to school with Mort Shuman, who wrote many of the Elvis songs later on, and did *Jacques Brel Is Alive and Well.* When I entered, Lou Gossett was graduating, and he was singing with a group. Neil Diamond lived across the street and went to Lincoln after me. All of us got so much from our teachers.

ANGELO BADALAMENTI: They made us feel special, worried about us, wondered what books we were reading. A teacher at Seth Low Junior High started me playing the French horn. I took it up in school and then went on to private lessons with a man who had played in the John Philip Sousa band. In high school, I played the piano and the French horn in the band and orchestra. On the basis of the French horn, I got a scholarship to Eastman School of Music. It was only because of the school system that I got the opportunities that made my musical career possible.

All through high school, I was busy writing songs. Before graduation, I went to Mrs. Greenwald. "I think I have something that could

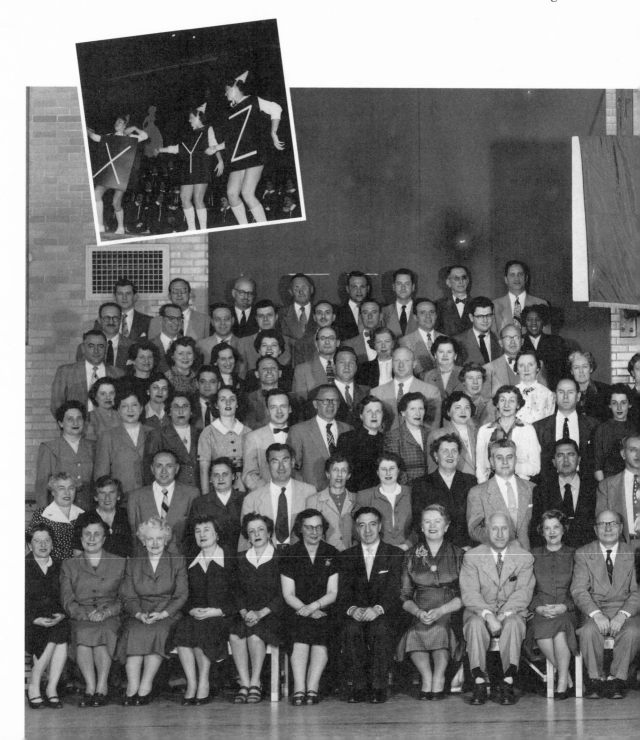

be the processional march for our graduating class. May I write it?"

"Absolutely, Angelo. Go for it. Do it."

I developed three themes. A friend of my brother's orchestrated it. And they used it. "Processional March composed by Angelo Badalamenti"—that's how it was listed on the graduation program.

That's what comes back when I think of high school: the creative environment, the quality of the teachers, the way they encouraged us: "Absolutely, Angelo. Go for it."

The Lafayette High School faculty in the mid 1950s.

CHAPTER 12

Hanging Out and Making It

WE'RE THE GIRLS OF SIGMA RHO
YOU'VE HEARD SO MUCH ABOUT.
WHENEVER WE GO MARCHING,
YOU HEAR THE PEOPLE SHOUT:
''THOSE ARE THE GIRLS OF SIGMA RHO
YOU'VE HEARD SO MUCH ABOUT . . . .''

—Club song

JOYCE SHAPIRO FEIGENBAUM: The key to belonging was being a member of one of the popular clubs. They were like mini-sororities, and getting in depended on superficial things like looks and personality and whom you knew. But if you belonged, you were "in," and you would announce that by wearing your club jacket, with the name across the back, when you walked up and down one of the big thoroughfares like Kings Highway on Friday nights.

BOB ERTEL: The Midwood crowd walked Avenue J from Coney Island Avenue to Seventeenth Street and gathered at Cooky's. After school, if the weather was bad, we'd go down to Arty's Poolroom, which we called Barricini's Basement in front of our mothers. A lot of older guys hung around there, and we enjoyed shooting pool and shooting the breeze with them.

A date was usually the movies: the Midwood on Avenue J, the Kingsway or the Avalon on Kings Highway. We double- and triple-dated all the time. As seniors, we migrated from Avenue J to Kings Highway, where the Madison, Lincoln, and Lafayette kids hung out.

LARRY STRICKLER: In *American Graffiti* they drove their cars; that's California. In Brooklyn, we walked. We walked Kings Highway from Coney Island Avenue to Ocean Avenue. We walked with a lilt, with one hand in our pocket, the other waving "hi." That's where we learned to schmooze. How was popularity measured in the Kings Highway area? By the time it took you to walk from Coney Island Avenue to Ocean Avenue. The shorter the time, the less popular you were. How long did it take me? Five days.

MARTY ADLER: A few blocks before Ocean Avenue, just past the Brighton el, was Dubrow's Cafeteria. That's where you ended up on a Friday night. If you were lucky enough to have a car, you kept it down to three guys so there'd be room in case you picked up some girls. The Madison and Midwood cheerleaders were there, and they were the prettiest. You'd take them to a movie or someone's party. Around midnight you'd drop by Dubrow's again to see if any of the other guys were around. You'd tell stories about what happened that night and hook up for a ball game the next day.

HERBY GREISSMAN: The Famous Cafeteria on Eighty-sixth Street under the West End el was a hangout for kids from Lafayette and New Utrecht. They'd give you a ticket when you went in, and when you ordered something they punched out the price. We would go in, get a ticket, go out, come back in again, and get a second ticket. Then we would take the cheapest thing for ten or fifteen cents, and that's what we used when it came time to pay the bill. But in between, we had the other ticket that we used to run up the tab. The big tab of a dollar-fifty or two dollars, we threw away. I'm sure everyone knew that gimmick. How they stayed in business, in my wildest dreams I can't imagine.

JOYCE SHAPIRO FEIGENBAUM: The kids converged on the tables in the front of the Famous. The old retired men occupied the tables in the back. Everyone stayed for hours on end. For me, it was a place of refuge away from my noisy, crowded apartment, where everybody was always yelling. I did my homework there.

BOB ERTEL: Gragnano's, on McDonald Avenue near Eighteenth Avenue, was a mecca for the New Utrecht and Brooklyn College crowds. It wasn't a cafeteria, but a pizza parlor—one of the first of its kind. There was no such thing then as buying pizza by the slice. Three or four kids would order a pie.

PHIL FAGIN: You could sit over a cup of coffee and a Danish for hours at the Famous Cafeteria on Eastern Parkway and Utica Avenue for a big twenty-five cents. The workers there were kibitzers. "A fly in your soup? It doesn't drink much." Or "Did you teach that fly how to do the backstroke?"

GAIL EISEMAN BERNSTEIN: Friday afternoons we'd rush home from Erasmus to get ourselves ready for our Friday night pilgrimage to Garfield's Cafeteria, on Church and Flatbush Avenues. It took awhile. First, you had to set your hair. I had put a streak in my hair with peroxide and ammonia, and I hung my head out the window so the sun would make it lighter. That was my dip. To get the right height on it, I put the bobby pins vertical to my head. Then I tied two Modess sanitary pads together, rolled the rest of my hair over them, put some gooey stuff on top, and waited for it to dry and harden. It came out a beautiful page-boy fluff. For a while I wore the Italian bob with spit curls—those little half-curls on the forehead, which I plastered with sugar and water to get them to stay. Then I put on makeup. I carefully drew the little line extending out from the corner of the eyes with a Maybelline pencil—doe eyes—and I put on lipstick, either Tattoo Orange or Tattoo Pink. Then I got dressed. We all wore skirts that were puffed up with crinolines. To make my horsehair crinolines stand out, I washed them in water and sugar and layered them one on top of the other over an umbrella. We wore nylon sweater sets: a short-sleeved sweater underneath and matching cardigan on top. If we wanted to look sexy, we wore the cardigan by itself, buttoned down the back, over one of the pointy bras: ice-cream bras, cone bras, carnival bras. We would tie a little kerchief around the neck or stick a dickey with our initials on it under the sweater. We wore loafers with bobby sox—the heavy wool sox from Davega. We folded them over and held them in place with a big rubber band around the top that cut off the circulation.

When we arrived at Garfield's, we never went inside. We stood on the corner and saw who came around. If someone interesting went in, we went in too. A girl could sit with a single Coke all night. We'd meet a lot of boys, but we never went anyplace after Garfield's. We'd give the boys our phone number and hope they called.

STEWIE STONE: Garfield's rice pudding with hot fruit sauce on top was the greatest delicacy in the world. But the food was secondary. The getting together was what mattered. Going from table to table on Friday night was like going from blanket to blanket on the beach.

Every high school crowd in Brooklyn had its own cafeteria, and every high school crowd in Brooklyn had its own section of the beach marked off by a jetty, a line of rocks, on each side. Ours was Bay 2 in Brighton. The closer to the sign you were, the hipper you were. And you didn't wear a bathing suit, you wore dungarees and a T-shirt.

BOB ERTEL: It was blanket-to-blanket from boardwalk to shore, especially when the tide was up and you had to move back a little farther. But you wouldn't lay down to relax or get a tan. The beach scene was standing on the sand and going into the water to horse around or cool off. It was a big social thing. The girls wore these latex one-piece bathing suits. By today's standards, they were not very revealing, but of course there were a couple of chesty girls who stood out.

MAX WECHSLER: The whole beach scene was one of sweat and suntan oil and saltwater—liquid stuff, sex. It was an environment that stimulated all the senses. There was so much to look at: the way the bathing suits fit, how much they revealed, the changing positions of the bodies on the blankets. The grainy sand always got into your bathing suit when you lay on the rough army blankets, discreetly making out under the sun. The beach was a turn-on.

"The whole beach scene was one of sweat and suntan oil and salt water — liquid stuff, sex."

MARNIE BERNSTEIN: The Lafayette kids stayed on Bay 7, at the end of Ocean Parkway. Portable radios were still pretty rare, but guys would bring down bongo drums, and we'd sit in a big circle and do calypso songs. Joyce and I swam out to the third barrel at the end of the rope. It was way over our heads, and we weren't such terrific swimmers, but somehow we never worried. We'd bob up and down sitting on the rope, look out at the endless horizon, and sing our own harmony to "Blue Moon."

JOYCE SHAPIRO FEIGENBAUM: On the Fourth of July in 1955, we were working out the parts to that song when Billy Barrett passed our blanket. He said to his friends, "These chicks can really sing"—the ultimate compliment—and sat down beside us. That's how we met him.

Billy was a Lenny Bruce–type character—hip, verbal, quick on the uptake. He'd say and do anything outrageous. Once we got caught in a traffic jam. Billy got out and started directing traffic, and everyone listened to him. Another time we were on the Sea Beach express going to the city. The train was crowded. All of a sudden, I look up and there's Billy, hanging from the bar overhead like a monkey. He was a skinny guy with a shock of black straight hair falling into his face, glasses that were forever sliding down his nose, a wide manic grin, and a wild laugh that sounded like a donkey braying. That doesn't exactly add up to a John Garfield. But all the girls were crazy about him.

MARNIE BERNSTEIN: I hadn't seen Billy for about six months when we met at Claire's engagement party. She was the first one in our crowd to get engaged, at the age of sixteen. But she was Syrian, and they all got married very young. I had started college by that time and brought along a boy I was dating, a medical student at Columbia P & S, no less. Billy cut in while we were dancing. "Where'd you get that 'yeshiva bucher' from?" he asked. Then he turned on the charm. "You look sensational, just like Eva Gabor. Wait till I tell Jerry [an old boyfriend]." That was it. I never saw the medical student again.

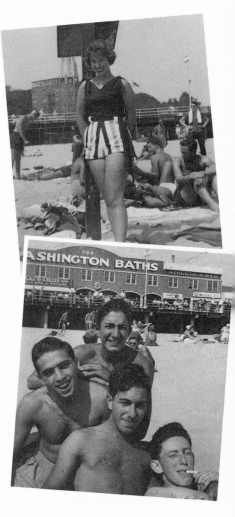

JOYCE SHAPIRO FEIGENBAUM: Billy and his friends were out of the mainstream. They weren't as serious and upwardly mobile as many of the other boys. They were into progressive jazz instead of rock 'n' roll. They had an irreverent sense of humor, would make fun of things we considered sacred, like religion or the president, shock us with their language. Larry Pino, one of them, was a soda jerk in the little candy store next to the Marboro Theater. He was a romantic who took himself very seriously and liked to swing around lampposts like he was Gene Kelly.

The Syrian-Jewish boys in Bensonhurst belonged to a club called the Silver Knights. Two of them took Stella and me to the Copacabana, where Martha Raye was appearing. It was an expensive date. After, they took us back to their clubroom, which was in a finished basement furnished with a few discarded and sagging couches. Stella and her date settled into one of them. Instead of an overhead light, there were lamps all over the room. My date, who was looking for his reward, was walking around switching all the lamps off. I took off my shoes, tiptoed behind him, and as soon as he switched a lamp off, I switched it back on.

Those guys were also atypical. They were terrific dancers and could do elaborate mambo and cha-cha breaks. They were also very sexually aggressive—except with women of their own kind, the ones they ended up marrying.

BILL FEIGENBAUM: Girls resisted sexual aggression. They fought hard to protect their virginity. They might do all kinds of things, which wasn't bad either, but not go "all the way." On the other hand, it was more rewarding in those days before sexual liberation. Guys felt more masculine, and I think girls felt more feminine. After, I missed the challenge of conquest.

NORMAN TIPOGRAPH: The spot for conquest was between Oriental and Manhattan Beach. It was called the Desert and was where all the young lovers went.

DORIS MODELL TIPOGRAPH: We took a blanket and some sticks, made a tent, and crawled underneath. It was hot!

NORMAN SPIZZ: When we had access to a car, we went to a little strip of beach off the Belt Parkway, just east of Sheepshead Bay, called Plum Beach. The water was polluted, and it smelled of fish, but it had a nice parking lot that overlooked Jamaica Bay. The big joke was we were going to watch the submarine races.

KARL BERNSTEIN: Our last Boy Scout meeting of the year was a cookout at Plum Beach. No Boy Scout is ever without his flashlight, and at Plum Beach, the kids ran around shining them into the cars.

GAIL EISEMAN BERNSTEIN: We stopped at Plum Beach and turned the headlights on the parked cars. We didn't see much, just steamy windows and people jumping apart.

TOM BOORAS: As kids, we were warned not to play on the docks of the East River near where we lived. But as teenagers, they became our favorite places for necking. At first we sat on boards, but once we got our fathers' cars, we would drive down and park at the end of the dock. It was a deserted area, but every once in a while a night watchman would come around and shine his light and get rid of you.

NORMAN SPIZZ: A lot was supposed to happen at all these lovers' lanes, but the girls of that era were not so willing.

JOYCE SHAPIRO FEIGENBAUM: Our undergarments were enough to inhibit anyone. They were as formidable as a suit of armor. Our bras were Exquisite Form, with the cups stitched around the tip to make our breasts look like they came to a point. When I bought my first bra, I couldn't fill it, so I stuffed it with tissues. There was no pantyhose then; our stockings were held up by a kind of girdle called the two-way-stretch. Under summer dresses, we wore a braselette—a one-piece foundation that was a combination strapless bra and girdle, with plastic bones running from top to bottom.

When we had parties in a finished basement, they'd turn the lights down low, and we'd dance to some doo-wop music. The guys would try to dry-hump, and the girls in their horsehair crinolines would struggle to avoid body contact. Along with the music, you'd hear the shifting crinolines: *swish, swish, swish.*

BOB ERTEL: The problem was finding a place to have parties and keep other people from crashing. So in my senior year, we formed a group called the Fabulous Fifteen and came up with the idea of naming a Girl of the Week. Her photo was taken, and she was entitled to have a party in her home.

JOE SIGLER: The beauty of Brooklyn was that if you were popular with the girls, you could go out with a girl who lived in the same building as another girl you went out with, and they wouldn't even know one another because it was so immense. You didn't need a car because everything was in the same area. But every guy wanted one.

BILL FEIGENBAUM: In 1958, my father bought me a 1939 LaSalle Cadillac. It had a running board, a pearlized steering wheel, and whitewall tires. I painted it bright red and drove down Ocean Parkway to Coney Island. There were always girls along the way. Once, eight of them piled in.

ELLIOT GUNTY: My brother Morty had a 1955 red Cadillac convertible. It was half a block long, with beautiful red-and-white leather seats and a white top. That June, he got a month's gig in Las Vegas. The night of my prom, a telegram arrived: "Be Careful! Signed: The Owner." The Caddy was mine for the prom and the month.

BOB ERTEL: I went to the 1956 Midwood senior prom with a girl named Sheila. I wore a white dinner jacket, and she wore a pastel-colored organza gown with a puffed-up skirt. She looked terrific. Together with two other couples we rented an "air-conditioned" limousine for a total of thirty-nine dollars for the night and debated over whether we should give the driver a five- or a ten-dollar tip.

After the prom at the Waldorf Astoria, the limo took us to the Latin Quarter, where we saw Johnny Ray. Then we went to Basin Street to see Ella Fitzgerald. We spent every buck we had. One of the gals lived in a big house, and she invited us to come back there for a breakfast party. And then we all went down to Brighton Beach. We probably slept on the beach. But we don't remember it quite that way. We were so strong, so full of energy, it seemed we just went right into the next day without any sleep.

STEWIE STONE: I went with this girl who had a red Buick convertible, and we parked in a deserted part of Canarsie. It was the sexiest—fooling around on the plastic seat covers of that Buick until the cops came and shone the lights on us.

I had the key to my father's dance studio, which had a comfortable couch. But my father would always leave something lying on the couch, and the next day if it had been moved, he'd want to know why I was there and what I was doing. So I had to find other places.

The first time I went with a girl to the Golden Gate Motel in Sheepshead Bay, I was still living at home. Every kid in Brooklyn lived at home. Nobody got their own apartment till they got married. As soon as I got into the motel room, I turned on the television. The

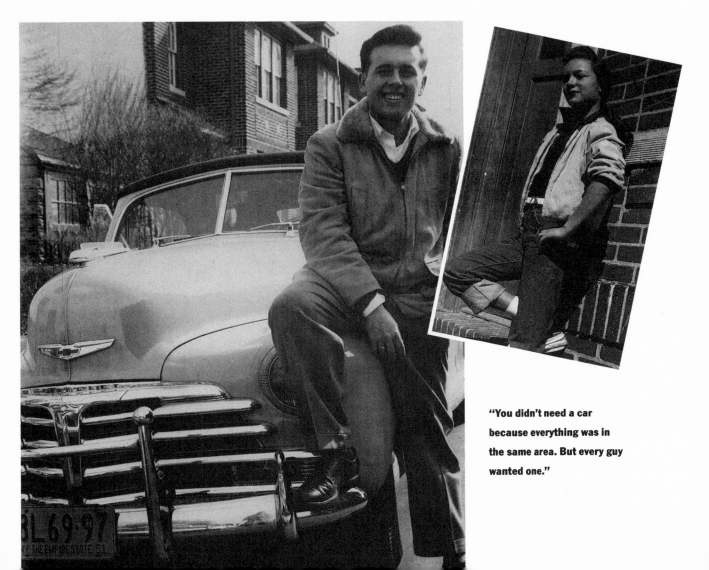

"You didn't need a car because everything was in the same area. But every guy wanted one."

girl was surprised. "What are you doing?" she asked. "Did we come here to watch TV?"

"I told my mother I was over a friend's house watching television," I explained, "and when she asks questions about the programs, I have to know what to tell her."

My mother asked questions, and I was more afraid of my mother than anything else. To this day, whenever I go into a motel room, I turn on the television.

JOEL MARTIN: I was with this girl from Erasmus who lived up the block from me. We were petting on a chaise lounge in the finished basement of her house. Suddenly we hear her mother's footsteps on the stoop. Panic! I can't describe it. Sheer terror! Worse than the scene in *Psycho*. The *clop-clop*ping into the house, her high heels on the linoleum floor overhead. The girl says, "Go, go, go!" Quickly I pull myself together and zip myself up. I hurt myself down there. Doubled up in pain, I go out the side door, run down the alley, up the block, and into my house. My mother, naturally, is awake.

"What's wrong with you?" she asks.

"Stomachache."

"How did you get a stomachache? I know—I warned you not to eat goyisha franks at Ebbets Field."

TOM BOORAS: In those days, kissing a girl with your mouth open was considered a mortal sin. Every Saturday I had to go to confession and admit to it. I would go into a very dark room with two confessional boxes and screens so the priest could not see me. After, the priest gave me absolution and told me what my penance was. Then he said, "OK, Tom, don't forget to be at the 10:15 mass tomorrow." I lived so close to the church, I couldn't be anonymous. Finally my friends and I got smart. We began going down to St. Peter's Church at the foot of Atlantic Avenue. Hispanic people had begun moving into that parish in the mid-fifties, and they had a Spanish-speaking priest. St. Peter's became the busiest place for confessions. All the Irish kids went there.

MARTIN SPITZER: We thought about sex and talked about it, but it was never outward and open, the way it is today. It was all innocent stuff, mostly kissing. We were a fraternity of Lincoln and New Utrecht kids. During the basketball season, we were always at the games. Then we'd be partying in rented finished basements. The cheerleaders would be down and everything—happy, happy occasions.

SHELLY STRICKLER: When rock 'n' roll first came out, people said it was far out and dangerous, that it would get us into trouble. But it was all so mild. What was the worst thing we did? Neck in the balcony?

I didn't like rock 'n' roll right away. I liked Joni James and Patti Page, Perry Como and Eddie Fisher. But we played the songs at parties in finished basements. We danced the Fish at the JCH. It worked itself into our crowds.

NEIL SEDAKA: Carole King went to Madison but hung out with the kids from Lincoln. Pizza was still new then, and one night we went to try it at Andrea's Pizza Parlor, on Brighton Beach Avenue. We were waiting for our order when someone put a nickel in the jukebox, and "Earth Angel" by the Penguins came on. We were mesmerized. The Penguins went "ooooooh," and we went wild. That was our first exposure to pizza and rock 'n' roll.

MURRAY THE K'S
HOLIDAY REVUE
FEATURING
BEN E. KING   LITTLE STEVIE WONDER
JAN and DEAN   THE DRIFTERS
THE SHIRELLES   GENE PITNEY
MIRACLES   THE ANGELS
THE DOVELLS   JAY and the AMERICANS
THE TYMES   THE CHIFFONS

ROGER GREEN: "The soul in the hole" was what we called a sunk-in section of the park adjacent to P.S. 44 on Madison Street in Bedford-Stuyvesant. Late summer nights, the local soul singers would gather there, get up on the park benches, and perform. All the kids in the neighborhood thought they could sing doo-wop and would try to outdo each other with songs like "Twinkle, Twinkle Little Star." Little Anthony and the Imperials came by before they were famous. It was early rock 'n' roll, rhythm and blues, a lot of a capella, a lot of call-and-response. Grown-ups from the tenements across the street leaned out the windows to listen. Young people gathered round. They'd

The old Brooklyn
Paramount, site of the
famous rock 'n' roll shows.

build up a little pit with loose bricks, stick a potato on a branch, cook it, and eat it while listening to the singing.

NEIL SEDAKA: We lived and breathed music. We sang doo-wop in the school gym and in the lobbies of apartment houses, which had wonderful echoes, on the street corners and outside the candy stores. Our music was an escape from the adult world; it was our own little club, our own little niche.

HOWARD RAPP: We did the fifties-style harmony to songs like "The Closer You Are." At first we were ten kids, then sixteen, then twenty, then thirty. When the people in the buildings complained, we moved on to another corner, and then another one. We also had a group of a lead singer and four backup guys. I was the first tenor. That was how high my voice was.

GAIL EISEMAN BERNSTEIN: We would get up at four in the morning, leave the house at five, walk down to Church Avenue, and take the IRT downtown to Nevins Street. From there, we'd walk to the Fabian Fox or Paramount and stand in line for the 10:00 A.M. rock 'n' roll show. We saw the Platters, the Penguins, Bill Haley and the Comets. Once Eddie Fisher was featured in an Alan Freed show.

We got seats in the front row, threw him mash notes, and screamed as he sang "Oh My Papa" and "Bring Back the Hands of Time."

HOWARD RAPP: The rock 'n' roll shows at the Brooklyn Paramount ran about ten days during the times the kids were off from school, five performances a day of three-hour shows, with one act coming out right after the other. It was kind of a throwback to vaudeville, except it was all music and there was so much audience participation. Kids sang along, danced in the aisles. The lines to get in were enormous, but no one minded.

Alan Freed and, afterward, Murray the K signed groups before they were popular and pushed their records on the air. By the time the show came on, the records were hits and the groups well-known. They picked the Brooklyn Paramount, I guess, because it was so close to Manhattan. What Alan Freed accomplished at the Brooklyn Paramount was great. But he got caught up in all kinds of scandals like payola and having kids out robbing cars during his rock sock hops. His TV show got canceled, and everyone disassociated from him.

In 1963, right after Labor Day, Murray the K had a show at the Brooklyn Fox, right down the block from the Paramount, which by then was part of Long Island University. My uncle Charlie Rapp managed a group of Filipinos called the Rockyfellers: four children, aged seven, nine, thirteen, twenty-two, and the father, who was about four-ten and played the biggest bass fiddle you could believe. They had a number-two record at the time: "Look at Killer Joe Go." Although I was only fourteen, I worked backstage as chaperon and office representative. Whenever I looked out the dressing-room window, I'd see mobs of kids behind barricades waiting for a glimpse of the stars. "Look," they screamed when they saw me, "it's one of the Rockyfellers." I'd go out for something to eat, and kids would be all over me for an autograph. I signed Tony's name, because we were the same age.

Stevie Wonder made his first appearance at that show. He was thirteen years old. From the way he acted backstage, I wondered if he was really blind. He had a way of knowing who different people were that was uncanny. It was like he had an extra sense. In a jam session, he sang a number, "Fingertips," that became his first hit record.

HERBY GREISSMAN: We played records in our clubroom, which was a finished basement on Sixty-fifth Street. We also played cards, smoked cigarettes, made out with girls, and hung out there when we played hooky from school. The monitor in my homeroom class marked me present whenever I played hooky. But one day she played hooky too, and my alibi went down the drain. My father happened to be home when the dean called and said, "Your son's not in school."

I'm in the clubroom playing cards. All of a sudden, one of the fellows runs in from off the street and says, "Herby, your father's coming!" I duck into a back room. My father comes in. "Where's Herby?"

"We haven't seen him, Mr. Greissman," my friends say. "He must be in school."

He leaves without a word. Later that day he asks me where I was.

I said I went to school. He says, "Who are you bullshitting? I was in the clubroom, and I saw three guys playing cards with four hands." That time, he caught me.

Another time when I played hooky and heard he was on the warpath, I ran out of the clubhouse down five blocks to Sixtieth Street. There I met the school bus on the way home. I got on, and when the school bus pulled up in front of my house, I nonchalantly got off. That time, he didn't catch me.

One Saturday, we hung around the candy store with nothing to do. Nobody had money. Everybody was hungry. One of the guys suggests we crash a wedding. It seemed like a good idea. So we got dressed up and went over to the Aperion Manor, on Kings Highway. On Saturday nights in the summertime, they don't start until late, so we got there just in time.

You know a wedding's not like a bar mitzvah, where everyone knows everyone. You got two sides. My friend goes up and kisses the bride, congratulates her. Whoever it was, we said we were from the other side. We ate whatever we liked from the smorgasbord. When they were about to start the ceremony, we gave back the yarmulkes and went home.

I was good at running because someone was always chasing me. Victor Gordon's candy store around the corner had a window opening up to the street so you could buy candy or a paper without going into the store. We drove Victor Gordon crazy. One Saturday night, we're breaking his chops, and he's really pissed. He takes a big soda glass and fills it with water to throw at us. All of a sudden, Casey walks by the window, all dressed up for his Saturday night date. Victor Gordon throws the water, and Casey gets soaked.

The candy store across the street was sold. This woman Molly took it over. She was tough, didn't want to live by the rules. What were the rules? To give us a glass of water during a stickball game. We taught her a lesson. Saturday night she got the delivery of the Sunday papers. We got them and ripped them in half and ran. Or we bought balloons, filled them up with water, went up on the roof of the building across the street, and bombed the store. Or we'd wait for a convertible to go by. Sometimes we'd miss, sometimes we wouldn't. As I said, I was always running.

CLARENCE NORMAN, SR.: I was always running when the gangs came around. There were the Nits, the Robins, the Beavers, the Social Jets. When they came on the block, guys like me disappeared. I lived on the bridge between Bed-Stuy and Williamsburg. But I spent most of my childhood between DeKalb Avenue and down-

Stevie Wonder made his first appearance in 1963 at Murray the K's rock 'n' roll show at the Brooklyn Fox.

town because I knew crossing over to Gates Avenue could be death. These guys had zip guns and knives.

BOB ERTEL: As teenagers, we became aware of gang activities in the neighborhood. One evening we were walking to our bench on Ocean Parkway—every bunch of kids had their bench, where they hung out—when a gang came charging at us. There must have been forty of them and six of us. We thought we were finished, but they pulled up and said, "Aw, it's only the East Fifth Street boys."

TOM BOORAS: Gangs were popular in the downtown area, organized according to territory and neighborhoods. Gowanus had the Gowanus Dukes. The Kane Street Midgets were the kids twelve and under. The Kane Street Stompers were fourteen to thirty years old. They were into knocking over garbage cans or giving cars flat tires—prank things.

HOWARD RAPP: I lived on Taylor Street between Bedford and Wythe. The Hellburners were on one side of Bedford Avenue, and the Phantom Lords were on the other side. My friends and I straddled the line, just wanting to play basketball and hang out at the Williamsburg YMHA. We all got beat up once in a while.

ANNETTE DE LUCIA-CLARK: There were all kinds of gangs in Red Hook: the Mau Mau Chaplins, the Corsair Lords, the Ambassadors, the Saints, the Ft. Greene Chaplains. I was one of the youngest members of the Rebelettes, the female part of the Rebels. It was integrated: Hispanic, black, white, Japanese, Mexican. We wore black-and-hot-pink jackets with our names printed across the back.

Guys in gangs could be vicious and violent but would rarely go out of their way to start something. It was more a guarding of the turf, something like *West Side Story*.

ALBERT VANN: Compared to the violence today, those gangs were very tame. In some ways, they were a healthy development. They reflected a high degree of organization, had a high regard for the neighborhood. You were only at risk if you didn't live in the neighborhood. Your elders, your seniors, they had no problems. They were well-respected.

ALAN LELCHUK: When I went with my father to the Eastern Parkway Arena to watch the fights, we knew we had to be more prudent on certain streets. There were gangs in Brownsville, but they didn't engage in random violence. They generally stayed on their own turf, except when they had gang fights.

CLARENCE NORMAN, SR.: Every May 30 there was a gang fight in Prospect Park. It was a known thing. We'd have a picnic on the Parade Ground and wait for it to start. We'd watch for a while, and then we'd all have to run.

LUIS COLMENARES: All told there were close to a hundred set for the gang fight at City Park, down just behind the projects area. It was the first time I was ever involved in anything like this. Everyone had chains and knives, bats and sticks. It was the Midgets, the Panthers, and some of the Angels against the Chaplins and Bishops.

We were there on this summer evening to fight these black kids, for what reason I don't know. But they weren't kids. They were men: six feet tall with eighteen-inch arms. They had guns and knives. Suddenly, Johnny Ferris comes out with a shotgun. The black guys stood there stiff. Johnny Ferris starts to scream: "You motherfuckers. Enough of this. I'm going to take all of you out." That was the first time I had ever heard the word *motherfuckers*. I didn't know what it meant, but it struck me that it was some kind of insult.

Then suddenly there was a *"BOOM!"* One of the Chaplins got wounded. Then there was a conference between the leaders of both sides. What started all the trouble was a rumor about a girl. Who started it, we didn't know. What girl, nobody seemed to know. Finally, it got settled and everybody went home.

ANNETTE DE LUCIA-CLARK: For weeks all the gangs were preparing for a gang fight in the Carroll Street Park. Kids were getting grease to put on their faces to protect against bites and scratches. There were the chains and the knives, the belts and the sticks. I was going along as part of the crowd, walking to the site of the fight with my girlfriend. "We must be out of our minds," I told her. "We can't go in there. What happens if we get killed?"

Then I joined the community center in my housing project, and it was a nice change from that kind of scene. We danced the lindy, the mashed potato, the fly, and the twist. We listened to Elvis and the Platters.

Miss Adams, a black counselor, suggested I compete in the Miss Gowanus Community Center Pageant. I was the only white girl who entered. The kids voted, and I won first place. I got a trophy and became eligible to compete in the citywide competition. I knew I could never enter, because one of the requirements was you had to make your own dress, and I had no money for anything.

But Miss Adams and her friend Mr. Johnson told me they would help. Mr. Johnson took money out of his own pocket and helped me buy white material. Their friends helped me sew it, and I actually wound up making a dress. It was, "Oh my God, me, Annette, made a dress?" I couldn't even read and write properly.

I had only had ragged hand-me-downs, dungarees, borrowed clothes—never anything nice like that before. I felt self-conscious and told the people at the community center I was dropping out. The whole thing was too high and mighty for me. But they would not let me. "You'll do fine," they insisted.

So I took part in the pageant and came in fourth runner-up in the city. Of course, the people at the Gowanus Community Center thought I should have finished higher. But for me, it was wonderful. Who would ever think that somebody in a poverty-ridden neighborhood, a gang member, a girl who grew up in an area where drugs and alcohol were on the street corners, could have such an experience? I had never thought I was pretty. But now I not only felt pretty, I believed I was different. I had assumed all of Brooklyn was like Gowanus. But now I saw there were other neighborhoods. I knew that I did not have to be part of a gang. I realized I could make choices.

ALBERT VANN: What kept me out of loopholes that young people can fall into was playing basketball. When we were not in school or working, we played. We played day and night, in the rain, in the cold. Patchen Park on Madison and Park, Kingston Avenue Park were places to show your stuff. In order to keep playing, you had to win.

It was difficult to win against those guys who were three or four years older, but we always tried.

So many came out of that basketball playing—Sihugo Green; Solly Walker of St. Johns; Frank Thomas, who was my teammate at Franklin K. Lane and is now president of the Ford Foundation; Connie Hawkins, who was a little behind us (we like to think we nurtured him along); Tommy Davis, who played for the Dodgers. Basketball was always preeminent for me. I played varsity basketball—junior high school through college.

HERB BERNSTEIN: We played at Wingate Field. When it got dark, we moved cars over and lit the court with headlights. Saturday mornings, I couldn't wait to get up and run over there. I played basketball on court number one, a privilege I got by being good. It was three-man ball, one basket against the fence. Great games, great ball players. There were lots of fights and lots of hassles. If you lost a game, you could sit and wait for four hours to get back on the court. So you wouldn't lose. You played till you dropped. Then you went to get a hamburger and french fries and went back to play some more. The girls used to come down, and we'd show off. It was a big social thing.

STARR FROST GOLDBERG: The boys were on the teams, and the girls were the cheerleaders, or they sat in the stands and watched their boyfriends play ball. Even if we were good at a sport, we would giggle through the game and try not to make ourselves look that good. We were afraid we might beat the boys.

"What kept me out of loopholes that young people can fall into was playing basketball."

STAN GOLDBERG: When the schoolyard closed, we moved on over to the JCH on Bay Parkway and Seventy-ninth Street. I was selected to play in the all-star basketball game of the Junior League there, and it was a big thrill.

MAX WECHSLER: My local basketball league team had an away game at the JCH. Coming by bus from Williamsburg into Bensonhurst was like a trip into an upscale neighborhood. It had trees, wide boulevards, cleaner streets.

Our coach was a tough guy who always told us to play physical, to bang the players on the other teams around. That was part of the secret of our success, although we had some talented players too. I considered myself one of them.

The game began. My matchup was against a guy who had long arms and curly black hair. I shook hands with him before the game started and said, "Good luck." He didn't answer. But about three minutes into the game, I could tell this guy was letting his basketball ability do his talking. He scored off me every time he got the ball— a couple of driving lay-ups, a jump shot, a set shot.

During a time-out, the coach yelled at me, "You're letting that guy eat you up alive. Smack him around a little. Maybe that'll slow him down."

I kneed him, elbowed him, pushed him. Nothing helped. He was like a machine out there. Like I said, I thought I was a fairly good basketball player. But he was in another league. My physical play fouled me out of the game early in the second half. When the game finally ended, he wound up scoring forty-five points off me and the two other guys who followed in my place. I found out later his name was Sandy Koufax.

That was part of growing up. You thought you were a hot-shot ball player, and then you came up against a Sandy Koufax. It was a testing ground, finding out what you were made of, how well you could take failure, where you should set your sights.

BOB ERTEL: Up and down our street in Borough Park, they graduated from high school and went to work. But at Midwood, people were taking the College Boards, discussing different colleges, applying to places like Princeton, Yale, Michigan—major-league stuff. Mrs. Bradshaw, the goddess of college admissions, took great care of the ones who had the best potential for the better schools. Out of the Fabulous Fifteen, our social group, twelve went to out-of-town schools, two went to CCNY Engineering, and I went to Brooklyn.

JIM SLEEPER: To go to college most anywhere else, you really had to have money. But the large concentration of socialist immigrants in New York believed you should be able to get a college education without having to pay for it. There was a very unusual coming together of certain forces in New York City in the thirties, forties, and fifties. The values of immigrant socialists combined with FDR's political clout to make this a city with incredible resources and tremendous vitality. That really stamped Brooklyn. A unique set of public colleges was created, among them, Brooklyn College.

Brooklyn College: the entrance and the sunken garden. "I looked to the right and to the left, and it was a very beautiful sight."

DONNA GEFFNER: All you needed was the grades: a 92 average for girls, an 88 average for guys—and we never thought to question the inequity of those criteria. For those of us from European backgrounds, this was a great opportunity. A registration fee of twenty-five dollars and a complete college education.

ALAN LELCHUK: Brooklyn College continued for me what I had with Jefferson and with the Dodgers—a strong sense of community, of excellence, of loyalty and fondness. You were going to college. Your father and mother had never gone, and you were bettering them.

Since my average in Jefferson wasn't high enough, I spent my first year at Brooklyn in night school. As it turned out, that was the best thing that happened to me in college. I joined up with the night-school magazine, *Nocturne*, where I met people in their thirties, veterans from World War II and the Korean War. It was a real literary brigade. Here were these mature guys with this seventeen-year-old kid on their hands who couldn't write his name. If I didn't know something, they didn't say shut up. They molded me. They gave me my first books to read, my indoctrination into literature. I began writing stories on the train. By the second year, I had earned good enough grades to matriculate into day school, but I remained with the *Nocturne*.

There was a real sense of excellence among the faculty. They were teachers, not celebrities going on television. I studied the classics. My Greek teacher was Vera Lachman, a Jewish lady who had escaped from Germany. She was very serious, very spare. I wrote plays in those days. She would take me to the lily pond in one of the sunken gardens that flanked the library. We would sit there and discuss the plays. It was exactly the educational experience one should get, being alone with a teacher in an isolated environment and talking about something that you were passionate about.

SOLOMON AIDELSON: I came to this country at the age of twenty-two, a Holocaust survivor. Nobody wanted to hear about the Holocaust at that time. No one wanted to touch the wounds. I had come from a very religious family and was ordained as a rabbi at a very young age, but I had no formal schooling since the first grade. What I wanted desperately was a secular education.

When I learned the Ford Foundation had given two million dollars to Brooklyn College to evaluate people who are self-taught, I applied, was accepted, and became a student at a regular college for the first time in my eventful life. It was a difficult and worrisome period, but it was also wonderful. In Eastern Europe, I had belonged to a sub-culture that had no relations with the main culture aside from buying and selling. Even in Brooklyn, I had been in all-Jewish surroundings. Now, I was in a different atmosphere.

Teaching during the day and going to school at night, I had very little time for leisure. But in the summers, when I didn't have to teach, I took the time to notice the campus. I looked to the right and to the left, and it was a very beautiful sight.

KARL BERNSTEIN: During my time, Brooklyn College was just four pink-brick Georgian buildings and a campus green we were not allowed to walk on. The library, La Guardia Hall, with its clock tower, dominated the whole scene. On either side of the library were sunken gardens: one had a lily pond, the other had a rose garden. Whitman, the performing arts center, opened in my senior year. Before that, all the way back to Flatbush Avenue was open campus. Behind the college, where Avenue H and Nostrand Avenue meet, there used to be experimental gardens with all kinds of plants and flowers and a little pond where biology majors worked on plant genetics. Walking around the campus, you felt like you were in an all-American out-of-town college, not in Brooklyn, New York.

Students Find Room Missing

Speech 19.1E was supposed to meet Tues. in 350W. That's what the schedule of clases said and that's where Speech 19.1E set out for, bright and alert.

Only one thing was wrong. The architect forgot to put a 350W in Whitman Hall. Such oversights happen all the time. so Speech 19.1E, undaunted, looked upstairs and downstairs in the big new building. They finally ended up on the roof. Only no 350W.

Somebody had the inspiration to call the speech department. "Yes," a voice said, "A mistake was made." The correct room was 023W.

Down to the catacombs of Whitman Hall trekked Epeech 19.1E to find 023W. It was a real challenge. But, alas, there was no 023W. Speechless, now, Speech 19.1E walked around in a state of traumatic shock.

A kindly student came around and cleared the matter up. It was all very simple. 023W was really inside 024W (not to be confused with 350W which doesn't exist at all). Spech 19.1E convened slightly late.

SHELLY STRICKLER: I missed out on a whole different acculturation not going away to college. I got on a different bus and went the other way with the same people I knew all my life. But my parents couldn't afford anything else, and I have to admit I got a first-class education. You went to public school, to high school, and then on to Brooklyn College. And you would be successful.

MIRIAM KITTRELL: My father said, "What are you crazy? What is this mishegoss? You have to go to college? Be a bookkeeper. Get married." But he couldn't stop me. I went to Brooklyn College. I worked in the lab, and I thrived.

ANGELO BADALAMENTI: We had our dreams, we worked at them, and we always talked about making it. Artie would tell me, "Angelo, you're gonna make it, I know you're gonna make it." I'd tell him, "Artie, you're gonna make it." We had this need to be successful, to step out of this lower-middle thing. What we had was not bad, but it wasn't enough. We knew there was a bigger, a greater world out there.

That World
Is Gone

STEWIE STONE: You thought things would never change. You'd hang out on the corner, go to the movies with your friends, grow up, get married, go over to your parents for dinner. You thought Brooklyn would always be Brooklyn.

IRVING RUDD: One night in the early fifties, Walter O'Malley was in his chauffeur-driven Buick headed home after a night game at Ebbets Field. Around the area of what is now the Meadowbrook Parkway, he got stuck in a traffic jam and noticed that a tremendous amount of traffic was headed west. "What's all that?" he asked the chauffeur.

"It's the people coming home from the trots, Mr. O'Malley."

O'Malley's ears perked. A counterattraction. Bingo! Smack! Click! O'Malley was a shrewd man. He already saw the demographics. Why were these thousands of people going to Roosevelt Field instead of Ebbets Field?

MAX WECHSLER: In August 1955, when the Dodgers were in first place blowing away all their opposition, stories appeared in the newspapers that the team had scheduled eight games for 1956 in Jersey City. That could have been another country. Fans protested on cardboard signs: "Leave us not go to Joisey." But people thought O'Malley was bluffing, throwing down the glove, making his move to pressure city officials to give him a new stadium in Brooklyn. They might play a couple of games in Jersey City, but the Dodgers leave Brooklyn? Unthinkable.

The Dodgers had gotten their name from the fans who once dodged the crisscrossing trolleys that converged on Ebbets Field. But trolleys were becoming rare in Brooklyn. More and more people were driving to the games, yet there was very little parking near the stadium, and auto vandalism was increasing. O'Malley had seen studies that predicted the area would soon be unsuitable for night games. And the ballpark, built in 1913, was in need of repair.

Robert Moses offered O'Malley a site for a new stadium by the Brooklyn-Battery tunnel. "It's a good site for *you*," O'Malley told Moses. "Everyone will have to pay a toll. But with a cemetery on one side and the river on the other, it's worse than Ebbets Field." He was offered a site in Flushing Meadows. "I might as well move to the West Coast," O'Malley said. "It won't be the Brooklyn Dodgers in Queens."

DORIS MODELL TIPOGRAPH: My father chaired the committee to "Keep the Dodgers in Brooklyn." Thousands of people took part in the protest parade he arranged. "If the Dodgers leave, that's the end of Brooklyn," he said.

PRECEDING PAGE
Henry Modell, the ultimate
Brooklyn Dodgers fan, in a
bittersweet moment. (Note
the *X* crossing out the *B* on
Henry's Dodgers cap.)

LUIS COLMENARES: Just before I started high school, the city told us we had to get out of our apartment. This guy came to the house. He was bald and wore eyeglasses. He had this large attaché case. He gave my mother some papers to sign. She refused. My mother and the other tenants were brought to the court building. Several times they went back and forth. The tenants were there. A bunch of lawyers was there. People asked questions. "Be quiet," they were told. "We're trying to conduct a hearing."

We were paying $27.50 a month for a seven-room apartment with two bathrooms. Concord Village was being built on the site of what had been a neighborhood lumberyard. They offered us a two-bedroom apartment there. Who could afford that?

We thought, Who the hell is doing this? We'd like to kill him. They said, "We're going to build these beautiful buildings, and you'll have first call on them." We got information about buying an apartment. I thought, Who the hell buys an apartment? You buy a house, not an apartment. But my mother had signed these papers and thought she would buy. Then she found it would cost $250 a month. She almost had a heart attack. Finally, to keep things simple, we left, moved up to Canada.

Blocks of beautiful old houses were bulidozed. One of them was where Walt Whitman set the type for *Leaves of Grass* back in 1855. Nobody cared about that or about all the people that got pushed out. A thriving ethnic neighborhood in Brooklyn Heights just got destroyed. In its place is Cadman Plaza Co-ops.

MATT KENNEDY: Our Coney Island neighborhood was a series of one-family houses. Many had Belgian brick fronts—that's a finer form of brick that was brought over in the ships as ballast; it lasts forever. When urban development began, these homes were condemned and the families forced out. They knocked down all the one-family houses and put up twenty-six-story buildings with balconies overlooking the ocean: low-income here, middle-income there, low-income here. Urban development and planning wiped out a very strong Coney Island neighborhood. All the mama-and-papa stores on Mermaid Avenue were killed off. There's no more shopping in the neighborhood. You don't go out after dark.

MURRAY HANDWERKER: The closing of Steeplechase was a big blow to Coney Island. Two square blocks closed up. Fred Trump wanted the land to build high-rise, middle-income housing. He wanted to change the zoning from amusement to residential. I felt it was important to have amusement zoning in a beachfront, boardwalk area. I fought him, and I beat him.

Robert Moses hated Coney Island. He wanted to wipe out the private amusement area. He tried to get the Cyclone torn down. He didn't want the Aquarium. When it was built, he had that overpass constructed connecting it to the subway to keep the people visiting the Aquarium from mingling with the crowds. I fought Moses also. I fought him all the way because I felt Coney Island had a place in New York.

When I think back on the old days in Coney Island, I think mostly of the people: Pat Auletta, Louis Gargiulo, the managers and workers at Nathan's. It was a joy. When the bureaucracy of the city of New York began bothering us, I lost enthusiasm. It was no longer a joy. That's when I stopped.

People complain to me that Nathan's frankfurters are not the same as the ones in Coney Island. I give them two reasons: one, the salt air; two, the three-quarter-inch U.S. Steel griddles we had. The thin griddles they use today don't hold the heat.

JUDY BERGER: The city took down twenty or thirty houses adjacent to Washington Cemetery on Twentieth Avenue that had belonged to lower-middle-class, predominantly Italian people who took great

It was hard to imagine the Dodgers not being Brooklyn.

pride in their neighborhood. The last high school to be built in Brooklyn, Franklin Delano Roosevelt, opened on that site in 1965. Black kids from out of the neighborhood were bused into the school. The day the building opened, "Niggers go home" was scrawled on the front. The ten-block walk the kids had to take from the F station on the subway became a gauntlet. They were frequently beaten up. But in the school, the student government leaders were black kids from out of the neighborhood.

JOAN MAYNARD: In the forties and fifties, Bedford-Stuyvesant was a stable, integrated neighborhood. But out on Long Island, white people were not buying fast enough into the new housing tracts. So the real estate interests shook things up. There was a conspiracy to destroy integrated, solvent neighborhoods to make money. Bed-Stuy went, and it went very fast.

WILLIAM THOMPSON: The speculating was a conscious and deliberate thing, no question about it. Starting in the 1950s, there was redlining and sophisticated blockbusting. The people who came in via blockbusting busted the houses up, rented out rooms, created illegal rooming houses.

JOAN MAYNARD: When a house became empty, it was rented to a family with a lot of social problems. People living nearby wanted to move out. The real estate interests moved in and bought these houses for cheap prices.

WILLIAM THOMPSON: The shutout was very subtle. Nobody said where you could and couldn't live, but where a bank might give a black person a mortgage on Hancock Street, it would never give him a mortgage in Bay Ridge. Blacks could only move out in concentric circles: to Crown Heights, then to East Flatbush, Flatbush. The ring has gotten bigger and bigger in Brooklyn, but the leaps have not been made. White people could move wherever they wanted to, and as redlining and blockbusting started to happen, they got out of the neighborhoods. That is what made them change.

JOAN MAYNARD: Many of the homeowners were older people who had struggled all their lives and tried so hard to keep the block up, but they could not get mortgages to make improvements on their homes. The banks decided who would get and who would not get. I saw this happening.

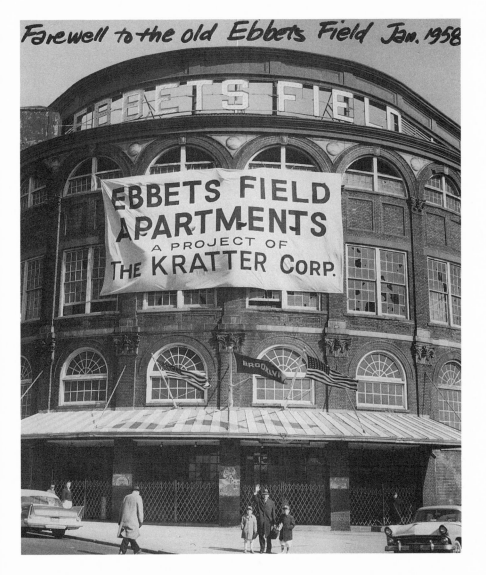

Farewell to the old Ebbets Field Jan. 1958

EBBETS FIELD
APARTMENTS
A PROJECT OF
THE KRATTER CORP.

BROOKLYN

"You thought things would
never change."

JIM SLEEPER: Bankers actually drew a red line on a map around the areas where they would not make mortgage loans. It was not a formal document, more a consensus of bankers looking over a map and saying, "That neighborhood's going bad. Let's not make any loans from here to here." If people in a certain neighborhood cannot get home improvement loans or can't get a mortgage loan to buy a house, then property values go way down. And people are panicked into selling and getting out. It is a death sentence to a neighborhood that has nothing to do with the creditworthiness of individual applicants. Redlining became a self-fulfilling prophecy.

HOWARD JONES: Coming out of an integrated experience, I always felt that as long as people lived together, knew each other,

The Brooklyn waterfront used to be like a company town.

things would be all right. Redlining changed all that. It stopped the mingling.

PHIL FAGIN: By 1963, most of the Jews and Italians had moved out of Brownsville. My father observed a few youngsters breaking into an apartment. They started to throw bricks at him. My father said it was time to go.

STEWIE STONE: The landlord started neglecting our building. My parents were living with exposed wires. We moved.

JOE SIGLER: After I got married, we lived in the same building on Ocean Avenue that my father and I had moved into when I was fourteen. Back then it had a doorman, nice furniture in the lobby. But over the years, the doorman went, the furniture went. Still, it was OK. My wife would walk the carriage in the park. In 1967, we moved to Rome. When we returned a year later, things had changed a lot. One of the buildings started taking in welfare people, and the next thing you knew there was a fire, and undesirable people started hanging out. My uncle Peter got mugged in the elevator. It wasn't what we wanted.

FRANK BARBARO: Red Hook, Carroll Gardens, South Brooklyn—I can remember when those waterfront areas used to be like a company town. Most of the longshoremen left their houses and walked five minutes to the pier. There were times when they weren't working.

They waited for the ship to come in. When it did, they worked twenty-four, thirty-six, forty-eight hours at a clip. It used to take three hundred to four hundred longshoremen a whole week to unload and load cargo on a single ship. Then they got that big paycheck. They paid off the loan shark, paid off the bookie, got Mama's wedding ring and the trumpet back from the hock shop, and paid off the clothing store for the new Easter outfits. It was a brutal life.

By the late fifties, people who had good jobs—bosses, superintendents—began moving out of the waterfront communities to the suburbs. By the sixties, most of the Italians had left. Today, fifty men unload and load maybe three times as much cargo in one day as three hundred to four hundred men did in one week years ago.

I go back to the old neighborhoods, and it's an eerie feeling. I remember the social halls, the pool halls, the music. At every party, there was somebody with a mandolin or a harmonica. I remember the vibrancy, the pulsating feeling of life and humanity. That world is gone.

JIM SLEEPER: The people in the first wave, those who left Brooklyn in the late forties and early fifties, were not fleeing crime and deteriorating neighborhoods. Suburbia was marketed. VA and FHA mortgages combined with the great interstate highway system made it attractive and possible to own a suburban home. People wanted to get out of their cramped, immigrant neighborhoods. They didn't want to live in the apartment above their parents. Theirs was a move to greener pastures, not flight from blockbusting.

The people in the second wave, those who left Brooklyn in the late fifties and into the sixties, moved out of anger and fear. The brokers and speculators had channeled in tenants in ways that made the neighborhoods undesirable. The first blacks that came in many cases were homeowners. But when the banks refused to lend them the money to build up their homes, the decline accelerated. Whereas earlier, white people moved from one neighborhood to another they thought was better—say, Brownsville to Flatbush—now there was a feeling that the whole borough was in peril. If they had the wherewithal, they went out to the Levittowns and less-expensive suburbs as best they could, or out to Queens when it was being developed in the postwar years. The minority newcomers were left stranded, high and dry. And obviously the departure of jobs—the breweries, the Navy Yard, the Dodgers—accelerated the decline. Chronic unemployment and all the things that go along with it came to be. The softened real-estate market triggered a cycle of deeper decay.

JOAN MAYNARD: The first drug that I heard about was marijuana. People called it Mary Jane. I knew a musician who used it. It was a scandal. Some entertainers were paid off in heroin. Then the mob brought it into the black community. The attitude they had was clearly expressed in the movie *The Godfather*: "They're not people anyway."

ALBERT VANN: Drugs broke up so-called gangs and led to the destruction of the strength of fundamental relationships in our community. They were the prime cause of the destabilization of the black family.

ROGER GREEN: The "soul in the hole," that gathering spot for local soul singers in the park on Madison Street, had originally been a source of release, a diversion, a coming together. But by the mid-sixties, the music had changed. Now it was expressing protest. Poets began coming through, and their poetry was very political. The "soul in the hole" became a reflection of the political and social changes that were occurring. There was more anger.

BOB LIFF: By the mid-sixties, the Brooklyn College campus was filled with a lot of civil-rights activity and protests against the Vietnam War. When a Navy recruiter set up a table in Boylan Hall, the campus leftists, many of them members of SDS, demanded another table. The college administration, which still bore the scars of former president Harry Gideons—the great red-baiter of the fifties—refused. There was an attempted sit-in. The administration called the cops, who started dragging people out. There was tremendous chaos. Most of the campus shut down. It made the first story on Huntley-Brinkley two nights in a row—which was how you measured things in those days.
   Brooklyn College was still largely Jewish then, although not the Brooklyn College that belonged to memory. It had a significant black student population and some brainy Asian kids. We pushed for open admissions. We sent ten busloads down to the March on Washington.

ROGER GREEN: There were people who were on the periphery of the civil-rights movement, who had a sense that here up North things weren't all that bad. But the assassination of Martin Luther King, Jr., in the spring of 1968 devastated them. It challenged them. The question of violence versus nonviolence became a serious debate.

ALBERT VANN: In 1967, I became acting principal at I.S. 271, in Ocean Hill–Brownsville. It was a transition time for the community. We began asking, What is taught? Who teaches? There was no African-

American history in the schools, and very few black teachers. The curriculum did not reflect us in any way. Our parents were not involved in the schools. We started the battle for community control of our schools, for decentralization.

HOWARD JONES: Ocean Hill–Brownsville was the first showcase of a community-run school. They would pick their own principal, pick their own faculty. In the fall of 1968, the teachers' union responded with a strike. To the people in the community, the majority of the people striking were white, and they were stopping them from starting a community school, which they needed to address their identity as blacks.

ABE LASS: That strike was over who was going to run the schools. It was a terrible period. There was great pressure to open the schools and conduct classes. By law, only the principal can do that. And I felt if anyone else would open the school, it would be over my dead body.

EVERETT KERNER: Ocean Hill–Brownsville created great animosity between those who thought the schools should be opened and

The Brooklyn-Queens Expressway plunged right through the heart of neighborhoods.

those who disagreed. Both staff and supervisors were out on the picket line. After it was all over, there were people in the same school who never spoke to one another again.

ABE LASS: Being on the picket line for almost two months, I had time to think of where the school system was going, and whether that's where I wanted to go. I took a long look down the pike, as they say, and saw nothing good was happening. When you put the responsibility for running a school system in the hands of people who are not teachers or administrators, I don't see anything good or promising on the horizon. Nobody has been able to demonstrate decentralization makes for better education. It makes for more jobs, more horse-trading, more corruption, more bad educational decisions—also more bickering and politicized situations in the lower schools—and it's passed along to the high schools. Nowhere else in the country does it exist. Once you give money and power to community groups, it's impossible to take it away without a revolution in the streets.

I decided then I was going to retire. I was only in my early sixties. It was almost unheard of at that time. But I didn't want any more of it. I had had it. This wasn't what teaching was about.

JIM SLEEPER: Ocean Hill–Brownsville broke the spine of the city's civic culture. People who had given their lives to the liberal vision found themselves deprecated and cursed. The political system was extending civil rights to people at the same time the economic

system was pulling the economic rug out from under them. They were
enraged, and they had a lot of scores to settle. On the other side, you
had Jewish people, Italians, and others who had struggled up from
their own ghettos and had managed to become something. The tragedy
was miscommunication and shouting back and forth. Brooklyn has
never really truly recovered.

HOWARD JONES: Ocean Hill–Brownsville was the downer, the
watershed. That was the flood. Nothing got better after that. People
could no longer live together. The melting pot that I grew up in was
gone.

ABE LASS: The teachers won the strike but lost the war. Right
after the strike they started busing kids. In '71, we got about a hundred
or so from Ocean Hill–Brownsville, where the strike had started. From
there it's all downhill.

RALPH GASARCH: I was teaching at Lincoln then and saw the
impact of change. It wasn't just busing, it was the skip-zoning that
brought in kids from out of the neighborhoods and the accompanying
tensions. Open-enrollment busing brings children to a school their
parents opt for. With skip-zoning, parents have no say. Many students
had to travel long distances because the school they were assigned to
was so far away, and they became a disruptive element.

JUDY BERGER: In 1968, black kids rampaged through FDR. We
had mounted police. The staff felt the principal was applying a double
standard by allowing the black kids to hang out and not the whites.
I felt the times they are a-changing. The liberalism I had as a high
school student was starting to be chipped away. It was hard to maintain
my youthful optimism. The high hopes and expectations had not
materialized.

ALBERT VANN: I put what happened in perspective. I understand
what happened, why it happened. I know changing society is not done
without upheaval and confrontation.

CLARENCE NORMAN, SR.: The Hasidic community was already in place in Crown Heights by the early sixties, as blacks were
coming in. We live side-by-side, next door to each other, in a truly
integrated community. However, the integration is parallel. It only
becomes interactive when there's a crisis. There have been serious
problems between the black and the Hasidim in Crown Heights, and

the media certainly has not helped. But there's vitality here, a lot of good middle-class black folk who plan to stay, a thriving Jewish community.

In 1967, with Crown Heights undergoing a transition, with a lot of whites moving out and blacks gradually moving in, our church purchased the Park Manor Catering Hall. Any Jewish person who came out of Brooklyn probably remembers it as the Twin Cantors, at 450 Eastern Parkway. The main banquet hall became our sanctuary. The upstairs banquet hall became our Sunday school. The bridal room became our chapel. Our church is *the* Baptist church in Crown Heights, with a membership of two thousand.

So many of the Jewish catering halls and synagogues have become churches. I look at what happened as a progression. Certain religious groups use a building. They move on. Others come in.

HELEN FRIED GOLDSTEIN: B'nai Israel of Bay Ridge was a distinguished synagogue, the only Conservative synagogue in the area for many years. Sometime in the 1960s, it was sold to a Protestant church. Not long after, I went inside. Against all reason, I expected to see my grandfather, tall and elegant, up on the *bima* before the Ark, as I had seen him so many times in the past. I expected to see his picture still hanging in the vestibule, for he had been a leading lay figure in the Conservative movement and this synagogue. It was heart-wrenching, because as far as I'm concerned that place belongs to my grandfather.

Brooklyn seen from above: "the whole density and intensity and diversity."

But then I entered the sanctuary and took a seat in one of the pews. I looked up at the Tiffany-like stained-glass windows, the sunlight spilling through the biblical scenes, and I imagined a little girl sitting there today, distracted by the brilliant colored light just as I used to be. It was all right. After all, it could have become an OTB parlor.

CHARLES HYNES: The sad part about Flatbush is that many of the Jews, Irish, and Italians who gave it great stability ran away as soon as they saw the first black face. People believed property values would drop, and they would not be able to sell their homes. That did not prove to be the case. My block is filled with people of color and all the others.

JIM SLEEPER: There's no question that some of the new immigrants are laying the same foundations in Brooklyn that other immigrants did generations before. Brooklyn had always been and remains an incubator, pumping out athletes, political leaders, impresarios, entertainers.

ROBERT MERRILL: Why did Brooklyn produce so many famous people? It was fighting life for space. The fact that we survived all this made us strong. As we grew older, we appreciated the finer things even more than the guy who lived in a quieter, less-crowded environment.

ALAN LELCHUK: Brooklyn occupied a place in the national mythology. People made jokes about it, but it was a universe unto itself. Now and then, Texas and Manhattan came in. But if the rest of the country had dropped out, that was all right. Brooklyn had enough fighting against itself, playing against itself, communing against itself.

MEL ALLEN: It was the poor working people of Brooklyn against the rich people of Manhattan. It was Brooklyn against the world. It was one of the five boroughs, but Brooklyn seemed to be a separate city. Maybe it was. Maybe it is.

FRANK BARBARO: When I first came to Bensonhurst, there was a wealth of Jewish organizational life: a Mr. & Mrs. club, a Hadassah club, a Deborah club. The temples were alive and used. The JCH was a hub of activity, supported by a lot of wealthy professional and business people. The Italian community was held together with CYOs,

How the city looked from the Brooklyn side in pre–World Trade Center days.

religious groups, people making novenas. Every church was overflowing. That was Bensonhurst.

Now synagogues are half-empty, maybe worse. The temples on Seventy-second and Bay Parkway and on Seventy-fifth Street have shut down. The kids moved to other neighborhoods; mama and papa stayed, mama died, or they decided to go to Florida. The cohesiveness of a group that interacted and interfaced and produced a dynamism is lost.

But Bensonhurst has held. Some of the Jews remain, and there are a lot of second-generation and recently arrived Italians who have built a very tightly knit community. The Italians are getting organization-minded; they're approaching the stage the Jews were in. We're in a hiatus, but we're getting there again.

And the old ethnic neighborhoods are being filled with recently arrived immigrants: Asians, Pakistanis, people from the Caribbean, Hispanics, Russian Jews. There may not be much interrelationship yet. But when these people are economically liberated, they will start their organizations and begin to interrelate with the other people.

ELI WALLACH: Some of the sections are coming back, even better than ever. There's a new cachet to Brooklyn.

NEIL SEDAKA: I go back. I ride on the Cyclone and still thrill to the first drop. I have a frank and french fries at Nathan's. I drive through the old neighborhood. I have to do it; it draws me. I'll never forget where I came from.

ABE LASS: So many have this terrible, terrible yen to come home again, to recapture the first fine careless rapture. In the mid-seventies, a Lincoln reunion in Los Angeles attracted people from all over the country, people who went back to the beginning of the school. What was it that brought people from all over to share memories of a school? What did the word *Lincoln* do to all these people?

JIM SLEEPER: There are dreams, mournful dreams. A sociologist calls this grieving for a lost home. I am convinced that countless people who left Brooklyn have felt that. The borough is haunted by ghosts for me—not because of past relatives, but simply at the thought of people who lived there and left, and also because the whole density and intensity and diversity just seizes me by the throat. Going to Lundy's, going to swim at the St. George Hotel, taking a trolley down to Coney Island and smelling the salt air even before you got there, the sense that the borough was like a vast empire with beaches and hills and woods in Prospect Park, with tenements and rows and rows of infrastructure. My greatest dream is to be able to get into a time machine and make it 1952 and just roam free across the borough.

"So many have this terrible, terrible yen to come home again." A serene stretch of Shore Road along the bay.

MARNIE BERNSTEIN: In 1993, I was invited to speak at the sixth-grade graduation of P.S. 226, a school I had graduated from in

1952. Driving down the Bensonhurst streets that hazy June morning, I felt I could so easily slip right back into the time of my childhood. Every house and driveway and yard and tree looked unchanged.

In the school auditorium, there was the same familiar sense of expectancy. Parents, serious and seemingly respectful of the event they were about to witness, filled all the available seats. Then the music teacher began to play "Pomp and Circumstance" on the old Knabe grand piano. Silently, I sang the still-remembered words— "Land of hope and glory, mother of the free . . ."—as the processional of sixth-grade graduates began. Two lines down the aisle of the old auditorium—one boys, one girls—in that same formal step, the toe of the back foot hesitating for a moment at the heel of the one in front before completing the step.

Another generation of children. Many new immigrants: Russians, Asians, Latinos; many more African Americans; also children with physical handicaps—invisible in my day. But in all the important ways, they are us, hopeful, repeating the same ritual in their navy skirts and pants, their white shirts and red ties, their fresh, sweet faces full of eagerness and optimism. Brooklyn as it was for me continues to be.

KARL BERNSTEIN: I search the borough for my past. I drive past an abandoned building on Atlantic Avenue in East New York. Once it was the Borden Dairy Plant; now, all that remains are two beautiful mosaics of Heidi and the cows on a yellow-brick wall. I walk up a ramp to the boardwalk in Coney Island past a wall that was once part of a bathhouse. It still is adorned with bas reliefs of mermaids and seahorses, and seashells. I pass the old Namm-Loeser store on Fulton Street and make out the name Frederick Loeser and Company, carved in stone above the plate glass window; that dates back to the time before Namm and Loeser merged. I ride down Surf Avenue and wonder why the red, yellow, and blue trolley poles are still standing so many years after the wires were cut down. Or why they never took up the trolley tracks that cross Rockaway Parkway at the subway terminal and run smack into a fruit stand, or dismantled the signal tower for the Norton's Point trolley at the Stillwell Avenue subway station or the trolley shelters at the Brooklyn end of the Williamsburg Bridge.

I pause at the old movie theaters, most of them converted to different use. The Claridge, on Avenue P, is a kosher catering hall. The Avalon, on Kings Highway, is a Pathmark drugstore. The Triangle, on Quentin Road across from Joyce Kilmer Square, is a furniture store, although it still has the marquee. The Jewel, which used to show foreign films when they first became popular, is a porno theater. The Vogue is a nursing home. The Midwood is a commercial building. But the funny thing is, in my mind's eye, I see them as they were.

I dream about home, and it's always the house in Brooklyn. I'm coming home on a cold day, and as I turn the corner from Kings Highway onto East Seventh Street, I brace myself for the cold wind I know will hit me in the face. I put my head down and pull my collar up and push through the wind till I pass the apartment house. Then it's OK, only a little bit farther to my house. Whenever I turned that corner, I knew I was home.

My grandmother had bought our two-family semi-attached house during the boom days of the twenties, brand-new. She wanted to buy a different house down the block, because it had a beautiful tree in front. To her dying day, she complained that they bought the house out from under her. But my father planted a silver maple for her. He tied it to keep it straight, and ultimately the rope got caught up in the tree. In the winter we could see it about ten feet off the ground.

Sometimes I go back and look at the house. The people who bought it have put in new windows. They opened up the roof with skylights. They took down walls. You wouldn't recognize it. But I do. I see it all just like it was. And best of all, the tree is still there.

P.S.

PAT COOPER: *President Roosevelt came down to Red Hook and made a speech, because they were starting work on the Brooklyn-Battery Tunnel. The teachers from P.S. 142 took all the kids to hear him.*

"My fellow Americans," he said, "we are going to give you this tunnel. It will cost thirty-five cents each way, but once this tunnel is paid, you will have it for nothing."

"He's a liar," I said to my friend. I was always a smart little kid.

"Once it's paid," the president repeated, "you will have it for nothing, and you will be closer to Manhattan."

"Who the hell wants to be closer to Manhattan?" I said.

Acknowledgments

Our special thanks to Judy and Joel Berger for reading an evolving manuscript and providing insightful feedback; to Gail and Karl Bernstein for a wealth of recall, photos, and artifacts; and to Doris Modell Tipograph and Norman Tipograph for a treasure trove of Modell and personal memorabilia.

We also thank for their interest and assistance Anthony Cucchiara, archivist and head of Special Collections, Brooklyn College Library; Lori Duggan Gold and the Brooklyn Botanic Garden; Frederic Frommer; Miriam Ginsberg; Roger Harris; Pearl Jackson; Charles Jones, director of public relations, New York City Technical College; Caroline Katz Mount; David Korman and St. Ann's Center for Restoration and the Arts; Clara Lamers of the Brooklyn Historical Society; John Manbeck, archivist and head of the Kingsborough Historical Society, Kingsborough Community College; Howard Rapp; Cathy Ryan of St. Francis College; Fiorenza Sigler; Gordon Silverman and the Jewish Community House of Bensonhurst; Roz Starr; Nat Weinstein; Gary Wojtas, director of public relations at the Brooklyn campus of Long Island University; and our agent, Don Congdon.

We are grateful to our aesthetically attuned editor, John Radziewicz, for once again being enthusiastically supportive and unfailingly correct in judgment; to Trina Stahl, who handled the impossibly complex job of designing this book, succeeded so admirably, and got an education about Brooklyn in the process; and to the staff at Harcourt—Dan Janeck, Christa Malone, Marcella Forster, Ginger Boyer, Steven Cooley, Maggie DeMaegd, and Candace Hodges—for their help and input.

Finally, our thanks to everyone who shared with us memories, perceptions, and photos. This is your life.

Picture Credits

Judy Berger: Pages xvi (top), 8 (middle), 21 (right), 37 (right), 83 (second from right), 108, 122, 143, 145 (bottom), 173 (left), 176, 181 (top), 182 (top), 183, 192 (bottom); Karl Bernstein: Pages iii (left and second from left), vii (top and bottom left, top right), xiii (top right), xvi–xvii (middle), xviii (top), 20 (left), 30 (inset), 31, 45 (top), 46 (bottom), 53, 57, 76 (bottom), 80, 83 (left), 94 (inset), 98, 104 (inset), 114 (middle), 126 (top and middle), 127 (left inset), 128 (bottom), 132, 150 (bottom), 165, 180, 182 (inset), 186, 191, 203 (top), 205 (top), 216, 218, 220, 238–39; Sam Bernstein: Pages xiii (bottom right), xiv (second from top), xv (top and bottom), 3 (inset), 8 (top and bottom), 76 (middle), 130, 145 (top); Bettmann Archive: Pages 3, 87, 146, 215; Frances Blum: Pages viii–ix (bottom), xiv (bottom), xvii (second from top), 2, 6 (middle), 32, 34, 73 (top), 77 (right), 110, 133, 154 (top, third from top); Tom Booras: Pages 56, 140 (top), 159, 198, 205 (bottom left), 214; Brooklyn Academy of Music: Pages 17 (middle), 64; Brooklyn Botanic Garden: Page 5 (both); Brooklyn College Library (courtesy of the Special Collections Department): Pages 9, 88, 97, 160, 167, 219 (both), 221 (both), 228, 231, 232, 237; Brooklyn Historical Society: Pages 35, 91, 94, 106, 210, 234; Jack Eagle: Page 65; Gail Eiseman Bernstein: Pages iii (far right), viii–ix (third from top), xvi (third from top), xviii–xix (second and fourth from top), 17 (second and fourth from left), 24, 44 (both), 46 (top), 48, 49, 51, 52, 54, 58, 66, 68, 70 (middle), 100 (bottom), 123, 124 (top), 158 (inset), 178 (bottom), 206 (top), 207 (left); Fagin Family Collection: Pages x (right), 18, 50 (bottom), 70 (top and bottom), 75 (both), 77 (left), 95, 112, 142; Bill Feigenbaum: Pages ix (second from top), 90; Frommer Collection: Pages iii (middle), vii (bottom right), viii (third from top), xiii (top and bottom left), xiv (third from top), xv (second from top), xviii (second from top), xix (top three), 6 (top), 15, 17 (left and right), 27, 28 (all), 32 (inset), 39 (top), 41 (top), 47, 60 (top), 64 (inset), 79, 100 (top), 118, 124 (bottom), 126 (bottom), 146 (inset), 154 (second from top), 162 (top), 173 (second from left, far right), 192 (top and middle), 193 (both), 196 (inset), 200 (middle), 202, 203 (middle and bottom), 204 (both), 205 (bottom right), 207 (inset), 211 (both),

Index

Rose's Celebrations

Rose's Celebrations

Rose Levy Beranbaum

WILLIAM MORROW AND COMPANY, INC.
New York

Library of Congress Cataloging-in-Publication Data

Beranbaum, Rose Levy.
Rose's Celebrations / Rose Levy Beranbaum.
        p.   cm.
    Includes index.
    ISBN 0-688-11946-8
    1. Holiday cookery.   I. Title.
TX739.B45   1992   92-19018
641.5′68—dc20   CIP

Printed in the United States of America

First Edition

1 2 3 4 5 6 7 8 9 10

BOOK DESIGN BY RICHARD ORIOLO

Acknowledgments

The photographs for this book were produced in a joyful creative atmosphere, thanks to the creative genius and gentle spirit of its photographer, *Amos Chan,* and the unique abilities and dedication of a wonderful team: art director: *Richard Oriolo;* illustrator: *Laura Hartman Maestro;* food stylists: *Rick Ellis, William Smith and Brett Kurzweil, Kevin Pavlina;* prop stylists: *Lanie Strahler, Mary Brannigan.* Special appreciation to *Deborah Weiss Geline,* chief copy editor; *Judith Sutton,* copy editor; *Terry Frishman,* of Creative Marketing Solutions, for her heirloom props that add so much to enhance the beauty of food. Also to *Rick Rodgers,* who cheerfully tested all the recipes innumerable times, giving so much of himself to each one; *Howard Helmer,* of The Poultry and Egg Board; and, as always, special love to *Maria D. Guarnaschelli,* who brought so many individual talents together to make this book what it is.

Holiday Celebrations

Winter

Spring

Summer

Fall

Special Categories

Note Regarding
Weights and Measures

As per my usual style, I have offered both volume measure and ounces and grams for ingredients where weighing would be desirable or in any way helpful. When buying produce or canned goods, for example, it is helpful to know the weight as this is how it is sold. Although most people, including myself, will not weigh 3 grams of parsley, the weight is useful for caterers who may want to make large multiples of the recipe.

I have rounded off the ounces to the nearest third of an ounce and the grams usually to the nearest whole number; therefore, *do not expect the mathematics of the avoirdupois system to correlate exactly with the metric system*. If you have a scale that does not have a digital readout, simply round off the ounces and grams to the nearest readable number. Although the weights are as precise as I could make them, in most instances, when cooking, they can be interpreted with far more flexibility than when measuring or weighing ingredients for baking.

My preferred plastic wrap for rolling pie dough and for wrapping things when they need to be airtight is Saran Wrap because it is very smooth (lies flat and does not get caught up in the dough) and is absolutely airtight. Many other wraps intentionally have microscopic "breathing" holes, designed to protect food items such as fruits and vegetables, which would mold if stored airtight.

Note Regarding
Plastic Wrap

I find that people's taste for salt varies widely and that mine falls in the middle range. Because salt flavors food more evenly when it is added early in the cooking process rather than added all at once at the very end, I offer a suggested amount rather than specify "season to taste." After trying one of my recipes, you will gain a sense of how my middle-range taste compares with yours and adjust all the other recipes accordingly if you like.

Note Regarding
Salt

I prefer to use unsalted broth and butter because doing so enables me to use as much of the ingredient as I want without adding more salt. A cup of salted canned broth, for example, contains almost a teaspoon of salt.

I usually use kosher salt rather than table salt to sprinkle on roasts because it distributes more evenly. There is no difference in flavor because kosher and table salt both come from exactly the same source. The only difference in flavor occurs in instances where the salt does not dissolve fully, as for example, in salads. The kosher salt, which is coarser, will remain in granules and therefore be perceived differently on the tongue.

If you would like to use kosher salt for these recipes, use the same amount *if using Morton brand. If using Diamond brand,* you will need 1¾ times the volume amount. (The weight is the same.)

Fine sea salt has a purer, almost "sweeter" flavor and can be used interchangeably by weight (or to taste). The volume, however, will vary from brand to brand.

 General Pointers for Success

- Whenever possible, taste as you cook and adjust the seasonings as necessary toward the end of cooking.
- Start checking roasts as soon as they appear cooked, well before the anticipated time, to gauge their progress and avoid overcooking.
- Choose the freshest seasonal ingredients.
- Cook recipes with love.

Introduction

Cooking has always provided a perfect balance to my baking career because baking requires inexorable precision. But when I cook, I am free to add a pinch of this or that, stir and taste along the way and throw exactness to the winds. Paradoxically, because of the inherent absence of precision that makes cooking seem so much easier and more forgiving than baking, writing about cooking is the more challenging of the two. In baking, it is possible to specify the basic ingredients such as type of flour, sugar, butter or milk, and these ingredients are all standardized. But in cooking there is a large variation in flavor, texture, moisture and fat content of the ingredients, all of which affect cooking times, not to mention the flavor and texture of the food. When you bake a cake, you cannot taste it partway through the cooking and decide what to add; when you are cooking, you must constantly taste, prod, evaluate and adapt. When you bake, you are, of necessity, a trusting slave to someone else's recipe; when you cook, you are free to improvise and make the recipe your own.

I love to bake as well as cook. To do only one would be to neglect a whole side of my personality. My editor, Maria, once said to me, "Rose, you celebrate life by cooking." I have to admit that I'm one of these people who, whether tired, angry, sad or even with a full stomach, is happiest when cooking. My goal as a writer, teacher and fellow human being is to share this pleasure.

There is little that gives me the comfort, well-being and joy that the wonderful smell of food emanating from the kitchen provides. There is a goodness to cooking and a warmth to enjoying food with family and friends. Nothing makes my heart soar more than my little greatniece Becky, eyes wide with wonder before my Passover cake, exclaiming, "Oh, that's so beautiful, how did you make it?" and really wanting to know, or my little nephew Alexander pronouncing the corn fingers so good he wonders if he could make some with me to take home to his parents.

The best part about food is that it is about nurturing and sharing. Good food, and the rituals that accompany it, is the finest tradition we can pass on to the next generation.

When I was growing up, going to a restaurant once a week on Sundays was considered a special treat. It's ironic that a home-cooked meal now has become, for most, the ultimate luxury. It doesn't have to be fancy to be enjoyable. In fact, some of the simplest recipes are my favorites if they are prepared with love and care and shared with those I love. I am convinced that cooking with love results in a different flavor because it's the little touches and involvement in the process that make the difference. Fancy is fun for special occasions but worthwhile only when the taste lives up to the elaboration. And if you are going to spend a lot of time and money, it's important to make the most of it by choosing quality ingredients and having the confidence that they will be used at their peak.

My credo is to get the maximum mileage of flavor from everything. This is best accomplished by getting the freshest and most flavorful ingredients and while intensifying and enhancing them, doing as little as possible to change them. I love new taste sensations that are not contrived and often get inspired by fabulous flavor combinations I experience during my travels around this country and abroad. But, like everyone else, over the years I have developed certain favorites, certain tastes I crave again and again that I keep going back to, that friends and family request as well. These are the recipes I have included in this book. This is what you'd be eating at my house if you came for dinner.

There is good to see happy faces
round a table full of good food.
Indeed, for good sounds,
I will put the song of
knives and forks
next to the song
of man.

—Richard Llewelyn,
How Green Was My Valley

Winter

❖ ❖ ◆ ❖

New Year's Eve

Oysters and Beurre Blanc in Puff Pastry Shells
Puff Pastry
Lemon Snow with Golden Grand Marnier Sauce

Winter Anniversary

Artichoke Flowers Filled with Truffled Pâté
The Elkins's 25th Anniversary Silver Snowflake Cake

Another Winter Special Occasion

The Copper Topper Cascade Mountain Cake

Valentine's Dinner

Prime Ribs of Lamb
Haricots Verts
Bulgur and Duxelles
Double Chocolate Sweetheart Cake

❖ ❖ ❖ ❖

Washington's Birthday

All-Seasons Cherry Pie
Perfect Flaky Cream Cheese Pie Crust

Winter Dinner for Friends

Butter and Sage Roasted Squab
Wild Rice and Chanterelles
Artichoke Hearts with Squab Livers
Cold Lemon Cream Soufflé
Cordon Rose Raspberry Sauce
Quick Raspberry Sauce

Winter Treat

"Levy's" Real Jewish Rye Bread

St. Patrick's Day

Beef and Barley Soupless
Butter-Roasted Parsnips

Oysters and Beurre Blanc in Puff Pastry Shells

I first ate oysters in beurre blanc at L'Archestrate, a former 3-star Parisian restaurant, and decided it was one of the most exciting and inspired flavor combinations I had ever tasted. When I returned to New York I worked for days to create a recipe with a presentation worthy of its flavor to teach in my hors d'oeuvre class. I discovered that the secret to plump flavorful oysters is not to cook them but merely to heat them essentially in their own liquor. I also discovered that the most delicious, silky, buttery yet astonishingly lilting beurre blanc can be made by reducing this flavorful liquid and then whisking in the butter.

The perfect container for all this melting loveliness is crisp, tender, flaky puff pastry shells, fashioned on the oyster shells. Making them is easy and fun and they can be prepared up to three days ahead. The puff pastry shells have the further advantage of transforming the oysters into finger food. A more simple but also attractive presentation is to serve the oysters in their own shells.

Over the years, I collected oyster shells whenever I would find ones with beautiful shapes. At oyster bars, I would ask for a "doggie bag" for my shells and, once home, would scrub them well. In the summer, I set them out in the garden for a month so the sun would bleach them and tiny insects would crawl into the outer crevices and clean up any oceanic debris that couldn't be reached with my brush. (It reminded me of Psyche befriending the insects and animals to accomplish the impossible tasks imposed by Venus, Cupid's mother, to make her worthy of receiving her wings and immortality.)

I so adore this recipe I reproduced it for my Aunt Ruth one year when visiting her in Florida. Ruth has almost every kitchen gadget available but she did not have pie weights to keep the center of the puff pastry from rising. It was then that I came up with the idea of using coins instead. Although it was an odd sight to see money baking in the oven, the coins worked even better than the pie weights as they were heavier and fewer were needed. (Copper pennies, in fact, are less expensive than aluminum pie weights and better conductors of heat.)

There is enough beurre blanc here for twenty-four oysters, should you want to double the recipe, or the extra can be served on the side. This recipe can be prepared before the company arrives as it is intended to be served at room temperature. It makes a dazzling New Year's Eve midnight supper.

Makes:
12 pieces
(serves: 4 to 6 as a first course)

Preheat the oven to:
425°F.
Baking time: 20 to 25 minutes

INGREDIENTS	MEASURE	WEIGHT	
	volume	*ounces*	*grams*
12 oysters, shucked (reserve liquor and shells)	·	·	·
1 recipe Puff Pastry (page 5) (*must be made with butter*)	·	20 ounces	567 grams
Court Bouillon (poaching liquid)			
dry white wine	1 liquid cup	·	·
reserved oyster liquor (from the shucked oysters)	about ⅔ liquid cup	·	·
tarragon wine vinegar	2 tablespoons	·	·
shallots, minced	2 tablespoons	0.25 ounce	9 grams
fresh tarragon, minced*	1½ teaspoons	·	·
Beurre Blanc			
reduced Court Bouillon (above)	2 tablespoons	·	·
cold water	1 tablespoon	·	·
unsalted butter, cut into ½-inch pieces, softened	8 tablespoons (1 stick)	4 ounces	113 grams
OPTIONAL: beluga caviar	·	1 ounce (or more if desired)	28 grams
OPTIONAL: dried seaweed for garnish	·	·	·

*Or ¼ teaspoon dried tarragon.

Pastry Shells
Scrub the concave bottom halves of the oyster shells well, using scouring powder and a stiff brush on the outside of the shell. (Once scrubbed clean, the shells can be reused indefinitely and can be washed in the dishwasher.)

On a floured surface, roll the puff pastry into a rectangle measuring 14 inches by 20 inches and about ⅛ inch thick. Cut 16 rectangular pieces (cut lengthwise into quarters and then crosswise into quarters) measuring 3½ inches by 5 inches (this is the correct size for oyster shells measuring 2½ inches by 4 inches at their widest points). You will need only 12 pieces; the remaining 4 can be frozen (well wrapped) for future use. Roll each piece so that it is a little under ⅛ inch thick. Use a fork to prick the pastry well all over.

Spray the inside of the oyster shells with nonstick vegetable shortening and press the puff pastry rectangles into the shells, being careful not to puncture the pastry as you near the point of the shell. With a sharp knife or scissors, trim off excess pastry. Place the prepared shells on a baking sheet, using crumbled pieces of foil where needed to prop the shells so that they are level (they must not tilt to the side or the pastry will not rise evenly and the pennies will spill out). Cover with plastic wrap (preferably Saran brand) and chill for at least 1 hour or up to 24 hours.

To bake, preheat the oven to 425°F.

Cut 12 rectangles of foil just slightly larger than the size of the pastry rectangles. Remove the plastic wrap from the pastry-covered shells and prick the pastry again with a fork. Press the foil rectangles into the pastry shells and fill with pennies or other coins (metal pie weights are not heavy enough and will pop out as the pastry rises). Bake for 15 to 20 minutes or until the pastry is set. Remove the foil with the weights and carefully unmold the pastry from the oyster shells. If not enough weights were used and the shells have risen in the centers, push them down gently to form the center impressions. Return the pastry shells, upside down, to the baking sheet and continue baking for about 5 minutes or just until golden and the centers, when turned right side up, appear to be cooked through, with no wet-looking pastry. Cool on a rack. Store in an airtight container at room temperature for up to 3 days.

Poached Oysters

In a heavy medium-size saucepan, combine all the ingredients for the court bouillon and bring it to a boil. Simmer for 2 to 3 minutes, then lower the heat to just below simmering and add the oysters. Poach gently for 2 to 3 minutes or just until the oysters swell. It is important not to overcook them. With a slotted spoon, remove the oysters to a bowl. They can sit at room temperature for about an hour before serving, but cover them once they cool.

Broth Reduction

Raise the heat and bring the poaching liquid to a boil. Boil rapidly until reduced to 2 tablespoons, about 20 to 30 minutes. The liquid will be thickened and slightly sticky. Set aside until ready to make the beurre blanc.

Beurre Blanc

If the court bouillon reduction has cooled, reheat it over the lowest possible heat until almost simmering. Add the 1 tablespoon of cold water, whisking rapidly. Remove the pan entirely from the heat and whisk in the first piece of the butter. Return the pan to the heat for just a few seconds, whisking rapidly. Remove it again and continue whisking until the butter has completely emulsified and no whole pieces remain. Add the next piece of butter, whisking rapidly. Continue in this way until all the butter is incorporated.

Return to the heat for 15 seconds, whisking rapidly. The sauce should be the consistency of heavy cream. Remove it immediately to a small bowl, preferably glass or ceramic, which will hold the heat. The beurre blanc can be held, covered, at room temperature for up to 2 hours or in a thermos for up to 6 hours. It will thicken slightly as it cools. (You will have ⅔ cup sauce.)

Final Assembly

Arrange the pastry shells on oyster or serving plates, using dried seaweed* if desired to keep the shells level. If the oysters are large, cut them in half before arranging them in the shells. Spoon a full teaspoon of the sauce over each oyster. If desired, place a small dollop of caviar toward the rounded tip. Pass the extra sauce. (I went whole hog and added lots of caviar in this picture because of New Year's, but the oysters are just as good without the luxurious caviar overlay.)

POINTERS FOR SUCCESS

- It's fine to use commercial puff pastry but it must be a variety that is made with butter. Other types of puff pastry do not have as attractive an appearance and the absence of buttery flavor makes them dull compared to the real thing and, to my mind, not worth eating.
- A simple device called the Smart Pin makes it easy to roll pastry evenly (available from Maid of Scandinavia, 800-328-6722). It is a rolling pin that comes with wooden circles of varying thickness that can be placed on either end of the pin to elevate it to the exact height you desire. Also available are rubber rings, which will fit most standard rolling pins.
- Rockport oysters from the state of Washington have especially beautiful fluted shells. Specialty oyster bars, such as the Union Square Café in New York City, sometimes offer them.

UNDERSTANDING

Too much heat will break down a beurre blanc. If this should happen, or if you have leftover sauce, use the beurre blanc to make a delicious béarnaise: Place 3 egg yolks in a small heavy pan over low heat and whisk rapidly until they begin to thicken. Very gradually dribble in the beurre blanc (which will resemble melted butter), whisking constantly. Remove from the heat.

*Ask your fish monger for seaweed. To remove any moisture that would soften the pastry, allow the seaweed to dry on paper towels for several hours.

Puff Pastry

*J*ust watching puff pastry come together and handling the satiny smooth dough is one of the most satisfying cooking experiences I know. Watching it rise is sheer magic. And the flavor and texture make all the labor worthwhile. Although the actual working time is short, you will need to be present for a four-hour period to complete the turns.

The finished pastry must be allowed to rest refrigerated for at least two hours. It is best if used by the next day, or it may be frozen for months.

I am very grateful to Bernard Clayton's The Complete Book of Pastry (Simon & Schuster) for the most important breakthrough in making even puff pastry at home: establishing the ideal temperature for the butter. Over the years, I have spent countless hours devoted to perfecting puff pastry. I have found that seven turns is the ideal for flaky and tender pastry. Six turns, however, is fine for molding oyster shells.

Makes: 1¼ pounds

INGREDIENTS *cold*	MEASURE *volume*	WEIGHT *ounces*	*grams*
unsalted butter, cut into ½-inch cubes, chilled, divided	1 cup (2 sticks)	8 ounces	227 grams
unbleached all-purpose flour, divided	1⅔ cups (dip and sweep method)	8 ounces	227 grams
salt	½ teaspoon	·	·
cold water	6 to 8 tablespoons	·	·
lemon juice, freshly squeezed	1 teaspoon	·	·

The Détrempe (Dough)

In a medium bowl, combine 2 tablespoons (1 ounce) of the chilled butter, a scant 1½ cups (7 ounces) of the flour and the salt. Rub this mixture between your fingers until it is very fine and grainy and no lumps of butter are discernible, about 5 minutes. Add 6 tablespoons of the cold water and the lemon juice and stir gently with a fork to incorporate it. The dough should be soft and clumpy. If necessary, add some or all of the remaining water by the tablespoon, adding only as much as necessary to form a soft dough.

Dump the dough out onto a floured surface and gently knead only until the dough holds together and looks fairly smooth. It should not become too elastic or it will be difficult to roll. Cover the dough and allow it to rest for 20 minutes at room temperature or up to 24 hours well wrapped in plastic wrap (preferably Saran brand) and refrigerated.

Butter Square   Place the remaining 14 tablespoons (7 ounces) of chilled butter on a sheet of plastic wrap and sprinkle with the remaining 3 tablespoons (1 ounce) of flour. Cover with a second sheet of plastic wrap and pound the butter lightly with a rolling pin to flatten and soften it. Remove the top sheet of plastic wrap and, using the bottom sheet of plastic wrap and your knuckles to avoid touching the butter directly, knead the butter and flour together. Work quickly and as soon as the flour is incorporated, shape it into a 4½-inch square no thicker than ¾ inch. At this point the butter should be cool but workable (about 60°F.). Use it at once or keep it cool. The butter must not be colder than 60°F. when rolled into the pastry or it will break through the dough and not distribute evenly.

The Dough Package

See pages 8-9.

Roll out the dough on a well-floured surface to a 6-inch square. Place the butter square diagonally in the center of the dough square (Fig. 1) and lightly mark the dough along the edges of the butter with the dull side of a knife (Fig. 2). Remove the butter and roll each marked-off corner of the dough into a 3-inch triangular flap (Fig. 3). The dough will be slightly elastic. Moisten the flaps lightly with water. Replace the butter on the dough (Fig. 4) and wrap it securely, stretching the flaps slightly to reach across the dough package (Fig 5). On a well-floured surface, keeping the dough seam side up and lightly floured, gently roll the dough package into a 6-inch by 12-inch rectangle (Fig. 6). Brush off all flour from the surface of the dough and fold it into thirds as you would fold a business letter (Fig. 7). This is the first "turn." Before each subsequent turn, move the dough so that the closed end is facing to your left (Fig. 8). Clean the surface, reflour it and roll and fold the dough a second time exactly the same way, but this time turn the dough over occasionally to keep the seams and edges even. Be sure to roll into all four corners of dough, and use a pastry scraper to even the edges.

Mark the dough with two fingertips (or knuckles if you have long nails) to indicate that two turns have been completed (Fig. 8). Wrap with plastic wrap and then foil, and refrigerate for 30 to 40 minutes. The dough must not chill for longer than 40 minutes or the butter will never distribute evenly.

Continue to roll and turn the dough, marking the turns with your fingertips and letting the dough rest for 30 minutes between turns. It is best to do only one turn at a time after the first two as the dough will become more elastic, and the best results are obtained when the dough is not forced and the layers not pressed together. (Do a total of six turns if molding on oyster shells; do seven if for another use.)

POINTERS FOR SUCCESS

• Plugra butter, which contains 82 percent butterfat, is produced by Hotel Bar Butter and is available in many specialty markets throughout the country. It produces an exceptionally light, flaky and tender puff pastry with a delicate, greaseless flavor. With Plugra, only six turns are necessary to achieve maximum height and tenderness.

Single turns as opposed to the "newer" double turns make it easier to control the shaping and layering of the pastry so that it will rise more evenly when baked.

Turns, or folds, create the layering of butter and dough. Six turns produce 729 layers; 7 turns, 2,187 layers. The more turns, the thinner the layers and the more tender and light the pastry. Once the pastry has been stretched to its maximum thinness, however, additional turns would destroy the layering and the pastry would not rise as well.

Unbleached flour contains more gluten-forming proteins, resulting in a stronger dough that can stand up well to this stretching process. Bread flour, with a higher protein content, makes a higher rise but a less tender pastry. The lemon juice relaxes the gluten, making the dough less stretchy and easier to roll.

UNDERSTANDING

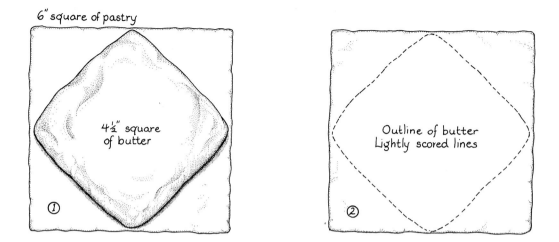

6" square of pastry

4½" square
of butter

①

Outline of butter
Lightly scored lines

②

3"

3"

3"

3"

③

④ 4½" square of butter

⑤

⑥ 4" 12"

⑦ Top

⑧ Top

Closed end

Mark number of turns with gentle indents

Lemon Snow with Golden Grand Marnier Sauce

This dessert is elegant, light and refreshing yet totally satisfying—the perfect ending to a heavy meal but equally delightful as the finale to a light midnight supper. In fact, it is probably the most perfect all-around dessert in my repertoire. It was this dessert I chose many years ago when I invited Lydie Marshall, owner of A La Bonne Cocotte cooking school in New York, and her husband, Wayne, for dinner. I was so nervous I curdled the sauce slightly but even then it was delicious.

When fresh raspberries are in season they make a lovely garnish. The snow pudding alone, however, without the sauce, makes a wonderful low-calorie, no-cholesterol dessert.

Serves: 8

Setting time: at least 3 hours

KEEPS:
5 days refrigerated.

INGREDIENTS *room temperature*	MEASURE *volume*	WEIGHT *ounces*	*grams*
Lemon Snow			
powdered gelatin	2¼ teaspoons (1 envelope)	0.25 ounce	7 grams
sugar	¾ cup	5.25 ounces	150 grams
lemon zest, finely grated	2 teaspoons	•	4 grams
lemon juice, freshly squeezed (2 lemons)	¼ liquid cup	•	•
boiling water	1¼ liquid cups	•	•
1 large egg white	2 tablespoons	1 ounce	30 grams
Golden Grand Marnier Sauce			
sugar	¼ cup	1.75 ounces	50 grams
salt	a dash	•	•
3 large egg yolks	3½ tablespoons	2 ounces	56 grams
heavy cream, cold, divided	1 liquid cup	•	•
milk	¼ liquid cup	•	•
Grand Marnier	¼ liquid cup	•	•
pure vanilla extract	½ teaspoon	•	•
OPTIONAL: fresh raspberries, candied violets or pomegranate seeds, for garnish	•	•	•

Lemon Snow

In a medium bowl, stir together the gelatin and sugar. Add the lemon juice and boiling water and stir until the sugar and gelatin are dissolved. Chill, stirring often, until the mixture mounds when dropped from a spoon. (The mixture may be either refrigerated or placed over a bowl of ice water with a little salt added to speed chilling.)

Add the egg white and, with an electric mixer set on high speed, beat until the mixture has doubled in volume and mounds when dropped from a spoon, 5 to 10 minutes. Fold in the lemon zest. Spoon the mixture into large wine goblets or dessert dishes. Chill for at least 3 hours to set.

Golden Grand Marnier Sauce

In a small heavy saucepan, stir together the sugar and salt. Add the yolks and stir to blend. Scald* ½ cup of the cream with the milk and, whisking constantly and vigorously, gradually add it to the yolk mixture. Cook over low heat, stirring constantly, until just below the boiling point (170°F. to 180°F.), 7 to 8 minutes. Steam will begin to appear. At once, remove from the heat and stir in the Grand Marnier and vanilla. Strain, and chill until cold. Shortly before serving, whip the remaining ½ cup of cream and fold it in. Spoon on top of the Lemon Snow (3 tablespoons per serving). Garnish with raspberries, candied violets or pomegranate seeds if desired.

POINTERS FOR SUCCESS

- The temperature and consistency of the gelatin mixture are crucial to achieving a fine foam that will not separate on chilling. To prevent separation, the mixture must not be beaten *until* it is thick enough and mounds when dropped from a spoon. If too thick, however, it will not form a fine foam. If the gelatin mixture begins to set before beating, briefly place the bowl over a bowl of hot water and stir constantly until the mixture begins to soften. Immediately set the bottom of the bowl directly into cold water to stop the heating immediately.

UNDERSTANDING

The sauce mixture must be heated adequately (to at least 160°F.) to thicken and prevent thinning out on setting, but for a silky smooth sauce that does not curdle, the mixture must not be allowed to boil. The boiling point of water is 212°F., but the other ingredients in the custard mixture lower the boiling point.

*Bring just to the boiling point (small bubbles will begin to appear around the edges).

Artichoke Flowers Filled with Truffled Pâté

These two-bite finger-food treats make great party fare for an anniversary or other very special occasion. The artichoke heart, filled with homemade pâté, is resting on five unattached artichoke leaves that create the illusion of a flower and make it easy to pick up. Artichoke Flowers was one of the favorite appetizers I taught when I ran the Cordon Rose Cooking School, perhaps because it was both decorative and delicious. Each bite provides a rush of flavor: the surprise of a creamy pâté center with underbite of vegetable and the deeply earthy flavor and artfully irregular shape of the truffle.

Makes: 12 hors d'oeuvres

TO SERVE:
Remove from the refrigerator at least 30 minutes before serving.

KEEPS:
Refrigerated, tightly covered, 3 days.

INGREDIENTS	MEASURE *volume*	WEIGHT	
		ounces	*grams*
12 baby artichokes	about 1¾ inches at the base	2 ounces each	56 grams each
salt	¼ teaspoon	•	•
Pâté			
OPTIONAL: fresh or jarred black truffle* *or* 6 small, ripe pitted olives for garnish	about 1-inch	1 ounce	28 grams
OPTIONAL: vegetable oil	about 1 tablespoon	•	•
goose fat or unsalted butter	1½ tablespoons	0.75 ounce	21 grams
1 shallot, finely minced	1 tablespoon	0.33 ounce	9 grams
2 large cloves garlic	1 tablespoon	0.25 ounce	7 grams
duck or chicken livers†	•	4 ounces	113 grams
cooked ham, diced	½ cup	2 ounces	57 grams
salt	⅛ teaspoon	•	•
black pepper, freshly ground	a few grindings	•	•
Cognac	1 tablespoon	•	•
heavy cream	1 tablespoon	•	•

*Jarred black truffles, while not as wonderful as fresh, can be quite delicious. If purchasing jarred black truffles, however, bring along a magnifying glass (I'm not kidding). If the words *tuber aestivum* (or *tartufo estivo*) are on the label, do not buy them; they are *summer* truffles and their interiors will be the color of the pâté. They are also much milder and less interesting in flavor.

†When I make duck, I freeze the duck liver to have for this preparation. Wrap airtight in plastic wrap (preferably Saran brand) and place in heavy-duty freezer bags with the air pressed out. I find they freeze well for several months.

In a large saucepan, place the artichokes and add enough boiling water to cover them by about 2 inches. Sprinkle them with the ¼ teaspoon of salt and cover them with a clean wet towel to keep them submerged. Boil rapidly, uncovered, for 12 to 15 minutes or until tender when pierced with a skewer. Drain immediately and plunge into ice water.

When cool enough to handle, remove the tough outer leaves. Cut off the stems to form flat bases. Carefully peel away one row of large leaves to form "petals." Peel away 1 or 2 rows of the dark green leaves until you reach the tender pale-green leaves that are not fibrous. Cut off the top of each artichoke, leaving about 1-inch-high leaves. With the tip of small spoon, or your finger, scoop out the inner leaves (I like to eat these as a snack). Scrape out any fuzz from the center of the artichoke.

Make [...] ical slashes into the inside of the leaves to enable them [...] open the leaves slightly to make a larger center. The [...] break open slightly but will come back together when [...] being filled with pâté.

Pâté

[...] rinse under cold running water, brushing lightly to [...] using a jarred truffle, drain it and reserve the juice. [...] to 12 large thin slices. Keep the slices covered with [...] the remaining truffle and cover with plastic wrap. (If [...]es, drain them and cut them in halves. Use a small knife [...]n attractive shape. Wrap them in plastic wrap.)

[...]et, over low heat, melt the goose fat or butter and sauté [...]ic until soft and translucent. Turn up the heat and cook [...] livers quickly, just until browned on all sides, about [...]ld still be rare inside. Add the Cognac and any reserved [...]ng the skillet to loosen browned-on particles. Add the [...], salt and pepper and cook for 1 minute. Use a food [...] chop the mixture finely and stir in the cream. Turn [...] pastry bag or heavy-duty freezer bag with the tip cut [...] and place about 2 teaspoons of pâté into the center of

[...]of the reserved large leaves, curved side up, on a serving [...]nted ends are out and the rounded ends touch at the [...]s. Place the pâté-filled artichoke bases on top of the [...]ormation.

[...]e with a truffle slice or black olive, shiny skin side up. [...]ll clean artist's brush to brush a little oil on the insides [...]served for décor and also on the truffle or black olive to keep them from drying. If not serving for several hours, cover with plastic wrap and refrigerate.

NOTE:
Baby chokes are available during the winter. Fresh black truffles are available from November through January.

POINTERS FOR SUCCESS

• Do not trim the outside of the truffle to make it smooth. The irregularity of shape is part of its charm.

FOOD **Editor:** Joe Yonan • **Deputy Director:** Marty Barrick • **S**[...] **Assistant:** Leigh Lambert • **To contact us** 202-334-7575 Mail: Food Section, The Wa[...] Washington, D.C. 20071

The Elkins's 25th Anniversary Silver Snowflake Cake

When my friends Judi and Paul Elkins celebrated their 25th wedding anniversary, I was unfortunately out of town, but I made this cake before my departure. Since their anniversary was in winter, and silver is traditional for a 25th anniversary, the snowflake motif seemed perfect. If the event you are celebrating falls on another time of year, simply changing the cutout to a different shape (stars or hearts, for example) will give a whole different look to the cake.

It is especially thrilling to cut into such a pristine-looking cake and discover the shock of dark dense chocolate hidden inside, so I chose Chocolate Oblivion Truffle Torte from The Cake Bible for the cake. The creamy bittersweetness of this flourless chocolate cake blends exceptionally well with the sweet chewiness of the rolled fondant. In fact, the whole experience is more like eating candy truffles than cake!

Preheat the oven to 425°F.

In a large metal bowl set over a pan of hot, not simmering, water (the bottom of the bowl should not touch the water) combine the chocolate and butter and let stand, stirring occasionally, until smooth and melted. (The mixture can be melted in the microwave on high power, stirring every 15 seconds. Remove when there are still a few lumps of chocolate and stir until fully melted.)

In a large bowl set over a pan of simmering water heat the eggs, stirring constantly to prevent curdling, until just warm to the touch. Remove from the heat and beat, using the whisk beater, until triple in volume and soft peaks form when the beater is raised, about 5 minutes. (To ensure maximum volume if using a hand mixer, beat the eggs over simmering water until they are hot to the touch, about 5 minutes. Remove from the heat and beat until cool.)

Using a large wire whisk or rubber spatula, fold ½ of the eggs into the chocolate mixture until almost incorporated. Fold in the remaining eggs until just blended and no streaks remain. Finish by using a rubber spatula to ensure that the heavier mixture at the bottom is incorporated. Scrape into the prepared pan and smooth with the spatula. Set the pan in the larger pan and surround it with 1 inch of very hot water. Bake for 5 minutes. Cover loosely with a piece of buttered foil and bake for 13 minutes. (The cake will look soft, but this is as it should be.)

Let the cake cool on a rack for 45 minutes. Cover with plastic wrap (preferably Saran brand) and refrigerate until very firm, about 4 hours.

*Available in art supply stores.

Serves: 12 chocolate lovers, 24 dinner portions

Make the cake, fondant and roses at least 1 day up to 2 weeks ahead

Preheat oven to: 425°F. Baking time: 18 minutes

EQUIPMENT:
8-inch springform pan at least 2½ inches high, buttered and bottom lined with buttered parchment or wax paper; outside of pan wrapped with a double layer of heavy-duty foil to prevent seepage; 10-inch cake or roasting pan to serve as a water bath; 8-inch cardboard cake round; a small piece of cardboard and an X-Acto knife to make the snowflake template; a small clean artist's brush; *optional:* a star burst stenciling tool* or toothpick tweezers

Chocolate Oblivion Truffle Torte

| INGREDIENTS | MEASURE | WEIGHT | |
room temperature	*volume*	*ounces/pounds*	*grams*
Chocolate Oblivion Truffle Torte			
bittersweet chocolate, preferably Lindt Excellence or Valrhona extra bittersweet*	8 3-ounce bars	1½ pounds	681 grams
unsalted butter	1½ cups	¾ pound	340 grams
9 large eggs	1¾ liquid cups	15.75 ounces (weighed without shells)	450 grams
Rolled Fondant	*(2½ pounds)*		
water	3 tablespoons	•	•
gelatin	1 tablespoon	•	10 grams
corn syrup	½ cup	5.75 ounces	64 grams
glycerine†	1 tablespoon	•	18 grams
solid white shortening	2 tablespoons	0.75 ounce	24 grams
powdered sugar	8 cups (lightly spooned into cup)	2 pounds	920 grams
Decoration			
3 marzipan roses and 2 rosebuds (page 19)	•	•	•
silver petal dust†	1 small vial	•	•
vodka or other high-proof clear drinking alcohol	a few drops	•	•
8 white chocolate rose leaves (page 21)	•	•	•
tiny silver dragées	½ teaspoon	•	•
Royal Icing (page 22)	(¾ cup)	•	•

*Available from Williams-Sonoma (415-421-4242).

†Available in cake-decorating supply houses such as Maid of Scandinavia (800-328-6722) and the Chocolate Gallery (212-675-2253).

To unmold: Wipe the outside of the pan with a hot, damp towel. Run a thin metal spatula around the sides of the cake and release the sides of the springform pan. Unmold the cake onto the cardboard round and refrigerate for at least 12 hours. Use a hot, wet spatula to smooth the surface of the cake so that it is perfectly smooth. Smooth the edges to bevel them slightly. Return the cake to the refrigerator.

In a 2-cup glass measuring cup, place the water. Sprinkle the gelatin over the top of the water and let the gelatin soften for at least 3 minutes. Place the measuring cup in a small saucepan of simmering water and stir the mixture for 2 to 3 minutes, until the gelatin is completely dissolved. (This can also be done in a few seconds in a microwave on high power.) Stir in the corn syrup and glycerine, then add the shortening and stir until almost completely melted. Remove from the heat.

Place the powdered sugar in a large bowl and make a well in the center. Add the gelatin mixture and stir with a lightly greased wooden spoon until blended. Mix with lightly greased hands and then knead vigorously in the bowl until most of the sugar is incorporated.

Turn the mixture out onto a lightly greased smooth surface such as Formica or marble and knead until smooth and satiny. If the fondant seems dry, add several drops of water and knead well. If it seems too sticky, knead in more powdered sugar. The fondant will resemble a smooth, well-shaped stone. When dropped, it should spread very slightly but retain its shape. It should be malleable like clay, soft but not sticky.

Wrap the fondant tightly with plastic wrap and place in an airtight container. It will firm slightly on standing.

Rolled Fondant

Marizipan for Modeling

Decorations

INGREDIENTS	MEASURE *volume*	WEIGHT	
		ounces	*grams*
almond paste	½ cup	5 ounces	142 grams
cornstarch	½ cup (lightly spooned into cup)	2 ounces	60 grams
powdered sugar	½ cup (lightly spooned into cup)	2 ounces	60 grams
corn syrup	3 tablespoons	2 ounces	62 grams

This marzipan is very easy to make in a food processor. It can also be made in a heavy-duty mixer such as a KitchenAid or kneaded by hand.

Mix together the almond paste, cornstarch and powdered sugar until it falls in fine crumbs. Add the corn syrup and process until well incorporated. (The mixture should not look greasy. If you do overmix, the marzipan will be usable if allowed to rest until the oil is reabsorbed.) Pinch a small amount to see if it holds together. If still too dry, add a few drops of corn syrup.

Dump onto a smooth counter or work surface and knead until very smooth and uniform in color. Wrap tightly with plastic wrap and place in an airtight container. Allow to rest for at least 1 hour before using.

Keep the marzipan well covered to avoid drying out while working with it. If the marzipan does become slightly dry and cracky, rub your fingers lightly with shortening and knead lightly. Cover tightly with plastic wrap and place in an airtight container.

Marzipan Roses

Makes: ¾ pound / 340 grams (1¼ cups)

STORE:
6 months refrigerated, indefinitely frozen. Allow to come to room temperature before kneading to prevent oil separation.

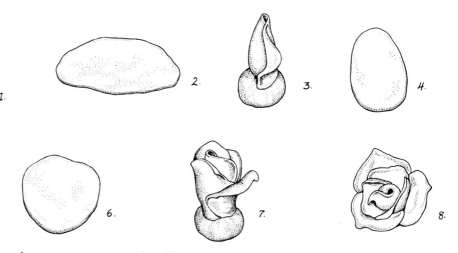

To shape roses: Begin by forming the center cone and base. Use the natural contours of your hand to form a pointed cone and pedestal base which will be removed after the rose is completed (Fig. 1).

Have ready a little bowl of water or lightly beaten egg white and a small artist's paint brush.

Roll out thin sheets of marzipan between 2 pieces of plastic wrap—but not too thinly because each piece will be rolled and shaped a second time. Keep the marzipan covered at all times to prevent drying.

Cut out a free-form rounded rectangle 2 inches long. Lift it from the plastic sheet and roll it a second time between plastic wrap to thin it (Fig. 2). Wrap it around the cone, overlapping to form a point and then folding it back. This is the closed bud of the flower (Fig. 3).

Cut three 1-inch rounds for petals. Remove each, 1 at a time, to a second set of plastic sheets and roll the upper section to thin the tip and form an oval shape (Fig. 4). Place around the bud, overlapping slightly and curving one side realistically back (Fig. 5). Paint tiny dabs of water or egg white toward the base to attach the petals. A small metal cuticle pusher is ideal for molding the petals and pushing them slightly away from the center bud.

For the second row of 3 petals, the rounds must be rolled slightly more elliptically because they have a wider circumference to cover. Cut three 1¼-inch rounds, again making the edges thinner than the base (Fig. 6). When the petals are in place, use a fingertip to form a center point and curve the sides slightly back (Fig. 7).

The completed rose (Fig. 8) will hold its shape well if placed in a bed of cornstarch to support the petals. When the marzipan sets and is firm enough to hold its shape, cut off the base with a small sharp knife. When the rose is thoroughly dry, use a small paint brush or dust atomizer to dust off the cornstarch.*

TIP: After rolling out and cutting the petals, use a fingertip to thin the edges of the petals. If the marzipan seems slightly soft and the petals droop, allow them to dry for a few minutes before applying them.

When the roses are completely dry, paint them with the silver petal dust.

*Marzipan roses can be purchased through Albert Uster Imports (800-231-8154).

Sprinkle a little petal dust into a small cup and add a few droplets of the vodka to dilute the "dust" and produce a thick "paint." Use a small clean artist's brush to apply the silver. Set any leftover aside for the rose leaves.

White summer coating (also known as compound chocolate)* is ideal for making the leaves as it does not require tempering. Simply melt it over hot, not simmering, water, stirring often.

   Select well-shaped rose leaves with no holes. Wash the leaves and dry them thoroughly. Each leaf can be used several times until it tears.

   Holding a leaf by its stem and supporting it underneath with a finger or the palm of your hand, use a small metal spatula or artist's brush to smooth an even layer of chocolate on the underside of the leaf (Fig. 1). Be sure to use the veiny underside as all the delicate lines will be imprinted on the chocolate. (Don't allow the chocolate to get on the other side of the leaf or the chocolate leaf may break when peeling off the leaf.)

   Carefully place the chocolate leaf on a baking sheet lined with foil, parchment or wax paper and refrigerate or freeze for 3 minutes, until set and no longer shiny. Add a second coat of chocolate for stability.

   To remove the chocolate from the leaf, peel back the stem end, touching the chocolate as little as possible (Fig. 2). If the chocolate adheres to the leaf, it has not set long enough.

   Add a few more droplets of the vodka to the silver petal dust and brush the silver gently onto the leaves.

Unwrap the fondant. You will need 1½ pounds (or about two thirds) of it. Some of the remainder can be used for the cutouts and the rest can be frozen for several months.

   Spray a smooth, clean work surface with nonstick vegetable spray. Also coat a large heavy rolling pin with the spray. Form the piece of fondant into a flat disc and roll it into a 13-inch by ¼-inch circle. Lift up and rotate the circle every 2 or 3 rolls to ensure that it is not sticking. If necessary, respray the work surface. Work quickly to keep the fondant from drying. If it is taking more than 3 or 4 minutes to roll out, cover the fondant with a few pieces of plastic wrap to keep it from drying.

   Remove the cake from the refrigerator. Slip your fists palm side down under the fondant being careful not to stretch or tear it. Lift the fondant onto the cake, covering it as evenly as possible. Using the palm of your hand, quickly smooth the top with a circular motion, starting from the center, to eliminate air bubbles. (Bubbles can be pierced with a needle and smoothed out if necessary.) Smooth the fondant gently against the sides, working from the top down with a semicircular motion, using both hands. The oil from your hands will give it a lustrous glow. With a pizza cutter or sharp knife, trim the bottom edge of the cake to remove the excess fondant.

Trace the snowflake template and transfer it to the cardboard. Use the X-Acto knife to cut it out.

*Available in cake-decorating supply houses such as Maid of Scandinavia (800-328-6722) and The Chocolate Gallery (212-675-2253).

Rose Leaves

Cover the Cake with Rolled Fondant

Snowflakes

Roll a small piece of the fondant on top of plastic wrap, ⅛ inch thick. Allow it to dry for at least 1 hour. Dust the surface lightly with powdered sugar to keep the template from sticking and lay the snowflake template on top. Using the tip of a sharp knife or the X-Acto knife, cut out the snowflake, following the template's design. Lift off the template and repeat as needed.

Royal Icing

INGREDIENTS room temperature	MEASURE volume	WEIGHT ounces	grams
Royal Icing			
meringue powder*	2 tablespoons	0.5 ounce	16 grams
water	¼ liquid cup	.	.
powdered sugar	2⅔ cups (lightly spooned into cup)	10.5 ounces	300 grams

In a large grease-free mixer bowl, preferably with the whisk beater of a heavy-duty mixer, beat the meringue powder and water on low speed until mixed. Add the powdered sugar and beat for 30 seconds or until the sugar is moistened. Increase the speed to medium high and continue beating for 5 to 8 minutes, until the icing forms stiff, glossy peaks when the beater is lifted. (The tips of the peaks should curve slightly.) Cover the bowl with a damp cloth to keep the icing from drying.

Decorating the Cake

FINISHED HEIGHT: 2½ inches

TO SERVE: Use a thin, sharp knife, dipped in hot water between each slice.

STORE: Room temperature.

POINTERS FOR SUCCESS

Chocolate Oblivion

Royal Icing

Use the plastic wrap to lift the snowflake and gently invert it and peel off the plastic wrap. Lightly brush the back of each snowflake with water and gently place it on the cake. Be sure to leave room for the roses.

It is best to apply the dragées to the fondant within a few hours of covering the cake, as the dragées will adhere. Alternatively, you can use a speck of royal icing to glue them in place but this is unnecessarily tedious. Use the stenciling tool or the pointed toothpick to mark the fondant for the silver dragées to form five-pointed star bursts. Lift each dragée using the tweezers; place it on the fondant and press it in.

Attach the roses and leaves to the fondant using the royal icing to hold them in position.

• For a moist airy texture, be sure to add the beaten eggs to the chocolate mixture and not the chocolate to the eggs.
• Wrapping the pan with foil keeps it watertight.
• The cake must be chilled thoroughly before unmolding.

• Only a very powerful electric hand-held mixer such as the Krupps or KitchenAid is strong enough to make royal icing without damaging the motor.

*2 large egg whites (¾ cup, 2 ounces/60 grams) can be used in place of the meringue powder and water.

The Copper Topper Cascade Mountain Cake

C-a-r-a-m-e-l. *The very sound of the word, not to mention the tantalizing aroma of burnt sugar, makes me long for it, so I created this cake with a soft, very moist crumb, filled and frosted with creamy caramel buttercream and topped with a crunch of caramel nut brittle.*

The cake was actually inspired by a cookie I heard about but have never tasted, from the Cascade Mountains in the state of Washington. Supposedly it was called "copper topper" because of its copper-colored caramel topping.

To honor the spirit of the mountains, I chose towering biscuit de Savoie cake layers (a butterless génoise) from the French Savoie because the cake can be made at high altitude since it has no chemical leavening. The brittle, broken into jagged pieces and inserted into the buttercream on top of the cake, is meant to resemble the mountain peaks. Store-bought peanut brittle, broken into pieces, can be used in its place.

This cake is for the caramel lover. It's even more delicious than it looks.

Serves: 16

Preheat the oven to: 325°F.
Baking time: 25 minutes

EQUIPMENT:
three 9-inch by 1½-inch round cake pans, bottoms greased and lined with parchment or wax paper (do *not* grease or flour the sides)

FINISHED HEIGHT:
3¾ to 4 inches

INGREDIENTS room temperature	MEASURE volume	WEIGHT ounces/pounds	grams
Biscuit de Savoie			
8 large eggs, separated			
yolks	4.5 fluid ounces	5.25 ounces	150 grams
whites	1 liquid cup	8.5 ounces	240 grams
superfine sugar, divided	1 cup	7 ounces	200 grams
pure vanilla extract	2½ teaspoons	·	·
warm water	1 tablespoon	·	·
sifted cake flour	1 cup + 2 tablespoons (sifted into the cup and leveled off)	4 ounces	113 grams
cornstarch	½ cup + 1 tablespoon (lightly spooned into the cup)	2.25 ounces	66 grams
cream of tartar	1 teaspoon	·	3 grams
Syrup			
sugar	¾ cup + 2 tablespoons	6 ounces	175 grams
water	1½ liquid cups	·	·
almond-flavored liqueur	3 fluid ounces (6 tablespoons)	·	·

INGREDIENTS *room temperature*	MEASURE *volume*	WEIGHT	
		ounces/pounds	*grams*
Caramel Silk Buttercream CRÈME ANGLAISE			
milk	1 liquid cup	•	•
1 large vanilla bean, split lengthwise, or ½ large Tahitian vanilla bean, split*	•	•	•
sugar	½ cup	3.5 ounces	100 grams
water	2 tablespoons	•	•
5 large egg yolks	3 fluid ounces	3.25 ounces	93 grams
ITALIAN MERINGUE			
sugar	⅓ cup + 2 tablespoons	3.25 ounces	92 grams
water	2 tablespoons	•	•
2 large egg whites	¼ liquid cup	2 ounces	60 grams
cream of tartar	¼ teaspoon	•	•
unsalted butter	2 cups	1 pound	454 grams
Copper Candy Topping			
sliced unblanched almonds (peels on)	½ cup	5.25 ounces	85 grams
sugar	1 cup	7 ounces	200 grams
water	¼ liquid cup	•	•

*A vanilla bean offers the most delicious flavor, but if not available, replace the bean with 1 teaspoon vanilla extract, added to the cooled *crème anglaise*.

Preheat the oven to 325°F.

In a large mixing bowl, preferably with the whisk beater of a heavy-duty mixer, beat the yolks and ⅔ cup of the sugar on high speed for 5 minutes or until the mixture is very thick and ribbons when dropped from the beater. Lower the speed and beat in the vanilla and water. Increase to high speed and beat for 30 seconds or until the mixture thickens again.

Stir together the flour and cornstarch. Sift over the yolk mixture without mixing in and set aside.

In another large mixing bowl, preferably with the whisk beater, beat the whites until foamy. Add the cream of tartar and beat until soft peaks form when the beater is raised. Gradually beat in the remaining ⅓ cup of sugar

Biscuit de Savoie

KEEPS:
The *biscuit* (without syrup) can be stored 2 days at room temperature, 5 days refrigerated and 2 months frozen.

and beat until stiff peaks form when the beater is raised slowly. Add one third of the whites to the yolk mixture and with a large balloon whisk, skimmer or rubber spatula fold until incorporated. Gently fold in the remaining whites.

Pour into the prepared pans. (They will be almost half full.) Bake for 25 minutes or until a cake tester inserted in the center comes out clean. Loosen the sides with a small metal spatula and unmold at once onto lightly greased racks; then reinvert to cool. The firm upper crust prevents falling and results in a light texture.

When ready to complete the cake, remove the crust with a long serrated knife by scraping it lightly across the top and bottom of each layer.

Syrup

In a small saucepan with a tight-fitting lid, bring the sugar and water to a rolling boil, stirring constantly. Cover immediately, remove from the heat and cool. Transfer to a liquid measuring cup and stir in the liqueur. If some of the syrup has evaporated, add enough water to equal 2 cups.

Sprinkle the syrup evenly over the tops and bottoms of the cake layers.* Cover them with plastic wrap while you make the buttercream.

Caramel Silk Buttercream

To Make the Crème Anglaise

Have ready a sieve suspended over a bowl near the range.

In a small saucepan, scald† the milk and vanilla bean. Remove from the heat and keep warm.

In a medium-size heavy pan, combine the ½ cup of sugar and the 2 tablespoons of water and stir until the sugar is fully moistened. Bring to a boil, stirring constantly. Cook without stirring until deep amber (360°F.). Immediately remove from the heat and slowly pour in the hot milk (reserving the vanilla bean). Return to low heat and cook, stirring, until the caramel is totally dissolved.

In a medium-size heavy noncorrodible saucepan, place the yolks, and gradually add the caramel mixture to them, stirring constantly with a wooden spoon. Cook over medium-low heat, stirring constantly, until just below the boiling point. The mixture will start to steam slightly and an accurate thermometer‡ will register 170°F to 180°F. Immediately strain through the sieve, scraping up any of the mixture clinging to the bottom of the pan.

Scrape the seeds from the vanilla bean into the custard, and cool to room temperature. (To speed cooling, put the bowl in another bowl or a sink partially filled with ice water.) Cover and refrigerate until ready to complete the buttercream, or up to 5 days.

To Make the Italian Meringue

Have ready a heatproof glass measure near the range.

In a small heavy saucepan (preferably with a nonstick lining), combine the ⅓ cup of sugar and the 2 tablespoons of water and stir until the sugar is fully moistened. Heat over medium heat, stirring constantly, until the

*After syruping, a *biscuit* layer becomes fragile and more prone to splitting when moved. Use a cardboard round or removable bottom of a pan to support it.
†Bring just to the boiling point (small bubbles will begin to appear around the edges).
‡The Cordon Rose candy thermometer is available through Dean & DeLuca (800-227-7714).

sugar dissolves and the mixture is bubbling. Stop stirring and reduce the heat to low. (If using an electric range, remove from the heat.)

In a mixing bowl, preferably with the whisk beater of a heavy-duty stand mixer, beat the egg whites until foamy. Add the cream of tartar and beat until soft peaks form when the beater is raised. Gradually beat in the remaining 2 tablespoons of sugar and beat until stiff peaks form when the beater is raised slowly.

Increase the heat under the syrup and boil until an accurate thermometer registers 248°F. to 250°F. (the firm-ball stage). *Immediately transfer the syrup to the glass measure to stop the cooking.*

If using a hand-held electric mixer, beat the syrup into the egg whites in a steady stream. Don't allow any syrup to fall on the beaters or they will spin it onto the sides of the bowl. If using a stand mixer, pour a small amount of syrup over the egg whites with the mixer off; then immediately beat at high speed for 5 seconds. Stop the mixer and add a larger amount of syrup. Beat at high speed for 5 seconds. Continue with the remaining syrup. For the last addition, use a rubber scraper to remove the syrup clinging to the glass measure. Lower the speed to medium and continue beating until completely cool, about 2 minutes.

Place the butter in a large mixing bowl and, preferably with the whisk beater, beat on medium speed for 30 seconds or until creamy. Gradually beat in the crème anglaise until smooth. Add the Italian meringue and beat until just incorporated. If the mixture looks curdled instead of smooth, it is too cold. Allow it to sit at room temperature to warm to 70°F. before continuing to beat. Or place the bowl in a hot water bath very briefly until the buttercream around the edge of the bowl just starts to melt. Remove at once and beat until smooth. Place in an airtight container. The butter-cream becomes slightly spongy on standing. Rebeat before using.*

Copper Candy Topping

KEEPS:
3 weeks at room temperature (if the humidity is low) in an airtight container.

On a lightly greased baking sheet, spread the almonds in a single layer. Set aside.

In a small heavy saucepan, combine the sugar and water and stir until the sugar is completely moistened. Bring the mixture to a boil over medium heat, stirring constantly until the sugar is dissolved. Increase the heat to medium high and boil undisturbed until the sugar begins to caramelize. It will begin to look like dark corn syrup and take on the characteristic smell of burnt sugar. (The temperature should be 370°F.) *Immediately* pour the caramel evenly over the nuts, covering as much of the nuts as possible. Allow the caramel to harden completely, 15 to 20 minutes. Remove it from the sheet and break it into pieces.

Assembling the Cake

Spread a little of the buttercream on a cake plate or 9-inch cardboard round and place a cake layer on top. Sandwich the cake layers with ¾ cup of the buttercream between each layer and frost the top and sides with the remaining buttercream. The cake will be about 3¾ to 4 inches high.

---

*Do not rebeat chilled buttercream until it has reached room temperature or it may curdle.

Arrange the Copper-Candy Topping on the cake top. (If you are planning to refrigerate or freeze the frosted cake, add the candy topping only after removing it from the refrigerator as it will become sticky if refrigerated.)

Serve the cake at room temperature or lightly chilled. Make sure that each serving contains a few pieces of the caramel nut topping. If the pieces become detached from the frosting, lay them decoratively on top of the cake.

POINTERS FOR SUCCESS

Biscuit de Savoie

- Use superfine sugar for the finest texture. (You can make it by processing granulated sugar in the food processor for a few minutes until fine.)
- Use cake flour without leavening.
- The bowl, beater and egg whites must be absolutely free of grease, including even a speck of egg yolk, for the egg whites to beat to stiff peaks.
- Using the correct amount of cream of tartar makes it possible to beat the whites very stiff without the risk of drying them and breaking them down.
- A large balloon whisk or slotted skimmer is ideal for folding in the flour with the least amount of air loss. If using the whisk, periodically shake out the batter which collects on the inside. Work quickly once the eggs are beaten so that they do not deflate. Fold the flour gently but *thoroughly* into the batter. Bake immediately after mixing.
- Use the correct pan size.
- For very even layers, wrap the cake pans with Magi-Cake Strips (available from Maid of Scandinavia, 800-328-6722).

Caramel Silk Buttercream

- Crème anglaise must be heated to at least 160°F. to thicken the egg yolks adequately. At temperatures over 180°F. the yolks will start to curdle and the cream may not be smooth.
- When cooking the caramel custard mixture, it is best to stir with a wooden spoon because a whisk will create air bubbles, making it difficult to judge when the mixture is done.
- The syrup for the Italian meringue must not get hotter than 250°F. or the whites will not incorporate air and thicken.

Copper Candy Topping

- When making the sugar syrup, be very careful not to allow any of the sugar to get on the sides of the pan. Before heating the mixture, make sure that all of the sugar has been moistened. This will prevent crystallization.

Prime Ribs of Lamb

Adelectable rack of lamb is very easy to make. The hard part is getting the butcher to give it to me the way I like it: chine bone intact and rib unfrenched (unscraped). Some of the most flavorful and crispiest meat is around the bone. Ever since I was three years old, I have preferred the bones to the meat. I used to wonder how I would ever be able to get married and still sit at the table enjoying the bones. When I met Elliott, much to my relief, not only was he a fellow bone lover, he did a better job on his than I did on mine. In fact, bones became the barometer of family relations. Elliott's children were not bone lovers, so whoever was most in favor at the moment got the bones discreetly passed over to his or her plate. To commemorate our mutual passion for bone nibbling, I always prepare rack of lamb for Valentine's Day.

Rack of lamb is one of the most elegant and impressive meals you can serve, yet it is extraordinarily simple to prepare as long as you have the timing right. If you don't feel comfortable with the "hand technique" (see below), an instant-read thermometer is all but infallible. I even made this recipe in the rustic setting of Wilbur Hot Springs in northern California last year. My cousin Joan and I were vacationing there for a weekend of hiking in the surrounding mountains, restorative sulfur baths and a good catch-up of our friendship. Wilbur is a place of spiritual quiet and beauty, with only kerosene lanterns as lights and a large communal kitchen with huge commercial ovens and spacious counters where people gather to prepare their individual dinners, respecting one another's privacy while cooperatively sharing oven time and space.

Joan brought the lamb and a fine red wine from her home in Berkeley; I brought the Dijon mustard and home-seasoned bread crumbs from New York. I surreptitiously glanced around to see what others were cooking. The variety was staggering, reflecting the different personalities of the guests. Most of the menus, however, seemed to be stir fries with "healthy" sorts of ingredients. But all around us, noses started twitching as the seductive, mingling aromas of lamb, fresh rosemary and garlic reached them. When I quietly (so I thought) demonstrated to Joan how to tell the consistency of the meat's doneness by using your own hand as a reference, suddenly people started to gather around. We suspected that it was probably the first rack of lamb to be cooked at Wilbur. But why not! The sweetest part was when, at table, I stood up to carve the rack, several people looked over and smiled longingly. I wanted to feed them all.

Serves: 4

Three hours before cooking, remove the rack of lamb to room temperature.

Preheat the oven to: 450°F.
Baking time: 35 to 40 minutes
Internal temperature (middle): 135°F.

INGREDIENTS room temperature	MEASURE volume	WEIGHT ounces/pounds	grams/kilograms
1 rack of lamb*	8 or 9 ribs	3¼ pounds	1 kilogram, 588 grams
3 medium cloves garlic	•	0.5 ounce	15 grams
salt	½ teaspoon	•	•
pepper, freshly ground, divided	¼ teaspoon	•	•
fresh bread crumbs†	¾ cup	1 ounce	32 grams
fresh parsley, preferably flat-leafed, minced	2 tablespoons	•	8 grams
fresh rosemary leaves, minced‡	2 teaspoons	•	•
Dijon mustard	3 tablespoons	2 ounces	54 grams

*I prefer to leave the chine bone intact and not to french the rib bones because this is some of my favorite eating. I do ask the butcher to trim most of the fat and to cut between the ribs at the base to facilitate carving.

†To make fresh bread crumbs, place bread in a food processor and process to fine crumbs.

‡Or 1 teaspoon dried rosemary.

At least 15 minutes before cooking, preheat the oven to 450°F.

Cut 1 piece of garlic in half and rub it all over the rack. Mince all 3 garlic cloves and set aside.

Sprinkle the rack with the salt and ⅛ teaspoon of the pepper and place it meat side down in a lightly oiled roasting pan. Roast for 20 minutes.

Meanwhile, in a small bowl, combine the bread crumbs, garlic, parsley, rosemary and the remaining ⅛ teaspoon pepper.

Turn the rack meat side up. Spread the upper meaty side of the roast with the mustard. Sprinkle with the bread crumb mixture, pressing to help it adhere. Roast for 15 to 20 minutes longer or until the crumbs are golden brown and an instant-read thermometer inserted toward the middle of the rack, but not touching the bone, registers 135°F. for medium rare, 140°F. for medium. If the bread crumbs look as if they are beginning to brown too much, tent the rack loosely with a piece of aluminum foil.

Allow the rack to rest for 10 to 15 minutes before carving.

Because a rack of lamb is so much smaller than a leg, the temperature will not continue to rise on standing, so it is brought to a slightly higher internal temperature for the same degree of doneness. The chops on either end will be slightly more done than the ones in the middle.

I fell in love with this Victorian table ornament, which is a prized family heirloom of my dear friend Elizabeth Field, who loaned it to me.

UNDERSTANDING

The Hand Test for Doneness

Try this even if you have an instant-read thermometer. The more often you practice, the more adept you will become. To use your hand as a guide for determining doneness, turn it sideways as if you were going to shake hands and make a tight fist. With the index finger of your other hand, press the muscled area between the thumb and index finger. It will feel very firm (Fig. 1). This is how well-done lamb should feel when pressed. Now relax your hand but keep it in a fist. Press the same area again and it will feel firm but no longer hard (Fig. 2). This is the consistency for medium. Now relax your hand completely. Press the same area again and it will feel soft (Fig. 3). This is the consistency for rare.

Haricots Verts

Serves: 4

In America, these tiny fresh string beans are reserved for special occasions simply because they are so much more expensive than the ordinary variety. When they are served to me, it always makes me feel like an esteemed guest.

INGREDIENTS	MEASURE volume	WEIGHT ounces	grams
haricots verts	·	8 ounces	227 grams
unsalted butter	1 tablespoon + 1 teaspoon	0.6 ounce	19 grams
salt	a light sprinkling	·	·
pepper, freshly ground	a grinding or two	·	·

Place a steamer insert in a large saucepan with a lid, and add water to come just under the steamer. Bring the water to a boil.

Add the haricots, placing them so that they lie next to each other. Cover and steam the haricots over low heat until just tender, 6 to 8 minutes.

Place the haricots on the dinner plates and place a teaspoon of the butter on top of each serving. Sprinkle with the salt and pepper.

Bulgur and Duxelles
(Mushroom Pilaf)

I first learned about duxelles at James Beard's cooking school over twenty-five years ago and placed it at once into that special category of culinary jewels that work magic to enhance other ingredients. This enrichment of finely minced mushrooms, slowly sautéed in butter until almost black, is wonderful to have on hand in the freezer for any number of dishes. In preprocessor days, it was necessary to use the largest chef's knife available for the laborious task of mincing the mushrooms. Now the task is reduced to a matter of seconds.

Duxelles does wondrous things to the wheatiness of bulgur. This dish is an excellent accompaniment to lamb, poultry or game.

Serves: 4

INGREDIENTS	MEASURE volume	WEIGHT ounces	grams
fresh mushrooms	4 lightly packed cups (after mincing)	12 ounces	340 grams
unsalted butter	4 tablespoons	2 ounces	57 grams
1 medium clove garlic, lightly smashed	·	·	5 grams
fine bulgur	1 cup	5.5 ounces	156 grams
salt	1 teaspoon	0.25 ounce	6.7 grams
sugar	¼ teaspoon	·	·
pepper, freshly ground	¼ teaspoon	·	·
boiling water	1½ liquid cups	·	·
parsley, preferably flat-leafed, minced	1 tablespoon	·	·

Clean the mushrooms by brushing off any dirt with a damp paper towel and cutting off the tough stem ends. If you are using a food processor, cut any large mushrooms in quarters. Process the mushrooms until finely minced, or finely chop using a large chef's knife.

In a large skillet over medium heat, melt the butter. Add the mushrooms and garlic and cook, covered, over low heat for 5 minutes. The mushrooms will release a lot of water. Uncover and continue cooking for about 30 minutes, stirring occasionally, until the mushrooms have turned dark brown and all the liquid has evaporated.

Add the bulgur to the skillet and sauté, stirring often, for 2 to 3 minutes. Reduce the heat to low. Sprinkle with the salt, sugar and pepper, add the boiling water and simmer, tightly covered, for 15 minutes. Fluff the mixture with a fork and allow it to stand, covered, for 5 minutes.

Sprinkle with the parsley before serving.

UNDERSTANDING

Never soak domestic fresh mushrooms in water to clean them, as any exposed gills act like little sponges to absorb water.

The processor releases a good deal of water from the mushrooms. Some people drain it off to speed up cooking time but I prefer to use it all for greater intensity of flavor.

Double Chocolate Sweetheart Cake

(Really the Final Word in Chocolate Cake)

As a chocolate consultant for a major food company, I was once asked how I would make a cake taste the most chocolatey possible if I had no limitations. This question, delightful to contemplate, was particularly interesting because cocoa makes the most chocolatey-tasting layer cake but chocolate mixed only with cream offers the fullest chocolate sensation. My answer was that I would make a cocoa layer cake with all yolks (which give the best flavor) and then inject it with my favorite eating chocolate. To further enhance the experience, I would have people eat it in a room filled with chocolate because what you smell while you're eating has a powerful effect on what you taste.

Soon after, I had a visit from Linda Foster Gomé, who had been head of the test kitchen at Ladies' Home Journal when I worked there. Linda has a marvelous sense of taste so I decided to try out part of my theory on her (the injecting part). I baked my favorite chocolate cocoa cake and as soon as it was done, poked holes in it and infused it with melted chocolate thinned with heavy cream. The result was this fabulously simple cake which is at once fudgey-moist and soft within, encased by a thin glaze of chocolate. For Valentine's Day I like to bake the cake in a heart-shaped pan and top it with fresh red raspberries, brightened with a gilding of currant jelly.

Serves: 8

Preheat the oven to: 350°F.
Baking time: 30 to 40 minutes

EQUIPMENT:
9-inch by 2-inch heart-shaped or round cake pan (8-cup capacity) or 9-inch springform pan, greased, bottom lined with parchment or wax paper and then greased again and floured; pastry bag and number 5 star tube, for optional décor

FINISHED HEIGHT:
1¾ inches

Preheat the oven to 350°F.

In a medium bowl, whisk together the cocoa and boiling water until smooth. Cover and cool to room temperature.

In another bowl, lightly combine the yolks, one quarter of the cocoa mixture and the vanilla.

In a large mixing bowl, combine the remaining dry ingredients and mix, preferably with the spade beater of a heavy-duty mixer, on a low speed for 30 seconds to blend. Add the butter and the remaining cocoa mixture. Mix on low speed until the dry ingredients are moistened. Increase to medium speed (high speed if using a hand mixer) and beat for 1½ minutes to aerate and develop the cake's structure. Scrape down the sides. Gradually add the egg mixture in three batches, beating for 20 seconds after each addition to incorporate the ingredients and strengthen the structure. Scrape down the sides.

Scrape the batter into the prepared pan and smooth the surface with a spatula. (The pan will be about half full.) Bake for 30 to 40 minutes or until a tester inserted near the center comes out clean and the cake springs back when pressed lightly in the center. *The cake should start to shrink from the sides of the pan only after removal from the oven.*

INGREDIENTS *room temperature*	MEASURE *volume*	WEIGHT *ounces/pounds*	*grams*
unsweetened cocoa (Dutch-processed)	¼ cup + 3 tablespoons	1.5 ounces	42 grams
boiling water	⅔ liquid cup	•	•
4 large egg yolks	2 full fluid ounces	2.5 ounces	74 grams
pure vanilla extract	¾ teaspoon	•	•
sifted cake flour	1½ cups + 1 tablespoon (sifted into the cup and leveled off)	5.5 ounces	156 grams
superfine sugar	1 cup	7 ounces	200 grams
baking powder	2½ teaspoons	•	12 grams
salt	½ teaspoon	•	3.5 grams
unsalted butter (must be softened)	9 tablespoons	4.5 ounces	128 grams
Chocolate Glaze			
bittersweet chocolate, preferably Lindt Excellence or Valrhona extra bittersweet*	1 3-ounce bar	3 ounces	85 grams
heavy cream	¾ liquid cup	•	•
fresh raspberries	2 pints	1 pound	454 grams
red currant jelly	¼ cup	2.6 ounces	77 grams
Whipped Cream Décor (optional)			
heavy cream	1 liquid cup	•	•
sugar	1 tablespoon	•	•
pure vanilla extract	1 teaspoon	•	•

*Available from Williams-Sonoma (415-421-4242).

   While the cake is baking, prepare the glaze: Break the chocolate into pieces and process in a food processor until very fine. Scald[†] the cream and, with the motor running, pour it through the feed tube in a steady stream. Process for a few seconds until smooth. (Alternatively, grate the chocolate, place it in a small bowl and stir in the scalded cream until uniform in color.) Transfer the chocolate glaze to a small bowl and keep warm.

   When the cake is baked, place it, still in the pan, on a rack and with a wooden skewer, poke holes all over the top. Use a brush to dab half of the chocolate glaze onto the cake, letting each application soak in before adding

[†]Heat just to the boiling point (small bubbles will appear around the edges).

the next. (This should take about 10 minutes.) Cover a cardboard round or a flat plate with plastic wrap or waxed paper and invert the cake onto it. Peel off and discard the parchment and poke holes all over the bottom of the cake. Dab with the remaining glaze, brushing a little onto the sides of the cake as well. Cool completely, for at least 1 hour, until the chocolate is firm to touch.

Invert the cake onto a 10-inch cardboard round or flat plate covered with plastic wrap. Peel off the plastic wrap from the cake, then reinvert onto a serving plate.

Place the raspberries close together to cover the surface of the cake, starting at the outside border and working in toward the center. You will actually need only about 1½ pints of raspberries but it's best to have extra so you can choose the most attractive ones.

In a small heavy saucepan, melt the currant jelly over low heat. Allow to cool to room temperature. Use a small brush to paint the currant glaze onto the raspberries.

If desired, whip 1 cup of heavy cream with 1 tablespoon of sugar and ½ teaspoon of vanilla extract. Use a number 5 large star tube and a pastry bag to pipe a shell border around the base of the cake.

 POINTERS FOR SUCCESS

- Use superfine sugar for the finest texture. (You can make it by processing granulated sugar in the food processor for a few minutes until fine.)
- Use cake flour without leavening.
- Use unsalted butter for the best flavor.
- Use fresh baking powder (under one year old).
- If using a hand-held mixer, beat at high speed.
- Use the correct pan size.
- For a very even layer, wrap the cake pan with a Magi-Cake Strip (available from Maid of Scandinavia, 800-328-6722).
- Do not overbake the cake.
- If planning to serve the cake without the raspberry topping, use a pastry brush to stipple the chocolate glaze after it is almost set for a more attractive appearance. You may also dust it lightly with cocoa or powdered sugar by placing the cocoa or sugar in a strainer, holding it over the cake and tapping the edge of the strainer with a spoon.

All-Seasons Cherry Pie

Washington's Birthday always makes me think of cherry pie, and thinking of cherry pie always makes me crave it. Washington's Birthday, however, does not fall around the fresh-cherry season. When I don't have any tart red pie cherries in the freezer, here's a special way I devised to use canned cherries for a pie, bringing out their best flavor.

SERVES: 6 to 8

Marinating time: 12 hours
Setting time: at least 4 hours
Preheat the oven to: 425°F.
Baking time: 20 to 25 minutes

INGREDIENTS *room temperature*	MEASURE *volume*	WEIGHT *ounces*	*grams*
Perfect Flaky Cream Cheese Pie Crust (page 42)	.	.	.
2 cans (16 ounces each) tart red pitted cherries, packed in water	.	.	.
Cherry Kijafa	¾ cup	.	.
sugar	¾ cup	5.25 ounces	150 grams
cornstarch	2 tablespoons	0.5 ounce	15 grams
salt	a pinch	.	.
almond extract	¼ teaspoon	.	.
lemon zest, finely grated	1 teaspoon	.	.

Pour the cherries into a colander set over a bowl and let them drain for 30 minutes. Press lightly to extract as much liquid as possible without crushing the cherries. Reserve ¼ cup of the cherry juice and discard the remainder.

In a medium noncorrodible saucepan, combine the reserved cherry juice, the Cherry Kijafa and the sugar. Stir to dissolve the sugar. Add the cherries and bring just to a boil over moderately high heat. Cover and remove from the heat. Cool to room temperature, then transfer the cherries and the liquid to a jar. Cover and macerate for 12 hours to overnight.

Preheat oven to 425°F. at least 15 minutes before baking time. Have the oven shelf at the lowest level.

On a floured pastry cloth or between 2 sheets of lightly floured plastic wrap (preferably Saran brand), roll the crust to 13 inches (⅛ inch thick). Transfer it to the tart pan. Fold in the excess, pleating and trimming if necessary. Press the pastry against the fluted edges of the pan. Cover the

Twelve hours ahead or night before

EQUIPMENT:
9½- to 10-inch by 1-inch tart pan with removable bottom

KEEPS: 2 days.

pastry lightly with plastic wrap and refrigerate it for at least 30 minutes or until very firm.

Line the pastry shell with foil and fill with pennies, aluminum pie weights or beans, making sure they are pushed up well against the sides. Bake for 15 minutes, remove the foil, prick the crust with a fork and continue baking 5 to 10 more minutes or until golden brown.

Pour the cherries back into a colander set over a bowl and let drain for 30 minutes. Reserve all liquid.

In a medium noncorrodible saucepan, boil the reserved liquid over high heat until it is reduced to 1 cup (5 to 8 minutes). Remove it to a bowl, cover and cool to room temperature.

In the same saucepan, stir together the cornstarch and salt. Gradually stir in the cooled cherry liquid. Add the cherries and bring to a boil over moderately high heat, stirring constantly. Reduce the heat to moderately low and simmer, stirring, for 1 minute, until the liquid is smooth and thick. Remove from the heat, stir in the almond extract and pour the cherries into the baked pastry shell. Using your thumb and forefinger, sprinkle the lemon zest evenly over the top. Cool to room temperature before removing it from the pan.

Allow the pie to set for at least 4 hours before serving.

- To transfer the crust to the pan, roll it loosely around the rolling pin. A cream cheese crust is more delicate and less flexible than other pie crusts and would crack slightly if folded into quarters.

POINTERS FOR SUCCESS

Perfect Flaky
Cream Cheese Pie Crust

Makes: pastry for a
9½-inch tart

KEEPS:
At least 2 days
refrigerated, 3 months
frozen.

This is my favorite pie crust. It is very similar in texture to my basic pie crust, but the addition of cream cheese makes it even easier to prepare because you never have to guess at how much water to add. And it gives it a flavor so delicious it is great to eat just by itself without any filling!

The food processor method is the easiest because the dough is handled less and stays colder, but the hand method will produce just as good a crust. Be sure to keep the ingredients cold to maintain flakiness. In summer I put the flour in a reclosable freezer bag in the freezer for at least thirty minutes before mixing the dough.

INGREDIENTS cold	MEASURE volume	WEIGHT ounces	grams
unsalted butter, divided	8 tablespoons	4 ounces	113 grams
bleached all-purpose flour	1 cup + 2 tablespoons (dip and sweep method)	5.5 ounces	156 grams
salt	¼ teaspoon	•	•
cream cheese	1 3-ounce package	3 ounces	85 grams
ice water	1 tablespoon + 1 teaspoon	•	•

Food Processor Method

Divide the butter into two parts: 2 tablespoons (1 ounce) and 6 tablespoons (3 ounces). Cut the butter into ½-inch cubes, keeping the two parts separate. Wrap each portion with plastic wrap (preferably Saran brand) and refrigerate for at least 15 minutes.

Place the flour and salt in a food processor with the metal blade and process for a few seconds to combine. Add the smaller amount of butter cubes and the cream cheese and process for 10 seconds or until the mixture ressembles coarse meal. Add the remaining butter cubes and process for 4 to 6 seconds or until the remaining pieces of butter are the size of small peas. Do not overprocess or the crust will not be flaky.

Add the ice water and pulse 4 times. The dough will be in moist fine particles which appear dry but should hold together when pinched with the fingers. Dump the mixture into a plastic bag and press the outside of the bag until the dough holds together. Knead the dough briefly in the bag until you can form a smooth ball.

Remove the dough from the bag, wrap it with plastic wrap and flatten it into a disc. Refrigerate it for at least 45 minutes or up to 2 days.

Place the flour and salt in a medium bowl and whisk to combine. Use a pastry cutter or two knives to cut the butter and cream cheese into the flour, the first addition into coarse meal, the second into small peas just as with the food processor method. When adding the ice water, sprinkle it on, tossing the mixture lightly with a fork. Use your hands to gather the dough together and knead it briefly on the counter until it forms a smooth ball. Wrap the dough with plastic wrap and flatten it into a disc. Refrigerate for at least 45 minutes or up to 2 days.

- Saran Wrap is the ideal plastic wrap for rolling the dough because it lies very flat.
- Don't fold the dough when transferring it to the pie plate because it cracks a little. Rolling it loosely around the rolling pin works best.

Hand Method

POINTERS FOR SUCCESS

Butter and Sage Roasted Squab

Serves: 6
Preheat the oven to: 425°F.
Baking time: 30 minutes
Internal temperature (thigh): 155°F.

EQUIPMENT:
shallow roasting pan about 18 inches long (a half-size sheet pan or a jelly-roll pan is perfect)

Squab is my favorite fowl. Its meat is full flavored, not at all gamey, and stands up to intense flavor accompaniments such as wild rice and chanterelles. Squab is most delicious when the breast is still rosy. Set the table with sharp knives and have ready a pair of shears to pass at the table to get through some of the more resistant joints. Actually, the ideal way to serve squab is to bone them whole, leaving only the wings and leg and thigh bones intact. This is a luxury for the guests but a time-consuming effort for the cook, and not really necessary when throwing an informal party for good friends who are not above using their fingers when necessary.

One squab is more than enough per serving, so I don't offer appetizers with a squab dinner and I keep the dessert light and refreshing.

If you prefer, Cornish game hens can be substituted.

INGREDIENTS	MEASURE	WEIGHT	
	volume	ounces	grams
6 squab*		15 to 18 ounces each	425 to 510 grams each
For optional stock: 1 bay leaf, 3 peppercorns, a few sprigs of thyme, ½ small onion, unpeeled			
2 large cloves garlic, cut in half and peeled			6 grams
unsalted butter, softened	2 tablespoons	1 ounce	28 grams
24 large sage leaves†			
salt	1 teaspoon	0.25 ounce	6.7 grams
black pepper, freshly ground	a few grindings		
cayenne pepper	about ⅛ teaspoon		
fresh thyme‡	1 bunch	1 ounce	28 grams

*Available at specialty markets and by mail order from 800-DARTAGN.
†I grow pineapple sage, which has beautiful markings, in my garden, and I freeze it for use throughout the year.
‡Or sprinkle ½ teaspoon dried thyme inside each squab.

At least 15 minutes before roasting, position an oven rack so that the roasting pan will sit in the upper third of the oven and preheat the oven to 425°F.

Remove the necks, gizzards and livers from the cavities of the squab. If desired, make a stock from the necks and gizzards by simmering them for about 30 minutes or until tender with the bay leaf, peppercorns, thyme sprigs and half onion in enough water to cover by 2 inches. Strain and reserve the stock for cooking the wild rice (page 48). (We like to eat the necks and gizzards.) Reserve the livers, refrigerated, for sautéing and filling the accompanying artichoke hearts (page 50).

Rinse the squab under cold running water, scraping out any remaining internal organs, and pat them dry with paper towels. Insert your fingers between the skin and flesh to loosen it over the legs and breasts.

Rub the squab all over with the cut garlic and then rub all over with the butter. Insert a sage leaf under the skin, in an attractive pattern, on each side of the breast and on each leg. Sprinkle each squab with the salt, pepper, and a pinch or two of cayenne pepper. Cut each piece of garlic in thirds and place two pieces in the cavity of each squab. Add a few branches of fresh thyme. Fold back the wing tips underneath the back. Tie together the legs only.

Roast the squab for 10 minutes. Lower the heat to 400°F. and continue roasting for 10 minutes or until an instant-read thermometer inserted in the thigh (not touching the bone) reads 155°F; when you tip the squab tailward the juices should run quite pink. If additional cooking is necessary, baste with the pan drippings and roast for another 5 to 10 minutes.

UNDERSTANDING

The squab is placed directly on the pan, rather than on a rack, because the metal conducts the heat well and cooks the backs. Because of the short roasting time, the backs would not cook adequately if the squab were on a rack.

Wild Rice and Chanterelles

Serves: 6

The voluptuous texture of chanterelle mushrooms is fabulous with wild rice. One August, when my cousins the Bushes (I'm not kidding) came to visit, they picked seven pounds of chanterelles in the semi-wild preserve adjoining our house. Marion has a business in White Plains, New York, called Wild Harvest. She gave me an on-the-spot lesson in chanterelle identification, showing me how to compare the blunted gills of the edible chanterelle with the sharp gills of its poisonous cousin. When I asked her if a person could die from eating the poisonous look-alike, her cryptically cautionary reply was, "No, but you get so sick you'd wish you would!" Wild mushroom picking is definitely for the experts. Fortunately, chanterelles are widely available in specialty markets.

That chanterelle windfall inspired this entire menu, which I prepared for the Bushes the following winter when the chanterelles became available in the market.

Using meat stock to cook the wild rice in this recipe turns the grains a dark rich brown that looks gorgeous against the pale orange of the mushrooms. This flavorful dish perfectly complements the rich flavor of squab.

INGREDIENTS	MEASURE		WEIGHT	
	volume		*ounces*	*grams*
wild rice	1 cup		6 ounces	170 grams
Glace de Viande (page 253)*	3 cubes		1.5 ounces	48 grams
water	3 liquid cups		•	•
salt†	¾ teaspoon		•	5 grams
chanterelle mushrooms		•	12 ounces	340 grams
unsalted butter	2 tablespoons		1 ounce	28 grams
minced shallot or onion	2 teaspoons		•	6 grams
1 clove garlic, smashed and peeled		•	•	5 grams
pepper, freshly ground	a few grindings		•	•
parsley, preferably flat-leafed, minced	1 tablespoon		•	•

*Or 3 cups unsalted beef broth or use 3 cups squab stock (page 45) and 1 beef bouillon cube, and omit the water.

†If using unsalted beef broth and a bouillon cube, add only ¼ teaspoon salt; if using broth that contains salt, omit the salt.

Place the wild rice in a strainer and run cold water through it until the water runs clear.

In a medium-size saucepan with a tight-fitting lid, bring the Glace de Viande and water (or broth and bouillon cube) to a boil. Simmer, covered, until the glace is dissolved. Measure the liquid and add enough water to equal 3 cups. Add the wild rice and salt, return the water to a boil and simmer over low heat, covered, for 50 to 60 minutes, stirring with a fork three or four times during the cooking. The rice should have puffed open and the liquid evaporated. If any liquid remains, raise the heat slightly and continue cooking briefly, uncovered, until dry. Cover the rice and keep warm.

Wash the mushrooms under cold running water to remove any dirt. Cut off the stem bottoms and any of the stem that may be tough. Slice each mushroom the long way into quarters; cut any larger mushrooms into sixths or eighths.

In a large heavy frying pan with a lid, heat the butter over medium heat until bubbling. Add the shallot or onion and cook, stirring often, for about 3 minutes or until translucent. Add the smashed garlic clove and mushrooms, cover and cook over low heat for about 10 minutes or until the mushrooms become tender. Continue cooking, uncovered, over medium-high heat, for 1 or 2 minutes, stirring often, until all the liquid evaporates and the mushrooms begin to glaze and brown lightly. Add this mixture to the cooked rice, then add the black pepper and toss lightly with a fork to blend. Taste and adjust the seasonings. Sprinkle with the parsley.

Pressure Cooker Method

I often cook the rice in a pressure cooker when I don't want to wait a full hour. It is a delightfully reliable method. Place the water and Glace de Viande cubes (or the stock and bouillon cube), rice and salt in the pressure cooker and lock the lid in place. Over high heat, bring the pressure to high. Lower the heat but maintain high pressure. Cook for 30 minutes. Place the pressure cooker in the sink and run cold water over the lid until the pressure is released. Open the lid away from your face, to avoid the steam. Then boil for a few minutes over medium-high heat to evaporate any remaining liquid. Depending on the rice and the size of the pot, this can take as long as 10 minutes.

POINTERS FOR SUCCESS

• If you are using a pot with a loose-fitting lid and the liquid evaporates before the rice is tender, add more boiling water. Some brands or harvests of wild rice may take as long as 70 minutes. The rice should be bloomed and open but some of the grains should be curled. If all the grains are open, flat and soft, with no crunch, they have been cooked too long.

NOTE: Uncooked wild rice stored in an airtight container keeps indefinitely without any nutritional or flavor loss.

UNDERSTANDING

Wild rice is the most unpredictable of all grains as far as cooking time and amount of liquid needed. It is therefore best to start with the minimum liquid and cooking time and add more if needed. Some people prefer to undercook the rice slightly, leaving some of the grains unopened and with more bite. I like the grains to be open but still curled. With continued cooking all the grains will open fully and flatten. I find this texture too soft to my taste. Wild rice expands four times in volume when cooked.

Glace de viande offers the best flavor because it is concentrated beef stock without salt. Next best is unsalted broth but it is very expensive.

Chanterelles do not absorb water as easily as do ordinary cultivated mushrooms so it's fine to rinse them under cold running water.

Artichoke Hearts with Squab Livers

Serves: 6

I created this recipe to take full advantage of the marvelous dividend you get when cooking squab: the liver. Deglazing the pan juices with the slightly sweet sting of raspberry liqueur makes an effortless and savory sauce. The artichokes can be cooked and trimmed early in the day and filled shortly before serving.

INGREDIENTS	MEASURE volume	WEIGHT	
		ounces	grams
6 large artichokes	.	12 to 14 ounces each	340 to 397 grams each
salt	¼ teaspoon + a pinch	.	.
6 squab livers	.	2.5 ounces	70 grams
unsalted butter, divided	1 tablespoon + 1½ teaspoons	0.75 ounce	21 grams
12 fresh sage leaves	.	.	.
pepper, freshly ground	a grinding	.	.
shallots, minced	1 tablespoon	0.3 ounce	9 grams
liqueur de framboise (raspberry liqueur)*	1 tablespoon	.	.

*Or 2 tablespoons sweet red vermouth.

Trim the stems from the artichokes so that about 1 inch remains for them to stand on above the water in the pot and set them upright in one or two pots just large enough to fit them standing upright.

Pour in about ½ inch of boiling water and sprinkle with the ¼ teaspoon of salt. Cover tightly and simmer over low heat until tender, adding more water if necessary. Very large artichokes can take as long as 1 hour and 15 minutes. Start testing after 40 minutes. To test for doneness, pierce the side of an artichoke with a metal cake tester or wooden skewer. It should meet with little resistance. When tender, the color will deepen and become more drab and when an artichoke is picked up with tongs, it will compress slightly.

Place the artichokes in a colander and allow them to cool enough so that you can handle them. Remove and discard the leaves and hairy inner choke. A small sharp knife or a grapefruit spoon works well for scraping away the choke without destroying the shape of the artichoke heart. Trim off enough of the stem so that the artichoke hearts will sit upright. If desired, trim the sides of the hearts (I prefer the rough natural look). Set them aside, covered, at room temperature.

Rinse the squab livers under cold running water and dry on paper towels.

In a medium-size heavy skillet over medium heat, melt 1 tablespoon of the butter. Add the sage leaves in a single layer and sauté them until lightly golden on both sides, about 1 minute for each side. Remove them carefully to paper towels. They will be crisp and fragile.

Add the remaining 1½ teaspoons of butter to the skillet and heat until bubbling. Add the squab livers. Sprinkle them with the pinch of salt and the pepper. Sauté the livers, stirring often, over medium high until browned, about 3 minutes. Be careful not to overcook them; they are most tender, juicy and delicious when still rosy inside. Remove them with a slotted spoon to a small bowl.

Lower the heat and add the shallots to the pan. Sauté them, stirring often, until softened and translucent, about 3 minutes. Remove from the heat and pour in the framboise (or vermouth), stirring to scrape up the browned bits. Pour over the squab livers.

When ready to serve, remove the squab livers to a cutting board and cut them into small cubes. Arrange 2 sage leaves in each artichoke heart so that they extend over the sides and place some of the liver and shallots in the center. Drizzle the pan juices on top.

UNDERSTANDING

Although the traditional French technique is to remove the artichoke leaves and trim the hearts before cooking, I prefer to do it afterward because I find that the hearts cook more evenly with the leaves still on to buffer them and it is easier to trim them.

Cold Lemon Cream Soufflé

I am thrilled with this recipe. It is lilting, refreshing and intensely lemony yet mellow and creamy at the same time. I created it for people who are concerned with the safety of eating raw eggs but discovered that cooking the eggs is actually a great improvement because it results in an extraordinarily voluptuous texture.

If you wish to make the soufflé less rich, it can be prepared with only half a cup of cream, or you can even omit the cream completely and it will still be delicious and "creamy." This is a fabulous dessert for entertaining as it freezes perfectly for up to six weeks and so can be made well ahead.

Serves: 10 to 12

Setting time: at least 4 hours

EQUIPMENT:
8-cup decorative mold (or a 6-cup decorative mold and wine goblets or dessert dishes for 1½ cups of the mixture), lightly sprayed with nonstick vegetable shortening or lightly oiled (Tupperware makes an excellent 6-cup mold with an upper lid to release the suction, which makes unmolding a dream.)

KEEPS:
5 days refrigerated, 6 weeks frozen.

| INGREDIENTS | MEASURE | WEIGHT | |
room temperature	volume	ounces	grams
heavy cream	1 liquid cup	•	•
Lemon Curd			
lemon zest, finely grated	2 teaspoons	•	4 grams
4 large egg yolks	¼ liquid cup	2.5 ounces	74 grams
sugar	¼ cup	1.75 ounces	50 grams
lemon juice, freshly squeezed	3 fluid ounces	•	•
unsalted butter, softened	4 tablespoons	2 ounces	57 grams
salt	a pinch	•	•
Light Italian Meringue			
powdered gelatin	1¼ teaspoons	•	•
water, divided	2 tablespoons + ¼ liquid cup	•	•
sugar, divided	¾ cup + 2 tablespoons	6 ounces	175 grams
4 large egg whites	½ liquid cup	4.5 ounces	120 grams
cream of tartar	½ teaspoon	•	•
OPTIONAL: Cordon Rose Raspberry Sauce (page 56) or Quick Raspberry Sauce (page 57) and fresh berries	•	•	•

In a large mixing bowl, place the heavy cream and refrigerate for at least 15 minutes. (Chill the mixer beater alongside the bowl.)

Lemon Curd

Put the lemon zest into a medium bowl, suspend a strainer over the bowl and set it near the range.

In a heavy noncorrodible saucepan, beat the yolks and sugar until well blended. Stir in the remaining ingredients (except the lemon zest). Cook over medium-low heat, stirring constantly, until the mixture is thickened and resembles hollandaise sauce (thickly coats a wooden spoon but is still liquid enough to pour). The mixture will change from translucent to opaque and begin to take on a yellow color on the back of a wooden spoon. It must not be allowed to boil or it will curdle. Whenever steam appears, remove the pan briefly from the heat, stirring constantly, to keep the mixture from boiling. When the curd has thickened, pour it at once into the strainer. Press with the back of a spoon until only the coarse residue remains. Discard the residue (or consider it the cook's dividend!). Stir to mix in the zest, and allow the lemon curd to cool completely.

When the lemon curd has cooled, beat the chilled cream only until the cream mounds softly when dropped from a spoon. Add the lemon curd and with a whisk or rubber spatula, fold the two together until the mixture is completely uniform. Cover the bowl tightly with plastic wrap (preferably Saran brand) and refrigerate.

Light Italian Meringue

Have ready a 1-cup heatproof liquid measure by the range.

In a small heatproof measuring cup, combine the gelatin and the 2 tablespoons of water and allow to sit for 5 minutes. Then set the cup in a pan of simmering water for a few minutes, stirring occasionally until the gelatin is dissolved. (This can also be done in a few seconds in a microwave on high power, stirring once or twice.)

In a small heavy saucepan, preferably with a nonstick lining, stir together the ¾ cup of sugar and the ¼ cup of water until the sugar is completely moistened. Heat, stirring constantly, until the sugar dissolves and the syrup is bubbling. Immediately stop stirring and turn down the heat to the lowest setting. (If using an electric range, remove from the heat.)

In a mixing bowl, preferably using the whisk beater of a stand mixer, beat the egg whites until foamy. Add the cream of tartar and beat until soft peaks form when the beater is raised slowly. Gradually beat in the remaining 2 tablespoons of sugar and beat until stiff peaks form when the beater is raised slowly.

Increase the heat under the syrup and boil the syrup until a thermometer registers 248°F. to 250°F. (firm-ball stage). Immediately pour into the glass measure to stop the cooking.

If using a hand-held electric mixer, beat the syrup into the whites in a steady stream. Don't allow any syrup to fall on the beaters or they will spin it onto the sides of the bowl. If using a stand mixer, pour a small amount of syrup over the whites with the mixer off, then immediately beat at high speed for 5 seconds. Stop the mixer and add a larger amount of syrup. Beat at high speed for 5 seconds. Continue with the remaining syrup. With the last addition, use a rubber scraper to remove the syrup clinging to the measure.

Lower the speed to medium, add the gelatin mixture and beat at medium speed until cool, about 2 minutes.

Use a large balloon whisk or rubber spatula to fold the Italian meringue into the lemon curd mixture in three parts. Spoon into the mold. Tap the mold on a counter to help settle the mixture and prevent large air bubbles at the bottom.

Refrigerate for at least 4 hours or freeze. Transfer the frozen soufflé from the freezer to the refrigerator at least 6 hours before serving.

To serve: Chill the presentation plate. Moisten the plate with water so that it will be easy to reposition and center the soufflé. Dip the mold in warm water for 20 seconds. If using the Tupperware mold, remove the large lid and invert it onto the plate. Remove the small upper lid. This releases the suction and the mousse will drop from the mold onto the plate. If using a mold without this upper lid, dip it in the warm water until the soufflé begins to slide when tilted. Release the suction by slipping a long spatula or knife blade between the soufflé and the side of the mold, all the way to the bottom of the mold.

Pour some of the optional raspberry sauce onto the top so that it drips decoratively down the sides or pour it in a pool around the base and center. Garnish with fresh seasonal berries if desired. Serve the remaining sauce on the side.

POINTERS FOR SUCCESS

Lemon Curd

- For finely grated zest, use a zester (a small implement with tiny scraping holes), a vegetable peeler or fine grater to remove the yellow portion only of the lemon rind. The white pith beneath is bitter. If using a zester or peeler, finish by chopping the zest with a sharp knife.
- If a lemon is heated (about 10 seconds in a microwave oven on high power) and then rolled around while pressing on it lightly, it will release a significantly greater quantity of juice.
- To prevent curdling, be sure to mix the sugar with the yolks before adding the lemon juice. Use a heavy noncorrodible pan that conducts heat evenly or a double boiler. To prevent curdling during cooking, do not allow the mixture to boil. Remove the curd immediately from the heat when thickened and strain at once, as the residual heat of the pan will continue to raise the temperature. (If you are working with an accurate thermometer,* the temperature of the thickened curd will be 196°F.)

Light Italian Meringue

- The syrup for the Italian meringue must not get hotter than 250°F. or the whites will not incorporate air and thicken.

*The Cordon Rose candy thermometer is available through Dean & DeLuca (800-227-7714).

Cordon Rose Raspberry Sauce

Makes: 1¼ cups
KEEPS:
10 days refrigerated,
1 year frozen.

T his tart, velvety, intensely flavored sauce is the essence of fresh raspberries. The secret is that the juice is concentrated to a quarter of its original volume but the pulp is not cooked at all.

INGREDIENTS	MEASURE	WEIGHT	
	volume	*ounces*	*grams*
raspberries, frozen with no sugar added	1½ 12-ounce bags	18 ounces	510 grams
lemon juice, freshly squeezed	1½ teaspoons	•	•
sugar	½ cup less 1 tablespoon	3 ounces	87 grams

In a strainer suspended over a deep bowl, thaw the raspberries completely. This will take several hours. (To speed thawing, place in an oven with a pilot light.) Press the berries to force out all the juice. There should be ⅔ cup.

In a small saucepan, boil the juice until it is reduced to 3 tablespoons. (Or reduce the juice in a microwave on high power.*) Pour the syrup into a lightly oiled heatproof cup.

Purée the raspberries and strain them through a food mill fitted with the fine disc. Or use a fine strainer to remove all the seeds. You should have ⅔ liquid cup of purée. Stir in the raspberry syrup and lemon juice. You should have 14 tablespoons (7 fluid ounces). Add the 7 tablespoons of sugar.† Stir until the sugar dissolves.

POINTERS FOR
SUCCESS

• Be sure to use unsweetened berries. Berries in syrup cannot be reduced as much because the sugar thickens the mixture before the intense flavor can be obtained.
• Raspberry seeds are very small and can pass through most food mills. The Cuisinart power strainer and sieve attachment removes all the tiny seeds in a matter of minutes and is easy to clean. The Squeezo tomato strainer with berry screen attachment, by Vitantonio, is also effective but not as easy to clean.

UNDERSTANDING

If using fresh berries, you will need to freeze and then thaw them in order to break down the cell membranes and exude some juice.

*If using a microwave, place the juice in a 4-cup heatproof glass measure or bowl to allow for bubbling.
†If you have less than ⅔ cup raspberry purée, decrease the sugar, using 1 tablespoon for each fluid ounce (2 tablespoons) of raspberry purée.

Quick Raspberry Sauce

This is a speedier version than the previous one because the fruit and juice are cooked together. It is also delicious but not quite as fresh tasting as the Cordon Rose Raspberry Sauce for which the fruit is not cooked at all.

Makes: about 1 cup

KEEPS:
10 days refrigerated,
1 year frozen.

INGREDIENTS	MEASURE volume	WEIGHT	
		ounces	grams
raspberries, frozen in light syrup	2 10-ounce packages	20 ounces	578 grams
sugar	¼ cup (or more to taste)	1.75 ounces	50 grams
lemon juice, freshly squeezed	2 teaspoons	•	10 grams
OPTIONAL: Chambord liqueur	1 tablespoon	•	•

Defrost the raspberries overnight in the refrigerator or for several hours at room temperature.

In a medium saucepan, combine the raspberries with the ¼ cup of sugar and bring the mixture to a simmer over medium-low heat. Cook, stirring often to avoid scorching, until reduced to about 1⅓ cups, 12 to 15 minutes.

Pass the mixture through a food mill fitted with the fine disc or a fine strainer to remove the seeds. Stir in the lemon juice and optional Chambord. Add more sugar, if desired, to taste.

• Raspberry seeds are very small and can pass through most food mills. The Cuisinart power strainer and sieve attachment removes all the tiny seeds in a matter of minutes and is easy to clean. The Squeezo tomato strainer with berry screen attachment, by Vitantonio, is also effective but not as easy to clean.

POINTERS FOR SUCCESS

"Levy's" Real Jewish Rye Bread

Makes: one 3½-pound round loaf, 6 inches high by 12 inches in diameter (5 inches by 10½ inches if baked in La Cloche)

Sponge time: at least 4 hours; up to overnight Rising time: 3 to 4 hours Preheat the oven to: 450°F. Baking time: 1 hour 20 minutes

Both my parents were raised in the Bronx, but when I was growing up, we lived in Manhattan. Whenever my father had an excuse to return to the Bronx, he never came home without a freshly baked loaf from his favorite bakery. My favorite was the rye bread, studded with constellations of caraway seeds. (I always complained when he brought home the seedless variety, which he would only do when they sold out of the caraway one.) My grandmother, who lived with us, would serve me slices spread thickly with unsalted butter, then paved with rounds of sliced red radishes and lightly sprinkled with kosher salt that she crushed between her thumb and index finger. To this day it is my favorite way to eat rye bread with one possible exception: When I bake it myself, I can have the first slice while it is still warm from the oven.

It has taken me years to get my rye bread to taste and feel just right. I like a wheaty flavor, with not so much rye that it becomes bitter, and a chewy texture that is not so dense it becomes pasty. I love using La Cloche, a large, unglazed, earthenware platter with a dome-shaped top. During baking, the bread rises to fill the dome, which gives it a lovely shape, moist texture and very crunchy top. The bread is still delicious when made free-form.

I like making bread entirely by hand because half the pleasure lies in the feel and touch of kneading it. But the quality will be equal if made with a heavy-duty electric mixer.

Proof the yeast: Crumble the fresh yeast into a small bowl and add ½ teaspoon of the sugar and ¼ cup of the water, warmed to a tepid 100°F.; if using dry yeast increase the temperature slightly to 110°F. Stir until the yeast is dissolved. Set aside in a draft-free spot for 10 to 20 minutes. The mixture should be full of bubbles; if not, the yeast is too old to be useful. Discard it and start again with fresh yeast.

Make the sponge: In a large bowl, combine the yeast mixture, 3 cups of the bread flour, 2 tablespoons of the remaining sugar and the remaining 2¾ cups of water. Whisk until very smooth, about 100 strokes. Cover with plastic wrap and allow to stand for 4 to 5 hours at room temperature or refrigerate overnight.

In a medium bowl, combine the remaining 2 cups of bread flour, the rye flour, the remaining 2½ teaspoons of sugar, the caraway seeds and salt. Stir into the sponge, add the oil and mix just until smooth. Mix in enough flour so that the dough is not sticky; then scrape the dough onto a lightly floured counter. Knead for about 10 minutes, adding bread flour as necessary to keep the dough from sticking. It should be very elastic, smooth and cool to the touch and jump back when pressed with a fingertip. If the

First thing in the morning or the night before

| INGREDIENTS | MEASURE | WEIGHT | |
room temperature	volume	ounces/pounds	grams/kilograms
fresh yeast* *or* dry yeast (*not* rapid-rise)	1 packed tablespoon 2½ teaspoons	0.75 ounce 0.25 ounce	17 grams 6.75 grams
sugar, divided	3 tablespoons	1.3 ounces	37.5 grams
water, divided	3 liquid cups	•	•
bread flour, divided	5 cups (dip and sweep method) + about 1½ cups for kneading	2¼ pounds	1 kilogram
rye flour	2 cups	6.75 ounces	190 grams
caraway seeds	¼ cup	1 ounce	28 grams
salt	1 tablespoon	0.70 ounce	20 grams
vegetable oil	1 tablespoon	•	•
cornmeal	about 2 teaspoons	•	•
OPTIONAL: unsalted butter, softened radishes, sliced kosher salt	•	•	•

*Fresh yeast causes dough to rise faster.

dough is too difficult to knead in one batch, divide it in half and knead one portion at a time until smooth, keeping the remaining dough covered. Then knead the two portions together until combined.

Form the dough into a ball and place it in a large oiled bowl. Turn to coat, tightly cover with plastic wrap (preferably Saran brand) or a damp towel and let rise for 1 hour or until doubled in bulk (it can take as long as 2 hours if the room is cold). Punch down the dough, knead it lightly and allow to rise a second time until doubled.[†] (The second rising takes about 45 minutes.)

Sprinkle the La Cloche bottom or a rimless baking sheet with about 2 teaspoons of cornmeal (or enough to cover lightly).

Roll the dough into an 8-inch ball and place it on the La Cloche bottom or baking sheet. Cover with a large inverted bowl or plastic wrap sprayed with nonstick vegetable shortening. Let the dough rise until doubled in bulk, about 1 hour to 1 hour and 15 minutes.

At least 30 minutes before baking, soak the top of La Cloche if using it. Preheat the oven to 450°F., and preheat a baking stone or cookie sheet.
Slash the top of the dough with a sharp knife or razor blade. (I like to

[†]If time allows, give the bread a third 45-minute rising before the final shaping.

make two long slashes about 6 inches apart in one direction and a second two long perpendicular slashes through them.) Place the soaked La Cloche top on top of the base if using and place on the preheated baking stone or sheet or slide the dough directly onto the baking stone.

Bake for 15 minutes, then lower the temperature to 400°F. and continue baking for 65 minutes or until the bread is golden brown and sounds hollow when rapped. (The baked bread will stay warm for 2 hours.)

NOTE: Do not use parchment on the bottom of the La Cloche unless it is greased or the bread will stick to it.

Electric Mixer Method

To make the sponge, place the ingredients in the mixer bowl of a 5-quart or larger heavy-duty mixer and, with the whisk attachment, beat for about 1 minute or until very smooth. Remove the whisk attachment, cover the bowl tightly with plastic wrap and let stand at room temperature for 4 to 5 hours or refrigerate overnight.

Using the dough hook paddle attachment, gradually stir in the remaining 2 cups of bread flour mixed with the rye flour, the remaining 2½ teaspoons of sugar, the caraway seeds and salt. Add the oil and mix just until smooth. Add additional bread flour, if necessary, and mix to form a soft rough dough. Change to the dough hook, scraping off any dough that clings to the paddle, and mix on medium speed until the dough is smooth and elastic, about 10 minutes. After the first 3 minutes, if the dough still appears sticky and has not begun to clean the sides of the bowl, add some additional bread flour a few tablespoons at a time. If the dough seems dry, add water 1 tablespoon at a time. Form the dough into a ball and proceed as above.

POINTERS FOR SUCCESS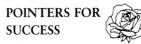

• Store the baked bread at room temperature or in the freezer and defrost to room temperature or reheat it. Do not refrigerate without warming it as the starch in the flour crystallizes when cold.
• Be sure to use bread flour. The larger amount of gluten-forming protein gives a significantly higher rise.

UNDERSTANDING

Preheating the baking stone or sheet causes the dough to hold its shape and start to rise immediately when placed directly on it in the oven. This technique results in the highest rise.

I added the 1 tablespoon of oil to lighten the texture of the bread because rye flour makes a much denser loaf. The 1 tablespoon of oil made a significant increase to the rise. It was Shirley Corriher who made this valuable contribution by telling me about experiments reported demonstrating this theory, although it is not yet understood exactly how the oil accomplishes this lightening of the dough. A very plausible hypothesis from my husband, Elliott, is that the oil coats the gluten strands, giving them more elasticity and further, acts as a sort of impermeable shield, coating the air cells, thereby keeping the carbon dioxide in longer, which increases the air spaces.

Beef and Barley Soupless

This recipe is dedicated to the Irish, God bless them, because of all the nationalities I can think of, it is the romantic, passionate and generous Irish who most welcome the world to celebrate with them. There is hardly a person who does not take pleasure in the wearing of the green on St. Patrick's Day, or thrill to the stirring wail of the bagpipes, or long to watch The Quiet Man *just one more time. Doesn't everyone want to be Irish, at least for one day of the year? I chose this recipe for St. Patrick's Day because barley is a much appreciated staple on the Irish table.*

This recipe came about because I have long loved beef and barley soup but wished I could have more of the barley and less of the liquid. One day I discovered that Elliott's mother, Bessie (whom I never had the fortune to meet), used to have a wonderful recipe for a barley casserole prepared with onions and beef broth. I added the cooked short ribs of beef (a very flavorful cut), some dried porcini mushrooms often used in the soup, little nublets of melting marrow for garnish, and I had the dish of my fantasy!

Serves: 9 to 10

I like to begin preparations the night before to make it easier to skim all the fat from the stock.

INGREDIENTS room temperature	MEASURE volume	WEIGHT ounces/pounds	grams/kilograms
beef marrow bones*	•	5 pounds	2 kilograms, 268 grams
short ribs, trimmed of excess fat	•	4 pounds	1 kilogram, 814 grams
beef broth (preferably College Inn)†	4 14.5-ounce cans (7¼ liquid cups)	58 ounces	1 kilogram, 644 grams
dried porcini mushrooms, rinsed under cold running water	•	1.5 ounces	43 grams
5 black peppercorns	•	•	•
1 large bay leaf	•	•	•
unsalted butter	4 tablespoons	2 ounces	57 grams
2 medium onions, chopped	2 cups	9 ounces	255 grams
sugar	a pinch	•	•
fresh mushrooms, sliced	5 cups	1 pound	454 grams
pearl barley	3 cups	21 ounces	600 grams
fresh parsley preferably flat-leafed, minced	2 tablespoons	0.25 ounce	7 grams

*Ask the butcher for hollow shinbones, as they have the most marrow.
†Or use 4 cubes Glace de Viande (page 253) and 7¼ cups water; add 1½ teaspoons salt.

To remove the marrow from the bones, run a skewer around the marrow to release it and push it out in one piece. Discard the bones. Place the marrow in a bowl of lightly salted cold water and refrigerate overnight to remove the blood.

In a large heavy casserole, place the short ribs, beef broth, dried mushrooms, black peppercorns and bay leaf. Bring to a boil and simmer, covered, for 1 hour. Cool for 1 hour. Remove the meat, mushrooms, peppercorns and bay leaf; discard the peppercorns and bay leaf and allow the beef, mushrooms and broth to cool. Refrigerate overnight.

The next day   Remove and discard the solid layer of congealed fat from the top of the broth. Remove the meat from the bones and add the bones to the broth. Bring the broth to a boil and boil until reduced to 6 cups. Discard the bones, and set the broth aside.

Meanwhile, cut the meat into large cubes. Chop the porcini into ½-inch pieces.

In a large heavy casserole, melt the butter. Add the onions, sprinkle with the pinch of sugar and sauté until lightly browned. Add the sliced fresh mushrooms and cook, covered, for 3 minutes. Uncover and continue cooking until the mushrooms are lightly browned, about 5 minutes. Add the barley and sauté for 2 to 3 minutes, stirring often. Add the reserved porcini mushrooms, beef cubes and 6 cups beef broth. Cover tightly and simmer for 1 hour or until all the broth has been absorbed and the barley is tender; if necessary, add a little water and continue cooking until tender. (You may also bake the casserole in a preheated 350°F. oven for 60 to 70 minutes.)

Meanwhile drain the marrow and cut it into ½-inch slices. Bring a medium saucepan of lightly salted water just to a simmer. Add the marrow and poach it just until translucent and soft, about 3 minutes. Be careful not to overcook the marrow or it will melt completely. Drain and set aside.

When ready to serve, top the beef and barley with the nublets of poached marrow and sprinkle with the minced parsley.

UNDERSTANDING   Barley generally needs double its volume in water or broth to hydrate; however if it has been sitting in your pantry for several years, it will require more water. I discovered some barley hidden in the back of my pantry, that is over 10 years old and requires 3½ times the volume of liquid to barley.

Butter-Roasted Parsnips

I first came to appreciate the special sweetness of winter parsnips when I was at college in Burlington, Vermont. Somehow parsnips don't have the same tenderness or sweet flavor except in cold weather so I wait until winter through early spring to make this simple, homey recipe. It's a lovely accompaniment to any flavorful meat, and perfect with the Beef and Barley Soupless to round out the St. Patrick's Day Dinner.

Serves: 6 to 8

Preheat the oven to: 350°F.
Roasting time: 60 to 70 minutes

INGREDIENTS	MEASURE volume	WEIGHT ounces/pounds	grams
parsnips, peeled	•	2 pounds	908 grams
chicken broth (preferably College Inn)*	1½ liquid cups	•	•
unsalted butter, cut into 8 pieces	2 tablespoons	1 ounce	28 grams
pepper, freshly ground	a few grindings	•	•

*Or use 2 cubes Glace de Volaille (page 256) dissolved in 1½ cups boiling water with ¾ teaspoon salt.

Cut off the root ends from the parsnips.

In a large heavy skillet, preferably cast iron, combine the broth and parsnips and dot with the butter. Grind the pepper over the parsnips. Roast for 30 minutes. Use tongs to turn the parsnips over, and continue roasting until the broth has evaporated and the parsnips are golden brown and tender when pierced with a skewer, 30 to 40 minutes longer. Remove any smaller ones as they are done and keep them covered in a serving dish.

Spring

Easter Dinner

Roast Leg of Lamb
Pan-Roasted Whole Potatoes with Rosemary and Lemon
Flageolets
Crème Brulée

Spring Luncheon

Vichyssoise
Crème Fraîche
Plain Wonderful White Bread

◆ ❖ ◆ ❖

Passover

Perfect Roast Chicken Stuffed with Spicy Matzoh Brei
Spicy Matzoh Brei
Carrots and Mushroom Sauté
Lavender Ice Cream

Mother's Day

Szechuan Swordfish Brochettes
Sesame Brown Rice
White Chocolate and Raspberry Nostalgia Cake
Pistachio Pavés

June Wedding Shower

Strawberry Champagne Punch

Roast Leg of Lamb

Lamb is Elliott's and my favorite meat and as we both particularly enjoy the flavor of leg of lamb, it is a dish I prepare several times during the year. When it's just the two of us, I make the shank half and serve the leftovers cold and thinly sliced, with crimson currant jelly that I make during the summer with currants from my one-hundred-year-old currant bush. I always used to reserve this jelly for glazing fruit for tarts, but when I had the pleasure of dining at the home of my British editor, Kyle Cathie, in London, she served her homemade currant jelly with grilled lamb chops and I immediately adopted the custom.

I always try to get the roast into the oven at least fifteen minutes before Elliott comes in the door because I know the pleasure he experiences stepping off the elevator and smelling the roasting lamb, rosemary and garlic, both hoping and knowing that it's coming from our apartment.

A whole leg of lamb is perfect for Easter dinner. It feeds a crowd and because of its shape, the same roast yields a full range of doneness, from rare to well-done—something to please everyone.

Although it is considered odd to serve two starches at the same meal, I am always torn between the two classics—roasted potatoes and flageolets—so I usually give in and serve them both.

Serves: 8 to 10

Two and a half to 4 hours before roasting, remove the roast from the refrigerator.

Preheat the oven to: 400°F.
Roasting time: about 2 hours
Internal temperature (middle): 130°F. to 135°F.

EQUIPMENT:
large roasting pan

INGREDIENTS	MEASURE volume	WEIGHT ounces/pounds	grams/kilograms
1 leg of lamb (ask butcher not to cut it at the shank joint)	.	7 pounds	3 kilograms, 175 grams
fresh rosemary leaves, divided	2 tablespoons	.	.
2 cloves garlic, peeled and cut into 10 thick slivers	.	0.5 ounce	14 grams
all-purpose flour	1 tablespoon	.	.
salt	2 teaspoons	0.5 ounce	13 grams
pepper, freshly ground	a few grindings	.	.

At least 15 minutes before roasting, preheat the oven to 400°F.

With a small, sharp knife, make ten ¾-inch-deep slits at even intervals in the roast. Reserve 1 teaspoon of the rosemary and insert the remaining rosemary and the garlic slivers into the slits in the lamb. Rub the top of the roast with the flour, sprinkle with the salt and pepper and sprinkle with the reserved rosemary. Roast for 10 minutes. Decrease the heat to 325°F. and continue roasting for about 1 hour and 45 minutes or until an instant-read thermometer, inserted toward the center of the roast, reads 130°F. to

135°F. for medium rare. The temperature will rise 5 degrees while standing. I find 135°F to 140°F. perfect as the final temperature.

Transfer the roast to a carving board and cover loosely with foil. Allow to stand for at least 20 minutes before carving to reabsorb its juices.

While the roast is resting, use the drippings in the roasting pan to prepare the Pan-Roasted Whole Potatoes with Rosemary and Lemon (page 71) and the Flageolets (page 72).

Use a long sharp knife held almost parallel to the bone to carve long, thin bias slices from the shank portion and from each side of the upper portion. Make sure that each serving contains a piece from each section so your guests may enjoy the variance in texture and flavor. Pass the meat juices in a gravy boat.

NOTE: Jane Freiman, in her wonderful book *Dinner Party* (Harper & Row), has instructions for home-aging supermarket meat. I find that prime lamb is more tender but slightly less flavorful than home-aged supermarket choice grade. If you buy prime meat, part of what you are paying for is its aging by the butcher. If you buy supermarket choice-grade meat, it benefits greatly from the following 3- to 5-day aging process: Place a roasting pan a little larger than the roast on a refrigerator shelf. Line it with a few paper towels to absorb the drippings. Unwrap the roast and place it, fat side up, on a shelf directly above the pan. Allow it to sit for 3 to 5 days. Trim off any dried areas. From a 7-pound roast you will lose about 1 pound in trimmings and liquid (about 15 percent of the weight) but you will gain greatly in flavor.

Pan-Roasted Whole Potatoes with Rosemary and Lemon

Serves: 8

Preheat the oven to: 400°F.
Roasting time: 10 to 15 minutes

T his recipe came to me over thirty years ago as a friend's childhood reminiscence. But she told it with such desire and nostalgia I soon felt as if it were my own. Betty Stark was raised by a very wealthy, very strict New England grandmother. Only once a year, on her birthday, was she allowed to chose whatever she wanted to eat. And every year it was the same favorites: leg of lamb, these roasted potatoes, string beans, and crisp meringues with vanilla ice cream and strawberries. I prepared this classic menu for years until I started substituting the flageolets for the string beans and the crème brulée for the meringues. But I have never been tempted to substitute anything for these tangy crispy potatoes.

INGREDIENTS	MEASURE *volume*	WEIGHT *ounces/pounds*	WEIGHT *grams/kilograms*
24 1½-inch potatoes	·	2¼ pounds	1 kilogram, 20 grams
rendered fat reserved from Roast Leg of Lamb (page 69)	2 tablespoons	·	·
fresh rosemary leaves, chopped*	1 tablespoon	·	·
lemon juice, freshly squeezed	2 teaspoons	·	·
salt	½ teaspoon	·	·
pepper, freshly ground	a few grindings	·	·

*Or 1 teaspoon dried rosemary.

Place a vegetable steamer in a large saucepan. Add water to come slightly under the bottom of the steamer and bring it to a boil. Place the potatoes in the steamer insert, cover the pan tightly, lower the heat and steam the potatoes until just barely tender, 15 to 20 minutes. A skewer or the tip of a sharp knife inserted into the potato should go in with a little resistance and the potatoes should still be firm. With tongs, remove the potatoes to a bowl of iced water and set them aside until cooled, about 5 minutes. Drain the potatoes well. Peel and set them aside on paper towels or refrigerate until ready to brown them.

When the roast leg of lamb is done, spoon 2 tablespoons of the roasting fat into a large heavy frying pan (preferably cast iron) that will hold the potatoes in one layer. Heat the pan over medium heat until the fat is bubbling hot. Add the potatoes, and sprinkle with the rosemary, lemon juice, salt and pepper. Sauté for 10 to 15 minutes, shaking the pan occasionally to brown the potatoes on all sides, until they are golden brown.

After purchasing potatoes, keep them in a cool place, but not in the refrigerator as they would develop an undesirable "sweet" flavor.

UNDERSTANDING

Roasting steamed potatoes in the oven more often than not overcooks the potatoes by the time the exterior is golden brown. Roasting them without precooking with moist heat results in a dry texture. Sautéing the potatoes offers the most control over the texture and degree of doneness.

Flageolets

Serves: 6 to 8

Preheat the oven to: 400°F.
Roasting time: 10 minutes

Most flageolets must be soaked before cooking, either overnight or with the quick-soaking method (see Pointers for Success).

These small, tender, celadon-hued French beans, the traditional accompaniment to lamb, are my favorite of all beans. They are not at all pasty and, when properly cooked, have a nice bite. It was a French chef from Limousin who taught me the simple but terrific technique of sautéing the cooked beans in the roasting pan of meat drippings. Michel held some strangely inventive theories about food. Perhaps the funniest of all was his explanation for why there are so many fat chefs: "Because they eat with their hands. There are large pores in the fingertips that absorb the food, which they handle all day, directly into the blood stream." Well, I was stupid enough to have asked! But Michel, who humbly insisted that he was not a chef but merely a cook, was a truly good one, and when I disregarded most of his old cuisinier's tales, I found some treasured trucs like this one.

INGREDIENTS	MEASURE		WEIGHT	
	volume		ounces	grams
dried flageolets*	2⅓ cups		16 ounces	454 grams
2 large garlic cloves, coarsely chopped		•	•	12 grams
2 to 3 fresh thyme sprigs†		•	•	•
salt	½ teaspoon, or more to taste		•	•
black pepper, freshly ground	½ teaspoon		•	•
cayenne pepper	a sprinkling		•	•

*These French beans are available in specialty food stores such as Dean & DeLuca.
†Or ½ teaspoon dried thyme.

Wash the flageolets and pick out and discard any stones or shriveled beans. Place them in a medium saucepan and add unsalted water to cover by 2 inches.

When ready to cook, drain off the water, rinse the flageolets and add fresh unsalted water to cover by 2 inches. Add the garlic and thyme sprigs and bring to a boil. Reduce the heat to low and simmer, partially covered until the beans are just tender but still firm, about 20 to 30 minutes. (If the beans are old they can take as long as 75 minutes.) Add more water if necessary so that the flageolets are always covered. Test a bean by cutting it in half to see if it is cooked through.

Remove the beans from the heat, add the ½ teaspoon of salt, and set aside in the saucepan. (Or drain off most of the liquid from the flageolets and cover them with plastic wrap, preferably Saran brand, to prevent cracking.)

When the leg of lamb is done and resting on a carving board, raise the oven temperature to 400°F. Drain off all but about 3 tablespoons of fat and drippings from the roasting pan (reserving 2 tablespoons for the Pan-Roasted Whole Potatoes if desired). Drain the flageolets, and discard the thyme sprigs. Add the flageolets and garlic to the roasting pan and stir to coat them well. Sprinkle with the black pepper, cayenne and salt to taste. Place the pan in the oven, and roast the flageolets for 10 minutes, stirring once or twice.

NOTE: If desired, 3 tablespoons of olive oil can be used in place of the lamb fat. If preparing flageolets without the lamb, a cube of Glace de Viande (page 253) or a bouillon cube dissolved in a little boiling water can replace the meat juices. Omit the salt if using the bouillon cube.

TO SOAK 8 HOURS OR OVERNIGHT:
Place the flageolets in a cool spot. If soaking overnight, refrigerate to keep the beans from fermenting.

TO QUICK-SOAK:
Bring the beans to a boil and boil for 2 minutes. Cover, remove from the heat and allow to sit for 1 hour.

POINTERS FOR SUCCESS

- Flageolets from a current crop (the information will be written on the package) require no soaking but should be brought to a boil in a large saucepan of water and drained, to avoid flatulence. If dried flageolets are over a year old they may be incapable of rehydration. The older they are, the longer they take to get tender, which means that it is necessary to give a range of time for doneness. It's best to start checking at the minimum time and continuing cooking as necessary.
- After 4 hours of soaking, beans are about 70 percent hydrated. They do not hydrate fully until about 8 hours. With the quick-soaking technique they hydrate almost as fully as after 8 hours.
- Flageolets, like other legumes, will never soften if they are salted during the cooking process. Once the flageolets are fully cooked, adding salt to the water keeps their outer shell from absorbing more water, thereby preventing them from further softening.
- For the most evenly tender but firm flageolets, overnight soaking is best, although the quick-soak method works almost as well.
- To keep the outer shell of the bean from splitting, the cooking water should be just barely simmering.
- Allowing the flageolets to cool in the cooking water keeps them moist and prevents splitting.
- The best way to drain the flageolets is with a slotted spoon so that they remain whole and uncrushed.

Crème Brulée

It has been said that the ideal test for the skills of a chef is the simple omelet, because it is the simple things that are the hardest to accomplish perfectly. I would say that the ideal test for a pastry chef is the simple crème brulée. For me, perfect crème brulée is cool and silky smooth, just firm enough to hold its shape when spooned, with a glass-hard thin, even, dark caramel topping.

It is rarely prepared exactly this way, I suspect because many restaurant chefs are too impatient to bake the custard slowly for one and a half hours or to pour on caramel cooked separately instead of melting sugar on top of the custard under the broiler or with a propane torch. But these two techniques are the secret of perfect crème brulée.

Before tiramisù *became the ne plus ultra trendy dessert, and crème brulée was still in the Number 1 position, all sorts of variations appeared. I disliked them all. I thought that one could not possibly improve on the sublime perfection of a perfectly made crème brulée–until I tasted Jim Dodge's version, containing four ripe raspberries that miraculously didn't seem to cook in the custard.*

My recipe for crème brulée was inspired by the first truly great one I ever experienced, at the Hayes Street Café in San Francisco. This part of the country is blessed with an exceptionally warm and generous food community I have always enjoyed and valued. No sooner did I beg for the recipe than it appeared at our table. The only changes I made were the addition of vanilla beans for the glorious flavor and subtle, barely perceptible crunch, and the method of caramelizing the topping. The restaurant's balance of sugar, cream and yolk and slow, even method of baking could not be improved upon.

Serves: 8

Up to 8 hours before serving,* make the caramel topping.

Unpreheated oven: 250°F.
Cooking time: 1½ hours
Chilling time: at least 1 hour

EQUIPMENT:
eight 5- to 6-ounce ramekins (about 3¼ inches by 1½ inches); roasting pan or baking pan large enough to hold the ramekins and at least 2 inches deep, lined with parchment

KEEPS: 2 days.

---

*If you have a high-humidity refrigerator such as a Traulsen or you live in a humid location, do not make the caramel until shortly before serving. Because the caramel heats up the crème, however, the crème then needs to be chilled for at least 1 hour before serving.

INGREDIENTS	MEASURE	WEIGHT	
	volume	*ounces*	*grams*
heavy cream	3 liquid cups	•	•
¼ Tahitian vanilla bean,* split lengthwise	•	•	•
½ Madagascar vanilla bean, split lengthwise	•	•	•
8 large egg yolks	scant ⅔ cup	1.25 ounces	150 grams
sugar	⅓ cup	2.33 ounces	67 grams
pure vanilla extract	¾ teaspoon	•	•
OPTIONAL: 32 raspberries	1 scant cup	3.5 ounces	100 grams
Caramel			
sugar	½ cup	3.5 ounces	100 grams
water	3 tablespoons	•	•

*Available in specialty food stores such as Dean & DeLuca. Or use a total of 1 Madagascar vanilla bean. If vanilla beans are unavailable, increase the vanilla extract to 1½ teaspoons.

Place the ramekins on top of the parchment in the roasting pan.

In a small saucepan, heat the cream and vanilla beans just until very hot. Do not boil. (Or heat in a heatproof glass measure in a microwave on high power.)

In a medium bowl, with a wooden spoon, stir together the yolks and sugar until blended. Remove the vanilla beans from the cream (do not discard) and gradually stir the heavy cream into the egg mixture; stir slowly to prevent bubbles. Strain the mixture through a fine strainer into a 4-cup glass measure or bowl, preferably with a spout.

With a sharp knife, scrape the vanilla seeds into the mixture. Stir gently to separate the seeds. (Fingertips work best for this.) Stir in the vanilla extract.

If adding the raspberries, place 4 in each ramekin. Pour the custard into the ramekins, and pour enough hot tap water around the ramekins to come halfway up their sides.

Set the pan in the oven and turn it on to 250°F. Bake, without opening the oven door, for 1½ hours. (A knife inserted into the center will not come out clean.)

Remove the ramekins from the hot water bath and allow them to cool.

Cover each ramekin tightly with plastic wrap (preferably Saran brand), being careful not to touch the surface of the custard with it. Refrigerate for at least 8 hours or up to 2 days. If liquid should form on the surface of the custards, blot it gently with paper towels.

Have ready a heatproof glass measure, sprayed with nonstick vegetable spray or greased, near the range.

In a heavy saucepan (preferably with a nonstick lining), stir together the sugar and water until the sugar is completely moistened. Heat, stirring constantly, until the sugar dissolves and the syrup is bubbling. Stop stirring completely and allow the syrup to boil undisturbed until it turns a deep amber (340° to 370°F. on a candy thermometer). Immediately remove from the heat and pour into the glass measure to stop the cooking.

Quickly pour a very thin layer of caramel (½ tablespoon) onto each custard. Rotate each ramekin quickly to spread the caramel evenly. It will bubble up but quickly settle into a glass-smooth glaze. If the caramel should become too thick to pour in thin layers, you can place it in the microwave for a few seconds on high power to reliquify it.

Refrigerate the crème brulée, uncovered, for at least 1 hour or up to 8 hours.

POINTERS FOR SUCCESS

- To prevent crystallization when making the caramel, do not allow any sugar crystals to get on the sides of the pan and be sure to moisten all the sugar with the water. Stop stirring entirely as soon as the syrup comes to a boil. If using a thermometer, be sure to rinse it and dry it if removing and then reinserting in the syrup. If any sugar remains on the thermometer, it will cause crystallization.
- If you have a problem with the caramel, such as making it too dark or pouring it too thick, simply allow it to cool and harden on the custard. Then lift it off and start again. (It will lift off in one piece, leaving the crème behind.)

UNDERSTANDING

The parchment in the water bath keeps the bottoms of the ramekins from coming into direct contact with the hot pan. The water bath equalizes the temperature and creates a moist environment.

The cream is heated to extract the maximum flavor from the vanilla beans. If not using the vanilla beans, you can add the cream without heating it, but bake the custards for 2 hours instead of 1½.

The higher the temperature of the caramel, the darker the color and the deeper the flavor. Too high, however, and there will be a burned flavor. If you do not have an accurate thermometer,* or it is not immersed adequately, it may read 370°F. when the temperature is actually much higher and the caramel may burn. Alternatively, you can gauge the color by sight, either using a white porcelain spoon to stir or placing a drop of the caramel on a white plate, but you must rinse off any utensil that has caramel or sugar syrup on it before reinserting it into the caramel or it will crystallize.

*The Cordon Rose candy thermometer is available through Dean & DeLuca (800-227-7714).

Vichyssoise
(Vicheeswahz)

F or years this cold creamed leek and potato soup created by Louis Diat, a famous French chef from the old Hotel Ritz Carlton in New York City, was a favorite spring and summertime first course or light supper. Gradually, as my taste sensibilities changed, I no longer felt comfortable about supping on so much cream. But then I eventually started longing for vichyssoise again and discovered that the richness of the flavor comes more from the potatoes and a good-quality chicken stock than from the cream. I usually stay away from "light" recipes because I prefer the moderation of smaller portions to flavor compromises, but here is one instance where light is appropriate. I use milk in place of the heavy cream and a final lacing of crème fraîche, topped with a sprinkling or constellation of freshly chopped chives. Together with the freshly baked bread, still warm from the oven, it provides a lovely menu with which to herald the spring.

Serves: 6
(makes about 8 cups)

Chilling time: at least 4 hours

KEEPS: 24 hours.

INGREDIENTS	MEASURE volume	WEIGHT ounces	grams
leeks (white part only), thinly sliced	4 cups	11.5 ounces	326 grams
unsalted butter	2 tablespoons	1 ounce	28 grams
½ large onion, thinly sliced	1⅓ cups	5 ounces	142 grams
2 large baking potatoes, such as Yukon gold or russets, peeled and thinly sliced	4 heaping cups	24 ounces	680 grams
cold water*	1½ liquid cups	·	·
low-sodium chicken stock†	2 liquid cups	·	·
salt	½ teaspoon	·	·
milk	2 liquid cups	·	·
Crème Frâiche (page 80) or heavy cream	½ cup	·	·
fresh chives, chopped, for garnish	2 tablespoons	0.25 ounce	7 grams

*Soak the potatoes in the cold water while you prepare the other ingredients.

†Homemade Glace de Volaille (page 256) makes the most delicious soup of all. Use 4 cubes, dissolved in 2 cups boiling water, and use a total of 1½ teaspoons salt.

Place the sliced leeks in a large bowl of cold water and stir well with your fingers to release any sand or dirt. Using a skimmer or slotted spoon, lift the cleaned leeks from the water, leaving the sand in the bottom of the bowl. Rinse well in a colander.

In a large heavy pot (at least 5 quarts' capacity), melt the butter. Sauté the leeks and onion until wilted. Add the potatoes along with the soaking water, the chicken stock and salt. Bring to a boil and simmer, covered, for 40 minutes or until the potatoes are very tender when pierced with a skewer or fork.

Purée the potato mixture in a food processor, in batches if necessary, and transfer to a large bowl (at least 3 quarts capacity). Add the milk and stir until well blended. Refrigerate until cold, at least 4 hours, or overnight. Stir in the crème fraîche until only small blobs remain. (This makes an attractive and delicious décor.) Sprinkle with the fresh chives.

POINTERS FOR SUCCESS

• After purchasing potatoes, keep them in a cool place, but not in the refrigerator as they would develop an undesirable "sweet" flavor.

Crème Fraîche

Makes: 1 cup

Thickening time: at least 12 hours; up to 36 hours

KEEPS: 3 weeks refrigerated. Crème fraîche continues to thicken on chilling.

This recipe produces a crème fraîche reminiscent of the enchanting varieties found in France. I prefer it to any of the commercial products available here. The proportion of one tablespoon of buttermilk to one cup of heavy cream results in a fresh, creamy taste with a gentle tang. Crème fraîche is wonderful for finishing sauces because, unlike sour cream, it does not curdle with heat.

INGREDIENTS	MEASURE *volume*	WEIGHT *ounces*	*grams*
heavy cream	1 liquid cup	.	.
buttermilk	1 tablespoon	.	.

Combine the cream and buttermilk in a jar with a tight-fitting lid and place it in a warm spot, such as the top of the refrigerator or near the stove. Allow to sit undisturbed for 12 to 14 hours or until thickened but still pourable. (Ultrapasteurized cream may take as long as 36 hours to thicken.)

Plain Wonderful White Bread

There is a satisfaction derived from the act of baking bread that I get from no other kitchen activity. Not for me a bread machine that would rob me of the pleasure of feeling the dough come to life under my hands. Just knowing that the bread dough is rising in a cool spot in the back room fills me with unspeakable contentment. Often, when I know I will be forced to sit all day proofing a manuscript, I reward myself by making bread so that I will have an excuse to get up every hour to check its progress and punch it down.

Perhaps the most exciting part about making bread is that the yeast is a dormant living organism that you bring to life, feeding it so that it will grow and expand, providing texture and flavor to the bread. It also seems utterly amazing that just flour, water, yeast and a bit of sugar and salt, judiciously proportioned, can be transformed into the most perfect loaf of bread.

Many years ago, when I was a freshman at the University of Vermont, I met a bearded backwoodsman the students called "Bert the beatnik." As he vigorously stirred his sourdough starter, he informed me that "a woman should be able to bake bread." I received this edict as a great fundamental truth and it aroused in me the feeling that I would never really be a woman if I hadn't at least made one loaf of bread. Seventeen is an age when girls ask each other how they will know when they are truly women. Some thought it would be when they lost their virginity, but I knew differently. Bread would do it. This was the early Sixties. Before hippies, before Vietnam, even before Julia Child.

I could make a meal of bread alone, fresh from the oven and spread with sweet butter, but who can resist the classic combination of bread and soup. Apart from being a delicious duo, it feels so basic and nourishing.

Makes: one 3½-pound round loaf, 6½ inches high by 10½ inches in diameter (5½ inches by 10 inches if baked in La Cloche)

Sponge time: at least 4 hours; up to overnight **Preheat the oven to: 450°F. Baking time: 1 hour 20 minutes**

INGREDIENTS	MEASURE	WEIGHT	
	volume	*ounces/pounds*	*grams/kilograms*
fresh yeast* *or* dry yeast (*not* rapid-rise)	1 packed tablespoon 2½ teaspoons	0.75 ounce 0.25 ounce	17 grams 6.75 grams
sugar, divided	1 tablespoon	0.50 ounce	12.5 grams
water, divided	3 liquid cups	.	.
bread flour, divided	7 cups (dip and sweep method) + about ½ cup for kneading	2 pounds, 6.5 ounces	1 kilogram, 99 grams
whole wheat flour	½ cup (dip and sweep method)	2.5 ounces	75 grams
salt	4 teaspoons	1 ounce	26 grams
cornmeal	about 2 teaspoons	.	.

*Fresh yeast causes dough to rise faster.

Proof the yeast: Crumble the fresh yeast into a small bowl and add ½ teaspoon of the sugar and ¼ cup of the water, warmed to a tepid 100°F; if using dry yeast, increase the temperature slightly to 110°F. Stir until the yeast is dissolved. Set aside in a draft-free spot for 10 to 20 minutes. The mixture should be full of bubbles; if not, the yeast is too old to be useful. Discard it and start again with fresh yeast.

Make the sponge: In a large bowl, place the yeast mixture, 3 cups of the bread flour, the remaining 2½ teaspoons of sugar and the remaining 2¾ cups of water. Whisk until very smooth, about 100 strokes. Cover with plastic wrap (preferably Saran brand) and allow to stand for 4 to 5 hours at room temperature or refrigerate overnight.

In a medium bowl, combine the remaining 4 cups of bread flour, the whole wheat flour and salt. Stir into the sponge and mix just until smooth. Mix in enough flour so that the dough is not sticky, then scrape the dough onto a lightly floured counter. Knead the dough for about 10 minutes. It should be very elastic, smooth and cool to the touch and jump back when pressed with a fingertip. If the dough is too difficult to knead in one batch, divide it in half and knead one portion at a time until smooth, keeping the remaining dough covered. Then knead the two portions together until combined. (You will have about 4 pounds of dough.)

Form the dough into a ball and place it in a large oiled bowl. Turn to coat, tightly cover with plastic wrap or a damp towel and let rise for 1 hour or until doubled in bulk (it can take as long as 2 hours if the room is cold). Punch down the dough and knead it lightly. Form the dough into a ball and allow to rise a second time in the oiled bowl, covered with plastic wrap or a towel.* (The second rising takes about 30 to 45 minutes.)

Sprinkle the La Cloche bottom or a rimless baking sheet with about 2 teaspoons of cornmeal (or enough to cover lightly).

Roll the dough into a 7-inch ball and place it on the La Cloche bottom or the baking sheet. Cover with a large inverted bowl or plastic wrap sprayed with nonstick vegetable shortening. Let the dough rise until doubled in bulk, about 1 hour to 1 hour and 15 minutes.

At least 30 minutes before baking, soak the top of La Cloche if using it. Preheat the oven to 450°F., and preheat a baking stone or cookie sheet.

Slash the top of the dough with a sharp knife or razor blade. (I like to make two long slashes about 6 inches apart in one direction and a second two long perpendicular slashes through them.) Place the soaked La Cloche top on top of the base if using and place on the preheated baking stone or sheet, or slide the dough directly onto the stone.

Bake for 15 minutes, then lower the temperature to 400°F. and continue baking for 65 minutes or until the bread is golden brown and sounds hollow when rapped. (The baked bread will stay warm for 2 hours.)

NOTE: Do not use parchment on the bottom of the La Cloche unless it is greased or the bread will stick to it.

First thing in the morning or the night before

---

*If time allows, give the bread three risings before the final shaping.

Electric Mixer Method

To make the sponge, place the ingredients in the mixer bowl of a 5-quart or larger heavy-duty mixer and, with the whisk attachment, beat for about 1 minute or until very smooth. Remove the whisk attachment, cover the bowl tightly with plastic wrap and let stand at room temperature for 4 to 5 hours or refrigerate overnight.

Using the dough hook paddle attachment, gradually add the remaining 4 cups of bread flour mixed with the whole wheat flour and salt. Mix just until smooth. Add additional flour, if necessary, and mix to form a soft rough dough. Change to the dough hook, scraping off any dough that clings to the paddle, and mix on medium speed until the dough is smooth and elastic, about 10 minutes. After the first 3 minutes, if the dough still appears sticky and has not begun to clean the sides of the bowl, add some additional flour a few tablespoons at a time. If the dough seems dry, add water 1 tablespoon at a time. Form the dough into a ball and proceed as above.

POINTERS FOR SUCCESS

- Store the baked bread at room temperature or freeze and defrost to room temperature or heat it. Do not refrigerate without warming it as the starch in the flour crystallizes when cold.
- Be sure to use bread flour. The larger amount of gluten-forming protein gives a significantly higher rise.

UNDERSTANDING

The small amount of whole wheat flour adds flavor without coarsening the texture.

Preheating the baking stone or sheet causes the dough to hold its shape and start to rise immediately when placed directly on it in the oven. This technique results in the highest rise.

Perfect Roast Chicken Stuffed with Spicy Matzoh Brei

Roast chicken, simple and familiar as it is, remains one of the most perfectly pleasing meals. When stuffed with a spicy matzoh brei, it is elevated to special occasion status, appropriate for the grandeur of a seder. For me, a chicken should be aromatic with herbs, moist and juicy with crisp golden skin. And roasting the chicken according to the special method described here produces an exceptionally moist breast and crisp skin.

I am a great believer in free-range chickens as they have far less fat and far more flavor. In the summer I get all my chickens from my friends Gus and Barbara at Pine Hill Farms in Hope, New Jersey. Now these chickens are as free range as you can get. I have seen Gus personally chase the chickens around the yard to make sure that they get enough exercise.

Passover has always been special for me, partly because I was born at that time of year so I felt, when I was growing up, that it was my personal holiday. But what is most special to me is the two nights of seders, not only the most lavish food-related ceremonies in all of Jewish tradition, but also a deeply meaningful celebration of survival and freedom from oppression. The annual retelling of escape of the Jews from Pharaoh's oppression, interwoven with the ritual communal consumption of symbolic ingredients (as pictured on the table), such as the horseradish to represent the bitterness of oppression and cinnamon-flavored chopped apples to represent the mortar used to build the pyramids, makes for an uplifting reaffirmation of life.

Memories of Passovers past include those I spent with my grandmother at a hotel in upstate New York. My parents did not keep the kosher tradition, and although my mother's mother, who lived with us, was Orthodox, she found it more convenient to go to a resort for a week rather than go through all the elaborate preparations required to make a house ready for Passover. Until I went to college, she always took me along. At the Empire Hotel, most families had their own table at dinner but because my grandmother and I were alone, we were seated with other people who did not come with large families. I'll always remember the sound of manishtana, *the four questions, coming from all corners of the room, being chanted at different intervals and with different tunes depending on the origins of the family and how quickly they progressed through the seder. As a child, it always seemed like the recounting of the story would never end and we would never get to eat.*

Since I married Elliott, we have always had the pleasure of seders spent with his large family, in which there are at least three men capable of correctly conducting a seder. Although tradition has yielded to a modified seder, in deference to the children's impatience, Elliott's brother Sam still takes great pride in the schmere *matzoh made by hand in the traditional method and presented to him each year by an Orthodox rabbi. Our sister-in-law Betty makes the best matzoh balls and gefilte fish, and I always bring the dessert.*

Serves: 3 to 4

For the crispiest skin, place the chicken on a rack, preferably V-shaped, in a pan to catch any juices and allow it to sit, uncovered, in the refrigerator overnight.

One hour before roasting, remove the chicken from the refrigerator.

Preheat the oven to: 425°F. Baking time: 60 to 75 minutes Internal temperature (thigh): 175°F. to 180°F.

This year, I plan to prepare my new recipe for matzoh-brei-stuffed chicken later in the Passover week. But we both enjoy it so much, I doubt if I will wait until the following Passover to make it again!

INGREDIENTS	MEASURE		WEIGHT	
	volume		*ounces/pounds*	*grams/kilograms*
1 chicken (preferably free range)			3.5 to 4 pounds	1 kilogram, 588 grams to 1 kilogram, 814 grams
1 large clove garlic, cut in half and peeled				6 grams
goose fat or unsalted butter	1 tablespoon		0.5 ounce	14 grams
salt	½ teaspoon			
black pepper, freshly ground	a few grindings			
cayenne pepper	a pinch or two			
Spicy Matzoh Brei (page 88)				
water	1 liquid cup			

At least 15 minutes before roasting, preheat the oven to 425°F.

Rub the chicken all over with the cut garlic and then with the goose fat or butter. Sprinkle the chicken inside and out with the salt, pepper and cayenne pepper. Spoon the stuffing into the chicken and secure the opening with a skewer. Fold the wing tips back under the back. Leave the chicken untrussed* and return it, breast side up, to the rack in the pan.

Roast the chicken for 45 minutes, basting every 15 minutes with the pan drippings. (Tilt the pan so that the drippings collect in one corner. Keep the oven door open as briefly as possible when basting. Do not include basting time in the 45-minute roasting time.)

Turn the chicken breast side down and continue roasting until done, 15 minutes longer for a 3½-pound bird, 30 minutes for a 4-pound bird. An instant-read thermometer inserted in the thigh, not touching the bone, should read 175°F. to 180°F.

Let the chicken rest on the rack for 15 to 30 minutes before carving so that it can reabsorb its juices and the skin remains crisp.

Meanwhile, skim as much fat as possible from the juices in the roasting pan. Add the water to the pan, and bring to a boil on top of the range, stirring to release the browned bits from the bottom of the pan. Boil, stirring constantly, until reduced to ⅓ cup. Pour into a gravy boat and serve with the chicken.

*Untrussed, chicken browns more evenly.

Spicy Matzoh Brei

**Makes: enough stuffing for
one 4-pound chicken
(serves: 2 as a brunch dish)**

Forget everything you have ever heard about matzoh brei and try this incredible recipe. It makes both an excellent brunch dish and a uniquely delicious golden brown stuffing for poultry. The texture is fluffy, silken and reminiscent of the lightest possible dumpling. Yet it is very easy to prepare.

Matzoh brei is a traditional Jewish fried matzoh and egg breakfast specialty prepared during Passover when leavened bread is forbidden. To my taste, the authentic version is pretty bland, one of those things that is an acquired taste. But this version is so enticing you don't have to have grown up eating it to enjoy it. The day I first made it, my friend Judith Blahnik was there, and she suggested using it to stuff a chicken. I will be forever grateful.

INGREDIENTS	MEASURE volume	WEIGHT ounces	grams
matzoh	1½ squares	1.7 ounces	50 grams
unsalted butter	1 tablespoon	0.5 ounce	14 grams
½ medium onion, chopped	¾ cup	3 ounces	85 grams
½ fresh jalapeño pepper, minced	•	0.25 ounce	7 grams
sugar	a pinch	•	•
1 medium clove garlic, minced	1 teaspoon	•	3.5 grams
1 large egg	3 tablespoons	1.75 ounces 50 grams (weighed without shell)	
water	1 tablespoon	•	•
salt	⅛ teaspoon	•	•
pepper, freshly ground	a grinding	•	•

Into a medium bowl, break the matzoh into pieces about 1 inch in size. Cover the matzoh with warm water and allow it to sit for a few minutes until it is soft. Drain the water, gently pressing out any excess from the matzoh.

In a medium skillet over medium heat, melt the butter. Add the onion and jalapeño pepper, sprinkle with the pinch of sugar and sauté, stirring occasionally, until the onion begins to brown. Add the garlic and sauté for

1 minute or until it softens. Add the matzoh and fry for about 3 minutes to dry it slightly.

Meanwhile, in a medium bowl, beat the egg with the water, salt and pepper.

To use as a stuffing, spoon the matzoh mixture into the egg mixture and stir until incorporated. To use as a brunch dish, add the egg mixture to the matzoh in the frying pan and fry on low heat, stirring often, until the eggs are set. Remove at once to a serving dish.

Carrots and Mushroom Sauté

Serves: 4

There is something wonderfully synergistic that occurs between the sweetness of carrots and the earthiness of mushrooms when they are browned slowly together in butter. I particularly love how this recipe came about. An old friend, Susan Doris, invented it when she was the mother of two active young boys.

Susan had a theory, dear to my heart, that the best way to keep one's husband interested in coming home on time every night is to cook something wonderful for dinner. In fact, she swore by it. So even though her boys kept her frantically busy, and funds were tight, she always managed to produce tempting dishes.

One night, while her mushrooms were sautéing and her carrots had just finished boiling, Susan found she needed a saucepan to warm a bottle of milk for the baby. Lacking another pan, she drained the carrots and dumped them into the mushrooms. She heated the bottle and then went to feed the baby, forgetting to turn off the heat under the frying pan. After about thirty minutes, when she went back to the stove, she found that the carrots and mushrooms had turned golden brown and were absolutely delicious. A new dish was born.

Carrots are a traditional part of the seder menu because they represent the idea of "merin," to increase.

INGREDIENTS	MEASURE	WEIGHT	
	volume	ounces/pounds	grams
6 medium carrots, scraped and cut into ⅛-inch rounds	3 cups	1 pound	454 grams
unsalted butter	2 tablespoons	1 ounce	28 grams
1 medium clove garlic, smashed and peeled	·	·	5 grams
fresh mushrooms, sliced	2 cups	6.5 ounces	184 grams
salt	½ teaspoon	·	·
pepper, freshly ground	¼ teaspoon	·	·
dried thyme	½ teaspoon	·	·
sugar	a pinch	·	·

In a medium saucepan, place the carrots and add boiling water to cover them by about 1 inch. Boil the carrots, partially covered, until tender-crisp, 5 to 8 minutes. Drain and set aside, covered.

Meanwhile, in a large heavy skillet over medium-low heat, melt the butter. Add the garlic and mushrooms. Cover and cook for about 5 minutes or until the mushrooms give up their liquid. Uncover and continue cooking, stirring occasionally, until the liquid evaporates, about 3 to 5 minutes.

Add the drained cooked carrots, salt, pepper, thyme and sugar and cook over low heat for 30 minutes, stirring three or four times. Increase the heat to medium high and cook, stirring often, until the carrots and mushrooms are golden brown, about 5 minutes.

Lavender Ice Cream

I tasted this ice cream for the first time in Florence, Italy, when I was visiting my friend Faith Willinger, of Cucina Toscana (a travel and food consulting service), who has been living there for over twenty years. Faith is one of the best spontaneous cooks I know. When you arrive at her beautiful apartment in the old city, you enter right into the large modernized dining room/kitchen and are immediately enveloped in comfort and nostalgic aromas. A fire is always flaming in the countertop-height wood-burning grill, Tuscan beans may be bubbling on the stove and at least ten different appetizers are likely to be in various stages of preparation.

Faith's kitchen is the social culinary hub of Florence. Purveyors from all over the country send their products for her to sample and evaluate and people come to her from all over the world for advice on where to eat and where to stay in Italy. Faith knows that I love to try different restaurants when I travel so she always sounds guilty when suggesting that we eat "at home," but the truth is I'd rather eat at her table, with her son Max and husband Massimo and assorted impromptu guests, than in any restaurant in Italy! One visit, however, Faith did succeed in having us eat dessert at one of her favorite restaurants, and it was there that I discovered the pure perfumed magic of lavender ice cream.

I always have an eye out for special flourless desserts for Passover. This subtly elegant ice cream is an inviting finale to the seder meal.

Makes: 5 to 6 cups (depending on the ice cream maker)

KEEPS:
Ice cream has the best texture within 3 days of freezing, but with the vodka this ice cream will maintain its texture for up to a week.

INGREDIENTS	MEASURE		WEIGHT	
	volume		*ounces*	*grams*
sugar, divided	¾ cup		5.25 ounces	150 grams
lavender flowers*	1 tablespoon + 1 teaspoon		·	·
8 large egg yolks	4.5 fluid ounces		5.25 ounces	150 grams
salt	pinch		·	·
heavy cream	3 liquid cups		·	·
milk	1 liquid cup		·	·
OPTIONAL: vodka	2 tablespoons		·	·

*Fresh lavender flowers can be frozen in an airtight jar for up to a year. If using dried lavender, use only 1 teaspoon and add it to the milk and cream mixture before bringing it to the boiling point. Allow the mixture to stand off the heat for 5 minutes before adding it to the egg yolks. The lavender will be strained out when the mixture is poured through the strainer, which is preferable when using the dried flowers. A source for dried lavender is Aphrodisia, 264 Bleecker Street, New York, New York 10014 (212-989-6440). Do not use potpourri as it has been sprayed.

In a food processor with the metal blade or a blender, process ¼ cup of the sugar with the fresh lavender until the lavender is in fine particles. Transfer the mixture to a medium mixing bowl, place it near the range and suspend a fine strainer over it.

In a small heavy noncorrodible saucepan, stir together the yolks, remaining ½ cup sugar and the salt until well blended, using a wooden spoon.

In another small saucepan (or a heatproof glass measure in a microwave on high power) scald* the cream and milk. Stir a few tablespoons into the yolk mixture, then gradually add the remainder, stirring constantly.

Heat the mixture, stirring constantly to just below the boiling point (170°F. to 180°F.). Steam will begin to appear and the mixture will be slightly thicker than heavy cream; a finger run across the back of a spoon dipped in the mixture will leave a well-defined track. Immediately remove from the heat and pour into the strainer, scraping up the thickened cream on the bottom of the pan. Cool in an ice-water bath or the refrigerator until cold, at least 2 hours, or overnight.

Stir in the optional vodka. Freeze in an ice cream maker according to the manufacturer's instructions. Allow the ice cream to ripen for at least 2 hours in the freezer before serving. If it is held longer and becomes very hard, allow it to sit in the refrigerator or at room temperature until softened and creamy.

POINTERS FOR SUCCESS

- Don't use a whisk to stir the yolk/cream mixture if not using an accurate thermometer[†] because the foam makes it difficult to see when the mixture is getting close to boiling.
- Do not heat the mixture above 180°F. or it will curdle. If overheated and *slight* curdling does take place, pour instantly into a blender and blend until smooth before straining.
- Do not add more than the recommended amount of vodka or the ice cream will not freeze.

UNDERSTANDING

The custard mixture must be heated adequately (to at least 160°F.) to thicken and prevent thinning out on setting, but for a silky smooth sauce that does not curdle, the mixture must not be allowed to boil. The boiling point of water is 212°F. but the other ingredients in the custard mixture lower the boiling point.

The vodka acts as antifreeze, preventing the formation of large ice crystals.

*Bring just to the boiling point (small bubbles will begin to appear around the edges).

[†]The Cordon Rose thermometer is available through Dean & DeLuca (800-227-7714).

Szechuan Swordfish Brochettes

When I think of swordfish, I am always reminded of when my brother was a little boy and my mother took us to Paddy's Clam House, a great fish restaurant in New York that used to be a traditional lunch spot for Macy's shoppers, as it was just down the street. When Michael heard that swordfish was on the menu he ordered it without hesitation but when the large flat fish steak arrived, he was visibly disappointed, immediately asking where the sword was. Thirty years later, I had the good fortune to be present to prevent his son's meeting the same fate. When Alexander ordered the swordfish, I said to him, "Wait! I bet you're ordering it for the sword. . . ." His incredulous response: "How did you know?"

No little boy would ever be disappointed by this swordfish recipe as it is served skewered on a "sword." (Although I'm certainly not recommending leaving it on the plate for them to play with.) But of course this is a recipe for children and grown-ups alike and is ideal for Mother's Day as children will take so much pleasure in helping to prepare it. The tangy orange/soy marinade, which was inspired by a dish served at Wilkinson's restaurant in New York, makes the fish wonderfully moist and tender. If you don't have a charcoal grill, the fish is also delicious broiled.

Serves: 6

Marinating time: 1 hour

EQUIPMENT:
12 metal or wooden skewers

INGREDIENTS	MEASURE	WEIGHT	
	volume	ounces/pounds	grams/kilograms
swordfish steaks, 1½ inches thick	.	3 pounds	1 kilogram, 361 grams
Marinade			
soy sauce	¼ liquid cup	•	•
orange zest, finely grated (from 1 navel orange)	2 tablespoons	0.5 ounce	12 grams
orange juice, freshly squeezed	¼ liquid cup	•	•
lemon juice, freshly squeezed	1 tablespoon	•	•
sesame oil	2 tablespoons	•	•
vegetable oil	2 tablespoons	•	•
tomato paste	2 tablespoons	•	•
2 large garlic cloves, minced	1 tablespoon	0.5 ounce	10.5 grams
pepper, preferably Szechuan,* freshly ground	½ teaspoon	•	•
fresh ginger, grated	1 teaspoon	0.2 ounce	6 grams

*If using Szechuan peppercorns, crush them in a mortar and pestle or put in a heavy-duty plastic bag and crush with a hammer.

INGREDIENTS	MEASURE	WEIGHT	
	volume	*ounces/pounds*	*grams/kilograms*
Vegetables			
2 medium red onions, cut into sixths	•	12 ounces	340 grams
2 small zucchini about 8-inches long, cut into 1-inch rounds	•	14 ounces	200 grams
2 red bell peppers, seeded and cut into 1½-inch pieces	•	6.25 ounces	175 grams

Cut the swordfish into 1½-inch chunks.

In a medium bowl, place all the ingredients for the marinade and whisk to blend well. Add the swordfish and stir to coat it. Cover tightly with plastic wrap (preferably Saran brand) and allow to sit at room temperature for about 1 hour.

Divide the vegetables evenly into 12 piles so that each skewer will have the same amount of each one. Place the swordfish on the skewers, alternating with the vegetables. Brush all over with the marinade.

Meanwhile, prepare a fire in a charcoal grill.

When the coals are ready, lightly oil the grill rack. (I like to heat the rack over the coals as they are heating so that it sears the fish.) Place the brochettes on the grill and grill, covered, for about 5 minutes. Turn the brochettes, brush again with the marinade and continue grilling for another 5 minutes or until the fish is opaque all the way through and tender when flaked with a fork.

• Don't allow the fish to marinate more than 1 hour or it will become too tender.

POINTERS FOR SUCCESS

Sesame Brown Rice

Serves: 6

Brown rice, in addition to being more healthful, also has a more pronounced flavor and (if not overcooked) a crunchier texture than white rice. I find that if too much water is added to brown rice it becomes pasty and altogether disagreeable, but if it's correctly prepared, we prefer it to white rice. The addition of toasted sesame seeds accentuates the slightly nutty flavor of the rice and perfectly complements the Asian-inspired swordfish brochettes.

INGREDIENTS room temperature	MEASURE volume	WEIGHT ounces	grams
water	4 liquid cups	•	•
salt	1 teaspoon	0.25 ounce	6.7 grams
brown rice	2 cups	13.5 ounces	386 grams
unhulled sesame seeds*	¼ cup	1.25 ounces	35 grams
cayenne pepper	⅛ teaspoon	•	•
unsalted butter, cut into 8 pieces	2 tablespoons	1 ounce	28 grams

*Available in health food stores.

In a medium-size saucepan with a tight-fitting lid, bring the water to a boil over high heat. Add the salt. Slowly, so that the water never stops boiling, pour in the rice. Reduce the heat to low, cover tightly and simmer for 35 to 40 minutes or until all of the water has evaporated and the rice kernels are firm but cooked through.

While the rice is cooking, in a small dry frying pan over low heat, heat the sesame seeds, stirring often for about 3 minutes to toast lightly and bring out their flavor. Allow them to cool completely.

In a food processor or blender, process the sesame seeds with the cayenne pepper until the seeds are slightly crushed. Remove them to a small bowl and set aside.

When the rice is cooked, add the crushed sesame seeds and cayenne and the butter, and use two forks to gently incorporate the seeds and butter into the rice.

UNDERSTANDING

Crushing the sesame seeds results in a great increase in flavor.

White Chocolate and Raspberry Nostalgia Cake

The design for this cake was inspired by an old-fashioned bedspread. It has an embroidered quality that is easy, though time-consuming, to accomplish. Because it is so unmistakably a feminine cake, I think it is ideal for Mother's Day. Pristine white rolled fondant encases tender, velvety white chocolate cake layers, filled with tart, silky smooth raspberry buttercream.

Serves: 16 cake lovers or 32 smaller eaters

Start preparing at least 3 days up to 4 days ahead

Preheat the oven to: 350°F. Baking time: 40 to 45 minutes

EQUIPMENT:
two 10-inch by 2-inch cake pans,* greased, bottoms lined with parchment or wax paper, then sprayed (sides and bottoms) with Baker's Joy or greased and floured, excess flour tapped out; 10-inch cardboard cake round*; ½-inch 5-petaled gum paste cutter*; small piece of soft foam; disposable pastry bags* or pastry bag and cake decorating coupler*; Number 1 and Number 2 round cake decorating tubes*

FINISHED HEIGHT:
4½ inches

STORE:
In a cool dry place; do not refrigerate.

*Available at cake-decorating supply stores such as Maid of Scandinavia (800-328-6722) and The Chocolate Gallery (212-675-2253).

INGREDIENTS *room temperature*	MEASURE *volume*	WEIGHT	
		ounces/pounds	*grams*
Rolled Fondant (double the ingredients and make 2 batches)			
lemon juice, freshly squeezed	2 tablespoons	•	•
water	1 tablespoon	•	•
powdered gelatin	1 tablespoon	0.35 ounce	10 grams
corn syrup	½ liquid cup	5.75 ounces	164 grams
glycerine*	1 tablespoon	•	18 grams
solid vegetable shortening	2 tablespoons	0.75 ounce	24 grams
powdered sugar	8 cups (lightly spooned into the cup)	2 pounds	920 grams
White Chocolate Cake			
white chocolate, preferably Lindt's Confectionery Bar, coarsely chopped	3⅓ 3-ounce bars	10 ounces	284 grams
8 large egg whites	1 liquid cup	8.5 ounces	240 grams
milk, divided	1⅓ liquid cups	•	•
pure vanilla extract	2½ teaspoons	•	•
sifted cake flour	5 cups (sifted into the cup and leveled off)	17.5 ounces	500 grams
superfine sugar	2 cups	14 ounces	400 grams
baking powder	2 tablespoons + ½ teaspoon	1 ounce	32 grams
salt	1¼ teaspoons	•	8 grams
unsalted butter (must be softened)	15 tablespoons	7.5 ounces	212 grams
Raspberry Neoclassic Buttercream RASPBERRY PURÉE			
raspberries, frozen with no sugar added	1 12-ounce bag	12 ounces	340 grams
lemon juice, freshly squeezed	1 teaspoon	•	•
sugar	⅓ cup	2.33 ounces	66 grams

*Available in cake-decorating supply stores such as Maid of Scandinavia (800-328-6722) and The Chocolate Gallery (212-675-2253).

INGREDIENTS *room temperature*	MEASURE *volume*	WEIGHT *ounces/pounds*	*grams*
BUTTERCREAM			
6 large egg yolks	3½ fluid ounces	4 ounces	112 grams
sugar	¾ cup	5.25 ounces	150 grams
corn syrup	½ liquid cup	5.75 ounces	164 grams
unsalted butter	2 cups	1 pound	454 grams
OPTIONAL: raspberry liqueur	2 tablespoons	·	·
red liquid food color	4 to 6 drops	·	·
Forget-me-nots			
reserved Rolled Fondant	·	·	·
violet paste food color*	·	·	·
blue liquid food color	·	·	·
30 silver dragées*	·	·	·
Royal Icing			
meringue powder†	2 tablespoons	0.5 ounce	16 grams
water	¼ liquid cup	·	·
powdered sugar	2⅔ cups (lightly spooned into the cup)	10.5 ounces	300 grams
moss green paste food color*	·	·	·
red and yellow liquid food color	·	·	·

*Available at cake-decorating supply stores such as Maid of Scandinavia (800-328-6722) and The Chocolate Gallery (212-675-2253).

†2 large egg whites (¼ liquid cup 2 ounces/60 grams) can be used in place of the meringue powder and water.

Prepare the fondant, the cake and the raspberry purée 2 days before decorating.

Make the buttercream, assemble the cake and cover it with fondant and make the forget-me-nots 1 day before decorating.

In a 2-cup glass measuring cup, combine the lemon juice and water. Sprinkle the gelatin over the top of the mixture and let the gelatin soften for at least 3 minutes. Place the measuring cup in a small saucepan of simmering water and stir the mixture for 2 to 3 minutes or until the gelatin is completely dissolved. (This can also be done in a few seconds in a microwave on high power.) Stir in the corn syrup and glycerine, then add the shortening and stir until almost completely melted. Remove from the heat.

Place the powdered sugar in a large bowl and make a well in the center. Add the gelatin mixture and stir with a lightly greased wooden spoon until blended. Mix with lightly greased hands and then knead vigorously in the bowl until most of the sugar is incorporated.

Turn out onto a lightly greased smooth surface such as Formica or marble and knead until smooth and satiny. If the fondant seems dry, add several drops of water and knead well. If it seems too sticky, knead in more powdered sugar. The fondant will resemble a smooth, well-shaped stone. When dropped, it should spread very slightly but retain its shape. It should be malleable like clay, soft but not sticky.

Wrap each batch of fondant tightly with plastic wrap (preferably Saran brand) and place in an airtight container. It will firm slightly on standing.

Position one rack in the top third and another in the bottom third of the oven, and preheat the oven to 350°F.

In a double boiler, melt the white chocolate over hot, not simmering, water, stirring frequently. (The water in the bottom container should not touch the upper container.) Remove the upper container and allow the chocolate to cool until tepid.

In a medium bowl, whisk together the egg whites, ⅓ cup of the milk and the vanilla.

In a large mixing bowl, preferably with the spade beater of a heavy-duty mixer, combine the dry ingredients and mix on low speed for 30 seconds to blend. Add the butter and the remaining 1 cup of milk. Mix on low speed until the dry ingredients are moistened. Increase to medium speed (high speed if using a hand-held mixer) and beat for 1½ minutes to aerate and develop the cake's structure. Scrape down the sides. Gradually add the egg white mixture in three batches, beating for 20 seconds after each addition to incorporate the ingredients and strengthen the structure. Scrape down the sides. Add the melted chocolate and beat to incorporate.

Scrape the batter into the prepared pans and smooth the surface with a spatula. (The pans will be about half full.) Bake for 40 to 45 minutes or until a tester inserted near the center comes out clean and the cake springs back when pressed lightly in the center. Halfway through the baking, switch the position of the cake layers for even baking. *The cakes should start to shrink from the sides of the pans only after removal from the oven.*

Let the cakes cool in the pans on racks for 10 minutes. Loosen the sides with a small metal spatula and invert onto greased wire racks. To prevent

Rolled Fondant (Make 2 Batches)

White Chocolate Cake

splitting, reinvert onto greased wire racks so that the tops are up and cool completely before wrapping airtight in plastic wrap.

Raspberry Purée

In a strainer suspended over a deep bowl, thaw the raspberries completely. This will take several hours. (To speed thawing, place in an oven with a pilot light.) Press the berries to force out all the juice. There should be a scant ½ cup.

In a saucepan, boil the juice until it is reduced to 2 tablespoons. (Or reduce the juice in a microwave* on high power.) Pour the syrup into a lightly oiled heatproof cup.

Purée the raspberries and strain them through a food mill fitted with the fine disc. Or use a fine strainer to remove all the seeds. You should have a scant ½ liquid cup of purée. Stir in the raspberry syrup and lemon juice. You should have 9 tablespoons (4.5 fluid ounces). Add the sugar.† Stir until the sugar dissolves. Cover with plastic wrap and refrigerate.

Raspberry Neoclassic Buttercream

Have ready a greased 1-cup heatproof glass measure near the range.

In a medium bowl, beat the yolks with the whisk beater of an electric mixer until light in color.

Combine the sugar and corn syrup in a small saucepan (preferably with a nonstick lining) and heat, stirring constantly, until the sugar dissolves and the syrup comes to a rolling boil. The entire surface will be covered with large bubbles. (If using a stand mixer, you can heat the sugar syrup while the yolks are beating.) *Immediately transfer the syrup to the glass measure to stop the cooking.*

If using a hand-held electric mixer, beat the syrup into the yolks in a steady stream. Don't allow any syrup to fall on the beaters or they will spin it onto the sides of the bowl. If using a stand mixer, pour a small amount of syrup over the yolks with the mixer turned off. Then immediately beat at high speed for 5 seconds. Stop the mixer and add a larger amount of syrup. Beat at high speed for 5 seconds. Continue with the remaining syrup. For the last addition, use a rubber scraper to remove the syrup clinging to the glass measure. Continue beating until cool. Be sure the mixture is *completely* cool before adding the butter because if the butter starts to melt, the buttercream will no longer firm correctly.

Gradually beat in the butter and ½ cup of the raspberry purée. (Any remaining purée may be frozen for several months and used for another purpose, such as a sauce.) Beat in the optional raspberry liqueur and the red food coloring.

Assembling the Cake

Unwrap the cake layers and remove the parchment paper from the bottom of the layers. If necessary, using a long serrated knife, trim the tops of the cake layers so that they are level. Slice each cake horizontally into 2 layers

---

*If using a microwave, place the juice in a 4-cup heatproof glass measure or bowl to allow for bubbling.

†If you have less than 9 tablespoons raspberry purée, decrease the sugar, using 1¾ teaspoons for each tablespoon of purée.

of equal thickness, making 4 layers. Using a metal cake spatula, spread a small amount of buttercream in the center of the 10-inch cardboard cake round and set the bottom layer of one of the cakes on top. Spread 1¼ cups of the buttercream over the layer. Place the second cake layer on top of the filling. Spread 1¼ cups of the buttercream over the layer. Place the third cake layer on top of the filling. Spread 1¼ cups of the buttercream over the layer. Top with the fourth cake layer, and press the layer gently into place.

Using a serrated knife, trim the top edge of the cake slightly. This will prevent the sharp edge of the cake from piercing the rolled fondant.

Cover the top and sides of the cake with a very thin layer of the remaining buttercream. Finish the top of the cake by holding the metal cake spatula at a slight angle and with several strokes, smooth the raised rim of buttercream around the edge toward the center of the cake until the top is completely smooth. Refrigerate the cake for 20 minutes while you prepare the rolled fondant.

Unwrap the two packages of fondant. Reserve one quarter of one of the two batches of fondant for making the forget-me-not flowers. Wrap the reserved fondant in a paper towel that has been rubbed with enough shortening to coat it well and then in plastic. Knead the remaining 2 pieces of fondant together into a ball. Continue to knead the fondant until it is malleable enough to roll. Form the fondant into a flat disc.

Spray a rolling pin and a clean, smooth work surface with nonstick vegetable spray. Roll the fondant into an 18-inch by ¼-inch circle, lifting up and rotating the fondant every two or three rolls to ensure that it is not sticking. If necessary, respray the work surface. Work quickly to keep the fondant from drying. If it takes more than 3 or 4 minutes to roll out, cover the fondant with a sheet of plastic wrap to keep it from drying.

Remove the cake from the refrigerator. Slip your fists palm side down under the circle of fondant, being careful not to stretch or tear it. Lift the fondant onto the cake, covering it as evenly as possible. Using the palm of your hand, quickly smooth the top with a circular motion, starting from the center, to eliminate air bubbles. (Bubbles can be pierced with a needle and smoothed out if necessary.) Smooth the fondant gently against the sides, working from the top down with a semicircular motion using both hands. The oil from your hands will give it a lustrous glow. With a pizza cutter or sharp knife, trim the bottom edge of the cake to remove the excess fondant. Form the trimmings into a ball and wrap them in plastic.

Transfer the cake to a serving plate. Roll about ⅔ cup of the reserve fondant trimmings into two 16-inch coils that are about ½ inch thick. Wrap the coils around the base of the cake and pinch the ends together with your fingers. Let the cake stand overnight at room temperature in a cool, dry place.

1   2   3

Forget-me-nots

Unwrap the fondant reserved for the forget-me-nots, and place it on a fresh piece of plastic wrap. Using the tip of a toothpick, place a small amount of the violet paste food color on the fondant. Squeeze a small amount of the blue liquid food color onto the fondant. Using the plastic wrap as a shield to prevent your fingers from getting stained by the food color, knead the color into the fondant. Add more paste or liquid color if necessary to make the fondant a violet-blue color.

Lightly spray a clean, smooth work surface with nonstick vegetable spray. Roll the piece of colored fondant into a 7-inch by 8-inch rectangle, ¹⁄₁₆ inch thick. Using the ½-inch five-petaled gum paste cutter, cut out 30 flowers (Fig. 1).

Using the pointed tip of a chopstick or a knitting needle, widen the flower petals by lightly pressing the center of each petal (Fig. 2).

One at a time, place a flower on the piece of soft foam. Using the rounded end of a chopstick, crochet needle, or a cotton swab, press gently into the center of each flower, forcing the petals to curve upward (Fig. 3). Press a silver dragée into the center of each flower. Let the forget-me-nots dry overnight in a cool, dry place.

Royal Icing

In a large, grease-free mixer bowl, preferably with the whisk beater of a heavy-duty mixer, beat the meringue powder and water on low speed until mixed. Add the powdered sugar and beat for 30 seconds or until the sugar is moistened. Increase the speed to medium high and continue beating for 5 to 8 minutes, until the icing forms stiff, glossy peaks when the beater is lifted. (The tips of the peaks should curve slightly.)

Divide the icing among four small grease-free bowls. Cover the bowls with damp cloths to keep the icing from drying.

Reserve one bowl of icing for making the white dots. Using the tip of a toothpick, place a small amount of the moss green paste food color into one of the bowls of royal icing. Using a small metal cake spatula, stir until the color is evenly blended to create a pale green icing. Squeeze a couple drops of red liquid food color into another bowl of icing. Stir until the color is evenly blended to create a pale pink icing. Squeeze a couple drops of the yellow liquid food color into another bowl of icing. Stir until the color is evenly blended to create a pale yellow icing. Keep all the bowls of icing covered with damp cloths to keep them from drying.

Let the icing sit for 2 hours before using. The icing will darken as it sits. If any becomes too dark after sitting, stir in a little of the white icing.

1   2   3

Decorating the Cake

Using the tip of a toothpick, outline an evenly spaced dotted scroll pattern on the top and sides of the cake. There is no specific scroll pattern to follow; but you should work out your own pattern before you start to mark the cake.

Fit a pastry bag with coupler or a disposable pastry bag with a Number 2 small round tube. Using a small metal cake spatula, fill the bag with the white icing. Pipe tiny white dots onto the marked outline of the scroll design (Fig. 1).

Pipe a small dot of the white icing on the back of each forget-me-not and affix it inside each scrolled area of the cake. Repeat using the remaining forget-me-nots, evenly spacing them around the bottom edge of the cake.

Fit another disposable pastry bag with a Number 1 small round tube and fill the bag with the green icing. Pipe green stems starting at the base of each forget-me-not (Fig. 2).

Fit another disposable pastry bag with a Number 2 small round tube and fill it with yellow icing. Pipe tiny five-petaled flowers (Fig. 3) on the top and sides of the cake, leaving space for pink flowers. Fit another pastry bag with a Number 2 round tube and fill it with the pink icing. Pipe tiny five-petaled pink flowers between the yellow flowers.

Serve the cake within 24 hours.

POINTERS FOR SUCCESS

White Chocolate Cake

- Follow the instructions carefully for melting the white chocolate so that it doesn't lump.
- Use superfine sugar for the finest texture. (You can make it by processing granulated sugar in the food processor for a few minutes until fine.)
- Use cake flour without leavening.
- Use unsalted butter for the best flavor.
- Use fresh baking powder (under a year old).
- If using a hand-held mixer, beat at high speed.
- Use the correct pan size.
- For very even layers, wrap the cake pans with Magi-Cake Strips (available from Maid of Scandinavia, 800-328-6722).
- Do not overbake the cake.

Royal Icing

- Only a very powerful hand-held electric mixer, such as the Krupps or KitchenAid, is strong enough to make royal icing without damaging the motor.

Pistachio Pavés
(pahVAY)

Makes:
4 dozen 3-inch cookies

Preheat the oven to:
375°F.
Baking time: 10 to 12
minutes

KEEPS:
1 month in an airtight
container at room
temperature or several
months frozen.

T*he special buttery and mildly exotic flavor of pistachio nuts is usually lost in a cookie, but these crescents are an exception because the dough is rolled in chopped pistachios. The pavés are literally paved with the lovely green nut. The pistachio lover will be yours for life if you make these cookies! And they are a good option for those who haven't the time or inclination to make a celebration cake for Mother's Day.*

INGREDIENTS	MEASURE	WEIGHT	
	volume	ounces	grams
shelled unsalted pistachio nuts,* divided	1¾ cups	9.25 ounces	262 grams
sugar	¾ cup	5.25 ounces	150 grams
unsalted butter, cut into pieces	2 cups	8 ounces	227 grams
1 large egg	3 tablespoons	1.75 ounces	50 grams (weighed without shell)
pure vanilla extract	2 teaspoons	.	.
bleached all-purpose flour	1¾ cups (dip and sweep method)	8.75 ounces	248 grams
salt	a pinch	.	.
OPTIONAL: green liquid food color	6 drops	.	.

*Unsalted pistachio nuts are available from Keenan Farms, Inc., P.O. Box 248, Avenal, California (209-386-9516). Roasted unsalted cashew nut pieces may be substituted for the pistachio nuts; omit the green food color.

At least 15 minutes before baking, place two oven racks in the upper and lower thirds of the oven and preheat the oven to 375°F.

Bring a small saucepan of water to a boil. Add ¾ cup (4 ounces/114 grams) of the pistachios and simmer for 1 minute. Drain and slip off the skins by squeezing the pistachios between your thumb and forefinger. Dry the nuts with paper towels.

Food Processor Method

In a food processor with the metal blade, process the ¾ cup peeled pistachios and the sugar until the nuts are ground powder fine. With the motor running, add the butter. Process until smooth and creamy. Add the egg and vanilla extract and process until incorporated, scraping the sides of the bowl. Add the flour and salt and pulse in just until blended. Pulse in the optional food color.

Electric Mixer
Method

Soften the butter. Grate the ¾ cup (4 ounces/114 grams) peeled pistachios powder fine. In a mixing bowl, cream the sugar and butter until fluffy. Add the grated nuts, then add the egg and vanilla extract and beat until blended. On low speed, gradually add the flour and salt and mix until incorporated.

Both Methods

Scrape the dough into a bowl and refrigerate for about an hour or until firm.

Chop the remaining 1 cup pistachios medium-fine and spread them on a smooth countertop.

Working with ¼ cup of the dough at a time, and leaving the rest refrigerated, measure out level tablespoons of dough. Roll each tablespoon of dough between the palms of your hands into a little log. When the dough starts to soften and get sticky, transfer the log to the nut-lined counter and continue rolling on the nuts until the log is 3 inches long and encrusted with nuts. Don't be alarmed that the dough is sticky; this enables it to pick up more nuts. Return the dough to the refrigerator if it softens too much for rolling.

Place the logs of dough, curving them slightly into crescent shape, at least 1 inch apart on cookie sheets. For the best shape, refrigerate for 5 minutes before baking.

Bake for 10 to 12 minutes or until the tops just begin to brown and the bottoms, when lifted, are brown. For even baking, rotate the cookie sheets from top to bottom and front to back halfway through the baking period.

Allow the cookies to cool on the sheets for a few minutes. Use a small, angled metal spatula or pancake turner to transfer the cookies to wire racks to cool completely.

Strawberry Champagne Punch
(For a Wedding Shower)

This is the most glorious celebratory punch I know. The first time I had it was when my cousin Marion was making it for an engagement party she was giving for her sister Sue. It was Marion who had introduced Sue to her future husband after he asked Marion that classic question, "Are there any more at home like you?" Marion happened to have the perfect response: "There is!" And she introduced him to her identical twin sister.

I had come early to the engagement party to help with the preparations and the first thing I noticed in the kitchen was the lovely perfume of fresh strawberries. Marion immediately showed me the large punch bowl and the strawberries marinating in the Moselle, which were responsible for the glorious aroma.

I have since served this punch for many different occasions and discovered, to my happy surprise, that what I thought to be a "lady's drink" is appreciated by men at least as much! The optional strawberry mint ice ring makes a stunning presentation and also serves to keep the punch sparkling cold.

Although delicious any time of year, this punch is at its very best in spring and summer, during strawberry season.

Wedding showers can be as casual or formal as you wish, from pot luck to catered. But even if you bring in all the food from the outside, making this champagne punch adds a special, personal touch.

Makes: about 1 gallon

Several hours or up to several days ahead, prepare the optional ice ring.

Marinating time: at least 1 hour; up to 4 hours ahead

EQUIPMENT:
4- to 6-cup ring or heart mold for optional ice ring

INGREDIENTS	MEASURE *volume*	WEIGHT	
		ounces/pounds	*grams*
Ice Ring (optional)			
1 bottle distilled water, cold	about 1 quart	·	·
fresh strawberries and fresh mint leaves, for garnish	·	·	·
Punch			
sugar, preferably superfine*	1 cup	7 ounces	200 grams
1 bottle Moselle wine	750 milliliters	·	·
fresh strawberries, hulled	1 quart	1 pound	454 grams
½ bottle red Bordeaux	375 milliliters	·	·
2 bottles California or Spanish Champagne	750 milliliters each	·	·

*Superfine sugar dissolves more easily but fine granulated will also work with more stirring.

Ice Ring

Pour about ½ inch of the distilled water into the mold and freeze until almost completely frozen. Arrange whole strawberries and mint leaves in the mold and press gently into the ice. Add enough water to come about halfway up the sides of the berries but not enough to float them. Freeze until the berries and mint are frozen into position. Then add water to cover the berries and mint and freeze.

Punch

At least 1 hour or up to 4 hours ahead, combine the sugar and Moselle and stir to dissolve the sugar. Add the strawberries, cover tightly with plastic wrap (preferably Saran brand) and allow to sit at room temperature for at least 1 hour.

When ready to serve, unmold the optional ice ring: Dip the bottom of the mold into cold water for a few moments and invert it onto a plate. Stir the Bordeaux into the punch. Slide the ice ring into the punch and then add the champagne.

UNDERSTANDING

Distilled water results in a clearer, less cloudy ice. If substituting tap water, be sure to allow it to sit in the refrigerator for at least an hour to help to prevent cloudiness.

An expensive Champagne is not necessary for this punch as the flavor is overridden by the other ingredients.

Summer

❖ ❖ ❖ ❖

Father's Day

Boeuf à la Ficelle
Horseradish Sauce
Steamed Baby Vegetables
Freckled Angel

Summer Country Breakfast

Blueberry Muffins

Fourth of July

Whole Poached Salmon
Doug Nester's Dill Mayonnaise
Steamed Potatoes
Watermelon Ice Cream Bombe

❖ ❖ ❖ ❖

Summer Lunch

Elliott's Favorite Three Bean and Corn Salad

Alexander's Birthday Party

Meatballs and Spaghetti
Checkerboard Fantasy Cake

Labor Day Barbecue

Barbecued Chicken
My Best Barbecue Sauce
Baked Potatoes with Sour Cream and Chives
Terry Frishman's Tomato Salad
Quintessential Corn Fingers
David Shamah's Back Porch Diet Lemonade
Double Chocolate Oriolos

Boeuf à la Ficelle
(BUHF ah la feeCELL)

Boeuf à la ficelle *is a traditional French technique for cooking beef tenderloin. It is called* à la ficelle *because the meat is tied with string (ficelle) and lowered into simmering beef stock, which sears in the juices and adds flavor. In the classic method, the ends of the string are tied to the handles of the pot so that the meat is suspended in the broth. As this requires a special pot and is awkward to accomplish, I have worked out an alternative method with excellent results.*

This method also works well with beef rib eye, which is more flavorful but higher in fat and not as buttery-tender. As a special treat, I sometimes coordinate this recipe with my making of Glace de Viande (page 253) and poach the beef in it before the final concentration—a fine benefit to both the beef and the glace!

I like to serve the beef with a variety of steamed fresh baby vegetables such as beets, turnips, carrots, snowpeas, new potatoes or sugar snaps. The baby vegetables are especially delicious and sweet in summer. They can be precooked early in the day and warmed before serving. A zippy simple cold horseradish sauce is my favorite accompaniment for both the beef and vegetables.

This is a menu specially tailored to please Dad for Father's Day. It is at once unfussy, elegant and hearty.

Serves: 6

Internal temperature (middle): 110°F.

EQUIPMENT:
long fish poacher with a rack or a large pot

INGREDIENTS *room temperature*	MEASURE *volume*	WEIGHT	
		ounces/pounds	*grams/kilograms*
homemade beef stock (page 253) or canned (preferably College Inn)	3 quarts (7 14.5-ounce cans)	101.5 ounces	2 kilograms, 878 grams
1 medium onion, quartered but unpeeled	·	6 ounces	170 grams
2 medium carrots, scraped	·	5.25 ounces	150 grams
celery tops with leaves, coarsely sliced	½ cup	1 ounce	28 grams
1 bay leaf	·	·	·
fresh thyme*	a few sprigs	·	·
1 12-inch-long beef tenderloin or rib eye roast, trimmed of fat and tied at 2-inch intervals†	·	3 to 3¼ pounds	1 kilogram, 360 grams to 1 kilogram, 475 grams

*Or ½ teaspoon dried thyme.

†Leave a long piece of string at either end to lift roast into and out of the broth.

In the poacher or pot, combine all the ingredients except the beef and bring to a boil. Simmer for 30 minutes, partially covered.

Add the roast, dangling the ends of the string over the side of the pot, and simmer, covered, for 15 to 20 minutes or until the internal temperature is 110°F. when an instant-read thermometer is inserted into the center of the beef. Remove from the broth. Allow it to sit for 10 to 20 minutes. The temperature will rise to 115°F. At this temperature, the roast will be very rare throughout. (If you prefer medium rare, bring it to 115°F., and it will rise to 120°F.)

The beef is excellent while still warm but equally delicious at room temperature.

NOTE: The poaching liquid can be reduced to about 1 cup and frozen indefinitely for reuse. If you use canned broth, however, it will be very salty so use only a small amount if adding to grain dishes and sauces.

Horseradish Sauce

Makes: 1 cup

Chilling time: at least 1 hour

KEEPS: 1 week refrigerated.

This is our favorite accompaniment to beef. It was created for the horse-radish lover and therefore has an undeniable bite. If you prefer a tamer variety, add more sour cream or whisk in some heavy cream, which will also serve to lighten it.

The sauce thickens on standing; prepare it at least 1 hour ahead, so that it will reach the desired consistency.

INGREDIENTS	MEASURE volume	WEIGHT ounces	grams
sour cream	½ cup	4 ounces	113 grams
prepared horseradish	½ cup	4.5 ounces	125 grams
Dijon mustard	2 teaspoons	0.5 ounce	12 grams
sugar	2 teaspoons	·	·
white pepper, preferably freshly ground	a few grindings	·	·
salt	a big pinch	·	·
fresh bread crumbs*	2 teaspoons	·	·

*To make fresh bread crumbs, place a piece of bread in the food processor and process it to fine crumbs.

In a small bowl, stir together all of the ingredients. Cover tightly and refrigerate until serving time.

Steamed Baby Vegetables

In summer, baby vegetables are at their sweetest and make a special treat. I steam them to make the most of their tender texture and flavor and I serve them plain with only a sprinkling of fresh chervil or parsley. When vegetables are this fresh and young, they need no gilding, although I do dip the potatoes in the horseradish sauce I serve with the beef.

The vegetables can be prepared ahead and reheated just before serving, which is a great convenience for a party like a Father's Day dinner.

Serves: 6

INGREDIENTS	MEASURE volume		WEIGHT ounces	grams
18 1½-inch new potatoes*		•	18 ounces	510 grams
18 baby carrots		•	8 ounces	227 grams
18 baby beets		•	10.5 ounces	300 grams
snow peas	1 cup		4 ounces	113 grams
salt	¼ teaspoon		•	•
pepper, freshly ground	⅛ teaspoon		•	•
fresh whole chervil leaves or parsley, preferably flat-leafed, minced	2 tablespoons		0.25 ounce	8 grams

*If only larger potatoes are available, cut them in half.

Place a vegetable steamer in a medium saucepan. Add water to come slightly under the bottom of the steamer and bring it to a boil. Place the potatoes in the steamer and cover tightly. Lower the heat and steam until just tender when pierced with the tip of a sharp knife, about 10 to 15 minutes. With tongs, transfer the potatoes to a bowl of iced water and set aside until cooled, about 5 minutes. Drain well and set aside on paper towels.

Add water to the saucepan if necessary, and steam the baby carrots until just tender when pierced with the tip of a sharp knife, about 10 minutes. Transfer to a fresh bowl of iced water. Cool, drain and set aside on paper towels.

Add water to the pan if necessary, and steam the baby beets until just tender when pierced with the tip of a sharp knife, about 15 to 20 minutes. Transfer to a fresh bowl of iced water. Slip off the peel and drain well. Cut off the root ends and trim the stems. Set aside on paper towels.

The potatoes, carrots and beets can be prepared up to 1 day ahead, covered and refrigerated. Remove the vegetables from the refrigerator 1 hour before serving.

Shortly before serving, place the vegetable steamer in the pot; add water to come slightly under the bottom of the steamer and bring it to a boil. Place the beets and snow peas on separate 12-inch squares of aluminum foil. Place the baby carrots and new potatoes in separate mounds in the steamer and nestle the beets in their foil on top, keeping the foil open. Cover and steam for 5 minutes. Nestle the snow peas in their foil next to the beets, cover and continue steaming for 3 minutes or until the snow peas are bright green and all the vegetables are heated through.

Transfer the vegetables to a warmed serving platter and season with the salt and pepper. Sprinkle with the chervil or parsley.

UNDERSTANDING

Steaming the beets and snow peas in foil contains them and keeps the beet juice from running and coloring the other vegetables. Exact steaming time will vary according to the size of the vegetables.

NOTE: A 9¾-inch steamer insert is the standard size, but a 12-inch steamer in a 10-inch or larger saucepan is ideal for this recipe.

Freckled Angel

My son, Michael, loved two cakes when he was growing up: Duncan Hines chocolate and angel food. This was a variation I created for him, to combine his favorite texture with his favorite flavor. Adding the bitter chocolate is great for tempering the inevitable sweetness of angel food cake. These days I often make this cake for family members and friends who are trying to watch their cholesterol. Eating this cake, they feel at once quite indulged and virtuous. I am pleased to provide this special recipe as an excellent option for a Father's Day dessert.

Serves: 14

Preheat the oven to:
350°F.
Baking time: 40 minutes

EQUIPMENT:
ungreased 10-inch two-piece tube pan

INGREDIENTS *room temperature*	MEASURE *volume*	WEIGHT	
		ounces	*grams*
sugar, preferably superfine, divided	1½ cups	10.5 ounces	300 grams
sifted cake flour	1 cup (sifted into the cup and leveled off)	3.5 ounces	100 grams
salt	¼ teaspoon	•	•
16 large egg whites	2 liquid cups	17 ounces	480 grams
cream of tartar	2 teaspoons	•	6 grams
pure vanilla extract	4 teaspoons	•	•
unsweetened chocolate, grated*	•	2 ounces	56 grams

*To grate chocolate, make sure that it is cold or it will melt rather than form fine particles. You can use a hand grater, Mouli grater or a food processor. If using a food processor, break the chocolate into small pieces before processing.

At least 15 minutes before baking, position an oven rack at the lowest level and preheat the oven to 350°F.

In a small bowl, combine ¾ cup of the sugar, the flour and salt and whisk to blend well. Sift the remaining sugar onto a piece of waxed paper.

In a large mixing bowl, preferably with the whisk beater of a heavy-duty mixer, beat the egg whites until frothy. Add the cream of tartar and beat until soft peaks form when the beater is raised. Gradually beat in the sifted sugar, and beat until very stiff peaks form when the beater is raised slowly.

Dust the flour mixture over the beaten whites ¼ cup at a time, and with a large wire whisk, slotted skimmer or large rubber spatula, fold it in quickly but gently. It is not necessary to incorporate every speck, until the last addition. Add the vanilla and grated chocolate and fold them in until evenly incorporated.

Spread a thin layer of batter onto the sides of the tube pan to ensure smooth sides. Pour the rest of the batter into the pan. (It will reach almost

FINISHED HEIGHT:
4 inches high in the middle.

KEEPS:
3 days at room temperature wrapped airtight; 10 days refrigerated; freezing toughens the texture.

COMPLEMENTARY ADORNMENTS:
A light sprinkling of cocoa. Lacy drizzles of melted chocolate or fresh flowers.

to the top.) Run a small metal spatula or knife through the batter to prevent air pockets and smooth the surface. Bake for 40 minutes or until golden brown, a cake tester inserted in the center comes out clean and the cake springs back when lightly pressed. (During baking, the center will rise above the pan but it sinks when the cake is done. After cooling it will be level with the sides of the pan. The surface will have deep cracks like a soufflé.)

Immediately invert the pan, placing the tube opening over the neck of a soda or wine bottle to suspend it well above the counter, and cool the cake completely in the pan, about 1½ hours.

Loosen the sides with a long metal spatula and remove the center core of the pan. Dislodge the cake from the bottom and center core with a metal spatula or thin sharp knife. (A wire cake tester works well around the core. To keep the sides attractive, press the spatula against the sides of the pan.) Invert the cake onto a flat plate covered with plastic wrap and reinvert it onto a serving plate.

For the fluffiest texture, use an angel food fork or two forks back to back to cut the cake. Alternatively, use a serrated knife but hold the cake gently without compressing it as you cut.

 POINTERS FOR SUCCESS

- The bowl, beater and egg whites must be absolutely free of grease, including even a speck of egg yolk, for the egg whites to beat to stiff peaks.
- Using the correct amount of cream of tartar makes it possible to beat the whites very stiff without the risk of drying them and breaking them down.
- A large balloon whisk or slotted skimmer is ideal for folding in the flour with the least amount of air loss. If using the whisk, periodically shake out the batter that collects on the inside. Work quickly once the egg whites are beaten so that they do not deflate. Fold the flour gently but *thoroughly* into the batter.
- After mixing, bake immediately in an *ungreased* pan.
- After baking, immediately invert the pan so that it is suspended well above the counter so that the cake doesn't steam and fall out of the pan.

Blueberry Muffins

A good blueberry muffin is one of life's most perfect things. To my mind it should be moist, tender, fine-textured, just barely sweet, but sweet enough to balance a generous amount of plump tangy berries suspended in it. Several summers ago, I set out to create the perfect blueberry muffin. We enjoyed my different versions throughout the summer until I finally hit upon the balance I was after. I have to admit that the most important element, the proper degree of moistness, came about entirely by accident when I was making a half batch and forgot to halve the milk. To my amazement, the additional liquid did not make the texture heavy or pasty as it would in a cake. The next time, I cut it back only slightly and had everything I was looking for in a blueberry muffin. I am also indebted to Elizabeth Alston's Muffins (Clarkson Potter) for the lovely idea of mashing some of the berries into the batter and making the tops crunchy with a sprinkling of sugar and nutmeg.

I like to serve these muffins to guests for breakfast in the country. I measure the ingredients the night before and, in the morning, quickly mix and bake them to serve with the freshly squeezed orange juice and coffee.

Makes: 8 muffins

Preheat the oven to: 375°F.
Baking time: 20 to 25 minutes

EQUIPMENT:
A muffin tin lined with foil or paper liners, lightly sprayed with nonstick vegetable shortening.

KEEPS:
3 days at room temperature, 3 months frozen.

| INGREDIENTS | MEASURE | WEIGHT | |
room temperature	*volume*	*ounces*	*grams*
unsalted butter	4 tablespoons	2 ounces	57 grams
sugar	¾ cup	5.25 ounces	150 grams
lemon zest, finely grated	1½ teaspoons	•	3 grams
1 large egg	3 tablespoons	1.75 ounces	50 grams (weighed without shell)
pure vanilla extract	½ teaspoon	•	•
fresh blueberries, rinsed and dried, divided	1¼ cups	5.5 ounces	155 grams
bleached all-purpose flour	1 cup (dip and sweep method)	5 ounces	145 grams
baking powder	1 teaspoon	•	4.9 grams
salt	¼ teaspoon	•	•
milk	⅓ liquid cup	•	•
Topping			
sugar	¾ teaspoon	•	•
nutmeg, grated	⅛ teaspoon	•	•

Preheat the oven to 375°F.

In a large mixing bowl, with an electric mixer set on medium speed, cream the butter, sugar and lemon zest until light and fluffy, about 5 minutes. Beat in the egg and vanilla.

In a small bowl, mash ¼ cup of the berries. Beat this into the butter mixture.

In a small bowl, whisk together the flour, baking powder and salt. Add half the flour mixture with half the milk and, using a rubber spatula, fold it in. Repeat with the remaining flour and milk, folding in just until the flour disappears. Fold in the remaining 1 cup of blueberries.

Spoon or pipe* the batter into the muffin cups, filling them almost to the top.

Topping

In a small bowl, stir together the sugar and nutmeg for the topping. Place it in a small strainer and, using a spoon to help press it through, dust it over the top of each muffin.

Pour a little water into any empty muffin cups to prevent uneven baking. Bake for 20 to 25 minutes or until the muffins spring back when pressed lightly in the center. Unmold the muffins onto wire cake racks to cool, top sides up. Serve warm or at room temperature.

POINTERS FOR SUCCESS

- For finely grated zest, use a zester (a small implement with tiny scraping holes), a vegetable peeler or a fine grater to remove the yellow portion only of the lemon rind. The white pith beneath is bitter. If using a zester or peeler, finish by chopping the zest with a sharp knife.
- Frozen blueberries can be substituted for fresh. Do not defrost or rinse.

---

*I find it easiest to scrape the batter into a heavy-duty gallon zip-seal bag, zip it shut and cut off the tip of one of the bottom corners. It functions as a disposable piping bag.

Whole Poached Salmon

Ideal for a large summer party such as Fourth of July, moist and flavorful whole poached salmon makes a stunning presentation. Although a little time-consuming, it is well worth the effort because the results are so elegant and delicious, it feeds many people and it requires no last-minute preparation. A smaller salmon is easy to do in a roasting pan, a larger requires a long fish poacher unless you sacrifice the head or cook it separately.

The first time I made this recipe was for a college course in international foods. I could hardly afford the price of the fish but wanted desperately to impress the hell out of Professor Tarantino, who had once been a chef and seemed to think that we college students weren't serious enough about food. In fact, I wanted to make him eat his words.

I was dating a French chef at the time, who went into shock when I told him I was planning to present the fish unadorned except by a beautiful pink aspic to enhance the color of its flesh. "Tu vas servir le poisson tout nu?" he questioned, voice and eyebrows raised in Gallic horror. When I realized this translated as "You're going to serve the fish naked!," I teased him by asking if he wanted me to put panties on it. "Ah, non!" Instead he showed me what he had in mind. I, who had wondered how I was going to lift the chilled poached fish onto the plate in one piece, watched in awe as Michel planted himself authoritatively in front of it and with two large and experienced hands lifted it in one assured movement, while pronouncing it "bien cuit" (well cooked). I glowed from behind him with hidden pride.

Having worked for several years as a chef on board a major cruise line, Michel was adept at performing the intricacies of elaborate classic French garde manger (a form of décor intended to enhance the visual appeal of the food while preserving its freshness). He showed me how to "dress" the fish with leaves of leek, tomato roses and an arbor of gracefully twisted strips of lemon peel, still attached to lemon halves on either side, arching over the fish. It was so breathtaking even my teacher was hesitant to cut it. He made me do the honors. And to this day I am continuing to do them, as this dish is one of my all-time favorite party foods.

Serves: 12 to 14

Start preparing at least 1 day up to 2 days ahead

Preheat the oven to: 350°F. Cooking time: 35 minutes Internal temperature (middle): 120°F.

EQUIPMENT:
long fish poacher or large roasting pan, 11 inches by 16 inches; large rack that fits in the pan or poacher; cheesecloth, preferably the elasticized tube variety; heavy-duty foil; instant-read thermometer

INGREDIENTS	MEASURE *volume*	WEIGHT *ounces/pounds*	*grams/kilograms*
1 whole cleaned salmon about 28 inches long with head*	·	6½ to 7 pounds	3 kilograms to 3 kilograms, 175 grams
unsalted butter	2 tablespoons	1 ounce	28 grams
1 large onion, chopped	2 cups	9 ounces	255 grams
2 large carrots, thickly sliced	1 heaping cup	5.75 ounces	163 grams
2 celery stalks with leaves, thickly sliced	1⅔ cups	5.5 ounces	155 grams
fresh parsley, preferably flat-leafed, coarsely chopped	1 packed cup	1.5 ounces	40 grams
2 bay leaves	·	·	·
8 black peppercorns	·	·	·
4 cloves	·	·	·
fresh thyme leaves†	1 tablespoon	·	·
salt	½ teaspoon	·	·
chicken broth (preferably College Inn)	5 liquid cups (3 13.75-ounce cans)	41 ounces	1 kilogram, 169 grams
water	4 liquid cups	·	·
vermouth or dry white wine	1 liquid cup	·	·
2 large egg whites	·	·	·
2 crushed eggshells	·	·	·
powdered gelatin	1½ tablespoons	0.5 ounce	14 grams
OPTIONAL: red liquid food color	a drop or two	·	·
OPTIONAL: blanched chives or leek greens, tomato roses (page 131), watercress or lemon zest and spinach leaf "cup," for garnish	·	·	·

*My first choice is King salmon; it is fatter, larger and fuller flavored than silver or Norwegian salmon.
†Or 1 teaspoon dried thyme.

If you are using a poacher, the salmon cooks on top of the range. *If using a roasting pan, preheat the oven to 350°F. 15 minutes before cooking.*

Rinse the salmon under cold running water and pat dry with paper towels. Wrap in plastic wrap (preferably Saran brand) and refrigerate.

In a large casserole or the fish poacher, melt the butter over medium heat. Sauté the onion, carrots, celery and parsley for about 3 minutes, stirring occasionally, until the onion is wilted. Add the bay leaves, peppercorns, cloves, thyme, salt, broth, water and vermouth or wine and simmer for 20 minutes.

While the broth is cooking, remove the dorsal fin at the center of the back of the salmon by making a small cut on either side of it and pulling it forward along with the bones that extend for about ¾ inch into the back. Cut off the pectoral fins behind the gills. Wrap the salmon in cheesecloth (if using the elasticized tubing, encase the salmon in it).

If using a roasting pan, place the salmon on the rack in the pan on an angle so that the head overhangs one corner and the tail, the opposing corner. Wrap the head and tail in foil to protect them. Pour the hot cooking broth over the fish. Use a large sheet of aluminum foil to cover the fish, crimping it tightly around the edges of the roasting pan. Place the pan in the oven and cook for 35 minutes.

If using a fish poacher, place the salmon on its rack and lower it into the simmering broth. Add about 6 cups boiling water or enough to come halfway up the sides of the salmon, and cover with the lid. Simmer for about 35 minutes (5 to 5½ minutes a pound).

To test for doneness: Insert an instant-read thermometer into the thickest section of the salmon. (If using the roasting pan, insert it right through the foil.) The thermometer should read 120°F. (The salmon will continue cooking as it cools in the broth.) Allow the fish to cool in the broth for 2 to 3 hours so that it will be firm enough to transfer without damage.

Use the cheesecloth to lift the salmon onto a large platter or tray. Cover it tightly with plastic wrap and refrigerate for at least 2 hours, or overnight. Strain the cooking liquid into a large bowl, cover tightly with plastic wrap and refrigerate for several hours or overnight, until the fat has solidified on the surface. Several hours or up to 1 day before serving, remove and discard all traces of fat from the cooking liquid. Strain the liquid through cheesecloth into a large saucepan, and bring it to a boil and boil until reduced to 3 cups. Add the egg whites and crushed eggshells and simmer for about 3 minutes, ladling the broth through the egg white to clarify it. (The egg whites will coagulate, forming a sort of filter.) Strain the broth through cheesecloth into a medium bowl, preferably a white one so that you can see the color of the broth. Whisk in the gelatin and a drop or two of red food color, if desired, to achieve a pale pink hue. Cover the bowl tightly and set it aside while preparing the salmon.

Fold back or cut away the cheesecloth from the salmon. Remove the skin from the top side of the salmon and scrape away the grayish fat. Use the cheesecloth to flip the salmon over onto a large sheet of foil. Peel off the remaining skin and use a damp paper towel to remove all traces of fat or any remaining skin. Use the foil to flip the salmon onto a serving platter. (The top side is usually the most attractive side.)

Place the bowl of clarified fish broth (aspic) in a larger bowl filled with iced water and stir often until syrupy (when dropped from a spoon it just starts to mound slightly). Immediately remove it from the iced water and spoon some of the aspic over the fish, coating the entire fish. Pour some of the remaining aspic around the fish so that it coats the plate.

Garnish the top of the salmon with pieces of blanched chives or leek to resemble leaves and with tomato roses. Refrigerate until set, about 30 minutes.

Spoon another coating of aspic over the decorations on the salmon. If the aspic has started to set, warm it over a bowl of hot water until smooth and chill it again over ice. If desired, chill the remaining aspic, chop it finely and place it around the salmon as a garnish.

Cover the eye with a leaf of watercress or a small bit of lemon zest. If desired, arrange a few spinach leaves next to the salmon to serve as a "cup" and spoon some of Doug Nester's Dill Mayonnaise (page 132) into it. Chill the salmon until serving.

NOTE: For a 9½-pound salmon, which will serve 18 to 21, make 1½ times the recipe, but use 1 large can of chicken broth (46 ounces), 1 teaspoon salt and 2 tablespoons gelatin. Cook for 50 minutes. Reduce broth to 4 cups.

TO MAKE TOMATO ROSES:
Use a small serrated knife or small sharp knife to peel the skin from a tomato. Start by making a horizontal cut at the base, about ¼ inch thick (Fig. 1). Keeping this base attached, angle the knife and cut around the tomato in concentric circles, removing the skin in a spiral (Figs. 2 and 3). Then starting at the end of the spiral, coil the skin until you reach the base (Fig. 4). Center the rose on its base (Fig. 5).

1

2

3

4

5

Doug Nester's Dill Mayonnaise
(From Dean & DeLuca)

Makes: about 1½ cups
KEEPS:
1 week refrigerated.

This is the most perfect cold dill sauce for fish I have ever tasted. I have to control myself to keep from eating it by the spoonful! It is herby, lemony and tangy with a lovely background of mustard. I tasted it one day, when buying fish at Dean & DeLuca, my favorite neighborhood specialty store (considered by many to be the father of all American specialty stores). It had been created as an accompaniment to their wonderful fresh fish. I was "hooked" immediately, and thrilled to get the recipe from Doug. I scribbled it down on a paper bag before I could forget or he could change his mind.

The recipe as Doug gave it to me went something like this: Make a safflower oil mayonnaise with Dijon mustard—enough to almost fill a food processor. Add a bunch of spinach, a bunch of watercress and two bunches of dill. I thought I had it until I discovered that each bunch of herbs varied enormously. Actually, the exact amount of herbs isn't really important. Feel free to vary it as you will, but here is how I fix it.

INGREDIENTS *room temperature*	MEASURE *volume*	WEIGHT *ounces/pounds*	*grams/kilograms*
1 large egg	.	1.75 ounces	50 grams (weighed without shell)
lemon juice, freshly squeezed	1 tablespoon + 1 teaspoon	.	.
Dijon mustard	1 tablespoon + 2 teaspoons	1 ounce	32 grams
salt	¼ teaspoon	.	.
white pepper, freshly ground	¼ teaspoon	.	.
sugar	¼ teaspoon	.	.
safflower oil	1¼ liquid cups	.	.
fresh dill, washed and dried, stems removed	½ loosely packed cup	0.5 ounce	14 grams
fresh spinach leaves, washed and dried, coarsely chopped	½ loosely packed cup	0.5 ounce	14 grams
watercress, washed and dried, stems removed	½ loosely packed cup	0.75 ounce	21 grams

In a food processor, place the egg, lemon juice, mustard, salt, pepper and sugar. Process for a few seconds to mix. Then, with the motor on, very slowly pour in the oil. By the time all the oil has been added, the mayonnaise will have thickened. Add the dill, spinach and watercress and pulse until finely chopped, scraping the sides of the bowl once or twice.

All ingredients for the mayonnaise must be at room temperature or it will not emulsify into a smooth mixture. For a thicker mayonnaise, use 2 yolks in place of the whole egg. One egg can absorb as much as 1⅓ cups of oil. Less oil will make it less thick but more stable so that it will keep longer. It is fine to use some olive oil, but do not use all olive oil or it will separate sooner.

UNDERSTANDING

Steamed Potatoes

*T*he most evenly cooked potatoes, firm throughout without being over-cooked, are small potatoes that are steamed. They make excellent potato salad but my favorite way of eating them is cold, sliced and dipped into dill mayonnaise.

I especially enjoy presentations where the food becomes an intrinsic part of the décor such as the way these potato slices, suggesting the scales of a fish, garnish the salmon.

Makes: 14 servings

INGREDIENTS	MEASURE *volume*	WEIGHT *ounces/pounds*	*grams/kilograms*
42 1½-inch red-skin potatoes, scrubbed (if only larger ones are available, cut them in half)	.	4 pounds	1 kilograms, 814 grams
salt	2 teaspoons	0.5 ounce	13 grams

Place a vegetable steamer in a large saucepan. Add water to come slightly under the bottom of the steamer and bring it to a boil. Place the potatoes in the steamer and cover tightly. Lower the heat and cook just until tender when pierced with the tip of a sharp knife, about 15 to 20 minutes. (If the saucepan is not large enough and the potatoes are piled on top of each other, the ones on the top will take longer.)

With tongs, transfer the potatoes to a bowl of iced water and set aside until cooled, about 5 minutes. Drain well and place on paper towels. Use a sharp knife to cut the potatoes into even slices.

• After purchasing potatoes, keep them in a cool place, but not in the refrigerator as they would develop an undesirable "sweet" flavor.

POINTERS FOR SUCCESS

Watermelon Ice Cream Bombe

When I was growing up, I was blessed with an extraordinary great-aunt. Pauline Kozma was a dedicated high school French teacher who also worked at the American Association to the UN where she one year received the Eleanor Roosevelt Award for having performed the most foreign service. Her husband, elegantly old-fashioned Uncle Leslie, was an importer of wine and spirits. Although I adored them both, they lived in such a rarefield and gracious manner that a visit to their exquisite apartment in Riverdale always held many unknown terrors for me. I was brought up in a much more casual, child-oriented environment. I didn't know not to put my feet on the chair rungs, or my hands on the walls, or not to pick up a chicken drumstick with my fingers. And I had certainly not experienced food that had wine or liqueur in it. But around the time I was in junior high school and could travel on my own up to the Bronx, Aunt Polly took it upon herself to civilize and educate me in the finer ways. The afternoon would usually begin with a detested French lesson and then proceed to some other cultural discussion. Dinner would be the final lesson, and one day, when Polly asked me if there was anything I couldn't tolerate to eat, I immediately presented her with a lengthy verbal list. She asked with great surprise if I could possibly be allergic to all those things and when I explained that it was simply a question of extreme distaste, her horrifying response was, "That's no excuse," and she proceeded to serve one of them (canned asparagus—horror of horrors). If only I could return to those dinners now, with my passion for speaking French and my more mature palate. (Though I still wouldn't want canned asparagus, even if imported from France.)

The one thing I almost always enjoyed about dinner was dessert. Hannah, the housekeeper, had been a pastry chef in the city of her origin, Vienna. She told stories about separate restaurant kitchens devoted to the brewing of coffee so as not to contaminate its flavor. My favorite of her desserts was her ice cream bombe. Hannah had become a little lazy and used store-bought pistachio ice cream and raspberry sorbet and chocolate chips for pits but I have recreated the recipe directly from my fantasy, making everything from scratch. The ganache seeds are ideal because they don't harden even on freezing and they really do resemble the real thing. Either way, this is a spectacular and fabulously delicious dessert, perfect for the Fourth of July, partly because watermelon is so very American and partly because the word bombe is suggestive of fireworks!

Serves: 8

Freezing time: at least 6 hours

EQUIPMENT:
watermelon mold, at least 6-cup capacity (about 9 inches long)

KEEPS:
Ice cream has the best texture within 3 days of freezing but with the Kirsch will maintain its texture for up to a week.

| INGREDIENTS | MEASURE | WEIGHT | |
	volume	ounces	grams
Pistachio Ice Cream	*(2½ cups)*		
4 large egg yolks	¼ liquid cup	2.5 ounces	74 grams
sugar	½ cup	3.5 ounces	100 grams
unsalted pistachio nuts,* finely ground	⅓ cup	1.75 ounces	50 grams
heavy cream	1½ liquid cups	·	·
milk	½ liquid cup	·	·
OPTIONAL: Kirsch (cherry eau de vie)	1 tablespoon	·	·
green liquid food coloring	4 drops	·	·
Raspberry Sorbet	*(2¼ cups)*		
raspberries, frozen with no sugar added	2 12-ounce bags	24 ounces	680 grams
lemon juice, freshly squeezed	1 tablespoon	·	·
sugar	1 cup	7 ounces	200 grams
OPTIONAL: Chambord liqueur	2 tablespoons	·	·
Chocolate Ganache Seeds	*(65 seeds)*		
bittersweet chocolate, finely chopped	⅔ of a 3-ounce bar	2 ounces	56 grams
heavy cream	1 tablespoon	·	·

*If you can only find salted nuts, place them in a strainer and rinse them in hot tap water; dry with paper towels.

Pistachio Ice Cream

Have a medium bowl ready near the range.

In a small heavy noncorrodible saucepan, stir together the yolks, sugar and pistachio nuts until well blended, using a wooden spoon.

In another small saucepan, scald† the cream and milk to the boiling point. (Or use a heatproof glass measure in a microwave on high power.) Stir a few tablespoons into the yolk mixture, then gradually add the remainder, stirring constantly.

Heat the mixture, stirring constantly to just below the boiling point (170°F. to 180°F.). Steam will begin to appear and the mixture will be slightly thicker than heavy cream; a finger run across the back of a spoon dipped in the mixture will leave a well-defined track. Immediately remove

†Bring just to the boiling point (small bubbles will begin to appear around the edges).

from the heat and pour into a bowl, scraping up the thickened cream on the bottom of the pan. (Strain if desired; I like the small pieces of pistachio in the ice cream.) Cool in an ice-water bath or the refrigerator until cold, at least 2 hours.

Stir in the optional Kirsch and the food coloring. Freeze in an ice cream maker according to the manufacturer's instructions. Allow the ice cream to ripen for at least 2 hours in the freezer until firm but spreadable before assembling in the bombe. Makes 2½ cups.

In a strainer suspended over a deep bowl, thaw the raspberries completely. This will take several hours. (To speed thawing, place in an oven with a pilot light.) Press the berries to force out all the juice. There should be 1 cup.

In a small saucepan, boil the juice until it is reduced to ¼ cup. (Or reduce the juice in a microwave* on high power.) Pour into a lightly oiled heat-proof cup.

Purée the raspberries and strain them through a food mill fitted with the fine disc. Or use a fine strainer to remove all the seeds. You should have 1 liquid cup of purée.

Stir in the raspberry syrup and lemon juice. You should have 1⅓ liquid cups. Add the sugar.[†] Stir until the sugar dissolves. Stir in the Chambord if desired.

Process in an ice cream maker according to manufacturer's instructions. Freeze the sorbet in a covered container for at least 2 hours or until fairly firm. Makes 2¼ cups.

In the upper container of a double boiler set over hot, not simmering, water on low heat, melt the chocolate. (Or melt the chocolate in a microwave on high power, stirring every 10 seconds.) Stir in the cream until smooth and uniform. Use an offset metal spatula to spread the chocolate in a thin layer on wax paper. Allow it to harden at room temperature for several hours or place it in the freezer just until firm, about 20 minutes.

Using the sharp tip of a knife or an elliptical canapé cutter,[‡] form the seeds. Place the sheet of seeds in the freezer until very hard.

Separate the seeds from the chocolate sheet by sliding a knife or metal spatula under the chocolate—the seeds will pop out. Place them on wax paper. Return them to the freezer until hard. Makes about 65 seeds.

Chill the watermelon mold.

Fold half the ganache seeds into the raspberry sorbet.

Spread the pistachio ice cream in the bottom and up the sides of the chilled mold (just to the edge of the decorative part). Freeze for about 30 minutes or until firm.

Raspberry Sorbet

KEEPS:
Sorbet has the best texture within 3 days of freezing but with the Chambord will maintain its texture for up to a week.

Chocolate Ganache Seeds

*If using a microwave, place the juice in a 4-cup heatproof glass measure or bowl to allow for bubbling.

†If you have less raspberry purée, decrease the sugar, using 2¼ teaspoons sugar for each tablespoon of raspberry purée (three-fourth the volume of sugar to purée).

‡Ateco makes a canapé set that contains a ⅞-inch-long cutter.

Fill the center of the mold with the sorbet. Cover tightly and freeze for at least 6 hours or up to a week. (If you have not added the Kirsch and Chambord, freeze no longer than 3 days, or ice crystals will form.)

To unmold, invert the mold onto a serving plate. Run a towel under warm water and wring it out. Drape it evenly over the mold and allow to sit for about 30 seconds. Run the towel under warm water a second time and drape over the mold. Repeat as necessary until when you lift away the mold the bombe slides out. Immediately set it in the freezer for 5 to 10 minutes.

Use a sharp knife dipped in hot water to slice the bombe. Set each slice on a plate and place the remaining chocolate seeds on the raspberry sorbet, pressing them in slightly. If your freezer is very cold and the ice cream and sorbet are still very solid, allow the slices to sit on the plates for 5 to 10 minutes before serving, as the bombe is the most delicious when just beginning to melt slightly.

UNDERSTANDING

The pistachio custard mixture must be heated adequately (to at least 160°F.) to thicken and prevent thinning out on setting, but for a silky smooth sauce that does not curdle, the mixture must not be allowed to boil. The boiling point of water is 212°F. but the other ingredients in the custard mixture lower the boiling point.

The Kirsch and Chambord act as antifreeze, preventing the formation of large ice crystals in the ice cream and sorbet.

POINTERS FOR SUCCESS

Pistachio Ice Cream

- Don't use a whisk to stir the yolk/cream mixture if not using an accurate thermometer because the foam makes it difficult to see when the mixture is getting close to boiling.
- Do not heat the mixture above 180°F. or it will curdle. If overheated and slight curdling does take place, pour instantly into a blender and blend until smooth before straining.
- Do not add more than the recommended amount of Kirsch or the ice cream will not freeze.

Raspberry Sorbet

- Do not add more than the recommended amount of Chambord or the sorbet will not freeze.

Elliott's Favorite Three Bean and Corn Salad

I created this recipe for Elliott when he briefly went on a low-cholesterol diet, because he so loves beans and highly seasoned food and never feels he's missing something when he eats this dish. But now I make it several times each summer because the fresh corn in season adds a touch of both color and sweetness we wouldn't want to do without.

This salad is a delicious one-dish meal to have with friends for a summer luncheon.

Wash the beans and pick out and discard any stones or shriveled beans. Place each type of bean in a separate medium saucepan and add unsalted water to cover by 2 inches.

When ready to cook, drain off the water, rinse the beans and add fresh unsalted water to cover by 2 inches. Bring to a boil, reduce the heat to low and cook at a bare simmer, partially covered, until the beans are just tender but still firm. Add more water if necessary so that the beans are always covered. Test a bean by cutting it in half to see if it is cooked through. Flageolets take from 20 to as long as 75 minutes, black beans 30 to 45 minutes and chick-peas 45 to 55 minutes. Remove the beans from the heat and add ¼ teaspoon salt to each pan. Allow the beans to cool completely in the cooking liquid. (Or drain most of the liquid from the beans and cover them with plastic wrap to prevent cracking.)

Cook the pasta in lightly salted boiling water as per the package directions, 8 to 9 minutes. Drain, and rinse under cold water and drain again.

Place the well-drained pasta in a medium bowl. Add the corn, onion and sundried tomatoes and mix together.

In a 3-quart bowl, whisk together the reserved sun-dried tomato oil and all the ingredients for the vinaigrette. Add the bean mixture and mix until evenly coated with the vinaigrette. Cover the bowl tightly and set aside for 2 hours at room temperature or refrigerate for up to 3 days, stirring occasionally. If the salad has been refrigerated, bring to room temperature before serving. Shortly before serving, garnish with fresh basil sprigs if desired.

Pressure Cooker Method

This is a speedy way to cook dried beans but because cooking time varies with each batch, start with the minimum time and then continue final cooking without pressure until tender. Soak the beans as above. Bring the pressure cooker up to full pressure and cook for 10 minutes. Stop the pressure at once by running cold water over the lid. Test a bean by cutting it in half to see if it is cooked through. Continue cooking if necessary until tender.

Serves: 4 as a main course, 8 as a side dish (makes: 10 cups)

Marinating time: at least 2 hours

Most beans (see Pointers for Success) must be soaked before cooking, either overnight or with the quick-soaking method.

KEEPS:
Leftover bean salad freezes well for up to 3 months but the pasta should be removed as its texture alters.

TO SOAK 8 HOURS OR OVERNIGHT:
Place the beans in a cool spot. If soaking overnight, refrigerate to keep the beans from fermenting.

TO QUICK-SOAK:
Bring the beans to a boil and boil for 2 minutes. Cover, remove from the heat and allow to sit for 1 hour.

| INGREDIENTS | MEASURE | WEIGHT | |
	volume	ounces	grams
dried black beans	1¼ cups	8 ounces	227 grams
dried chick-peas	scant ⅔ cup	4 ounces	113 grams
dried flageolets*	scant ⅔ cup	4 ounces	113 grams
salt	¾ teaspoon	•	•
fusilli pasta	1½ cups	4 ounces	113 grams
fresh cooked corn, cut off the cob (3 medium ears)	1¾ cups	9 ounces	255 grams
1 medium onion, chopped	1½ cups	6.75 ounces	191 grams
18 half pieces sun-dried tomatoes in oil, drained (2 tablespoons oil reserved) and chopped	¾ cup	3.5 ounces	100 grams
Vinaigrette			
olive oil	¼ liquid cup	•	•
cider vinegar	3 tablespoons	•	•
sugar	a pinch	•	•
cayenne pepper	a sprinkling	•	•
black pepper, freshly ground	½ teaspoon	•	•
salt	1 teaspoon	0.25 ounce	6.7 grams
Dijon mustard	1½ teaspoons	0.3 ounce	9 grams
garlic, minced (3 medium cloves)	4 teaspoons	0.5 ounce	14 grams
fresh basil, minced	2 tablespoons	•	10 grams
fresh parsley, preferably flat-leafed, minced	2 tablespoons	0.25 ounce	7 grams
OPTIONAL: fresh basil sprigs, for garnish	•	•	•

*These French beans are available in specialty food stores such as Dean & DeLuca. If desired, they can be replaced by additional black beans. Do not use pea beans or navy beans as they tend to be slightly pasty when cold.

• Beans from a current crop (this information will be written on the package) require no soaking but should be brought to a boil in a large saucepan of water and drained to avoid flatulence. If dried beans are over a year old they may be incapable of rehydration. The older they are, the longer they take to get tender, which means that it is necessary to give a range

POINTERS FOR SUCCESS

of time for doneness. It's best to start checking at the minimum time and continuing cooking as necessary.

- After 4 hours of soaking, beans are about 70 percent hydrated. They do not hydrate fully until about 8 hours. With the quick-soaking technique they hydrate almost as fully as after 8 hours.

- Beans will never soften if they are salted during the cooking process. Once the beans are fully cooked, adding salt to the water keeps their outer shell from absorbing more water, thereby preventing them from further softening.

- For the most evenly tender but firm beans, overnight soaking is best, although the quick-soak method works almost as well.

- To keep the outer shell of the beans from splitting, the cooking water should be just barely simmering.

- Allowing the beans to cool in the cooking water keeps them moist and prevents splitting.

- The best way to drain the beans is with a slotted spoon so that they remain whole and uncrushed.

- Marinating the beans for at least 2 hours allows the flavors to penetrate, making it unnecessary to flavor the beans during cooking.

- To cook the corn, boil it in a pot of unsalted water for 9 minutes or until just tender. Salt added during cooking toughens corn.

Meatballs and Spaghetti

There's no meal I enjoy more than a well-made spaghetti and meatball dinner. This is one dish that is practically impossible to have right if not homemade because upscale restaurants don't bother with it and the kind of restaurants that do don't give it the attention it deserves.

My preference is for a high proportion of bread crumbs in the meatballs so they hold their shape and have substance. I also favor hot sausages and red pepper flakes in the tomato sauce but as this is a favorite family meal, I usually have to forgo the spice for the sake of tender young palates. The tomato sauce, however, whether made with fresh tomatoes or canned, is so flavorful, I hardly miss the extra spice. This is a favorite menu for my nephew Alexander's birthday party because kids and grown-ups alike love it and because his birthday, August 23, is right at the height of the fresh tomato season.

Serves: 8

KEEPS:
The sauce keeps 5 days refrigerated, 3 months frozen.

INGREDIENTS	MEASURE *volume*	WEIGHT	
		ounces/pounds	*grams/kilograms*
Meatballs			
ground beef, pork and veal (ground together)	1 pound ground round, 8 ounces ground pork, and 8 ounces ground veal	2 pounds	907 grams
3 large eggs	5 fluid ounces	5.25 ounces (weighed without shells)	150 grams
dry bread crumbs	1½ cups	6 ounces	172 grams
milk	½ liquid cup	•	•
Parmesan cheese, freshly grated	⅔ cup	2 ounces	56 grams
parsley, preferably flat-leafed, minced	¼ cup	0.5 ounce	15 grams
fresh basil, minced*	¼ cup	0.75 ounce	20 grams
garlic, minced (1 large clove)	1½ teaspoon	•	5 grams
salt	1 teaspoon	0.25 ounce	6.7 grams
black pepper, freshly ground	½ teaspoon	•	•
cayenne pepper	⅛ teaspoon	•	•
Sauce			
Italian plum tomatoes†	•	10 pounds	4.5 kilograms, 36 grams
tomato paste	¼ cup	2.25 ounces	65 grams
2 beef bouillon cubes (or 2 cubes Glace de Viande, page 253, + 1 teaspoon salt)	•	•	•
salt	1 teaspoon	0.25 ounce	6.7 grams
black pepper, freshly ground	¼ teaspoon	•	•
OPTIONAL: red pepper flakes	½ to 1 teaspoon (to taste)	•	•
Angostura bitters	1 teaspoon	•	•
sugar	1 tablespoon	•	12.5 grams
OPTIONAL: 3 sun-dried tomatoes, minced	2 tablespoons	0.75 ounce	20 grams

*Or 1 tablespoon dried.

†Or one 28- to 32-ounce can Italian plum tomatoes plus 2 cups canned tomato sauce, a total of two 6-ounce cans tomato paste and 1 cup water.

INGREDIENTS	MEASURE volume	WEIGHT	
		ounces/pounds	*grams/kilograms*
Italian sausage links, sweet or hot, pricked with a fork	.	1 pound	454 grams
olive oil, divided	3 tablespoons	.	.
½ medium onion, coarsely chopped	½ cup	2.25 ounces	64 grams
garlic, minced (1 large clove)	1½ teaspoons	.	5 grams
dry red wine	½ liquid cup	.	.
fresh oregano, minced*	1 tablespoon	.	2.5 grams
fresh basil, minced*	1 tablespoon		5 grams
spaghettini or spaghetti	.	1.5 pounds	567 grams
freshly grated Parmesan cheese, for serving	.	.	.

*Or 1 tablespoon dried.

In a large bowl, combine all the meatball ingredients and, using your fingers or a wooden spoon, blend them together. Cover and refrigerate.

Peel and seed the tomatoes[†]: Bring a large pot of water to a boil. Blanch the tomatoes in the simmering water for 1 minute. Empty them into a colander to drain. Remove the skin, using the tip of a sharp knife or your fingers. It should slip off easily.

Cut the tomatoes into quarters and remove and discard the seeds and cores, reserving any liquid. Chop the tomatoes coarsely using a large knife or the food processor. Place them in a large Dutch oven along with the reserved liquid. You should have about 8 cups of tomatoes. Cook over medium-high heat until reduced to about 7 cups. Add the tomato paste.

(If using canned tomatoes, drain the tomatoes in a strainer over a bowl, reserving the liquid. Cut the tomatoes into quarters, over the strainer. Remove and discard the seeds and cores, reserving the liquid. Place the tomatoes in a large Dutch oven, add the reserved liquid, the 2 cups tomato sauce, the 2 cans tomato paste, and the 1 cup water and proceed as directed.)

Reduce (or turn on) the heat under the tomatoes to low. Add the bouillon cubes (or Glace de Viande and salt), pepper, optional pepper flakes, Angostura bitters, sugar and optional sun-dried tomatoes and let simmer while you prepare the remaining ingredients.

In a large heavy frying pan over medium heat, sauté the sausages until browned, about 10 minutes. Remove them to paper towels to drain and set aside. Discard the fat from the pan and set the pan aside.

[†]For speed and efficiency, I like to use a Squeezo strainer, a device that removes the skin and seeds without blanching, leaving only the crushed tomato pulp.

Use a meatball shaper or measure about 3 tablespoons of meat mixture per meatball and form 24 meatballs slightly less than 2-inches in diameter. Set aside uncovered (they will develop a slight crust, which helps to keep the shape better when frying).

Heat 1 tablespoon of the oil in the frying pan over medium-low heat and sauté the onion until golden, about 5 minutes. Add the garlic and sauté, stirring constantly, for about 1 minute or until softened. With a spoon, transfer the onions and garlic to the simmering tomato sauce.

Raise the heat under the frying pan to medium and add the remaining 2 tablespoons of oil. Add the meat balls, in two batches so as not to crowd, and brown them, dislodging them gently with the edge of a pancake turner and shaking the pan gently to turn them and keep them as round as possible, about 7 minutes. With a slotted spoon, transfer the meat balls to the simmering tomatoes.

Discard the fat in the pan and, off the heat, deglaze the pan with the wine, stirring and scraping up the browned bits on the bottom of the pan. Stir into the simmering tomatoes, cover partially and simmer over low heat for 1½ hours, stirring occasionally. Add water if the sauce seems to be getting too thick.

Cut the sausages in half crosswise and add them to the sauce along with the oregano and basil. Simmer for 30 minutes longer, adding water if necessary. There should be about 5 cups of sauce. Skim off any fat that has risen to the surface and discard.

Meanwhile, cook the pasta in boiling water, with 1½ tablespoons salt, according to the package directions. Heat the serving plates.

Drain the pasta thoroughly and place it on the warm serving plates. Place 3 meatballs and 1 sausage piece on top of each serving and top with a heaping half cup of sauce. Pass grated Parmesan on the side.

NOTE: I like the sauce to be thick enough to coat the spaghetti well. If the consistency seems too thin at the end of the cooking time, remove the meatballs to a bowl, raise the heat and reduce the sauce to the desired consistency. Be sure to stir often because as the sauce thickens it burns more easily.

Cooking in a Crock Pot

I love to make this recipe in a crock pot because I only have to stir once to equalize the heating and there's no risk of scorching the tomato sauce. I don't like to leave the meatballs and sauce in the pot all day on low, however, as the meatballs overcook. Turn the crock pot to high and proceed as directed above. If using fresh tomatoes, cook until reduced to 6 cups (instead of 7). If using canned tomatoes, omit the water. Cook the meatballs and sauce for 2 hours on high, stir, add the sausage, oregano and basil, lower the heat to low and continue cooking for 2 hours.

POINTERS FOR SUCCESS

- Ground round, which is 85 percent lean, makes a more juicy meatball than sirloin or cuts that are leaner.
- To keep the meat from sticking to the meatball shaper or your fingers, rinse the shaper or your fingers with cold water before each meatball.

Checkerboard Fantasy Cake

Serves: 12

Preheat the oven to: 350°F.
Baking time: 25 minutes

EQUIPMENT:
2 large pastry bags; 2
Number 9 round cake
pastry tubes (¾ inch in
diameter); set of three
9-inch by 1-inch
checkerboard cake pans,
greased, Checkerboard
cake bottoms lined with
parchment or wax paper
and then greased again and
floured

FINISHED HEIGHT:
3¾ inches

KEEPS:
2 days at room
temperature, 5 days
refrigerated, 2 months
frozen.

T*his delightful trompe l'oeil of downy yellow and chocolate checkerboard cake from* The Cake Bible *is the one I choose for my nephew Alexander's annual visit. When he was about to be seven years old, he started the happy tradition of spending his birthday week with us at our house in Hope, New Jersey. He takes great pride in his being grown-up enough to take the flight from San Francisco on his own, thanks to the airline's "young flyers club."*

It seems to me that the highlights of the week for him are diving at least fifty times a day at the local pool, playing with the kids and baby animals at a nearby dairy farm, getting reacquainted with his East Coast cousins at his birthday party and baking with his aunt. Last year he planted himself behind my work island and announced that he wanted to make a mixture entirely on his own. When asked why, he explained, "I want to see what it's like to be Rose Levy Beranbaum—a boy Rose Beranbaum." When he finished making the "fudge" he allowed as to how he thought it was fun being me, to which I replied, "You're right!" (Especially the week he's there.)

The silky smooth chocolate buttercream I use on the cake is a favorite for children and adults. It's easy and fun to spread into big swirls. Alexander especially loves helping with this part of the cake (not to mention cleaning the bowl).

INGREDIENTS	MEASURE	WEIGHT	
room temperature	*volume*	*ounces/pounds*	*grams*
Checkerboard Cake			
extra bittersweet or bittersweet chocolate, preferably Lindt Excellence or Valrhona	1 3-ounce bar	3 ounces	85 grams
4 large eggs	6 full fluid ounces	7 ounces (weighed	200 grams without shells)
milk, divided	1⅓ liquid cups	•	•
pure vanilla extract	1 tablespoon	•	•
sifted cake flour	4 cups (sifted into the cup and leveled off)	14 ounces	400 grams
superfine sugar	2 cups	14 ounces	400 grams
baking powder	2 tablespoons	•	29.5 grams
salt	1 teaspoon	0.25 ounce	6.7 grams
unsalted butter (must be softened)	1 cup	8 ounces	227 grams
Chocolate Neoclassic Buttercream			
6 large egg yolks	3½ fluid ounces	4 ounces	112 grams
sugar	¾ cup	5.25 ounces	150 grams
corn syrup	½ liquid cup	5.75 ounces	164 grams
unsalted butter	2 cups	1 pound	454 grams
bittersweet chocolate, preferably Lindt Excellence, melted and cooled	2 3-ounce bars	6 ounces	170 grams

Preheat the oven to 350°F.

In the upper container of a double boiler, melt the chocolate over hot, not simmering, water, stirring frequently. (Or melt in a microwave on high power, stirring every 10 seconds.) Remove the upper container from the heat and set aside.

In a medium bowl, whisk together the eggs, ⅓ cup of the milk and the vanilla.

In a large mixing bowl, combine the dry ingredients and with an electric mixer on low speed, mix for 30 seconds to blend. Add the butter and the remaining 1 cup of milk. Mix on low speed until the dry ingredients are moistened. Increase the speed to medium (high speed if using a hand-held electric mixer) and beat for 1½ minutes to aerate and develop the cake's structure. Scrape down the sides of the bowl. Gradually add the egg mixture in three batches, beating for 20 seconds after each addition to incorporate the ingredients and strengthen the structure. Scrape down the sides of the bowl.

Divide the batter between two bowls putting slightly more batter in one than in the other (1¾ pounds/793 grams in one bowl, 1½ pounds/680 grams in the other). Stir the melted chocolate into the smaller batch of batter until uniform in color.

Fill two large pastry bags fitted with large number 9 tubes with the two batters.*

Place the divider rings in one of the prepared pans and pipe batter into each section, alternating batter colors. The batter should fill the pan about half full. Using a small metal spatula or the back of a spoon, smooth the top of the batter. Carefully lift out the divider and rinse it off. Pipe batter for the second layer, alternating the colors (i.e., if you started with yellow for the outside ring, for the first layer, start with chocolate). Pipe the batter for the third layer exactly like the first.

Bake for 25 minutes or until a tester inserted near the center comes out clean and the cakes spring back when pressed lightly in the centers. *The cakes should start to shrink from the sides of the pans only after removal from the oven.*

Let the cakes cool in the pans on racks for 10 minutes. Loosen the sides with a small metal spatula and invert the cakes onto greased wire racks. To prevent splitting, reinvert so that the tops are up and cool them completely.

Chocolate Neoclassic Buttercream

Have ready a greased 1-cup heatproof glass measure near the range.

In a medium bowl, beat the yolks with the whisk beater of an electric mixer until light in color.

Combine the sugar and corn syrup in a small saucepan (preferably with a nonstick lining) and heat, stirring constantly, until the sugar dissolves and the syrup comes to a rolling boil. The entire surface will be covered with large bubbles. (If using a stand mixer, you can heat the sugar syrup while the yolks are beating.) *Immediately transfer the syrup to the glass measure to stop the cooking.*

If using a hand-held electric mixer, beat the syrup into the yolks in a steady stream. Don't allow any syrup to fall on the beaters or they will spin it onto the sides of the bowl. If using a stand mixer, pour a small amount of syrup over the yolks with the mixer turned off. Then immediately beat at high speed for 5 seconds. Stop the mixer and add a larger amount of syrup. Beat at high speed for 5 seconds. Continue with the remaining syrup. For the last addition use a rubber scraper to remove the syrup clinging to the glass measure. Continue beating until cool. Be sure the mixture is *completely* cool before adding the butter because if the butter starts to melt, the buttercream will no longer firm correctly.

*You may use glass measuring cups to pour the batter into the pans, but pastry bags are faster and easier to use.

Gradually beat in the butter. (The buttercream will not thicken until almost all of the butter has been added.) Beat in the cooled melted chocolate. Makes 4 cups.

To assemble the cake, stack the layers so that the outside colors alternate, using a very thin coating of the buttercream to make the layers adhere without disturbing the checkerboard effect. With a small metal spatula, swirl the remaining buttercream onto the top and sides of the cake.

POINTERS FOR SUCCESS
Checkerboard Cake

- Use superfine sugar for the finest texture. (You can make it by processing granulated sugar in the food processor for a few minutes until fine.)
- Use cake flour without leavening.
- Use unsalted butter for the best flavor.
- Use fresh baking powder (under a year old).
- If using a hand-held mixer, beat at high speed.
- To keep the serving plate clean, slide 3 or 4 long narrow pieces of waxed paper between the cake and the plate before frosting. Slip them out after frosting.

Chocolate Neoclassic Buttercream

- The syrup must come to a rolling boil or the buttercream will be too thin.
- Using a hand-held beater makes it easier to pour the syrup around the spinning beater.
- The chocolate must be fluid but not warm when added to the buttercream because if it starts to melt the butter, the buttercream will never firm correctly.

UNDERSTANDING

A slightly higher proportion of baking powder than usual is used for this cake because the pans are only 1 inch high.

The batter is thick enough to pipe through a pastry bag, making filling the special sections of these pans quick and easy.

I use melted chocolate instead of cocoa because it is more convenient to add to the batter and also because its less intense chocolate flavor blends better with the more subtle yellow cake.

Barbecued Chicken

Barbecued chicken is a summer favorite for friends, family or just the two of us and makes frequent appearances throughout the barbecue season, from the moment the dust cover comes off the Weber grill. This is our traditional Labor Day barbecue.

Serves: 4 to 6

INGREDIENTS	MEASURE *volume*	WEIGHT	
		ounces/pounds	*grams/kilograms*
2 3- to 3½-pound chickens	.	6 to 7 pounds	2 kilograms, 722 grams to 3 kilograms, 175 grams
lemon juice, freshly squeezed (2 lemons)	about ¼ liquid cup	.	.
salt	1 tablespoon	0.25 ounce	20 grams
cayenne pepper	2 teaspoons	.	.
black pepper, freshly ground	a few grindings	.	.
4 medium cloves garlic, smashed and peeled	.	0.75 ounce	20 grams
My Best Barbecue Sauce (page 154)	2 cups	19.5 ounces	560 grams
OPTIONAL: mesquite chips, for the grill	a handful	.	.

Rinse the chickens under cold running water and dry with paper towels. Cut into serving pieces: I like to cut the chicken at all the joints, cutting the breast and back section into halves. If desired, the chicken can be cut into quarters, or the leg and thigh and the wing sections can be left intact.

Place the chicken pieces in a large bowl and sprinkle with the lemon juice, salt, cayenne and black pepper, tossing to coat them well. Add the garlic cloves, cover tightly and refrigerate until 1 hour before grilling.

A day ahead or at least 2 hours ahead, marinate the chicken.

Use indirect heat to grill: Place the coals on both sides of the grill away from the center, and light them.

When the coals are ready, sprinkle them with the soaked mesquite. Lightly oil the grill rack and place the chicken on it, skin side up, so that most of it is not directly over the coals; the dark meat pieces should be closer to the coals than the white meat. Grill, covered, for 10 minutes. Turn the chicken skin side down and continue grilling, covered, for 5 minutes. Brush with the barbecue sauce and continue grilling, covered, for 5 minutes. Turn the chicken skin side up. Brush with sauce, cover, close the vents and leave on the grill for 5 minutes. (If you are using an electric grill, turn it off.) Serve with extra sauce.

At least 1 hour before grilling, place the mesquite in a small bowl with water to cover.

NOTE: If you are using larger chickens or grilling on a cool or windy day the chicken can take as long as 45 minutes to cook. Wait until the chicken is almost done (when pierced with a knife the juices run clear) before applying the barbecue sauce to prevent burning.

Real hardwood charcoal is now available in many supermarkets throughout the country or mail order from Nature's Own (800-289-2427). It burns hotter and results in more flavor. Gas grills simply do not provide the flavor produced even by ordinary charcoal.

My Best Barbecue Sauce

Makes: 3 cups

This zesty, sweet-sour tomato sauce clings nicely to chicken, ribs or brisket. It keeps so well I often make a huge batch to use for the whole barbecue season: Memorial Day to Labor Day.

INGREDIENTS	MEASURE	WEIGHT	
	volume	ounces	grams
tomato chili sauce	1 12-ounce bottle	12 ounces	340 grams
tomato purée	1 liquid cup	·	·
Worcestershire sauce	⅓ liquid cup	·	·
cider vinegar	¼ liquid cup	·	·
light brown sugar	¼ tightly packed cup	2 ounces	54 grams
vegetable oil	1 tablespoon	·	·
1 medium onion, coarsely chopped	1⅓ cups	6 ounces	170 grams
1 large clove garlic, smashed and peeled	·	·	6 grams
dry mustard	1½ teaspoons	·	·
pepper, freshly ground	½ teaspoon	·	·

KEEPS:
Several months refrigerated.

Pour the chili sauce into a 2-quart heavy saucepan. Fill the bottle with water and shake well to free any chili sauce remaining in the bottle. Pour the water into the sauce. Add all the remaining ingredients and bring to a boil. Simmer, uncovered, over the lowest possible heat, stirring often to prevent scorching, until the sauce has reduced to 3 cups, about 1 to 1½ hours. Let cool.

Pour the sauce into a jar and cover tightly.

Baked Potatoes with Sour Cream and Chives

Serves: 6

Preheat the oven to: 400°F
Baking time: 50 minutes to
1 hour

EQUIPMENT:
6 potato nails, optional

What could be more easy to make, more delicious—and more unattainable at most restaurants—than a simple well-baked potato? Maybe the problem is that baked potatoes are so humble that chefs who would know what to do with them wouldn't dream of putting them on the menu, and less pretentious cooks often take advantage of the potato's forgiving nature by baking them way ahead of serving, wrapping them in foil and holding them for so long they turn steamy and weirdly sweet tasting.

I could make a meal of a well-baked potato: one with crisp skin, a mealy dry and fluffy interior, squeezed open to receive a large pat of sweet butter or a dollop of sour cream, freshly ground pepper, and chopped chives fresh from the garden by the grill. In fact, this is just what I did this year for lunch every day when skiing in Sun Valley, Idaho. They sure know how to bake potatoes there, but after all if they don't, who would?

I almost always serve baked potatoes with barbecue of any sort, putting them on the side of the grill for about ten minutes to pick up a hint of smoke from the coals.

INGREDIENTS	MEASURE volume	WEIGHT ounces/pounds	grams/kilograms
6 Idaho potatoes, about 5 inches long	.	3 pounds	1 kilograms, 360 grams
olive oil or olive oil spray	about 2 tablespoons	.	.
salt	to taste	.	
pepper, freshly ground	to taste	.	.
sour cream	1 cup	8 ounces	242 grams
chives, finely chopped	2 tablespoons	0.25 ounce	7 grams

Preheat the oven to 400°F.

Pierce each potato a few times. If desired, insert the potato nails lengthwise through the potatoes. Wipe or spray the potatoes lightly with the oil. Place them directly on the oven rack and bake for 20 to 30 minutes. Use tongs to turn them over and continue baking until tender when pierced with a fork. If desired, place them on the side of the barbecue grill for 10 minutes.

When ready to serve, make a long slash lengthwise down the center of each potato. Push the ends of the potato together slightly to fluff up the insides. Sprinkle with salt and pepper to taste.

Serve the sour cream and chives on the side.

**POINTERS FOR
SUCCESS**

UNDERSTANDING

• After purchasing potatoes, keep them in a cool place, but not in the refrigerator as they would develop an undesirable "sweet" flavor.

The potatoes are pierced to prevent the steam that builds up in their interiors from bursting them.

Oil allows the skins to crisp without becoming hard and dry.

Potato nails conduct the heat to the center of the potato, speeding up the cooking.

Terry Frishman's Tomato Salad

Serves: 6

By *Labor Day, I've gotten a tiny bit past the delight of eating fresh tomatoes right off the vine, still warm from the sun, because by September, I usually have a bumper crop and am looking for some exciting new way to serve them. When our friends Terry and Garry invited us for dinner, as we entered the dining room, the garlicky, herby aroma of these tomatoes infused the atmosphere. This dressing makes even out-of-season tomatoes quite delicious.*

INGREDIENTS	MEASURE volume	WEIGHT ounces/pounds	grams/kilograms
6 ripe tomatoes, sliced ¼ to ½ inch thick	.	3 pounds	1 kilogram, 361 grams
garlic, minced (1 medium clove)	1 teaspoon	.	3.5 grams
2 scallions, thinly sliced (green and white parts)	⅓ cup	1 ounce	28 grams
fresh parsley, preferably flat-leafed, minced	2 tablespoons	0.25 ounce	8 grams
balsamic vinegar	2 tablespoons	.	.
olive oil	⅓ liquid cup	.	.
salt	¼ teaspoon	.	.
pepper, freshly ground	⅛ teaspoon	.	.

On a large serving platter, arrange the tomato slices. Sprinkle them with the garlic, scallions, parsley, vinegar and olive oil and allow to sit for at least 1 hour at room temperature.

Shortly before serving, sprinkle the tomatoes with the salt and pepper.

Quintessential Corn Fingers

I had been collecting corn bread recipes for years but each one I tried was a disappointment, mainly because the texture was invariably coarse instead of the fine soft texture I'd been seeking. I was beginning to think that great corn bread, particularly corn fingers (the corn bread is baked in a mold that forms miniature corncob shapes), was a figment of my imagination until two years ago when I finally reached the end of my quest: The corn fingers at Campton Place in San Francisco are my idea of perfection. Tender, fine grained, slightly sweet with little nublets of corn in each bite and glad surprises of occasional hot pepper flakes, the corn fingers dissolve in your mouth yet have a full corn flavor. I know San Franciscans who love the food at Campton Place but return with mainly one thing in mind: to eat more of those corn fingers!

I was invited to lunch at Campton Place on Tuesday, October 17, 1989, by my friend Bernadette Vaughn. "Sasha," I said, "I forgot how wonderful these corn fingers are. In fact, they are the best I have ever eaten. I'd give anything for the recipe." "Why don't you ask them for it; I'm sure they'll give it to you," was her nonchalant reply that inspired me with the courage to ask the maitre d' for the recipe. And after lunch it appeared, perfectly typed on the beautiful pale gray Campton Place stationary with the swan logo. I was in heaven.

I protectively took the recipe back to my hotel room on Nob Hill before going to an appointment a few blocks below at the Portman Hotel—which is where I was when the earthquake hit. Anyone who has ever been in a natural disaster will tell you that the events immediately preceding and following it are marked as in a picture frame with indelible clarity. What I remember most is the absolute suddenness, the shockingly total lack of control and helplessness in the face of enormous unreasonable force. Then weak knees, fear and a desire to take some action. And finally, when the worst was over, the inevitable thought surfaced: "Where is that precious corn finger recipe and, if worse came to worst, would they give it to me a second time or was it just a fluke that was never meant to be after all?"

The following day, accompanied by my brother and a porter, I walked up the many flights of stairs in the disabled, vacated hotel, perched on the very top of Nob Hill. The massive walls were cracked all the way up to the top floor, and one of the walls in my room had a long jagged crack in it. As I looked out the window, with a panoramic view of the city below, fear gripped me again and I began to feel lightheaded. I threw my things into my bags as fast as I could but this time folded *the recipe and put it in my purse, where it stayed until I reached home. When I studied the recipe the secret of its tender texture and rich flavor was immediately apparent: heavy cream and a little extra sugar.

Makes: 12 to 13 corn fingers

Preheat the oven to: 425°F. Baking time: 15 minutes

EQUIPMENT:
2 cast-iron corn finger molds, sprayed with nonstick vegetable shortening or lightly greased (or bake in two batches using 1 mold)

KEEPS:
Corn fingers freeze well for several weeks. Wrap each airtight in plastic wrap and place in heavy-duty freezer bags. To reheat from frozen, warm in a preheated 400°F. oven for 7 minutes.

Recently, my friend Joceleine Daquin came from France to visit her daughter, Ariane, and I invited them for dinner. Since the Daquins come from the Southwest of France I thought it would be especially appropriate to make them something with American Southwest inspiration so I made the corn fingers as hors d'oeuvre. After two bites, Joceleine looked at me with wide entreating eyes and said, "We have a lot of corn in Gascogny and I have been looking for a recipe for good corn fingers for years. They are never so tender and delicious. Would you possibly give me the recipe for our restaurant?"

Now there are four places in the world where you will be able to find these corn fingers: Campton Place in San Francisco, Chez André Daquin in Auch, France, my house in Hope, New Jersey, and your own home. Here is the recipe: keep it in a safe place!

INGREDIENTS	MEASURE	WEIGHT	
	volume	*ounces*	*grams*
yellow cornmeal (preferably stone-ground)	½ cup	2.25 ounces	64 grams
bleached all-purpose flour	½ cup (dip and sweep method)	2.5 ounces	75 grams
sugar	2 tablespoons + 2 teaspoons	1 ounce	33 grams
baking powder	1¼ teaspoons	•	6 grams
salt	½ teaspoon	•	•
hot pepper flakes	½ to 1 teaspoon (to taste)	•.	•
fresh cooked corn, cut off the cob (2 small ears)	1 cup	5 ounces	142 grams
unsalted butter, melted	4 tablespoons	2 ounces	57 grams
heavy cream	⅓ liquid cup	•	•
milk	⅓ liquid cup	•	•
1 large egg, separated:			
yolk	1 tablespoon + ½ teaspoon	0.65 ounce	18.6 grams
white	2 tablespoons	1 ounce	30 grams

Preheat the oven to 425°F. Five to 10 minutes before the batter is ready, preheat the molds.

In a medium bowl, stir together the cornmeal, flour, sugar, baking powder, salt and hot pepper flakes. Add the corn and stir until coated.

In a small glass measuring cup or bowl, lightly whisk together the butter, cream, milk and egg yolk.

In a medium bowl, beat the egg white until soft peaks form when the beater is lifted slowly.

Stir the egg yolk mixture into the corn mixture just until moistened. There should still be some lumps remaining. Fold in the egg white just until incorporated.

Spoon or pipe the batter into the molds, filling them almost to the top. (If piping, use a pastry bag fitted with a plain ½-inch-wide tube.) Use a small metal spatula or the back of a teaspoon to smooth the batter if necessary. Fill any empty depressions half full with water.

Bake for 15 minutes or until the tops are golden brown. To unmold, loosen the sides of each corn finger with a small metal spatula. Place a wire rack over one of the molds and invert together. Repeat with the second mold. These corn fingers are so tender they require care to avoid breaking them while still warm.

Serve warm or at room temperature.

POINTERS FOR SUCCESS

- To cook the corn, boil it in a pot of unsalted water for 9 minutes or until just tender. Salt added during cooking toughens corn. Vacuum-packed corn kernels, drained, can be substituted for the freshly cooked corn.
- Piping the batter is neater and faster than using a spoon. A pastry bag works best for this batter because it is stiffer than a heavy-duty plastic bag.

UNDERSTANDING

Filing any empty depressions in the molds with water prevents the heat from being drawn to those areas and adds moisture as well.

David Shamah's Back Porch Diet Lemonade

Serves 6

Lemonade is the most refreshing nonalcoholic drink I know. Because it is so easy to drink gallons of it, and so much sweetness is necessary to balance the lemon juice, my friend David has come up with an excellent solution.

This is the only time I use a sugar substitute for anything. But the lovely, fresh flavor of freshly squeezed lemon juice overrides it.

I make this so often in the summer I keep the recipe on the refrigerator door.

INGREDIENTS	MEASURE volume	WEIGHT ounces	grams
lemon juice, freshly squeezed (about 6 to 8 lemons)	1 liquid cup	.	.
cold water	4 liquid cups	.	.
15 packets* Equal (NutraSweet)	2 tablespoons	0.5 ounce	15 grams
6⅛-inch-thick lemon slices (cut from the center section of 1 lemon)	.	.	.

*Or for nondietetic lemonade, ¾ cup (5.25 ounces/150 grams) superfine sugar.

In a large pitcher, combine the lemon juice, water and Equal and stir until the powder is dissolved. Add the lemon slices.

To serve, place a few ice cubes in each glass and pour the lemonade over them. Use tongs to place a lemon slice in each glass.

POINTERS FOR SUCCESS

• To extract more juice from lemons, warm them first for 10 minutes in a low oven or for about 20 seconds in the microwave. Roll them on the counter to break down the membranes and release more juice before cutting them open.
• For one serving: 2 tablespoons lemon juice, ½ cup water and ¾ teaspoon NutraSweet (or 1½ tablespoons superfine sugar).

UNDERSTANDING

Equal (NutraSweet) is 6 times as sweet as sugar.

Double Chocolate Oriolos

These amazing cookies are named for Richard Oriolo, beloved art director and designer of all of my books, because he simply cannot eat enough of them. Perhaps it's because they are intensely chocolatey and buttery yet extraordinarily light, and so easy to swallow. The chocolate buttercream topping is silky smooth under its crown of crunchy toasted walnuts. It stays spreadably soft for hours at room temperature but hardens overnight or on refrigeration just enough to be able to stack the cookies for packaging.

This cookie has it all—guaranteed to become part of your permanent collection.

Makes: 34 2¼-inch cookies

Preheat the oven to: 325°F.
Baking time: 20 to 25 minutes
KEEPS:
3 weeks at room temperature, several months frozen.

INGREDIENTS	MEASURE volume	WEIGHT ounces	grams
Chocolate Cookies			
walnuts, divided	½ cup + ⅔ cup	4.25 ounces	120 grams
unsalted butter, cold	10 tablespoons	5 ounces	142 grams
unsweetened cocoa, preferably Dutch-processed	¼ cup (lightly spooned into the cup and leveled off)	0.75 ounce	23 grams
powdered sugar	⅓ cup (lightly spooned into the cup and leveled off)	1.33 ounces	38 grams
granulated sugar	⅓ cup	2.33 ounces	66 grams
bleached all-purpose flour	¾ cup (dip and sweep method)	3.75 ounces	109 grams
Chocolate Walnut Buttercream	½ cup		
bittersweet chocolate, preferably Lindt	1 3-ounce bar	3 ounces	84 grams
unsalted butter, softened	3 tablespoons	1.5 ounces	43 grams
corn syrup	½ teaspoon	•	•
pure vanilla extract	½ teaspoon	•	•

At least 15 minutes before baking, place two oven racks in the upper and lower thirds of the oven and preheat the oven to 325°F.

Place the walnuts on a cookie sheet and toast them in the oven for 10 minutes, stirring occasionally, until lightly browned.

Cut the butter into 1-inch cubes, and wrap and refrigerate.

In a food processor with the metal blade, process ½ cup (1¾ ounces/50 grams) of the walnuts, the cocoa and the powdered and granulated sugars until the walnuts are finely ground. Add the butter and pulse in until absorbed. Add the flour and pulse in until there are a lot of little moist crumbly pieces and no dry flour particles remain.

Dump the dough into a plastic bag and press it together. Remove the dough from the bag and knead it lightly until it holds together.

Food Processor Method

Soften the butter. Grate ½ cup of the walnuts very fine. Sift the cocoa.

In a medium bowl, whisk together the grated walnuts, cocoa and sugars.

In a large bowl, cream the butter with the sugar mixture until light and fluffy. With the electric mixer or your fingers, mix in the flour until incorporated. (If using the mixer, add the flour in two parts.)

Electric Mixer Method or by Hand

Measure scant tablespoons of dough. Roll each tablespoon of dough between your palms to form a 1-inch ball. Place them 2 inches apart on ungreased cookie sheets. Use the bottom of a glass tumbler, dipped in granulated sugar, to flatten each cookie to about 1½ inches in diameter.

Bake the cookies for 20 to 25 minutes or until they are firm enough to lift from the sheets but still soft when pressed lightly on top. (Do not overbake.) For even baking, rotate the cookie sheets from top to bottom and front to back halfway through the baking period. Cool the cookies on the sheets for 2 minutes. Transfer them to racks to cool completely.

While the cookies are baking, prepare the chocolate buttercream topping: In the upper container of a double boiler set over hot, not simmering, water over low heat, melt the chocolate. (Or melt in a microwave on high power, stirring every 10 seconds.) Remove the upper container from the heat before the chocolate is fully melted and stir until blended. Stir in the butter, 1 tablespoon at a time, until blended. If necessary, return briefly to the heat but do not allow the mixture to become too hot or the butter will separate. Stir in the corn syrup and vanilla. Let the buttercream stand at room temperature for about 1 hour or until thick enough to spread.

Chop the remaining ⅔ cup of toasted walnuts medium-coarse.

Use a small metal spatula to spread the buttercream on the cookies. Sprinkle the nuts on top. Allow the topping to set overnight at room temperature or refrigerate for 30 minutes before storing the cookies in airtight containers.

For Both Methods

Toasting the walnuts enhances their flavor.

The butter in the chocolate topping not only enhances the flavor, it also creates the satiny texture and completely keeps the chocolate from streaking when it sets.

UNDERSTANDING

Fall

❖❖❖❖

Columbus Day

Lamb Osso Buco
Risotto Milanese
The Best All-American Apple Pie
Perfect Flaky Cream Cheese Pie Crust
Triple Vanilla Lover's Ice Cream
Caramel Sauce

Halloween

English Gingerbread

Election Day

Orange Election Day Cheesecake

Thanksgiving

Graavlax with Sweet Mustard Dill Sauce
Turkey with Sausage and Chestnut Stuffing
Rick Rodgers's Rolled Herbed Turkey Breast
Mom's Healthy but Delicious Coleslaw
Cranraspberry Sauce
Low-Profile Pecan Pie
Perfect Flaky Cream Cheese Pie Crust

❖ ❖ ❖ ❖

Hanukkah

*Celia's Pure Potato Latkes
Rosy McApple Sauce
Orange Glow Chiffon Cake*

Holiday Cheer

*The Cannonball
Hot Buttered Rum Cider*

Christmas Tree Cookies

*Stained Glass
Traditional Rolled Christmas Sugar Cookies
Gingerbread People
Christmas Wreaths*

Christmas Eve

Petrossian Blini and Caviar

Christmas Dinner

*Sage and Thyme Roasted Goose
Salt and Pepper Wild Rice
Cousin Marion's Pickled Grapes
Chocolate Raspberry Trifle
Bourbon Pecan Butter Balls*

Lamb Osso Buco

Ibegan... started making osso buco with lamb instead of veal because lamb marrow is my favorite, and much to my delight, I found I prefer the rich intense flavor the lamb shanks give to the dish rather than the more delicate, less assertive flavor of the traditional veal.

This hearty meal is for when the cooler weather arrives. I chose it for Columbus Day because it is an example of Italian inspiration and American innovation.

Serves: 6

INGREDIENTS	MEASURE *volume*	WEIGHT	
		ounces/pounds	*grams/kilograms*
all-purpose flour	¼ cup	1.25 ounces	36 grams
salt	1¾ teaspoons	0.4 ounce	12 grams
pepper, freshly ground	½ teaspoon	•	•
6 lamb shanks, about 16 ounces each, each sawed crosswise into 2 pieces (have the butcher do this)	•	6 pounds	2 kilograms, 722 grams
olive oil, divided	¼ liquid cup	•	•
unsalted butter	2 tablespoons	1 ounce	28 grams
3 small carrots, scraped and chopped	1 cup	4.5 ounces	128 grams
celery, finely chopped (about ¼ stalk including leaves)	¼ cup	1 ounce	30 grams
1 medium onion, chopped	1 cup	4.5 ounces	128 grams
garlic, minced (1 small clove)	1 teaspoon	•	3.5 grams
tomato sauce	1 8-ounce can	8 ounces	227 grams
dry white vermouth or white wine	1 liquid cup	•	•
dried basil	1 teaspoon	•	•
dried thyme	½ teaspoon	•	•
1 bay leaf	•	•	•
Gremolada			
lemon zest, finely grated	1 teaspoon	•	2 grams
fresh parsley, preferably flat-leafed, minced	2 tablespoons	0.25 ounce	8 grams
garlic, minced (1 small clove)	½ teaspoon	•	•

On a large plate, mix the flour with the salt and pepper. Roll each piece of lamb shank in the flour mixture and shake off the excess. Reserve any remaining flour.

Heat a large heavy frying pan, preferably cast iron, over medium-high heat until hot. Add 1 tablespoon of the oil and heat until a film appears over the oil. Add only as much lamb as will fit without crowding and brown on all sides, about 8 to 10 minutes, adding more oil as necessary to keep the lamb from sticking. Remove the lamb to a bowl and set it aside. Pour off the fat and discard it.

In the same pan, heat the butter until bubbling. Sauté the carrots, celery and onion for about 5 minutes or until the onion is softened and translucent. Sprinkle on any remaining flour mixture, stir in the garlic and cook, stirring, for about 30 seconds.

Stir in the tomato sauce, vermouth or white wine, basil, thyme and bay leaf. Add the shanks and bring to a boil. Reduce the heat to low, cover and simmer for about 1¾ to 2 hours or until tender, turning the shanks once after 45 minutes. A knife inserted into the meat should enter easily but the meat should not be falling off the bone. If the sauce becomes too thick, add a few tablespoons of boiling water.

While the shanks are cooking, prepare the gremolada: Combine the lemon zest, parsley and garlic and chop together until very finely chopped and well blended.

When the shanks are done, add the gremolada to the pan and turn the shanks. Cover, remove from the heat and allow to sit for 5 to 10 minutes before serving.

Arrange the shanks on a warmed serving dish. (If the sauce seems too thin, boil over moderately high heat, stirring constantly, until reduced to about 2 cups.) Spoon the sauce over the shanks.

 POINTERS FOR SUCCESS

- For finely grated zest, use a zester (a small implement with tiny scraping holes), a vegetable peeler or a fine grater to remove the yellow portion only of the lemon rind. The white pith beneath is bitter. If using the zester or peeler, finish by chopping the zest with a sharp knife.

Risotto Milanese

I have known Lorna Sass, author of several excellent cookbooks, for over twenty years, in fact since before either of us was involved with food as a profession.

When Lorna sent me her cookbook Cooking Under Pressure (William Morrow, 1989), she included a little note saying: "Be sure to try the risotto." Yes! The pressure cooker is the ideal way to make pearly risotto with a creamy-firm texture. Using the pressure cooker means nine minutes of cooking without stirring as opposed to twenty to thirty minutes with constant stirring, and the results are perfect. Since risotto is too wonderful to miss, here are both methods.

Serves: 6 as a side dish

INGREDIENTS	MEASURE volume	WEIGHT ounces	grams
saffron threads	⅛ teaspoon	•	•
salt	½ teaspoon, plus more to taste*	•	•
low-salt chicken broth†	2¼ liquid cups‡	•	•
olive oil	2 teaspoons	0.25 ounce	9 grams
unsalted butter, divided	4 teaspoons	0.66 ounce	19 grams
shallots, minced, or onions, minced	1 tablespoon 2 tablespoons	0.25 ounce 0.6 ounce	9 grams 18 grams
Arborio rice	1 cup	6.75 ounces	190 grams
vermouth or dry white wine	¼ liquid cup	•	•
pepper, freshly ground	to taste	•	•
Parmesan cheese, freshly grated	¼ cup	0.5 ounce	14 grams
OPTIONAL: grated Parmesan cheese, for serving	•	•	•

*Omit the salt if using salted broth.
†Or 3 cubes Glace de Volaille (page 256), dissolved in 2¼ cups boiling water.
‡If not using a pressure cooker, you will need 3 cups broth plus ⅔ cup water.

Chop the saffron threads into small pieces. Add the saffron and salt to the chicken broth. (If you are not using a pressure cooker, heat the broth and water and keep covered to prevent evaporation.)

In a pressure cooker or a medium-size saucepan over medium-low heat, heat the oil with 2 teaspoons of the butter. Sauté the shallots, stirring often, for about a minute or until translucent. Add the rice and sauté, stirring constantly to coat the rice with the oil, for about 2 minutes or until lightly glazed. Stir in the vermouth (most of it will evaporate).

If using a pressure cooker, add the broth. Lock the lid in place and over high heat, bring the pressure to high. Lower the heat but maintain high pressure. Cook for 9 minutes. Place the pressure cooker in the sink and run cold water over the lid until the pressure is released. Open the lid away from your face to avoid any steam. A little liquid will still be visible. Use a wooden spoon to stir it into the rice, scraping to release any grains that may have stuck to the bottom. (If not using a pressure cooker, add the hot broth about ⅓ cup at a time, and cook, stirring frequently, until each addition has been absorbed before adding more. You may not need all the liquid, or you may need slightly more. When done, the rice should be creamy and tender but with still a little bite. A grain cut in half will be opaque in the center.)

Sprinkle the rice with the pepper. Add the ¼ cup of grated cheese and the remaining 2 teaspoons of butter and stir until blended. Add salt to taste. Serve at once. (If you need to hold the rice for a short period of time, cover it and set it aside before adding the pepper, cheese, butter and salt.)

Pass extra grated Parmesan if desired.

NOTE: One of my favorite special additions to risotto is a small amount of poached marrow cut into ¼-inch pieces and served on top of each portion. The heat of the risotto will soften the marrow. To prepare the marrow, purchase beef bones, preferably from the shin. Run a skewer around the marrow to release it from the bone and push the marrow out in one piece. Place the marrow in a bowl of lightly salted cold water and refrigerate it overnight to remove the blood. Drain the marrow and cut it into ¼-inch slices. Poach it in lightly salted water for 3 minutes or until translucent and soft. Be careful not to overcook the marrow or it will melt completely. Drain and set aside.

To serve this risotto as a fabulous appetizer during white truffle season (November to December), shave thin slices of truffle over each portion.

The design of pressure cookers has improved vastly since my first one, which had been a wedding present to my mother in the 1940s and which she had always been afraid to use. My two favorite models are manufactured by Cuisinarts and Kuhn-Rikkon.

UNDERSTANDING

Low-salt broth is preferable to ordinary broth, which has about 1 teaspoon of salt per cup. If you use ordinary broth, even if omitting the added salt, the risotto will still be saltier than if you used the low-salt broth and the added ½ teaspoon of salt.

The Best All-American Apple Pie

My first apple pie was an apple sauce pie, but not because that was what I wanted it to be. It was because I used my then-favorite eating apples: McIntosh. I had envisioned a pie like ones I had seen in photos, where the crust was highly domed and dimpled from the abundance of apple slices piled high within, so I peeled, cored, sliced and mounded as many apples as would fit the bottom crust without sliding out and carefully draped the top crust over them. The baked pie turned out beautifully golden and majestically high. I could hardly wait for it to cool enough to slice into it. But when I did, I was shocked and disappointed to see that the crust stood alone, towering above a thin layer of melted apples. Apparently the apples had stayed firm long enough for the crust to set and hold its shape and then the high moisture content of the apples (which makes them so delightfully juicy to eat raw) caused them to soften and dissolve. That was when I learned my first lesson about apple pie: Much depends on the type of apples and a juicy apple like a McIntosh is not a good baking apple.

Years later, newly married, we bought a country house that had only three quarters of an acre of land, but on it resided a magnificent one-hundred-year-old Baldwin apple tree. We were warned by the previous owners that this old-fashioned tree produced apples that were perfect for pies, but only every third year and that when this third year arrived, it would produce so lavishly we would not know what to do with all the apples that would end up dropping from the tree, rotting only to be crushed underfoot.

I waited anxiously for that third year of my apple tree's season. I turned on the huge upright freezer in the basement weeks in advance in anticipation of filling it with unbaked apple pies. And as the apples started turning from solid green to a faint blush of pink, I made my second apple pie. The apples were perfect, but they were sitting in a puddle of juices that soaked the bottom crust, despite the tapioca I had sprinkled on it before adding the apples. I considered adding more cornstarch to the filling but disliked the idea of corrupting the texture and flavor of the apples. That was when inspiration struck. Why not reduce the juices! I had noticed that while sitting with the sugar and spice mixture, the apple slices had begun to excude liquid. I surmised that by concentrating this liquid, the sugars would caramelize slightly and the liquid would become syrupy, so that the baked filling would be juicy but not runny. My fruit pies have never been the same since. I found that not only does this technique work for apples, it also is excellent for peaches and nectarines or any other juicy fruit. And only about half the usual amount of thickener is required. In fact, when making buckles, I use no thickener at all.

I went on to make twenty-four apple pies that season, some with Cheddar cheese in the crust, the rest with just a plain flaky butter crust, which in the end we preferred. When I baked the first of the pies I had frozen I discovered the third great secret: Fruit pies baked from frozen have crisper bottom crusts. (The reason is that the bottom crust, being closer to the bottom of the pan,

Serves: 8

Preheat the oven to: 425°F. Baking time: 50 to 60 minutes

EQUIPMENT:
9-inch pie plate

KEEPS:
2 days at room temperature.

starts to bake before the fruit has defrosted and bakes longer than it would normally.)

Three years later, when the next bumper apple crop appeared, I went back into production but time allowed only making six pies, so I offered baskets of apples as gifts. And then we found our dream house a few miles away, up in the mountains, surrounded by acres of hemlock, pine and maple—but no apple trees. So for my fall apple pies I buy local apples like Macoun, Stayman-Winesap, Cortland or Jonathan. Other great baking apples I've discovered that are available around the country are Rhode Island Greening, York Imperial, Northern Spy and Newtown Pippin. My cousin Sue, who always brings the Thanksgiving apple pie, likes to combine three or four varieties of apple. She also adds brandy-soaked raisins to her filling. In the winter, I use Granny Smith apples from the market, which also make a marvelous pie using the concentration technique.

A few weeks ago we decided (some three years after having sold the old house) to take a ride over to see if the "new" owners had changed the landscaping. When we drove by we both gasped and cried out in unison: "The Baldwin apple tree!" The beloved old apple tree had disappeared. Not even a stump remained. I guess the new owners must have experienced that third year of rotting apples underfoot and put their foot down. In any event, they sure couldn't have been pie bakers.

Make this pie whenever you have the yearning. Or, if ever you want to sell your house, have it baking in the oven as prospective buyers come to visit: The aroma of apples, butter and cinnamon emanating from the oven permeates the house like none other and makes anyone feel truly at home.

For an extra-special treat, serve the pie à la mode with creamy vanilla ice cream and a generous pool of amber caramel sauce.

INGREDIENTS	MEASURE *volume*	WEIGHT *ounces/pounds*	*grams*
Perfect Flaky Cream Cheese Pie Crust (page 176)	1 recipe	•	•
apricot preserves	3 tablespoons	2 ounces	56 grams
2½ pounds apples (about 6 medium), peeled, cored and sliced ¼ inch thick*	8 cups	2 pounds (cored and peeled)	907 grams
lemon juice, freshly squeezed	1 tablespoon	•	•
light brown sugar	¼ cup (firmly packed)	2 ounces	54 grams
granulated sugar	¼ cup	1.75 ounces	50 grams
ground cinnamon†	1½ teaspoons	•	•
nutmeg, preferably freshly grated	¼ teaspoon	•	•
salt	¼ teaspoon	•	•
unsalted butter	2 tablespoons	1 ounce	28 grams
cornstarch	1 tablespoons + 1 teaspoon	0.5 ounce	13 grams

*To core apples, cut them in half and use a melon baller to scoop out the core. Then slice each half in half and then each piece into 3 or 4 slices; slices must be no thicker than ¼ inch.
†If you prefer a milder cinnamon flavor decrease the cinnamon to ½ to 1 teaspoon.

In a small saucepan, heat the apricot preserves until melted and bubbling. (Or heat in a glass measure in a microwave oven.) Strain into a small cup. Allow to cool to tepid.

Remove one disc of pie dough from the refrigerator. Using a pastry cloth and a rolling pin fitted with a sleeve rubbed with flour, or two sheets of plastic wrap (preferably Saran brand) or wax paper sprinkled lightly with flour, roll the dough into a circle about 13 inches in diameter and about ⅛ inch thick. Trim it to an even 12 inches in diameter. Transfer the dough to the pie plate by rolling it loosely around the rolling pin and unrolling it over the plate.

Brush the pastry with the apricot preserves. Cover it loosely with plastic wrap and set it aside in a cool place or refrigerate it.

In a large bowl, combine the apples, lemon juice, sugars, cinnamon, nutmeg and salt and toss to mix. Allow to sit for 30 minutes to 1 hour. Transfer the apples to a colander suspended over a bowl to capture the liquid. The mixture will exude about ½ cup of liquid.

In a small saucepan (preferably lined with a nonstick surface), reduce this liquid, with the butter, to ⅓ cup. (Or spray a 4-cup heatproof measure with nonstick vegetable spray, add the liquid and butter and reduce in the microwave.) Allow the liquid to cool for about 10 minutes or until warm.

Meanwhile, toss the apples with the cornstarch. Pour the liquid over the apples, tossing gently. Transfer the mixture to the pie shell.

Roll out the top crust to a 12-inch circle. Moisten the edges of the bottom crust with water and place the top crust over the fruit. Use scissors to trim the edges of the top crust, leaving an overhang slightly larger than the bottom pastry (Fig. 1). Tuck the overhang under the bottom crust border and press down well all along the edge to seal it (Fig. 2). Crimp the border using a fork or your fingers (Fig. 3) and slash the top of the pie in several places (Fig. 4). Refrigerate the pie for 1 hour. (If time allows freeze for at least 12 hours before baking. This ensures a crisp bottom crust.)

At least 15 minutes before baking, position an oven rack at the lowest level, place an oven stone or cookie sheet on it and preheat the oven to 425°F.

Place the pie on the baking stone in the oven and bake for 50 to 60 minutes or until the juices bubble through the slashes and the apples feel tender but not mushy when a cake tester or small sharp knife is inserted through a slash. Shield the edges of the crust with foil after about 40 minutes. If baking from frozen, bake for 1 hour and 15 minutes.

Serve warm or at room temperature, with Triple Vanilla Lover's Ice Cream (page 179) and warm Caramel Sauce (page 181) if desired.

- The apples must be sliced thinly so that they lie close together. Thick slices allow air space between them; then, as they cook and soften, the air space disappears and the apples sink lower in the pan, leaving a gap between them and the crust.

TO MAKE A FOIL SHIELD: Make a 12-inch ring of aluminum foil (preferably heavy duty), using a ruler as a guide to cut a 12-inch circle. Cut out the center to leave a 2½-inch-wide ring. Crimp it all around the outside so that it will curve down over the sides of the pastry border.

POINTERS FOR SUCCESS

1

3   4

Makes: pastry for a two-
crust 9-inch pie

KEEPS:
At least 2 days
refrigerated, 3 months
frozen.

Perfect Flaky
Cream Cheese Pie Crust

| INGREDIENTS | MEASURE | WEIGHT | |
cold	volume	ounces	grams
unsalted butter, divided	12 tablespoons	6 ounces	170 grams
bleached all-purpose flour	1⅔ cups (dip and sweep method)	8.25 ounces	234 grams
salt	⅜ teaspoon	.	.
cream cheese (chilled)	1½ 3-ounce package	4.5 ounces	128 grams
ice water	2 tablespoons	.	.

Divide the butter into two parts: 3 tablespoons (1.5 ounces) and 9 table-spoons (4.5 ounces). Cut the butter into ½-inch cubes, keeping the two parts separate. Wrap each portion with plastic wrap (preferably Saran brand) and refrigerate for at least 15 minutes.

Food Processor Method

Place the flour and salt in a food processor with the metal blade and process for a few seconds to combine. Add the smaller amount of butter cubes and the cream cheese and process for about 15 seconds or until the mixture resembles coarse meal. Add the remaining butter cubes and process for 4 to 6 seconds or until the remaining pieces of butter are the size of small peas. Do not overprocess or crust will not be flaky.

Add the ice water and pulse 4 times. The dough will be in moist fine particles which appear dry but should hold together when pinched with the fingers. Dump the mixture into a plastic bag and press the outside of the bag until the dough holds together. Knead the dough briefly in the bag until you can form a smooth ball.

Remove the dough from the bag and divide it in half. Wrap each piece of dough with plastic wrap and flatten it into a disc. Refrigerate it for at least 45 minutes or up to 2 days.

Hand Method

Place the flour and salt in a medium bowl and whisk to combine. Use a pastry cutter or two knives to cut the butter and cream cheese into the flour, the first addition into coarse meal, the second into small peas just as with the food processor method. When adding the ice water, sprinkle it on, tossing the mixture lightly with a fork. Use your hands to gather the dough together and knead it briefly on the counter until it forms a smooth ball. Divide the dough into two equal parts, wrap each piece with plastic wrap and flatten it into a disc. Refrigerate for at least 45 minutes or up to 2 days.

• Saran Wrap is the ideal plastic wrap for rolling the dough because it lies very flat.
• Don't fold the dough when transferring it to the pie plate because it is likely to crack a little. Rolling it loosely around the rolling pin works best.

The secret to success is incorporating the cream cheese and part of the butter into the flour, which keeps the flour from absorbing too much water and forming gluten, which would make the crust tough. The remainder of the butter is incorporated in larger pieces, which serve to separate the layers, resulting in the desired flakiness.

Very little water is needed because the cream cheese is 51 percent water. The addition of a small amount of water activates a little gluten, strengthening the structure just enough to prevent cracking (which would result in leaking of the filling) when the crust is baked. This pie crust does not shrink or distort as much because there is less gluten development than usual.

Flattening the dough into a disc before refrigerating makes it easier to roll without cracking. The dough is rested to relax the gluten, making it less elastic and easier to roll. Chilling firms the butter, preventing sticking during rolling and the need for extra flour, which would toughen it.

For a two-crust pie, I divide the dough in half because I like the top crust, which gets the crispest and most delicious, to be thicker than the bottom crust. (The bottom crust is rolled 1 inch larger.)

Triple Vanilla Lover's Ice Cream

The secret to having intensely pure vanilla flavor without bitterness is to use vanilla seeds as well as extract. Since I love the deep, full flavor of the Madagascar bean and the floral quality of the Tahitian bean, I use both. The optional vodka is flavorless but serves to keep the ice cream velvety even after a week in the freezer.

Makes: 5 to 6 cups (depending on the ice cream maker)

Freezing time: at least 2 hours

INGREDIENTS	MEASURE volume	WEIGHT	
		ounces	*grams*
8 large egg yolks	4.5 fluid ounces	5.25 ounces	150 grams
sugar	¾ cup	5.25 ounces	150 grams
salt	a pinch	·	·
heavy cream	3 liquid cups	·	·
milk	1 liquid cup	·	·
1 Tahitian vanilla bean,* split lengthwise	·	·	·
1 Madagascar vanilla bean, split lengthwise	·	·	·
pure vanilla extract	2 teaspoons	·	·
OPTIONAL: vodka	2 tablespoons	·	·

*Available in specialty food stores such as Dean & DeLuca (800-227-7714). If Tahitian vanilla beans are unavailable, use a total of 3 ordinary (Madagascar) vanilla beans.

Have a fine strainer suspended over a medium mixing bowl ready near the range.

In a small heavy noncorrodible saucepan, stir together the yolks, sugar and salt until well blended, using a wooden spoon.

In another small saucepan (or in a heatproof glass measure in a microwave on high power), scald† the cream, milk and vanilla beans. Stir a few tablespoons into the yolk mixture, then gradually add the remainder, stirring constantly.

Heat the mixture to just below the boiling point (170°F. to 180°F.). Steam will begin to appear and the mixture will be slightly thicker than heavy cream; a finger run across the back of a spoon dipped in the mixture will leave a well-defined track. Immediately remove from the heat and pour into

KEEPS:
Ice cream has the best texture within 3 days of freezing but with the vodka will maintain its texture for up to a week.

†Bring just to the boiling point (small bubbles will begin to appear around the edges).

the strainer, scraping up the thickened cream on the bottom of the pan. Remove the vanilla beans and scrape the seeds into the custard. Stir to separate the seeds (fingertips work best for this). Return the pods to the custard until ready to freeze. Cool in an ice-water bath or the refrigerator until cold, at least 2 hours, or overnight.

Remove the vanilla pods. Stir in the vanilla extract and the optional vodka. Freeze in an ice cream maker according to the manufacturer's instructions. Allow the ice cream to ripen for at least 2 hours in the freezer before serving. If it is held longer and becomes very hard, allow it to sit refrigerated or at room temperature until softened and creamy.

POINTERS FOR SUCCESS

- Don't use a whisk to stir the custard mixture if not using an accurate thermometer because the foam makes it difficult to see when the mixture is getting close to boiling.
- Do not heat the custard mixture above 180°F. or it will curdle. If overheated and *slight* curdling does take place, pour instantly into a blender and blend until smooth before straining.
- Do not add more than the recommended amount of vodka or the ice cream will not freeze.

UNDERSTANDING

The custard mixture must be heated adequately (to at least 160°F.) to thicken and prevent thinning out on setting, but for a silky smooth sauce that does not curdle, the mixture must not be allowed to boil. The boiling point of water is 212°F. but the other ingredients in the custard lower the boiling point.

The vodka acts as antifreeze, preventing the formation of large ice crystals.

Caramel Sauce

This sauce is for the caramel lover—like myself! It's equally wonderful over ice cream, yellow cake or apple pie. It is just thick enough when hot, but not clumpy or sticky as it cools on the plate. Don't be afraid of making caramel. If you follow the simple but important rules below it will be easy. Do be careful when making it not to have any small children about and to give it your undivided attention. Caramel burns are extremely painful.

Makes: 1¼ cups

INGREDIENTS *room temperature*	MEASURE *volume*	WEIGHT	
		ounces	*grams*
sugar	1 cup	7 ounces	200 grams
water	¼ liquid cup	.	.
heavy cream	½ liquid cup	.	.
unsalted butter	2 tablespoons	1 ounce	28 grams
pure vanilla extract	1 teaspoon	.	.

In a heavy saucepan, with at least a 5-cup capacity (ideally with a nonstick lining) stir together the sugar and water until the sugar is completely moistened. Heat, stirring constantly, until the sugar dissolves and the syrup is bubbling. Stop stirring completely and allow the syrup to boil undisturbed until it turns a deep amber (about 370°F. on a candy thermometer). Immediately remove from the heat, and slowly and carefully pour the cream into the caramel. Be careful: It will bubble up furiously.

Use a wooden spoon to stir the mixture until smooth. If any lumps develop, return the pan to the heat and stir until they dissolve. Stir in the butter. The mixture will be streaky but will become uniform after cooling slightly and stirring.

Pour the caramel into a serving pitcher and allow it to cool for 5 minutes. Gently stir in the vanilla extract.

KEEPS:
3 days at room temperature, at least 3 months refrigerated. To reheat: Scrape it into a microwave-safe container and microwave on high power for 1 minute, stirring twice. Alternatively, place it in a pan of simmering water and heat, stirring occasionally, until warm, about 7 minutes.

POINTERS FOR SUCCESS

• To prevent crystallization, do not allow any sugar crystals to get on the sides of the pan and be sure to moisten all the sugar with the water. Stop stirring as soon as the syrup comes to a boil. If using a thermometer, be sure to rinse it and dry it if removing and then reinserting in the syrup. Any sugar remaining on the thermometer will cause crystallization.

• After the caramel is prepared, do not stir it too much as this could eventually cause crystallization.

UNDERSTANDING

I adore the flavor of caramel so I like to have as much depth of flavor as possible without any burned flavor. I like to bring the caramel up to 380°F. for maximum flavor. The darker you make the caramel, the less sweet it will seem but you risk burning it if you don't have an absolutely accurate thermometer.*

It's best to have the cream and butter at room temperature to avoid splattering when added to the hot caramel.

*The Cordon Rose candy thermometer is available through Dean & DeLuca (800-227-7714).

English Gingerbread

Kyle Cathie, the clever and discerning British editor of the UK version of The Cake Bible, *informed me in no uncertain terms that a book could not be called a "cake* bible" in England if it did not contain the beloved *gingerbread. So when I went to England to retest all the cakes using British flour and ingredients, I developed this gingerbread recipe. It is a moist, spicy cake with an intriguing blend of buttery, lemony, wheaty and treacly flavors and an appealing alternative for people who stay away from gingerbread because of the molasses. Cut into squares and decorated with pumpkin faces it makes a delightful "treat" for Halloween.*

Makes: 16 2-inch squares

Preheat the oven to: 325° F.
Baking time: 50 to 60 minutes

INGREDIENTS room temperature	MEASURE volume	WEIGHT	
		ounces	grams
unsalted butter	½ cup	4 ounces	115 grams
golden refiner's syrup	1¼ liquid cups	8 ounces	230 grams
dark brown sugar	¼ cup (firmly packed)	2 ounces	60 grams
orange marmalade	1 heaping tablespoon	1.5 ounces	40 grams
2 large eggs	3 fluid ounces	3.5 ounces	100 grams (weighed without shells)
milk	⅔ liquid cup	•	•
cake flour	1 cup (lightly spooned into the cup)	4 ounces	115 grams
whole wheat flour	1 cup minus 1 tablespoon (lightly spooned into the cup)	4 ounces	115 grams
baking powder	1½ teaspoon	•	7.5 grams
powdered ginger	1 teaspoon	•	•
ground cinnamon	1 teaspoon	•	•
baking soda	½ teaspoon	•	2.5 grams
salt	a pinch	•	•
Lemon Syrup			
lemon juice, freshly squeezed	2 tablespoons	•	•
unsalted butter (softened)	2 tablespoons	1 ounce	28 grams
sugar	3 tablespoons	1.3 ounces	38 grams

Preheat the oven to 325°F.

In a small heavy saucepan over medium-low heat, stir together the butter, golden syrup, sugar and marmalade until melted and uniform. Set aside and let cool until just barely warm; then whisk in the eggs and milk.

In a large bowl, whisk together all the remaining ingredients. Add the liquid mixture to the dry ingredients, stirring with a large spoon or rubber spatula just until the batter is smooth. Pour the batter into the prepared pan, filling it no more than half full (see Pointers for Success).

Bake for 40 to 50 minutes or until a tester inserted near the center comes out clean and the cake springs back when pressed lightly in the center. *The cake should start to shrink from the sides of the pan only after removal from the oven.*

While the gingerbread is baking, make the syrup. In a small pan, stir together the lemon juice, softened butter and sugar. Heat, stirring, until the butter is melted and the sugar dissolved.

Brush half the syrup on to the top of the hot gingerbread. Let cool in the pan on a rack for 10 minutes.

Loosen the sides of the gingerbread with a small metal spatula and invert onto a greased wire rack. Brush the bottom with the remaining syrup. To prevent splitting, reinvert so that the top is up.[†]

For extra moistness, cover the cake with plastic wrap (preferably Saran brand) while still hot and allow it to cool. For the most even moisture distribution, wrap airtight and set aside for 24 hours before serving.

To decorate the cake with a pumpkin motif, cut the cake into 2-inch squares. Lay the template on top of one of the pieces of cake and sprinkle it with powdered sugar. Lift off the template and repeat with the remaining cake pieces. (To make the template, trace the design and use an X-Acto knife to make the cutouts for the eyes, nose and mouth [Fig. 1].)

- Some metal pans slope inward and are less than 8 inches across at the bottom. In that case it is necessary to use a 9-inch square pan or fill the pan only half full and bake the excess batter as cupcakes. (The capacity of the pan should be 8 cups.)
- Use cake flour without leavening.
- Use unsalted butter for the best flavor.
- Use fresh baking powder (under one year old).
- For very even layers, wrap the cake pans with Magi-Cake Strips (available from Maid of Scandinavia, 800-328-6722). Do not overbake the cake.

EQUIPMENT:
8-inch square cake pan, preferably metal,* greased, bottom lined with parchment or waxed paper, then greased and floured

FINISHED HEIGHT:
about 2 inches

KEEPS:
2 days at room temperature, 5 days refrigerated, 2 months frozen.

POINTERS FOR SUCCESS

*If using glass, reduce oven temperature to 300°F.

[†]The British like their gingerbread moist and sticky. To achieve that consistency, invert it instead onto a large flat plate covered with a larger piece of plastic wrap, brush the cake with the syrup and cover it with the plastic wrap.

Orange Election Day Cheesecake

My editor, Maria Guarnaschelli, adores the combination of chocolate and orange so I created this cake for her. A true orange taste is hard to achieve but this cheesecake and orange curd pack a powerful orange punch.

The design of this cake came about when I was decorating a cheesecake for the press party for The Cake Bible *in the fall of 1988. I had an inspiration to encircle the cake with a train of elephant-shaped cake cutouts because they are my favorite animal. But as it was an election year, and my purpose was to enhance the cake, not to make a political statement, I alternated the elephants with donkeys. My five-year-old nephew was so intrigued with the shapes that I used the cutters the next day to make him animal-shaped peanut butter and jelly sandwiches! If ever you want to get your kid to eat something he or she is resisting, put it between bread and cut it into a favorite shape. It will work for at least one bite!*

The elephant and donkey motif makes this a fun cake to serve when friends come to watch the election returns. The creamy orange cheesecake is so delectable it will satisfy both Democrats and Republicans.

Serves: 8 to 12

Make the biscuit *and* **cheesecake at least 1 day up to 2 days ahead**

EQUIPMENT:
17-inch by 12-inch jelly-roll pan, greased, bottom lined with a nonstick liner or parchment (liner should extend slightly over the sides) and then greased again and floured; 2- to 2½-inch-high elephant and donkey cookie cutters; 8-inch by 2½-inch or higher springform pan, greased, outside of the pan wrapped with a double layer of heavy-duty foil to prevent seepage; 10-inch cake pan or a roasting pan to serve as a water bath

INGREDIENTS *room temperature*	MEASURE *volume*	WEIGHT	
		ounces/pounds	*grams*
Biscuit			
cocoa, preferably Dutch-processed	¼ cup	0.75 ounce	23 grams
boiling water	¼ liquid cup	•	•
pure vanilla extract	¾ teaspoon	•	•
4 large eggs	¾ liquid cup	7 ounces (weighed without shells)	200 grams
1 large egg yolk	3½ teaspoons	0.5 ounce	18 grams
superfine sugar, divided	⅔ cup + 1 tablespoon	5 ounces	145 grams
sifted cake flour	⅓ cup (sifted into the cup and leveled off)	1.25 ounces	33 grams
cream of tartar	¼ teaspoon	•	•

INGREDIENTS room temperature	MEASURE volume	WEIGHT ounces/pounds	grams
Cheesecake			
cream cheese (softened)*	2 8-ounce packages	1 pound	454 grams
sugar	1 cup	7 ounces	200 grams
1 large egg	3 tablespoons	1.75 ounces	50 grams (weighed without shell)
2 large egg yolks	2 full tablespoons	1.25 ounces	37 grams
orange zest, finely grated, divided (from about 5 navel oranges)	3 tablespoons + 1 teaspoon	0.75 ounce	20 grams
pure vanilla extract	1½ teaspoons	.	.
salt	¼ teaspoon	.	.
sour cream	2 cups	17 ounces	484 grams
heavy cream	1 liquid cup	.	.
Orange Curd			
orange juice, freshly squeezed (from about 3 oranges)	1 liquid cup	.	.
unsalted butter (softened)	4 tablespoons	2 ounces	57 grams
4 large egg yolks	2 full fluid ounces	2.5 ounces	74 grams
sugar	½ cup	3.5 ounces	100 grams
(orange zest reserved from the cheesecake)	(4 teaspoons)	.	(8 grams)
salt	a pinch	.	.
Ganache Glaze (optional)			
bittersweet chocolate, preferably Lindt Excellence, finely chopped	1⅓ 3-ounce bars	4 ounces	113 grams
heavy cream	⅓ liquid cup + 1 additional tablespoon if necessary	.	.
OPTIONAL: Cointreau	1 teaspoon	.	.

*Don't be tempted to use the more expensive "natural" cream cheese. Philadelphia brand, available even in Japan, offers the best and most consistent flavor and texture for this cake. Cream cheese without gums will aerate more, yielding more volume and less creaminess.

Position an oven rack in the lower third of the oven, and preheat the oven to 450°F.

In a small bowl, with a rubber spatula, stir together the cocoa and boiling water until smooth. Stir in the vanilla and cover tightly with plastic wrap (preferably Saran brand).

Separate 2 of the eggs, placing the yolks in one large mixing bowl and the whites in another. To the yolks, add the additional yolk, the remaining 2 eggs and ⅔ cup of the sugar. Beat, preferably with the whisk attachment of a heavy-duty mixer, on high speed 5 minutes or until thick, fluffy and tripled in volume. Add the cocoa mixture and beat for a few seconds until incorporated.

Sift the flour mixture over the egg mixture and set it aside.

Beat the egg whites until foamy. Add the cream of tartar and beat until soft peaks form when the beater is raised. Beat in the remaining 1 tablespoon of sugar and beat until stiff peaks form when the beater is raised slowly. With a large rubber spatula, fold one third of the whites into the batter until all of the flour is incorporated. Gently fold in the remaining whites. Pour the batter into the prepared jelly-roll pan and use an offset metal spatula to level it.

Bake for 7 minutes or until a cake tester comes out clean and the cake is springy to the touch. Loosen the edges with a small metal spatula or sharp knife and, lifting by a long edge of the liner or parchment overhang, gently slide the cake from the pan onto a flat surface. Cover with a clean dish towel and allow to cool.

Use the bottom of an 8-inch cake pan or an 8-inch cardboard round and the tip of a knife to trace an 8-inch circle in one end of the *biscuit*. Use scissors to cut it out. With the cookie cutters, stamp out 8 shapes. Wrap them with plastic wrap and set them aside. *You can glaze the cutouts with the ganache a day before serving or just several hours before, but be sure to leave time to allow the glaze to set so you can lift the cutouts without marring the glaze.*

Preheat the oven to 350°F.

Place the chocolate *biscuit* round in the bottom of the prepared 8-inch pan.

In a large mixing bowl, beat the cream cheese and sugar, preferably with the whisk beater, until very smooth, about 3 minutes. Beat in the egg, then the yolks, beating until smooth and scraping down the sides once or twice. Add 2 tablespoons of the orange zest, the vanilla and salt and beat until incorporated. Beat in the sour cream and heavy cream just until blended.

Pour the batter into the prepared pan. Set the pan in the larger pan and pour 1 inch of very hot water into the larger pan.

Bake the cake for 45 minutes. Turn off the oven (without opening the door) and let the cake cool for 1 hour. Remove it to a rack and cool to room temperature, about 1 hour. Cover with plastic wrap and refrigerate overnight.

Biscuit

One day ahead, make the Chocolate biscuit and the cheesecake.

Preheat the oven to: 450°F. Baking time: 7 minutes

Cheesecake

Preheat the oven to: 350°F. Baking time: 1 hour and 45 minutes

Orange Curd

Spray a 4-cup heatproof measure with nonstick vegetable spray or grease it lightly. Add the orange juice and microwave on high power until reduced to 2 tablespoons, about 15 minutes. Watch closely toward the end as the juice gets very syrupy and reduces quickly. (Or boil it in a medium saucepan on the range, stirring often to prevent burning.) Stir the butter into the concentrated orange juice. Cool to room temperature.

In a heavy noncorrodible saucepan, beat the yolks and sugar with a wooden spoon until well blended. Stir in the orange juice mixture, the 4 teaspoons of reserved orange zest and the salt. The mixture will be very thick. Cook over low heat, stirring constantly, until thickened and resembling mayonnaise, 4 to 5 minutes. The mixture should thickly coat a rubber spatula but still be liquid enough to pour. It will change from translucent to opaque and begin to take on a lovely orange color on the rubber spatula. It must not be allowed to boil, or it will curdle. Whenever steam appears, remove the pan briefly from the heat, stirring constantly to keep it from boiling. An accurate thermometer will read 180°F. to 185°F.* (Tilt the pan so that it is adequately immersed.) When the curd has thickened, pour it at once into a bowl.

Allow the orange curd to cool for about 5 minutes. Reserve 2 tablespoons to attach the chocolate *biscuit* cutouts, and pour the rest onto the cheesecake while it is still hot, using an offset metal spatula to spread it quickly to form a smooth film. If it is too thick to pour, stir in up to 2 teaspoons of warm water. Chill for at least 2 hours. (It is best to place the cake in an airtight container so that it doesn't absorb odors from the refrigerator, but do not cover it with plastic wrap as it will mar the smooth surface.)

To unmold, wipe the sides of the pan with a hot, damp towel. Run a small metal spatula between the sides of the cake and the pan and release and remove the sides of the springform. Place the cake on a serving plate and refrigerate until shortly before serving.

Ganache Glaze

At least 1 hour or up to 6 hours before serving, prepare the ganache glaze.

Place the chocolate in a small heavy saucepan with a lid. Place ⅓ cup of the cream in a small saucepan, and scald† it. (Or pour into a heatproof glass measure and heat in the microwave.) Pour it over the chocolate, cover tightly and allow it to rest for 5 minutes to melt the chocolate.

Gently stir the mixture until uniform in color, trying not to create air bubbles. Pass it through a fine strainer and stir in the optional Cointreau. Allow the glaze to cool until just tepid. Makes ¾ cup.

Place the animal-shaped cutouts on a rack set in a pan to catch the glaze.

To check the consistency of the glaze: At a tepid temperature, a small amount of glaze should mound a bit when dropped from a spoon before smoothly disappearing. If the glaze is too thick and the mound remains on the surface or if the glaze seems curdled, warm the remaining 1 tablespoon of cream and add it by the teaspoon.

Spoon a heaping tablespoon of glaze over each cutout so that it cascades down the sides, being sure that the upper side of each cutout is well covered

---

*The Cordon Rose candy thermometer is available through Dean & DeLuca (800-227-7714).

†Bring just to the boiling point (small bubbles will begin to appear around the edges).

as these will show when placed on the cake. If necessary, use a small metal spatula or artist's brush to apply the glaze to any areas missed or to break any air bubbles. Set the rack and pan in a cool spot and allow the glaze to set so that you can touch it without leaving a mark.

Up to 2 hours before serving, lift each glazed cutout, handling the glazed surfaces as little as possible, and apply a little of the reserved orange curd to the underside of the cutouts to help them adhere to the curved sides of the cake. Press each one gently in place, placing them evenly around the sides of the cake. If the cutouts are slightly higher than the sides of the cake, carefully paint a little of the chocolate glaze on any exposed areas on the bottom sides.

To serve, cut the cake with a knife that has been wiped and dipped in hot water between each slice.

POINTERS FOR SUCCESS

Chocolate Biscuit

- If you forget to cover the cocoa and water mixture and it dries out, add water a few droplets at a time until it is soft enough to form soft peaks when lifted with the spatula.
- Use superfine sugar for the finest texture. (You can make it by processing granulated sugar in the food processor for a few minutes until fine.)
- Use cake flour without leavening.
- The bowl, beater and egg whites must be absolutely free of grease, including even a speck of egg yolk, for the egg whites to beat to stiff peaks.
- Using the correct amount of cream of tartar makes it possible to beat the whites very stiff without the risk of drying them and breaking them down.
- Work quickly once the eggs are beaten so that they do not deflate.
- Fold the flour gently but *thoroughly* into the batter.
- Bake the *biscuit* immediately after mixing.
- Use the correct pan size.

Orange Curd

- If an orange is heated (about 10 seconds in a microwave oven on high power) and rolled around while pressing on it lightly, it will release a significantly greater quantity of juice.
- To prevent curdling, be sure to mix the sugar with the yolks before adding the orange juice. Use a heavy noncorrodible pan that conducts heat evenly or a double boiler. To prevent curdling during cooking, do not allow the mixture to boil. Remove the pan immediately from the heat when the mixture is thickened and empty it into a bowl at once as the residual heat of the pan will raise the temperature. (If you are working with an accurate thermometer, the temperature of the thickened curd will be 180°F. to 185°F.)
- Be sure to cook the orange zest with the rest of the ingredients, and do not strain it out, as it is necessary for flavor.

Ganache-Glazed Cutouts

- It is best to apply the *biscuit* cutouts after removing the cake from the refrigerator as refrigeration dulls the glaze. Alternatively, you can replace 2 tablespoons of the cream in the glaze with corn syrup to add sheen and keep it from cracking when refrigerated.

Graavlax with
Sweet Mustard Dill Sauce

W hen I tasted this for the first time, I asked my Canadian sister-in-law Alice where she had bought it, because I thought it was the best "lox" I had ever eaten. When I found out she had made it I immediately asked for the recipe. The mustard dill sauce is a wonderful tangy accompaniment, although I love the pure salmon flavor so much I often eat it plain. After the curing process is complete, all of the seasoning is wiped off, but the flesh absorbs a slight peppery sweetness accented by the dill.

The recipe is utterly simple to make. You just have to remember to turn the seasoned salmon at the beginning and end of each day.

One year I made this graavlax for my New York family's Thanksgiving. It disappeared from the plate within five minutes of having been set on the coffee table, but afterward I was accused of not doing my part because everyone thought that instead of cooking something from scratch I had "gone out and bought expensive lox." So if the idea is impressing the relatives—don't make this recipe.

Serves: 12

Marinating time: at least 3 days up to 4 days ahead

KEEPS:
About 10 days refrigerated.

INGREDIENTS	MEASURE *volume*	WEIGHT	
		ounces/pounds	*grams/kilograms*
center-cut King or Norwegian salmon, cut into 2 fillets, boned	•	3 pounds (boned)	1 kilogram, 361 grams (boned)
sugar	¼ cup	1.75 ounces	50 grams
kosher salt*	¼ cup	2.5 ounces	72 grams
white peppercorns, coarsely cracked	2 tablespoons	0.75 ounce	20 grams
1 bunch fresh dill, stemmed and coarsely chopped†	1 loosely packed cup	0.75 ounce	21 grams
Sweet Mustard Dill Sauce			
light brown sugar	¼ cup (firmly packed)	2 ounces	54 grams
Dijon mustard	¼ cup	2.5 ounces	72 grams
chopped fresh dill (reserved from salmon)	2 tablespoons	0.25 ounce	7 grams

*If using Morton's kosher salt or table salt, use 2 tablespoons plus 1 teaspoon.
†Reserve 2 tablespoons for the sauce.

Use tweezers or needle nose pliers to remove any small bones from the salmon.

Place one piece of the salmon, skin side down, in a shallow glass, stainless steel, or ceramic container so that it lies perfectly flat. Mix the sugar, salt and peppercorns together. Sprinkle three quarters of the dill and three quarters of the seasoning mixture on the salmon. Cover with the remaining piece of salmon, skin side up, and sprinkle the remaining seasoning mixture and dill over the top. Cover the salmon tightly with plastic wrap (preferably Saran brand) and then with heavy-duty foil and weight with a plate and weights. The more the salmon is compacted, the more velvety the texture of the flesh and the easier it will be to slice. Refrigerate for 3 to 4 days, turning every 12 hours. (Do not pour off the liquid that accumulates.)

Drain the salmon, scrape off the seasoning mixture and pat the salmon dry with paper towels.

To serve, place each piece of salmon skin side down on a cutting board. With a long, thin knife (the ideal knife is hollow ground), slice on the bias as thinly as possible. Freezing the salmon for 10 minutes also helps the slicing process.

Sweet Mustard Dill Sauce

In a small saucepan, place the brown sugar and the Dijon mustard and stir over low heat until the sugar is dissolved and the sauce is smooth. Add the 2 tablespoons of reserved dill. Serve warm or at room temperature.

UNDERSTANDING

Salting the salmon is an ancient preserving technique because it draws out the water. The liquid must not be drained off until the end because the salt, which is needed to draw out more water, is dissolved in this liquid. The longer the salmon sits, the more "cured" or flavored it becomes. Kosher salt is ideal because the coarse crystals do not dissolve as quickly.

Turkey with
Sausage and Chestnut Stuffing

I have been making turkey every year for the past fifteen years. Although we always celebrate Thanksgiving at Aunt Margaret's or at cousin Marion and Marty's, my turkey tradition got started after I married Elliott and discovered he received an annual gift of a large turkey. It always seemed to arrive at a time when I was most busy, yet I have never resisted the temptation of stopping whatever I was doing to prepare it together with all the trimmings!

Over the years I have experimented with different roasting techniques and stuffings. One year I read in a magazine that Julia Child liked to remove the breast and cook it separately. She explained that with the traditional method, by the time the rest of the bird was cooked, the breast was overcooked. Since I thoroughly agreed, I tried the technique and loved it. Removing the breast but leaving the skin intact provides lots more room for the stuffing, which I like to bake in the bird for extra flavor. If your family prefers dark meat you can simply slice the breast and freeze it to use in place of veal for scaloppine. But for white meat lovers, my friend Rick Rodgers, author of The Turkey Cookbook (Harper Collins), has created a special recipe that produces a moist flavorful breast that can be baked alongside the turkey.

The stuffing has also evolved over the years. Chestnuts add an earthy spicy and sweet note that I adore. My husband likes the extra crunch and flavor of walnuts. We both like the giblets (though the kids never did and always went hunting through their stuffing to pick them out and fork them over to us). I prefer a somewhat dry stuffing with each component separate as opposed to a moist pasty one. Of course more liquid can be added if you prefer a moister stuffing. I also happen to prefer the texture and flavor of prepared seasoned bread cubes to making my own, though I do add extra fresh thyme and sage. My daughter, Beth, added the technique of shaping the sausage into tiny balls. This somehow adds to the flavor.

The nicest thing I can tell you about this stuffing, however, happened one year when Beth made Thanksgiving. When I tasted her stuffing I proclaimed it the best I had tasted. Her answer was, "It's your recipe!"

Serves: 14 to 18 with the breast, 8 to 10 without the breast (see page 201)

Preheat the oven to: 325°F.
Roasting time: 4 to 5 hours
Resting time: 30 minutes to 2 hours
Internal temperature (thigh): 175°F

INGREDIENTS	MEASURE *volume*	WEIGHT	
		ounces/pounds	*grams/kilograms*
1 turkey	•	17 pounds	7 kilograms, 711 grams
2 cloves garlic, halved and peeled	•	•	•
goose fat or butter	2 tablespoons	1 ounce	28 grams
salt	1 teaspoon	0.25 ounce	6.7 grams
pepper, freshly ground	several grindings	•	•
Turkey Stock			
reserved turkey breast bones, gizzard and neck	•	•	•
goose fat or vegetable oil	2 tablespoons	•	•
1 large onion, coarsely chopped	2 cups	9 ounces	255 grams
2 large carrots, coarsely chopped	1 cup	4 ounces	113 grams
2 celery ribs, coarsely chopped	1 cup	4 ounces	113 grams
water	2 liquid cups	•	•
4 parsley sprigs	•	•	•
dried thyme	½ teaspoon	•	•
5 black peppercorns	¼ teaspoon	•	•
1 bay leaf	•	•	•
Stuffing			
2 pounds fresh chestnuts, shelled and peeled*	4 cups	1¼ pounds (peeled)	567 grams (peeled)
milk	2 liquid cups	•	•
seasoned bread cubes	8 cups (preferably 1 7-ounce bag of cubes + 4 ounces cornbread)†	11 ounces	312 grams
OPTIONAL: reserved turkey giblets			
sweet sage sausage, casings removed if necessary	•	1 pound	454 grams

*This amount takes into account that a few will be bad and have to be discarded. Chestnuts can be spoiled without showing any indication on the shell. Look for solid, glossy chestnuts or use peeled frozen or vacuum-packed jarred ones. Fresh chestnuts in the shell will keep refrigerated for about a month.

†Packaged unsweetened cornbread for stuffing, **not** corn muffins.

| INGREDIENTS | MEASURE | WEIGHT | |
	volume	*ounces/pounds*	*grams/kilograms*
goose fat or butter, divided	6 tablespoons	3 ounces	85 grams
1 large onion, coarsely chopped	2 cups	9 ounces	255 grams
sugar	a pinch	•	•
fresh mushrooms, sliced	5 cups	1 pound	454 grams
coarsely chopped walnuts	2 cups	8 ounces	228 grams
fresh sage, chopped	3 tablespoons	0.35 ounce	7 grams
fresh thyme, leaves	¼ cup	0.25 ounce	8 grams
black pepper, freshly ground	1 teaspoon, or to taste	•	•
cayenne pepper	a pinch	•	•
reserved turkey stock (page 197) or chicken broth (preferably College Inn)	¾ liquid cup*	•	•
Gravy			
reserved turkey stock (page 197) or chicken broth	4 liquid cups	•	•
unsalted butter	2 tablespoons	1 ounce	28 grams
all-purpose flour	2 tablespoons	0.66 ounce	18.5 grams

*If baking the stuffing separately, increase the chicken broth by ¾ cup (or use water to bake the stuffing).

If desired, prepare the turkey and some of the stuffing components the night before and refrigerate. Note that to make the Rolled Herbed Turkey Breast (page 201) at the same time as the turkey, you need two ovens.

At least 15 minutes ahead of roasting, preheat the oven to 325°F.

Rinse the turkey with cold running water and drain well.

Using sharp scissors, make a longitudinal cut through the breast skin, from the point of the breast all the way to the neck opening. Pull back the skin so that the entire breast section is exposed, being careful not to tear the skin. Use sharp shears to cut off each section of breast meat, including the bone. Use a sharp knife to slice the breast meat from the bone, keeping each breast whole, and reserve the bones for the stock. Wrap and refrigerate the breasts for later use.

Using a trussing needle or a large needle and heavy brown thread, stitch together the breast skin, using an overhand stitch. Sew the neck skin flap to the back of the turkey: This will become what is usually the neck cavity.

Turkey Stock

Using a heavy cleaver or knife, chop the breast bones into 2-inch pieces.

In a large saucepan, heat the goose fat over medium-high heat. Add the giblets (not the liver), breast bones and neck and cook, stirring often, until browned, about 10 minutes. Add the onion, carrots and celery and cook until the onions are softened. Pour in the water and bring to a simmer. Skim off any foam on the surface.

Add the parsley, thyme, peppercorns and bay leaf and simmer, uncovered, for at least 4, preferably 6, hours. If you plan to use the gizzard and neck in your stuffing or gravy, remove them when they are tender. The neck takes about 1 hour and 15 minutes, the gizzard about 1½ hours. Remove the meat from the neck and return the bones to the stock. Finely chop the meat and refrigerate. If you like turkey liver in your stuffing or gravy, add it during the last 5 to 10 minutes of cooking.

Strain the stock, discarding the bones and vegetables but reserving the liver if desired. Cut the gizzard and liver into small cubes. Cover and refrigerate.

Measure the stock. You should have 6 cups. If you have more, boil to reduce it to 6 cups. If less, add water to bring it to 6 cups. Cool the stock to room temperature. Cover and refrigerate.

When the fat has solidified on the surface of the stock, scrape it off. You will need 4 cups of stock for the gravy, 1 cup for the turkey breast rolls and ¾ to 1 cup for the stuffing.

Peel and cook the chestnuts (this can be done up to 3 days ahead).   **Stuffing**

Using a chestnut cutter or a sharp paring knife, cut an X through the skin on the flat side of each chestnut. In a large saucepan, place the chestnuts and cold water to cover and bring to a boil. Simmer for a few minutes, then turn off the heat. Remove the chestnuts a few at time, for peeling. Remove both the outer shell and as much of the inner skin as possible. I like to use scissors to cut through the shell, especially the hard top part.

Rinse out the saucepan, and add the peeled chestnuts and milk. Simmer, covered, until the chestnuts are easily pierced with a cake tester, 20 to 40 minutes, depending on how dry the chestnuts are. Add more milk if necessary to keep them barely covered. Cool and then drain the chestnuts, discarding the milk.

Into a gallon-size bowl, crumble the cooked chestnuts. Add the bread cubes and optional cooked giblets (liver, neck and gizzard) and set aside.

Into a large frying pan, over medium heat, pinch off small pieces of the sausage, about ½ inch in size. Fry the sausage pieces until lightly browned. Remove them to the bowl of chestnuts, using a slotted spoon, and drain away the fat.

Add 4 tablespoons of the goose fat or butter to the frying pan and melt over medium heat. Add the onion and sprinkle with the pinch of sugar. Fry, stirring often, until golden brown and caramelized. Add the sliced mushrooms and cook, covered, for about 3 minutes or until they exude their liquid. Uncover and continue cooking for about 5 minutes, until the liquid evaporates and the mushrooms begin to brown. Transfer this mixture to the stuffing bowl. Add the walnuts, sage, thyme, black pepper and cayenne. Toss the mixture to blend it well.

Heat the reserved ¾ cup of broth with the remaining 2 tablespoons of goose fat or butter and sprinkle it over the stuffing in four additions, tossing lightly each time. Taste and adjust the salt and pepper if necessary. The stuffing will be very dry at this point because it will not have absorbed the juices from the turkey. Makes 12 cups.

Spoon the stuffing into the turkey. Do not pack in the stuffing as it will expand during baking. (Any leftover can be sprinkled with a little extra broth or water and baked in a separate pan, covered, for 30 to 40 minutes. Removing the cover for the last 15 minutes gives a crunchy top.) Tuck the turkey legs into the band of skin (the "hock lock" usually provided) and tie the wings to the sides of the bird, or truss in the following manner: Place a long piece of twine under the turkey, near the tail. Bring it up over the ends of the legs, cross it over and bring each piece down under the leg ends, bringing the legs together. Pull each end of the twine toward the back of the bird so that the twine runs along the sides of the bird, under each leg and across the wings, holding them in place. Knot the twine securely at the back of the bird. If you like crisp back skin, place a strong rack in the roasting pan to support the turkey. Place the turkey on the rack or directly in the pan. Rub the cut sides of the garlic cloves all over the turkey and then rub it with the 2 tablespoons of goose fat or butter. Sprinkle it all over with the 1 teaspoon of salt and the ground pepper.

Roast the turkey for 3 hours or until an instant-read thermometer inserted in the thigh (not touching the bone) reads 175°F. If the turkey starts getting too brown, tent it with a piece of aluminum foil, preferably heavy duty. Allow the turkey to rest for at least 30 minutes before carving.

Gravy

Pour off the pan drippings into a glass measuring cup or bowl and let them stand for 5 minutes. Skim off the fat that rises to the surface. Return the juices to the roasting pan and pour in the 4 cups of the reserved turkey stock. Place the roasting pan on the range and reduce the juices to 2 cups, stirring and scraping often to dislodge the delicious browned bits on the bottom and sides of the pan, 15 to 20 minutes.

Meanwhile, in a medium saucepan, melt the 2 tablespoons of butter over low heat. Whisk in the 2 tablespoons of flour and cook, without browning, whisking constantly, for 1 minute.

Whisk in the reduced stock and bring it to a boil. Cook, whisking often, until thickened, about 5 minutes. Pour the gravy into a sauceboat.

NOTE: I do not include salt in the list of stuffing ingredients because commercial bread crumbs contain salt and the stock may also be salty. Season to taste.

If you are not making gravy, reduce the stock to 1 cup and freeze it for the next turkey.

Rick Rodgers's
Rolled Herbed Turkey Breast

Y*ou will need a second oven to bake this turkey breast at the same time as the turkey with sausage and chestnut stuffing.*

Serves: 6 to 8

INGREDIENTS	MEASURE volume	WEIGHT ounces/pounds	grams/kilograms
2 whole turkey breast halves, boned (see page 197)	.	6 pounds	2 kilograms, 722 grams
fresh parsley, preferably flat-leafed, minced	¼ cup	0.50 ounce	15 grams
2 to 3 shallots, minced	2 tablespoons	0.66 ounce	18 grams
fresh sage, minced	2 tablespoons	.	5 grams
salt	½ teaspoon	.	.
pepper, freshly ground	¼ teaspoon	.	.
prosciutto, thinly sliced	.	3 ounces	85 grams
pancetta, thinly sliced	.	4 ounces	113 grams
Turkey Stock (page 197)	½ liquid cup	.	.

In a small bowl, combine the parsley, shallots, sage, salt and pepper.

On a flat surface, place one of the boned turkey breasts, boned side up. Using a sharp knife, butterfly the breast by making 2 or 3 horizontal cuts into the thickest parts of the meat, cutting toward the edges and leaving the piece closest toward the edge attached. Open each piece like a book. Cover the breast with a sheet of plastic wrap and pound it with a meat pounder or rolling pin to an even thickness. It should measure about 12 inches at its widest point.

Place half of the prosciutto over the turkey and sprinkle it with half of the herb mixture. Starting at a short side, roll up the breast into a cylinder. Drape half the pancetta over it and tie it crosswise in several places with kitchen twine. Repeat the procedure with the other breast and remaining prosciutto, herbs and pancetta.

Place the rolled breasts in a baking dish. Cover tightly and refrigerate until 2 hours before roasting.

Up to a day ahead, stuff the turkey breasts.

Two hours before roasting, remove the turkey breasts from the refrigerator and bring to room temperature.

Preheat the oven to: 350°F. Baking time: 70 to 80 minutes

EQUIPMENT:
kitchen twine, 9-inch by 13-inch baking dish

At least 15 minutes before roasting, preheat the oven to 350°F.

Pour the turkey stock into the baking dish. Roast the turkey breasts for 60 to 70 minutes (20 to 25 minutes per pound) or until an instant-read thermometer inserted in the center of a breast reads 160°F. Allow the breasts to stand for at least 10 minutes before slicing.

Mom's Healthy but Delicious Coleslaw

Serves: 6

Marinating time: at least 1 hour; up to 8 hours

W hen I was growing up, "good for you" invariably applied to things I did not want to eat. There were, however, a few exceptions, the main one being our family's special version of coleslaw, invented by my grandmother who lived with us and did the cooking. Rather than the usual creamy dressing, it was prepared with equal parts of freshly squeezed lemon juice and oil. It wouldn't be the same without the minced garlic and in recent years, my mother's much appreciated addition has been currants for little bursts of sweetness and chopped avocado, which adds a slight creaminess and lusciousness of flavor.

Years ago I bought my mother a food processor to ease the preparation by speeding the grating of the cabbage and carrots. She tried it several times but we all agreed that the hand grating added something to the texture so she returned to the old way and I breathed a sigh of relief.

When I was a child, this coleslaw often accompanied family meals and we all enjoyed it on top of buttered rye bread. But because it was such a family favorite, it always appeared (and still does) at holiday dinners as well. Its savory freshness and lightness in face of all the heavier fare makes it an ideal side dish. It wouldn't be Thanksgiving, in fact, without cousin Sue's apple pie and mom's coleslaw.

Any leftover coleslaw is still delicious, though less crisp, the following day but that's the storage limit once the dressing has been added. I know because I always go home with a jar of the leftover. I guess I must have grown up; the fact that it's healthy food actually pleases me now.

INGREDIENTS	MEASURE	WEIGHT	
	volume	ounces	grams
green cabbage (shredded with a knife or 4 mm. Cuisinarts slicing disc)	3 cups	10 ounces	284 grams
4 medium carrots, coarsely shredded	1½ cups	5 ounces	142 grams
green bell pepper, chopped	½ cup	2.3 ounces	65 grams
dried currants	¼ cup	0.5 ounce	14 grams
olive oil, preferably light	¼ liquid cup	·	·
lemon juice, freshly squeezed*	¼ liquid cup	·	·
1 large clove garlic, minced	1½ teaspoons	·	5 grams
OPTIONAL: avocado, diced	½ cup	2.5 ounces	70 grams

*Lime juice makes a nice variation.

In a 2-quart bowl, place the cabbage, carrots, green pepper and currants. In a glass measuring cup, measure the oil and lemon juice; add the garlic and mix lightly. Pour the dressing over the vegetable mixture and toss to mix well. Add the avocado and toss lightly.

Cover the coleslaw tightly and refrigerate it for at least 1 hour before serving. The coleslaw is best eaten the same day.

NOTE: The vegetable mixture, except the avocado, can be prepared a day ahead and refrigerated.

Cranraspberry Sauce

Makes: 5 cups

Chilling time: at least 8 hours

This is my number-one favorite cranberry sauce. The addition of raspberry purée adds a lovely extra dimension to the traditional whole cranberry sauce. Lemon juice provides freshness and sparkle. I like to make a large quantity to ensure that there will be enough to accompany the leftover turkey. I wouldn't enjoy the turkey as much without this sauce.

INGREDIENTS	MEASURE volume	WEIGHT ounces	grams
Raspberry Purée			
raspberries, frozen with no sugar added	1 12-ounce bag	12 ounces	340 grams
sugar	¼ cup + 1½ teaspoons	2 ounces	56 grams
Cranberry Sauce			
fresh cranberries	6½ cups	24 ounces	680 grams
water	1 liquid cup	.	.
sugar	1¾ cups	12.25 ounces	350 grams
lemon zest, finely grated	1 tablespoon + 1 teaspoon	0.25 ounce	8 grams
lemon juice, freshly squeezed (about 1½ large lemons)	3 tablespoons	.	.

In a strainer suspended over a deep bowl, thaw the raspberries completely. This will take several hours. (To speed thawing, place in an oven with a pilot light.) Press the berries to force out all the juice. There should be a scant ½ cup.

In a microwave on high power,* or a small saucepan (preferably with a nonstick lining), boil the juice until it is reduced to 2 tablespoons. Pour it into a lightly oiled heatproof cup.

Purée the raspberries and strain them through a food mill fitted with the fine disc. Or use a fine strainer to remove all the seeds. You should have a scant ½ liquid cup of purée. Stir in the raspberry syrup. You should have 9 tablespoons (4.5 fluid ounces). Add ¼ cup plus 1½ teaspoons sugar.[†] Stir until the sugar dissolves. Refrigerate.

Wash the cranberries and drain them thoroughly.

In a medium saucepan, combine the water and the 1¾ cups of sugar and bring to a boil, stirring constantly. Add the cranberries and simmer for 10 minutes, stirring occasionally. Remove from the heat and stir in the lemon zest and juice. Cool to room temperature.

Stir in the raspberry purée.

- Raspberry seeds are very small and can pass through most food mills. The Cuisinart power strainer and sieve attachment removes all the seeds in a matter of minutes and is easy to clean. The Squeezo Tomato Strainer with berry screen attachment, by Vitantonio, is also effective but not as easy to clean.
- For finely grated zest, use a zester (a small implement with tiny scraping holes), a vegetable peeler or a fine grater to remove the yellow portion only of the lemon rind. The white pith beneath is bitter. If using the zester or peeler, finish by chopping the zest with a sharp knife.
- If a lemon is heated (about 10 seconds in a microwave oven on high power) and rolled around while pressing on it lightly, it will release a significantly greater quantity of juice.

KEEPS:
At least 1 month refrigerated, several months frozen.

POINTERS FOR SUCCESS

---

*If using a microwave, place the juice in an oiled 4-cup heatproof glass measure or bowl to allow for bubbling.

[†]If you have less raspberry purée, decrease the sugar, using 1 tablespoon for each fluid ounce of purée.

Low-Profile Pecan Pie

I have long adored pecan pie but bemoaned its cloying sweetness. My so-lution was to make it in a tart pan, which offers a more equitable balance of crust to filling. I also increased the amount of nuts in proportion to filling, which results in more of the pecan flavor and less of the sugar. Lyle's English refiner's syrup instead of the usual corn syrup adds both a more beautiful, richer golden color and a less sugary, more lilting flavor.

Softly whipped cream, barely sweetened but perfumed with bourbon, is a fabulous complement. Serve it on the side, though some will insist on having it right on top!

Serves: 6

Preheat the oven to: 350°F.
Baking time: 35 to 40 minutes
Setting time: 1½ hours

EQUIPMENT:
9½-inch by 1-inch tart pan with removable bottom (preferably black steel)

INGREDIENTS	MEASURE	WEIGHT	
	volume	ounces	grams
Perfect Flaky Cream Cheese Pie Crust (page 210)	1 recipe	•	•
pecan halves	1½ cups	6 ounces	170 grams
4 large egg yolks	2 full fluid ounces	2.5 ounces	74 grams
Lyle's refiner's syrup or dark corn syrup	⅓ liquid cup	•	•
light brown sugar	½ cup (firmly packed)	3.75 ounces	108 grams
unsalted butter, melted	4 tablespoons	2 ounces	57 grams
heavy cream, cold	¼ liquid cup	•	•
salt	a pinch	•	•
pure vanilla extract	1 teaspoon	•	•
Chocolate Lace Topping			
bittersweet chocolate, finely chopped	⅓ of a 3-ounce bar	1 ounce	28 grams
heavy cream, cold	2 tablespoons	•	•
bourbon	½ teaspoon	•	•
Bourbon Whipped Cream (optional)			
heavy cream	1 liquid cup	•	•
sugar	½ teaspoon	•	•
bourbon	1 tablespoon	•	•
pure vanilla extract	¼ teaspoon	•	•

KEEPS:
3 days at room
temperature.

At least 15 minutes before baking, position an oven rack at the lowest level, place an oven stone or cookie sheet on it and preheat the oven to 350°F.

Using a pastry cloth and rolling pin sleeve rubbed with flour, or two sheets of plastic wrap (preferably Saran brand) or wax paper sprinkled lightly with flour, roll the dough into a 13-inch or slightly larger circle about ⅛ inch thick. Cut out a 13-inch circle. Dust the pastry lightly with flour and lift it by rolling it loosely around the rolling pin. Unroll it over the tart pan and arrange it in the pan without stretching the pastry. Use scissors to trim the overhang to about 1 inch. Fold down the excess to reinforce the sides, pleating the sides where necessary, and cut away the excess. Press the pastry against the fluted sides of the pan.

Arrange the pecan halves rounded sides up, in the bottom of the pie crust. Cover the pastry with plastic wrap and refrigerate it for at least 30 minutes or overnight.

In a medium-size bowl, combine the egg yolks, syrup, brown sugar, butter, cream, salt and vanilla. Stir to combine them well and dissolve any lumps of sugar. Pour the filling slowly over the nuts. Place the tart pan on a baking sheet to catch any butter that may leak from the pastry and place on the baking stone.

Bake for 35 to 40 minutes, or until the filling is puffed and golden and the pastry has begun to brown lightly. The filling will shimmy very slightly when moved. Allow the pie to cool completely on a rack before removing from the pan, about 1½ hours.

Chocolate Lace Topping

In a small microwave-proof bowl, or the top of a double boiler set over hot, not simmering, water, place the chopped chocolate. (Do not allow the water to touch the bottom of the upper container.) Heat the chocolate, stirring often until melted, and remove it from the heat. If using a micro-wave, stir every 15 seconds.

Pour the cream over the chocolate and stir until smooth. Stir in the bourbon. Pour the mixture into a reclosable quart-size freezer bag and close it securely. Use it immediately, before it cools. Cut off a small corner from the bag. Drizzle swirls of chocolate over the top of the cooled pie. (You will not need all of the topping. Any leftover is delicious on ice cream.)

Whipped Cream Topping (optional)

In a large mixing bowl, place all the topping ingredients, and refrigerate for at least 15 minutes. (Chill the mixer beater alongside the bowl.)

Beat only until soft peaks form or the cream mounds softly when dropped from a spoon. Serve alongside the pie.

POINTERS FOR SUCCESS

• To transfer the crust to the pan, roll it up over the rolling pin as a cream cheese crust is more delicate and less flexible and would crack slightly if folded in quarters.

NOTE: For a more beautiful appearance, precooking the pastry shell and the filling separately and then straining the filling before cooking them together results in a clear shiny filling. For this method: *At least 15 minutes before baking, preheat the oven to 425°F.*

Line the pastry shell with foil and fill with pennies, aluminum pie weights or beans, making sure they are pushed up well against the sides. Bake for 15 minutes, remove the foil and weights and prick the shell with a fork. Continue baking for 5 to 10 minutes or until golden brown. Cool.

Reduce the oven temperature to 350°F.

Have ready a strainer suspended over a small bowl near the range.

(The butter should be softened but does not have to be melted.) In a medium-size noncorrodible saucepan, combine the egg yolks, syrup, brown sugar, softened butter, cream and salt. Cook over moderately low heat, stirring constantly with a wooden spoon without letting the mixture boil, until it thickens enough to coat the spoon heavily, or until it measures 180°F. on an accurate candy thermometer,* 7 to 10 minutes. Strain at once into the small bowl and stir in the vanilla.

Arrange the pecan halves, top sides up, in the bottom of the baked pie crust. Pour the filling over the nuts.

Bake for 20 to 25 minutes, or until the pie is puffed and golden.

TIP: For 2 rectangular pies that will serve 24 for Thanksgiving or other holiday dinners when delicious, easy-to-serve desserts are always appreciated, use two 13-inch by 4-inch rectangular flan forms with bases and multiply the recipe by 1½ times, using a total of 8 ounces of pecans. I like to use smaller pecans so that I can line them up in short parallel rows, which makes for easiest cutting (2 rows per serving). (I worked out the exact volume of the flan forms using the mathematical formula πr^2 ["pi" r squared]. It was the first time I had used it since high school and it seemed fitting to be using it at last for a pie!)

---

*The Cordon Rose thermometer is available through Dean & DeLuca (800-227-7714).

Makes: pastry for a
9½-inch tart

KEEPS:
At least 2 days refrigerated,
3 months frozen.

Perfect Flaky
Cream Cheese Pie Crust

| INGREDIENTS | MEASURE | WEIGHT | |
cold	volume	*ounces*	*grams*
unsalted butter, divided	8 tablespoons	4 ounces	113 grams
bleached all-purpose flour	1 cup + 2 tablespoons (dip and sweep method)	5.5 ounces	156 grams
salt	¼ teaspoon	•	•
cream cheese	1 3-ounce package	3 ounces	85 grams
ice water	1 tablespoon + 1 teaspoon	•	

Food Processor Method

Divide the butter into two parts: 2 tablespoons (1 ounce) and 6 tablespoons (3 ounces). Cut the butter into ½-inch cubes, keeping the two parts separate. Wrap each portion with plastic wrap (preferably Saran brand) and refrigerate for at least 15 minutes.

Place the flour and salt in a food processor with the metal blade and process for a few seconds to combine. Add the smaller amount of butter cubes and the cream cheese and process for 10 seconds or until the mixture ressembles coarse meal. Add the remaining butter cubes and process for 4 to 6 seconds or until the remaining pieces of butter are the size of small peas. Do not overprocess or the crust will not be flaky.

Add the ice water and pulse 4 times. The dough will be in moist fine particles which appear dry but should hold together when pinched with the fingers. Dump the mixture into a plastic bag and press the outside of the bag until the dough holds together. Knead the dough briefly in the bag until you can form a smooth ball.

Remove the dough from the bag, wrap it with plastic wrap and flatten it into a disc. Refrigerate it for at least 45 minutes or up to 2 days.

Hand Method

Place the flour and salt in a medium bowl and whisk to combine. Use a pastry cutter or two knives to cut the butter and cream cheese into the flour, the first addition into coarse meal, the second into small peas just as with the food processor method. When adding the ice water, sprinkle it on, tossing the mixture lightly with a fork. Use your hands to gather the dough together and knead it briefly on the counter until it forms a smooth ball. Wrap the dough with plastic wrap and flatten into a disc. Refrigerate for at least 45 minutes or up to 2 days.

 POINTERS FOR SUCCESS

• Saran Wrap is the ideal plastic wrap for rolling the dough because it lies very flat.
• Don't fold the dough when transferring it to the pie plate because it cracks a little. Rolling it loosely around the rolling pin works best.

Celia's Pure Potato Latkes

In my family, it wouldn't be Hanukkah without latkes (potato and onion pancakes) with apple sauce. We love them so much we make them the main dish! It's the one time of the year I am charmed to see both my parents collaborating in the kitchen, and since I gave them a Cuisinart, they get more enjoyment than ever out of the project.

Most people would agree that the best latkes are the ones your mother makes but I really do think these are the best. Perhaps it's because of the Idaho potatoes, which hold together better than the usual waxy type and result in a much less oily potato cake. When my friend Diane, who also grew up on latkes, tasted these I said, "Admit it! Aren't these the best you ever tasted?" Her response was priceless: "Please! My mother is still alive."

This recipe actually comes from an old and dear family friend, Celia Hindin, who is no longer alive. Celia grew up in Russia. She claimed they understand potatoes better there. She taught my mother this simple way of making potato pancakes using only potatoes and onion grated so fine it disappears into the potatoes. But it was to me that she left her magnificent sterling silver latke spoon. She claimed that the best latkes are prepared using a silver spoon to drop them into the hot fat. To this day I am unsure if this is based on a scientific reaction (after all, Celia was a laboratory technician) or pure bubameisis (old wives' tale from the Old Country).

Traditionally, according to the kosher laws, when latkes are to be served with a fish meal, they are fried in oil and served with sour cream; when served with meat, they are fried in chicken fat and served with apple sauce.

These potato pancakes are lighter and more rustic and lacy than the traditional ones made with the addition of flour and egg. My mother, who always fries them in oil, also rejoices in the fact that they are far healthier this way but I modify that somewhat by the flavorful addition of goose or chicken fat! My father likes using the food processor to shred the potatoes because he says the potatoes exude more water, enabling them to hold together better.

Latkes are most delicious when freshly made so in our family we fry up a batch just before we are about to eat and then we take turns popping up to spoon in and turn over subsequent batches while we are eating.

Makes: about 20 latkes

| INGREDIENTS | MEASURE | WEIGHT | |
room temperature	volume	ounces/pounds	grams/kilograms
4 large Idaho potatoes	•	2¾ pounds	1 kilogram, 134 grams
1 large onion, peeled	•	8 ounces	227 grams
salt	½ teaspoon	•	•
pepper, freshly ground	¼ teaspoon	•	•
goose fat, chicken fat, vegetable oil or a mixture, divided	¼ cup	•	•

In a food processor fitted with the coarse shredding disc or on the large shredding holes of a hand grater, shred the potatoes. Squeeze them well to rid them of as much water as possible and place them in a large bowl.

With the medium shredding holes of a hand shredder, shred the onion.* When you get to the end and shredding becomes difficult, remove the root end and chop the remainder finely by hand. Add the onion to the bowl. Add the salt and pepper and stir to mix well. More liquid will be exuded and the mixture should be squeezed and drained thoroughly.

In a large heavy frying pan (I use a 12-inch cast iron pan) over medium heat, heat 2 tablespoons of the fat or oil until a slight haze appears on the surface. Drop heaping serving spoons (¼ cups) of the mixture into the oil, flattening them very slightly with the back of the spoon. Leave a little space between the pancakes for ease in turning. They should be about 2½ inches in diameter and will flatten slightly on cooking.

Cook for about 7 minutes or until they start to turn golden brown around the edges. Turn and continue cooking for another 5 to 7 minutes or until the second side is golden brown. If the fat starts smoking at any point or the latkes start to brown too much in spots, lower the heat and remove the frying pan briefly from the heat. Remove the latkes and drain on several layers of paper towels. Continue with the remaining latke mixture, adding 2 tablespoons of fat or oil to the pan per batch.

- After purchasing potatoes, keep them in a cool place, but not in the refrigerator as they would develop an undesirable "sweet" flavor.
- Shred the potatoes shortly before frying so that they don't discolor.
- Chilling the onion before shredding helps to prevent tearing.
- Shred the onion shortly before frying to maintain its sweet flavor.
- Do not wash the shredded potatoes—the starch is necessary to hold them together.
- Salt is essential in this recipe as it causes the potatoes to exude water, which creates an even golden brown color when frying them.

*Celia was a stoic and used the coarse grating holes on a four-sided grater. If tearing eyes bothers you too much, use the coarse grating holes—the potato pancakes will still be delicious.

NOTE: A grater consists of tight, rough round holes or points and results in tiny pieces of the grated substance. A shredder consists of open, partially rounded holes and results in longer pieces of the shredded substance.

POINTERS FOR SUCCESS

Rosy McApple Sauce

Cold, silky smooth, tart fresh apple sauce is the perfect accompaniment to crisp hot potato latkes. This apple sauce is the most lovely shade of pink, because it is cooked with the colorful skins of the apples left on, and mildly spicy because it is cooked with a whole cinnamon stick.

You will be surprised to know what strong feelings I have about such a simple gentle dish as apple sauce. It was over apple sauce that I made my first stand as a child of two years of age. I remember, I think, that it was scary but that my aversion was such that I had to do it. From my highchair I cried out to my grandmother in despair, "I don't want Aunt Margaret to feed me; she gives me yumps in the apple sauce!"

Growing up, I can't remember a time when Grandma didn't have an enamel saucepan of apple sauce cooling under the sink, but I would never eat any because she made the lumpy variety. Since she wasn't willing to strain it, she had to buy baby apple sauce for me.

In all these years, my taste in apple sauce has never changed, except that now I can make it myself and have the delicious fresh flavor and the smooth texture.

INGREDIENTS *room temperature*	MEASURE *volume*	WEIGHT	
		ounces/pounds	*grams/kilograms*
6 medium McIntosh apples	•	2 to 2¼ pounds	907 grams to 1 kilogram, 21 grams
sugar	½ cup, or more to taste	3.5 ounces	100 grams
lemon juice, freshly squeezed (1 large lemon)	2 tablespoons	•	•
1 3-inch cinnamon stick*	•	•	•

*Use the supermarket variety; the specialty store cinnamon sticks have a much more intense flavor and, if available, would require only about 1 inch for the same results.

Wash the apples well but do not peel them. Cut them in quarters and cut away the cores. Cut each quarter in half lengthwise and then crosswise and place them in a heavy medium-size saucepan with a tight-fitting lid. Add the ½ cup sugar and the lemon juice and toss to blend. Add the cinnamon stick and set aside for 20 minutes. (About ½ cup of liquid will be exuded from the apples.)

Heat over medium heat just until the liquid starts to boil. Reduce the heat to very low, cover tightly and cook for 20 minutes. Stir the apples and continue cooking, covered, for another 20 minutes, stirring two or three times. The apples should have softened completely. Remove the pan from the heat and allow to cool until warm or room temperature.

Remove and discard the cinnamon stick. Pass the apples through a fine sieve, such as a strainer, Cuisinart power strainer, Squeezo Tomato Strainer with the fine screen or a food mill. (A food mill will result in a coarser apple sauce.) Stir in more sugar by the teaspoonful if desired. Refrigerate, tightly covered, until serving time.

• If you want a very smooth apple sauce and you don't have the Cuisinart power strainer, first use the finest disc of a food mill and then use a fine strainer (pushing the apples through a fine strainer alone requires much more effort). With the power strainer, however, you can have the finest apple sauce in minutes. Once again, toques off to Carl Sontheimer!

POINTERS FOR SUCCESS

Orange Glow Chiffon Cake

Serves: 14

Preheat the oven to:
325°F.
Baking time: 55 minutes
Cooling time: 1½ hours

The only truly traditional Hanukkah dessert is suf ganiyot, *a deep-fried jelly doughnut originating from Israel, but I don't serve them for Hanukkah. After stuffing ourselves with latkes, the last thing any of us wants is a deep-fried doughnut! We prefer far lighter and refreshing fare such as this moist, airy, festive chiffon cake from* The Cake Bible.

INGREDIENTS room temperature	MEASURE volume	WEIGHT ounces	grams
sifted cake flour	2¼ cups (sifted into the cup and leveled off)	8 ounces	225 grams
superfine sugar, divided	1½ cups	10.5 ounces	300 grams
baking powder	2 teaspoons	·	10 grams
salt	½ teaspoon	·	3.5 grams
safflower oil	½ liquid cup	·	·
7 large eggs, separated, + 3 additional whites:			
yolks	½ liquid cup	4.5 ounces	130 grams
whites	1¼ liquid cups	10.5 ounces	300 grams
orange zest, finely grated	2 tablespoons	·	12 grams
orange juice, freshly squeezed	¾ liquid cup	·	·
pure vanilla extract	1 teaspoon	·	4 grams
cream of tartar	1¼ teaspoons	·	4 grams

EQUIPMENT:
ungreased 10-inch two-piece tube pan

FINISHED HEIGHT:
4½ inches high in the middle

STORE:
3 days at room temperature wrapped airtight, 10 days refrigerated, 2 months frozen.

Preheat the oven to 325°F.

In a large mixing bowl, combine the flour, all but 2 tablespoons of the sugar, the baking powder and salt and beat for 1 minute to mix well. Make a well in the center. Add the oil, egg yolks, orange zest, orange juice and vanilla and beat for 1 minute or until smooth.

In another large mixing bowl, preferably with the whisk beater of a heavy-duty mixer, beat the egg whites until frothy. Add the cream of tartar and beat until soft peaks form when the beater is raised. Beat in the reserved 2 tablespoons of sugar and beat until stiff peaks form when the beater is raised slowly. Gently fold the egg whites into the batter with a large balloon wire whisk, slotted skimmer or large rubber spatula until just blended.

Pour the batter into the tube pan (the batter will come to 1 inch from the top) and bake for 55 minutes or until a cake tester inserted in the center comes out clean and the cake springs back when lightly pressed in the center. Invert the pan, placing the tube opening over the neck of a soda or wine bottle to suspend it well above the counter and cool the cake completely in the pan, about 1½ hours.

Loosen the sides with a long metal spatula and remove the cake and center core of the pan. Dislodge the cake from the bottom and center core with a metal spatula or thin sharp knife. (A wire cake tester works well around the core. To keep the sides attractive, press the spatula well against the sides of the pan.) Invert the cake onto a greased wire rack and reinvert it onto a serving plate.

To serve, sprinkle lightly with powdered sugar if desired and or garnish with fresh flowers. Serve at room temperature or lightly chilled, and cut with a serrated knife.

POINTERS FOR SUCCESS

- Use superfine sugar for the finest texture. (You can make it by processing granulated sugar in the food processor for a few minutes until fine.)
- Use cake flour without leavening.
- For finely grated zest, use a zester (a small implement with tiny scraping holes), a vegetable peeler or fine grater to remove the orange portion only of the orange rind. The white pith beneath is bitter. If using a zester or peeler, finish by chopping the zest with a sharp knife.
- If an orange is heated (about 10 seconds in a microwave oven on high power) and rolled around while pressing on it lightly, it will release a significantly greater quantity of juice.
- The bowl, beater and egg whites must be absolutely free of grease, including even a speck of egg yolk, for the egg whites to beat to stiff peaks.
- Using the correct amount of cream of tartar makes it possible to beat the whites very stiff without the risk of drying them and breaking them down.
- A large balloon whisk or slotted skimmer is ideal for folding in the flour with the least amount of air loss. If using a whisk, periodically shake out the batter that collects inside. Work quickly once the eggs are beaten so that they do not deflate.
- Bake immediately after mixing in an *ungreased* pan.
- After baking, immediately invert the pan so that it is suspended well above the counter so that the cake doesn't steam and fall out of the pan.

The Cannonball

When we were looking for a new house, Claire Cannon, a charming and ebullient realtor in Blairstown, New Jersey, showed us around the area. I never wanted it to end because she made house hunting so much fun. But Claire quickly found us our dream house and on Christmas of that year invited us to a party at hers. When I tasted this cheese ball, I knew I was going to have to get the recipe because it was so special. Claire said she put in the carrots and celery to make it healthful. Fortuitously, they also contribute a delicious crunch, and the horseradish and onion add the delightful zip that keeps you going back for more. I dubbed it "the cannonball," not inappropriate for the recipe of such a dynamo.

Makes: one 7-inch cheese ball

Chilling time: at least 1 hour

KEEPS:
About 3 days refrigerated after which the celery and carrots lose some of their crunch.

INGREDIENTS *room temperature*	MEASURE *volume*	WEIGHT *ounces/pounds*	*grams/kilograms*
cream cheese	2 8-ounce packages	1 pound	454 grams
mayonnaise	¼ cup	2 ounces	54 grams
Parmesan cheese, freshly grated	⅓ cup	0.5 ounce	15 grams
onion, finely chopped	2 tablespoons	0.5 ounce	16 grams
prepared horseradish	1 teaspoon	·	·
carrot, finely chopped	2 tablespoons	0.5 ounce	16 grams
celery, finely chopped	2 tablespoons	0.5 ounce	16 grams
salt	½ teaspoon	·	·
OPTIONAL: walnuts, chopped medium coarse	1 tablespoon to 1¼ cups	0.25 to 5 ounces	7 to 142 grams
OPTIONAL: a few large leaves of radicchio, for garnish	·	·	·

In a large mixing bowl or an electric mixer, blend all the ingredients except the nuts. Place the mixture on a large piece of plastic wrap (preferably Saran brand). Bring up the edges of the plastic and using the wrap and your hands, form the mixture into a ball. Place it in a small, deep bowl to help hold its shape and then refrigerate for at least 1 hour.

If desired, when firm, roll the cheese ball in the 1¼ cups of chopped nuts to coat evenly, pressing on the nuts to make them adhere. Alternatively, press a few nuts gently into the top. For a dramatic presentation, arrange radicchio leaves on a serving dish and place the cheese ball in the center. Refrigerate until serving time.

NOTE: Lightly toasting the walnuts brings out their flavor. Place the chopped walnuts on a baking sheet and bake in a 350°F. oven for about 10 minutes or until their color deepens slightly.

POINTERS FOR SUCCESS

- For the most attractive appearance, place the chopped nuts in a strainer and toss them lightly to sift out the smaller pieces. (These can be used for cookie making.)

Hot Buttered Rum Cider

This is a traditional cold weather drink for country weekends and holiday parties alike. I start making it as soon as the first cold snap is in the air and the apple cider presses start to work at the local farms. The hot mingling flavors of citrus, rum and sugar seem to warm you from the bottom up. I'm giving the recipe for one serving because it is easiest to measure out the amounts into each individual cup. But heat the cider for any number of servings all together in a kettle or saucepan.

Serves: 1

INGREDIENTS	MEASURE *volume*	WEIGHT	
		ounces	*grams*
pure maple syrup	1 teaspoon	·	·
dark brown sugar	1 teaspoon (firmly packed)	·	·
unsalted butter	1 teaspoon	·	·
dark rum	3 tablespoons (1½ fluid ounces)	·	·
lemon quarter, seeded	·	·	·
1 thick orange slice, halved and seeded	·	·	·
3 cloves	·	·	·
unpasteurized apple cider	⅔ liquid cup	·	·
1 long cinnamon stick*	·	·	·
OPTIONAL: long strips of orange zest to wrap around cinnamon stick,† for garnish	(1 orange yields 2 to 3 long strips)	·	·

*Available during the holiday season at specialty food stores.

†A "stripper," available in gourmet equipment stores such as Williams-Sonoma, is the best implement for making long strips of orange zest. Zest means the colored part only, not the bitter white pith beneath.

In a large mug, combine the maple syrup, brown sugar, butter and rum. With the tip of a knife, remove any pits. Squeeze the lemon wedge into the mug and then drop it in.

Use a metal skewer to poke 3 holes into the orange rind. Press the cloves into the holes and add this to the mug. If desired, coil orange zest strips around the cinnamon stick. Place the cinnamon stick in the mug.

In a saucepan or microwave oven, heat the apple cider just until small bubbles form around the sides. Pour into the mug and use the cinnamon stick to stir.

Stained Glass

This is a cookie and a candy all in one. The cookie component is a crisp sugar-butter cookie. The candy panes, made of crushed sour balls, add a sweet fruity flavor and crunch.

Makes: about 4 dozen 3-inch cookies

Preheat the oven to: 350°F. Baking time: 10 to 12 minutes

EQUIPMENT:
cookie sheets lined with aluminum foil, then sprayed with nonstick vegetable cooking spray or greased; rolling pin; 3-inch round cookie cutters and small canapé cutters

| INGREDIENTS | MEASURE | WEIGHT | |
	volume	ounces	grams
bleached all-purpose flour	2¾ cups (dip and sweep method)	13.75 ounces	390 grams
baking powder	½ teaspoon	•	•
salt	½ teaspoon	•	•
sugar	⅔ cup	4.75 ounces	132 grams
unsalted butter	1 cup	8 ounces	227 grams
about half a large egg, lightly beaten	2 teaspoons	•	•
pure vanilla extract	1½ teaspoons	•	6 grams
lemon extract	⅛ teaspoon	•	•
sour balls	1 package (1 cup)	6.5 ounces	184 grams

Food Processor Method

In a small bowl, whisk together the flour, baking powder, and salt.

In a food processor with the metal blade, process the sugar until it is very fine. Cut the butter into a few pieces and add it with the motor running. Process until smooth and creamy. Add the egg and extracts and process until incorporated, scraping the sides of the bowl. Add the flour mixture and pulse in, just until the dough begins to clump together.

Electric Mixer Method

Soften the butter. In a mixing bowl, cream together the sugar and butter until fluffy. Add the egg and extracts and beat until blended. In a small bowl, whisk together the remaining dry ingredients. On low speed, gradually add them to the butter mixture and mix just until the dough can be gathered into a ball.

For Both Methods

Scrape the dough onto a sheet of plastic wrap (preferably Saran brand) and use the wrap, not your fingers, to press the dough together to form a thick flat disc. Wrap it well and refrigerate for at least 30 minutes, preferably no longer than 3 hours.

Place 2 oven racks in the upper and lower thirds of the oven.

Separate the sour balls into individual colors and pulverize them separately in a blender or food processor. Place each color in a small container and set aside.

Using about a quarter of the dough at a time, roll out the dough to ⅛-inch thickness between 2 sheets of plastic wrap or on a lightly floured counter. Cut out cookies with a 3-inch cookie cutter, spraying or greasing the cutter as needed to prevent sticking. With a small, angled metal spatula or pancake turner, transfer the cookies to the prepared cookie sheets. If you are planning to hang the cookies, make small holes with the blunt end of a wooden skewer.

Cut out shapes for the stained glass in each cookie with small cutters or with a small sharp knife. Use the tip of a small sharp knife to fill the holes with candy pieces, filling just to the top of the dough.

Bake for 10 to 12 minutes or until the cookies are lightly browned and the candy has melted completely. For even baking, rotate the cookie sheets from top to bottom and front to back halfway through the baking period. Watch carefully toward the end of baking to see that the candy does not start to caramelize and turn brown.

Allow the cookies to cool completely on the sheets. Carefully peel off the aluminum foil.

STORE:
In an airtight container, between sheets of wax paper, at room temperature.

KEEPS:
Several weeks.

SMART COOKIE

- Saran Wrap is the ideal plastic wrap for rolling the dough because it lies very flat. Wax paper is the second choice.
- For precise cutouts, chill the dough after the impressions are made and remove the cutout with the tip of a sharp knife after the dough has firmed enough for each cutout to come out in a clean piece.
- If you are using a blender to pulverize the sour balls, drop the balls with the motor running in order to keep them from getting stuck under the blades.
- Allow the cookie sheet(s) to cool completely before using for the next batch.
- Distribute the cookies evenly around the cookie sheet. Avoid crowding the cookies into one section of the cookie sheet, leaving a large area bare.

Traditional Rolled Christmas Sugar Cookies

T*hese sugar cookies can be as simple or as decorative as your fancy dictates. The dough is ideal for rolling and cutting into special shapes. Now is the time to get out your favorite Christmas cookie cutters.*

Makes: about 4 dozen 3-inch cookies

Preheat the oven to: 350°F. Baking time: 8 to 12 minutes

EQUIPMENT: nonstick or buttered or greased cookie sheets; rolling pin; cookie cutters

INGREDIENTS	MEASURE *volume*	WEIGHT	
		ounces	*grams*
bleached all-purpose flour	2¼ cups (dip and sweep method)	11.25 ounces	320 grams
salt	¼ teaspoon	•	•
sugar	¾ cup	5.25 ounces	150 grams
unsalted butter	12 tablespoons	6 ounces	170 grams
1 large egg	3 tablespoons + ½ teaspoon	1.75 ounces	50 grams (weighed without shell)
lemon zest	1 tablespoon (finely grated)	•	6 grams
pure vanilla extract	1 teaspoon	•	4 grams
Edible Tempera Color (page 226)			
Royal Icing (page 226)			

Food Processor Method

In a small bowl, whisk together the flour and salt.

In a food processor with the metal blade, process the sugar until very fine. Cut the butter into a few pieces and add it with the motor running. Process until smooth and creamy. Add the egg, lemon zest, and vanilla extract and process until incorporated, scraping the sides of the bowl. Add the flour mixture and pulse in just until incorporated. If the mixture seems dry, add a few droplets of water and pulse in just until the dough begins to clump together.

Electric Mixer Method

Soften the butter. In a mixing bowl, cream together the sugar and butter until fluffy. Add the egg, lemon zest, and vanilla extract and beat until blended. In a small bowl, whisk together the remaining dry ingredients. On low speed, gradually add them to the butter mixture and mix until incorporated. Add water, a few drops at a time, only until the dough starts to come away from the sides of the bowl.

For Both Methods

Scrape the dough onto a sheet of plastic wrap (preferably Saran brand) and use the wrap, not your fingers, to press the dough together to form a thick flat disc. Wrap it well and refrigerate for at least two hours, preferably no longer than 3.

STORE:
In an airtight container at room temperature.

KEEPS:
For several months.

Place 2 oven racks in the upper and lower thirds of the oven.
     On a lightly floured surface, roll out the dough to a ⅛-inch thickness. Cut shapes using your favorite Christmas cookie cutters or homemade cardboard patterns or even freehand. With a small, angled metal spatula or pancake turner, transfer the cookies to the prepared cookie sheets. If desired, paint the cookies with Edible Tempera Color. If you are planning to hang the cookies, make small holes with the blunt end of a wooden skewer.
     Reroll the scraps, chilling them first, if necessary.
     Bake for 8 to 12 minutes or until the cookies begin to brown around the edges. For even baking, rotate the cookie sheets from top to bottom and front to back halfway through the baking period.
     Use a small, angled metal spatula or pancake turner to transfer the cookies to wire racks to cool before decorating with Royal Icing, dragées, sprinkles and glittering holiday edibles.

Edible Tempera Color

Lightly beat 2 large egg yolks and spoon equal amounts of them into 5 small bowls or cups. Use liquid food coloring to color each mixture. For yellow, use ½ teaspoon of yellow; for red, use ½ teaspoon of red; for green, use ¼ teaspoon of green; for blue, use ¼ teaspoon of blue; for black, use 1½ teaspoons of green, 1½ teaspoons of red and 5 drops of blue.
     Use a small clean paintbrush to paint the designs on the cookies before baking.

Royal Icing

INGREDIENTS	MEASURE	WEIGHT	
Do not make on a humid day	*volume*	*ounces/pounds*	*grams*
3 large egg whites	3 fluid ounces	3 ounces	90 grams
powdered sugar	4 cups (lightly spooned into the cup)	1 pound	460 grams

This recipe has an excellent consistency for piping. For painting, thin the icing with water.

In a large mixing bowl, place the egg whites and powdered sugar and beat, preferably with the whisk beater, at low speed, until the sugar is moistened. Beat at high speed until very glossy and stiff peaks form when the beater is lifted (5 to 7 minutes). The tips of the peaks should curve slightly. If necessary, more powdered sugar may be added. Keeps 3 days in an airtight container at room temperature. Rebeat lightly.

Royal Icing with Meringue Powder*

Replace the egg whites with 3 tablespoons of meringue powder and 3 fluid ounces (6 tablespoons) of warm water (this is approximately the amount of water contained in the eggs). Proceed as for basic Royal Icing. Keeps 2 weeks in an airtight container at room temperature. Rebeat lightly.

SMART COOKIE

- Cookies can be rolled to a ¼-inch thickness and underbaked slightly for a softer, chewier cookie.
- If the dough cracks while rolling it, cut it in quarters and allow it to soften until it is more malleable before continuing.
- Allow the cookie sheet(s) to cool completely before using for the next batch.
- Distribute the cookies evenly around the cookie sheet. Avoid crowding the cookies into one section of the cookie sheet, leaving a large area bare.

*Meringue powder is available through cake-decorating supply houses such as Maid of Scandinavia (800-328-6722) and the Chocolate Gallery (212-675-2253).

Gingerbread People

Makes: 19 dozen 2-inch by ¼-inch small cookies or 40 5-inch by 3-inch by ¼-inch large cookies

T*his gingerbread is delicious to eat and not too spicy, even for children. The cookies are perfect to string with bright fresh cranberries as garlands on the tree. Teddy bears and other favorite shapes are also fun to make.*

INGREDIENTS	MEASURE volume	WEIGHT ounces	grams
bleached all-purpose flour	3 cups (dip and sweep method)	15 ounces	425 grams
salt	¼ teaspoon	•	•
baking soda	1 teaspoon	•	5 grams
ground ginger	2 teaspoons	•	•
ground cinnamon	1 teaspoon	•	•
grated nutmeg	½ teaspoon	•	•
ground cloves	¼ teaspoon	•	•
dark brown sugar	¾ cup (firmly packed)	6.25 ounces	179 grams
unsalted butter	12 tablespoons	6 ounces	170 grams
unsulfured molasses (preferably Grandma's)	½ cup (use a greased liquid measuring cup)	5.5 ounces	161 grams
1 large egg	3 tablespoons + ½ teaspoon	1.75 ounces (weighed without shell)	50 grams
OPTIONAL: raisins, currants, decorative candies and Royal Icing (page 230)			

Preheat the oven to: 350°F.

Baking time: 8 to 10 minutes for small cookies 10 to 12 minutes for large cookies

EQUIPMENT: nonstick or greased or buttered cookie sheets; floured pastry cloth and floured rolling pin sleeve; rolling pin; gingerbread men and women cookie cutters and/or hearts or other shapes

In a medium bowl, sift together the flour, salt, baking soda, and spices, then whisk together to mix evenly.

In a food processor with the metal blade, process the brown sugar until fine. Cut the butter into a few pieces and add it with the motor running. Process until smooth and creamy. Add the molasses and egg and process until incorporated, scraping the sides of the bowl. Add the flour mixture and pulse in just until the dough begins to clump together.

Food Processor Method

Soften the butter. In a small bowl, sift together the flour, salt, baking soda and spices, then whisk together to mix evenly. In a mixing bowl, cream together the brown sugar and butter until fluffy. Add the molasses and egg and beat until blended. On low speed, gradually beat in the flour mixture until incorporated.

Electric Mixer Method

Scrape the dough onto a sheet of plastic wrap (preferably Saran brand) and use the wrap, not your fingers, to press the dough together to form a thick flat disc. Wrap it well and refrigerate it for at least 2 hours.

For Both Methods

Place 2 oven racks in the upper and lower thirds of the oven.

On a floured pastry cloth, roll out the dough to about ⅛-inch thickness. Use gingerbread cutters to cut out the dough. With a small, angled metal spatula or pancake turner, lift the cut dough onto the cookie sheets, placing the cutouts about 1 inch apart. If desired, make holes for hanging, either at the tops or hands, using the blunt edge of a wooden skewer.

Bake for about 8 to 10 minutes for the small cookies, up to about 10 to 12 minutes for the larger ones, or until firm to the touch and just beginning to color around the edges. For even baking, rotate the cookie sheets from top to bottom and front to back halfway through the baking period.

Cool the cookies on the sheets for about 1 minute. When they are firm enough to lift, use a small, angled metal spatula or pancake turner to transfer the cookies to wire racks to cool completely.

While the cookies are still hot and slightly soft, if desired, press raisins, currants, cinnamon red-hots or other candy into the dough (for eyes and buttons). They can also be attached, using dots of Royal Icing as glue, after the cookies have cooled. Royal Icing, either white or tinted with food coloring, can be used to pipe details or frilly borders. The icing can be thinned slightly with a few drops of water and used to paint decorative motifs on the baked cookies. For a very special, dramatic effect, cut out rectangular or other shape plaques from the dough and personalize them for use as place cards or even as menus or greeting cards. The writing can be done with piped Royal Icing. To create stands, cut and bake triangles of gingerbread and attach them with Royal Icing to the back of the gingerbread plaques. Allow the icing to dry at least 24 hours before standing the plaques upright.

STORE:
In an airtight container at room temperature.

KEEPS:
For several months.

NOTE: Gingerbread for a cathedral or house can be made even more sturdy by reducing the amounts of sugar and butter. Use ½ cup (4.25 ounces/120 grams) of firmly packed dark brown sugar and ½ cup (4 ounces/113 grams) of unsalted butter. For further stability plus a delicious flavor, spread melted bittersweet or semisweet chocolate onto the back of the baked, cooled gingerbread.

Royal Icing

INGREDIENTS *Do not make on a humid day*	MEASURE volume	WEIGHT	
		ounces/pounds	grams
3 large egg whites	3 fluid ounces	3 ounces	90 grams
powdered sugar	4 cups (lightly spooned into the cup)	1 pound	460 grams

Royal Icing

This recipe has an excellent consistency for piping. For painting, thin the icing with water.

In a large mixing bowl, place the egg whites and sugar and beat, preferably with the whisk beater, at low speed, until the sugar is moistened. Beat at high speed until very glossy and stiff peaks form when the beater is lifted (5 to 7 minutes). The tips of the peaks should curve slightly. If necessary, more powdered sugar may be added. Keeps 3 days in an airtight container at room temperature. Rebeat lightly.

Royal Icing with Meringue Powder*

Replace the egg whites with 3 tablespoons of meringue powder and 3 fluid ounces (6 tablespoons) of warm water (this is approximately the amount of water contained in the eggs). Proceed as for basic Royal Icing. Keeps 2 weeks in an airtight container at room temperature. Rebeat lightly.

SMART COOKIE

- If you like your gingerbread people soft, chewy and pudgy, roll the dough to ¼-inch thickness and underbake it slightly so that upon cooling the cookies remain soft.
- Well-chilled dough rolls easily on a floured surface without plastic wrap or a pastry cloth.
- Dough can also be rolled between plastic wrap layers but needs to be refrigerated after cutting as the dough becomes too soft to hold its shape well.
- Saran Wrap is the ideal plastic wrap for rolling the dough because it lies very flat. Wax paper is the second choice.
- Allow the cookie sheet(s) to cool completely before using for the next batch.
- Distribute the cookies evenly around the cookie sheet. Avoid crowding the cookies into one section of the cookie sheet, leaving a large area bare.
- Gingerbread is delicious and crunchy eaten plain. It becomes softer and equally delicious dunked in coffee, tea, or Cognac.

*Meringue powder is available through cake-decorating supply houses such as Maid of Scandinavia (800-328-6722) and the Chocolate Gallery (212-675-2253).

Christmas Wreaths

The crunchy, wheaty, sticky sweetness of these wreaths is quite delicious when freshly made. Air-dried, they make adorable tree ornaments.

Makes: 1½ dozen
2-inch wreaths

INGREDIENTS	MEASURE		WEIGHT	
	volume		*ounces*	*grams*
unsalted butter	½ cup		4 ounces	113 grams
30 large marshmallows	3 cups		7.25 ounces	208 grams
green liquid food coloring	1½ teaspoons		•	•
pure vanilla extract	1 teaspoon		•	4 grams
cornflakes	4 cups		5 ounces	140 grams
cinnamon red-hots (candies)	2 tablespoons		1 ounce	30 grams

Spray a medium saucepan with nonstick vegetable shortening or lightly grease it.

Melt the butter over low heat. Add the marshmallows and melt them over low heat, stirring constantly, until smooth (about 6 minutes). Remove the pan from the heat and whisk in the food coloring and vanilla extract until well blended. Stir in the cornflakes to coat them well. Keep the mixture warm by placing the saucepan in a large pot or skillet filled with 1 inch of very hot tap water. Replace the water as it cools.

Working quickly so the mixture does not harden, use the 2 spoons, or lightly greased fingers, to drop small (1 heaping tablespoon) mounds of the cornflake mixture onto the wax paper. With lightly greased fingers, quickly form cornflake mounds into wreaths with holes in the centers. Immediately, while the wreaths are still sticky, decorate the wreaths with red-hots. (The red-hots may also be attached in a more leisurely fashion by using small dabs of Royal Icing, page 230.)

When wreaths dry, they may be strung with nylon string or gold ribbons as tree ornaments.

• Do not use the microwave to melt the marshmallows unless you have an enormous microwave-proof bowl; marshmallows swell considerably on heating.
• For easy cleanup, place your spoons and whisk in the saucepan; fill it with water and bring it to a boil.

EQUIPMENT:
flat counter or cookie sheet, lined with wax paper, sprayed with nonstick vegetable cooking spray or lightly greased or buttered; 2 small spoons sprayed with nonstick vegetable cooking spray or lightly greased or buttered

STORE:
In an airtight container.

KEEPS:
For eating, about 1 month; as ornaments, indefinitely.

SMART COOKIE

Petrossian Blini and Caviar

There are people who think they don't like caviar because they have tasted only the lumpfish variety, which is like eating fish-flavored salt. But top-quality malossol (low-salt) sturgeon caviar has the freshness of an ocean breeze with just a hint of the sea's saltiness. I tasted it the first time when I was seventeen and my mother's friend Celia brought back a small jar from a trip to her native Russia. I was spoiled for life. Newly in love, though, I actually managed to save almost half of it for my boyfriend, who, much to my delight, thought he did not like caviar.

Petrossian, purveyor of some of the world's finest caviar, is one of the most romantic restaurants in New York. It is situated, appropriately, in a landmark building on the corner of 58th Street and 7th Avenue. From the outside it resembles a sand-dripping castle and from the inside a Fabergé jewel box. Although Petrossian also serves excellent meals (I experienced the reenactment of Babette's Feast there for my fortieth birthday), it is most known for its fine caviar, smoked salmon and other smoked fish. And the fabulous presentation is truly fit for royalty.

Gold serving spoons and pallets (not silver, which would react with the purity of the caviar) are used to lift the caviar, and icy vodka is ceremoniously poured to the very brim of the fluted glasses so that even one more drop would overflow. Beluga caviar is served only with toast points, as nothing must interfere with the perfection of its flavor, but the saltier pressed caviar is served with pillows of yeasty tender warm blini spread with cool thick crème fraîche.

The Petrossian blini recipe was given to me by Dro Proudian. Thousands of them are prepared each year to serve at the restaurant and also to ship mail order. These blini are so delicious they would make even less expensive caviar, such as red salmon caviar, more of a treat. What could be more perfect for Christmas Eve, or even perhaps a festive Christmas breakfast? For me, this is the ultimate way to celebrate the most important occasions.

Serves: 8 (makes: 32 3-inch blini)

Rising time: 1 to 1½ hours

EQUIPMENT: plett pan with 3- to 3½-inch round individual recesses or a heavy frying pan or griddle

INGREDIENTS	MEASURE	WEIGHT	
	volume	*ounces*	*grams*
Blini			
warm water	¼ liquid cup	•	•
sugar, divided	2 tablespoons	1 ounce	25 grams
fresh yeast *or* dry yeast (not rapid rise)	2¾ packed teaspoons 2¼ teaspoon	0.6 ounce 0.25 ounce	17 grams 7 grams
3 large egg yolks	scant 2 fluid ounces	2 ounces	56 grams
vegetable oil	6 tablespoons (3 fluid ounces)	•	•
bleached all-purpose flour	2 cups (dip and sweep method)	10 ounces	284 grams
salt	½ teaspoon	•	•
milk, warm	2 liquid cups	•	•
3 large egg whites	6 tablespoons (3 fluid ounces)	3 ounces	90 grams
cream of tartar	⅜ teaspoon	•	•
Crème Fraîche (page 80)	2 cups	•	•
caviar, preferably sevruga or osetra*	•	17.5 ounces	500 grams

*Available by mail order from Petrossian (800-828-9241).

Proof the yeast: Crumble the fresh yeast into a small bowl and add ½ teaspoon of the sugar and ¼ cup of the water, warmed to a tepid 100°F.; if using dry yeast increase the temperature slightly to 110°F. Stir until the yeast is dissolved. Set aside in a draft-free spot for 10 to 20 minutes. The mixture should be full of bubbles; if not, the yeast is too old to be useful. Discard it and start again with fresh yeast.

In a medium bowl, place the egg yolks and gradually whisk in the oil to form a thick emulsion resembling mayonnaise.

In a large bowl, whisk together the flour, remaining 5½ teaspoons of sugar and the salt. Whisk in the yolk mixture until mixed (it will not be moist). Whisk in the yeast mixture and then gradually whisk in the warm milk, whisking until smooth. (If the milk is too hot it will kill the yeast.)

Cover the mixture tightly with plastic wrap (preferably Saran brand) and set aside in a warm draft-free place for 1 to 1½ hours or until doubled in bulk and tiny bubbles appear all over the surface.

In a mixing bowl, beat the egg whites until foamy. Add the cream of tartar and beat until stiff peaks form when the beater is raised slowly. Using a large whisk or rubber spatula, fold the whites into the batter.

Heat the pan or griddle over medium heat until a drop of water sizzles when dropped onto the pan. Spray lightly with nonstick vegetable shortening or brush with oil. Pour a scant ¼ cup of batter into each plett pan indentation, filling them about half full, or pour the batter by ¼ cups into the frying pan or onto the griddle. Cook, adjusting the heat as necessary to avoid overbrowning, until the underside of each blini is golden brown and the upper side begins to dull, about 2½ minutes. Transfer the cooked blini to a baking sheet and keep them warm in a 200°F. oven until ready to serve.

Serve the blini with the crème fraîche and caviar on the side. The blini are delicious both warm and at room temperature.

NOTE: The blini can be prepared ahead of time and frozen. Allow the blini to cool, then stack them and wrap them first in plastic wrap and then heavy-duty foil. Allow them to defrost at room temperature. Arrange the blini in single layers on baking sheets and reheat them in a 350°F. oven for about 10 minutes or until heated through. You may also loosely wrap the blinis in paper towels in stacks of four and microwave on high power for 30 seconds. I find them to be delicious at room temperature as well.

UNDERSTANDING

Egg yolk and oil coat the flour, keeping it from forming as much gluten, which results in more tender blini.

Other traditional serving utensils for caviar are bone or mother of pearl, which do not affect the caviar's flavor.

Russian red salmon, also available from Petrossian, is smaller but less salty than the American variety. When caviar is salty, I counteract it with extra crème fraîche!

Sage and Thyme Roasted Goose

Goose, although not quite as tender as other fowl, more than makes up for it with its incomparable rich flavor—and the bonus of the best fat for cooking you will ever come by. I usually associate goose with a Dickensian Christmas, or at least cold weather time, but actually the best goose I ever had was one summer when my friends Gus and Barbara of Pine Hill Farms in New Jersey accidentally came by a baby goose, weighing less than five pounds. I think it was run over by a car; it reminded me of years before, when I was living in Washington Crossing, Pennsylvania, and my car hit a pheasant when I was on my way to work one morning. I took off after it, willingly skipping work, but never did catch a second glimpse of it. Probably just as well too; I would have had no idea (city girl that I was) what to do with poultry that didn't come cleaned and wrapped.

Barbara called me that summer afternoon, saying. "You take this goose; I don't know what to do with it." I offered to give her cooking instructions but she said, "Never mind; it's all yours." We had been about to leave for a trip, but given this windfall, Elliott agreed to postpone the departure by several hours.

Since it was the end of summer, and the garden was full of thyme and sage, I took large bunches of each and stuffed the cavity of the goose. Perhaps because the goose was so young and free range (actually wild), there was hardly any fat, and the herbs thoroughly permeated the flesh. The texture and flavor were extraordinary. I now use this same method for roasting larger geese. It's not quite the same but it is still quite wonderful.

Serves: about 8

Two hours before roasting, remove the goose from the refrigerator.

Preheat the oven to: 400°F. Baking time: 2 to 3 hours Internal temperature (thigh): 175°F. to 180°F.

EQUIPMENT: large roasting pan and rack

INGREDIENTS	MEASURE volume	WEIGHT ounces/pounds	grams/kilograms
1 goose		10 to 12 pounds	4 kilograms, 536 grams to 5 kilograms, 443 grams
kosher salt*	1½ teaspoons	0.3 ounce	9 grams
pepper, freshly ground	several grindings	.	.
1 whole head of garlic, cut in half horizontally		2.5 ounces	75 grams
2 large bunches thyme		2 ounces	56 grams
1 large bunch sage		1 ounce	28 grams

*If using Morton's kosher salt or table salt, use ¾ teaspoon.

If the goose is frozen, allow it to thaw in the refrigerator for 2 to 2½ days. My cousin Richard, a chemist, once thawed a turkey with two cycles in a dishwasher. This was before microwave defrosting, but probably a lot more even.

Remove all loose fat from the cavity and discard it or render it for future use (see Note). Remove the neck and giblets from the cavity and, if desired, simmer them for 2 to 3 hours with the beef broth for the Salt and Pepper Wild Rice (page 243) to enrich the broth. (Poach the liver in the broth for about 5 to 10 minutes as a special treat for the cook.)

Preheat the oven to 400°F.

Prick the goose all over, being careful not to go deeper than the fat layer. Sprinkle it inside and out with the salt and pepper. Place the garlic, thyme and sage in the cavity. Place the goose on the rack in the pan and tuck the wings back under the back. Pour ½ cup boiling water over the goose.

Roast for 30 minutes, then remove the pan from the oven (close the door so the heat does not escape). Drain off the fat and pour over another ½ cup of boiling water. Return to the oven for another 30 minutes. Drain and douse with boiling water. Reduce the oven heat to 325°F. and continue roasting for another 1 to 2 hours, draining the fat and dousing the goose with boiling water every 30 minutes, until an instant-read thermometer inserted in the thigh, not touching the bone, reads 175°F. to 180°F. When tilted tailward, the juices should run dark brown, not rosy. The temperature will rise about 5 degrees on sitting.

Allow the goose to rest for 30 minutes before carving. Return the thighs to the oven for about 10 minutes, or until no longer pink. If desired, turn up the heat to 400F. and roast the back section to crisp the skin. Garnish with seasonal fruits and herbs. After presenting the goose at the table, return it to the kitchen for carving. (It is difficult to carve a goose gracefully as the joints do not separate easily.)

NOTE: To render goose fat, process it in a food processor (or chop with a sharp heavy knife) into small pieces and place in a medium-size heavy saucepan. Add ¼ cup of water and cover tightly. Cook on the lowest possible heat for about 1 hour to 1 hour and 15 minutes or until the fat is rendered, leaving only small golden bits. Stir a few times during the cooking to prevent overbrowning which would give it an off flavor. The melted fat will keep refrigerated for several months and frozen for several years.

• Anyone who has ever encountered a tough goose knows just how tough it can be. This is more likely to happen with imported geese. For reliability regarding tenderness the National Goose Council recommends the frozen American goose available in supermarkets. Larger, 14-pound USDA geese are, amazingly, just as tender as smaller USDA geese but somewhat fattier. The only way you can be sure it is this variety is if it has the USDA grade

POINTERS FOR SUCCESS

A shield. A tip from Arianne Daquin of D'Artagnan: If you are buying a fresh goose, it will be at its best in the months before January. Farm-raised geese are born in May, so by January they may be too mature and no longer tender.

UNDERSTANDING

I prefer goose unstuffed because any stuffing becomes infused with the fat.

I drain off the fat every half hour before it begins to brown and save it for cooking. The rack makes collecting the fat easier. Dousing the goose with boiling water helps to release the fat and keeps the breast moist. I prefer to cook the goose only to 175°F. so that the breast remains juicy. This is a bit underdone for the thighs and back, but it's preferable to return them briefly to the oven than to overcook the breast.

Kosher salt is preferable to the finer table salt because it does not dissolve as readily when the boiling water is poured onto the goose.

Salt and Pepper Wild Rice

Because a dish that's 100 percent wild rice can be grassy tasting, I like to add a little white rice for lightening both the flavor and appearance. I do not recommend buying a commercial mix that includes both, because wild rice takes more than double the time to cook than does white so you end up with undercooked wild rice and overcooked white!

The intense flavor of wild rice works wonderfully with game and full-flavored poultry such as goose. I often bring it as a house gift to my friends the Brossolets, in France, because it is a native American product less available there and goes so magnificently with the game Max hunts. One year, when my friend Jean Pierre, owner of the enchanting Le Rivage hotel and restaurant in Orléans, was about to be married, I presented him with a big package of wild rice, saying, "In America we throw white rice on the bride and groom; but since you are not yet married, here is some wild rice instead." He served it for lunch with wild duck they had caught that morning. It was memorable.

Serves: 6

INGREDIENTS	MEASURE *volume*	WEIGHT	
		ounces	*grams*
boiling water	3 to 4 cups	•	•
Glace de Viande (page 253)*	3 cubes	1.5 ounces	48 grams
wild rice	1 cup	6 ounces	170 grams
salt, divided	¾ teaspoon + ⅛ teaspoon	•	•
long-grain white rice (preferably Uncle Ben's)	¼ cup	1.75 ounces	48 grams
boiling water	⅓ liquid cup	•	•
OPTIONAL: sliced mushrooms	2½ cups	8 ounces	227 grams
goose fat or butter	2 tablespoons	1 ounce	28 grams
OPTIONAL: shallot, minced *or* onion, minced	2 teaspoons 1 tablespoon	0.25 ounce 0.3 ounce	6 grams 9 grams
pepper, freshly ground	several grindings	•	•

*Or 3 cups unsalted beef broth and ¼ teaspoon salt; or 2 cups beef broth (preferably College Inn) plus 1 cup water, and omit salt entirely from the recipe.

Place the wild rice in a strainer and run cold water through it until the water runs clear.

In a medium-size saucepan, bring 3 cups of water and the Glace de Viande (or the broth) to a boil. Simmer, covered, until the *glace* is dissolved.

Remeasure and add water to equal 3 cups. Add the wild rice and ¾ teaspoon of the salt. Return the broth to a boil, then simmer over low heat, covered, for 50 to 70 minutes, stirring with a fork three or four times, until the rice puffs open. Add extra water if all the liquid evaporates before the rice is tender. If any water remains when the rice is done, raise the heat and continue cooking briefly, uncovered, until dry. Cover and keep warm.

Meanwhile, spray the inside of a small heavy saucepan with a tight cover with nonstick vegetable shortening, or butter it. Add the white rice, boiling water and the remaining ⅛ teaspoon salt, immediately cover and cook for 15 minutes on the lowest possible heat. Remove from the heat and allow the rice to sit for at least 5 minutes.

Scrape the white rice into the cooked wild rice and fluff lightly with a fork. Cover the rice tightly.

To prepare the optional mushrooms, while the rice is cooking, in a large, heavy frying pan with a lid, heat the goose fat or butter over medium heat. When bubbling, add the shallot or onion and cook, stirring often, for about 1 minute or until translucent. Add the mushrooms, cover and cook for about 5 minutes or until they give up their liquid. Continue cooking un-covered, stirring occasionally, until the liquid evaporates and the mush-rooms are lightly browned, about 5 minutes. Add this to the rice mixture. Add the pepper and toss lightly with a fork to blend. (If you omit the shallots and mushrooms, add the goose fat or butter and pepper to the rice mixture.) Taste and adjust the seasonings.

Pressure Cooker Method

I often use this method when I don't want to wait an hour for the rice. It is delightfully reliable. Place the water and Glace de Viande cubes or stock, the rice and salt in the pressure cooker and lock the lid in place. Over high heat, bring the pressure to high. Lower the heat but maintain high pressure. Cook for 30 minutes. Place the pressure cooker in the sink and run cold water over the lid until the pressure is released. Open the lid away from your face to avoid the steam. Then boil for a few minutes over high heat to evaporate any remaining liquid. Depending on the rice and the size of the pot, this can take as long as 10 minutes.

Uncooked wild rice stored in an airtight container keeps indefinitely without any nutritional or flavor loss.

UNDERSTANDING

Wild rice is the most unpredictable of all grains as far as cooking time and amount of liquid needed. It is therefore best to start with the minimum liquid and cooking time and add more if needed. Some people prefer to undercook the rice slightly, leaving some of the grains unopened and with more bite. I like the grains to be open but still curled. With continued cooking, all the grains will open fully and flatten. I find this texture too soft. Wild rice expands four times in volume when cooked.

Glace de Viande offers the best flavor because it is concentrated beef stock without salt. Next-best is unsalted broth but it is very expensive. Regular canned beef broth is very salty so only half the amount can be used, even when omitting added salt.

Cousin Marion's Pickled Grapes

Marion made this side dish for Thanksgiving one year and it was such a hit it has become a traditional part of the meal. The tanginess of the marinated grapes is a perfect foil for the richness of any fowl.

Makes: 3 cups

Marinating time: at least 24 hours; up to 1 week

INGREDIENTS room temperature	MEASURE volume	WEIGHT ounces	grams
seedless green grapes, washed and stemmed	1½ cups	9 ounces	255 grams
seedless red grapes, washed and stemmed	1½ cups	9 ounces	255 grams
sugar	1½ cups	10.5 ounces	300 grams
white wine vinegar	1 liquid cup	•	•
3 3-inch cinnamon sticks	•	•	•
3 cloves	•	•	•

Place the grapes in a glass bowl or jar. If using a glass jar, use one with a nonreactive lid or cover the lid with plastic wrap (preferably Saran brand).

In a small stainless steel or enamel-coated pan, bring the remaining ingredients to a boil, stirring occasionally. Simmer the mixture for 5 minutes, then pour it over the grapes. Stir, cover tightly with plastic wrap or the lid, and allow the grapes to stand overnight at room temperature.

The grapes will be ready to serve the next day but the flavor improves if marinated longer. To marinate longer, refrigerate as soon as the mixture is cool. Stir once a day to keep the grapes on the top moist. After 3 days, the grapes start to wrinkle slightly.

KEEPS:
Up to 1 week refrigerated.

Chocolate Raspberry Trifle

Serves: 10 to 12

Prepare the cake, syrup and the crème anglaise 2 days before serving. Assemble the trifle the day before serving. Pipe the topping the day of serving.

Preheat the oven to: 350°F. Baking time: 30 to 35 minutes

EQUIPMENT:
3-quart (100-ounce) trifle bowl; two 9-inch by 2-inch round cake pans, greased, bottoms lined with parchment or wax paper, then sprayed (bottom and sides) with Baker's Joy or greased and floured, with the excess flour tapped out; large pastry bag fitted with a large open star tube (Number 5)

KEEPS:
The trifle will still be delicious one day after the topping has been added. Since covering it with plastic would ruin its appearance, be sure to cover tightly any aromatic food in the refrigerator to prevent the cream from absorbing other flavors.

*C*hocolate and raspberry is one of my favorite combinations so one day when my friend Jan Kish suggested a trifle with these ingredients, I fell for it immediately. The dessert is as luscious as it looks. And it is perfect for holiday entertaining because it makes a stunning presentation and it is prepared the day ahead.

I like to have extra dessert at Christmastime because friends and family often drop over after their own traditional holiday dinner.

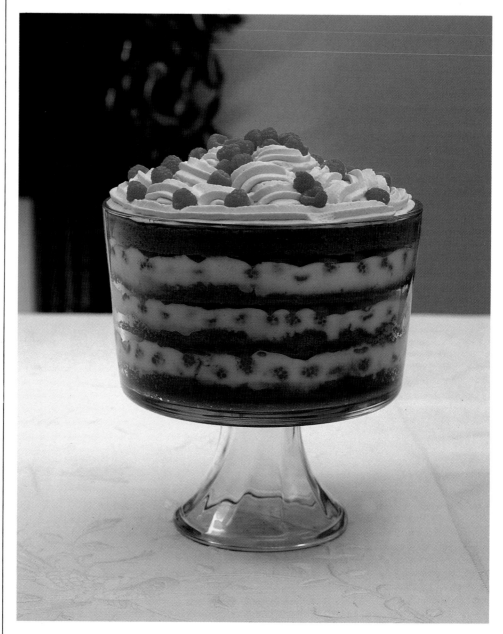

INGREDIENTS	MEASURE	WEIGHT	
	volume	*ounces/pounds*	*grams*
Moist Chocolate Génoise			
bittersweet chocolate, preferably Lindt Excellence or Valrhona extra bittersweet	2⅔ 3-ounce bars	8 ounces	227 grams
boiling water	1 liquid cup	•	•
8 large eggs	1½ liquid cups	14 ounces (weighed without shells)	400 grams
superfine sugar	1 cup	7 ounces	200 grams
sifted cake flour	1½ cups (sifted into the cup and leveled off)	5.25 ounces	150 grams
Raspberry Syrup			
sugar	¼ cup + 3 tablespoons	3 ounces	88 grams
water	¾ liquid cup	•	•
Chambord liqueur or water	3 tablespoons	•	•
Crème Anglaise			
sugar	6 tablespoons	2.63 ounces	75 grams
salt	⅛ teaspoon	•	•
12 large egg yolks	7 fluid ounces	7.75 ounces	223 grams
milk	3 liquid cups	•	•
1½ vanilla beans, cut in ½ lengthwise*	•	•	•
fresh raspberries	4 cups (4½ pints)	1 pound	454 grams
seedless raspberry preserves, divided	½ cup	5 ounces	145 grams
Raspberry Jam Cream Topping			
seedless raspberry preserves	1 cup	10 ounces	290 grams
Chambord liqueur or water	1 tablespoon	•	•
heavy cream	2 liquid cups	•	•
sugar	2 tablespoons	1 ounce	26 grams

*You may substitute 1 tablespoon vanilla extract for the vanilla bean, but the bean offers a fuller, more aromatic flavor. If using extract, add it after the sauce is cool. If using a Tahitian bean, use only ¾ of a bean.

Moist Chocolate Génoise

Preheat the oven to 350°F.

In a heavy saucepan, bring the chocolate and water to a boil over low heat, stirring constantly. Simmer, stirring, for 5 minutes or until the chocolate thickens to a puddinglike consistency. (If dropped from the spoon, it will pool slightly before disappearing.) Cool completely.

In a large mixing bowl, beat the eggs and sugar, preferably with the whisk beater of a stand mixer, on high speed for 5 minutes or until tripled in volume. (A hand-held mixer may be used but it will be necessary to beat for at least 10 minutes.)

Sift half the flour over the egg mixture and fold it in gently but rapidly with a slotted skimmer or large rubber spatula until some of the flour has disappeared. Fold in the remaining flour until all the flour has disappeared. Fold in the chocolate mixture until incorporated.

Pour the batter immediately into the prepared pans (they will be about two thirds full) and bake for 30 to 35 minutes or until a tester inserted in the center enters as easily as it does when inserted closer to the sides. Avoid opening the oven door before the minimum time or the cakes could fall. The cakes rise to the tops of the pans during baking and will sink slightly when done, pulling slightly away from the sides.

Loosen the sides of the cakes with a small metal spatula and unmold them at once onto lightly greased racks. Reinvert the cakes and allow them to cool. The firm upper crusts prevent falling.

When cool, wrap the cakes tightly in plastic wrap (preferably Saran brand) and store them at room temperature overnight.

Raspberry Syrup

In a small saucepan, with a tight-fitting lid, bring the sugar and water to a rolling boil, stirring constantly. Cover immediately, remove from the heat and allow to cool completely. Transfer the syrup to a liquid measuring cup and stir in the liqueur. If the syrup has evaporated slightly, add enough water to equal 1 cup plus 2 tablespoons of syrup.

Crème Anglaise

Have a fine strainer suspended over a medium bowl ready near the range.

In a medium-size heavy noncorrodible saucepan, stir together the sugar, salt and yolks until well blended, using a wooden spoon.

In a small saucepan, scald* the milk and vanilla beans. (Or heat in a heatproof 4-cup glass measure in a microwave on high power.) Stir a few tablespoons into the yolk mixture, then gradually add the remaining milk and vanilla beans, stirring constantly.

Heat the mixture, stirring constantly, to just below the boiling point (170°F. to 180°F.). Steam will begin to appear and the mixture will be slightly thicker than heavy cream; a finger run across the back of a spoon dipped in the mixture will leave a well-defined track. Immediately remove the pan from the heat and pour into the strainer, scraping up the thickened cream on the bottom of the pan. Remove the vanilla beans and scrape the seeds into the sauce. Stir to separate the seeds (fingers work best). For maximum flavor, return the pods to the sauce until ready to assemble the trifle.

*Bring just to the boiling point (small bubbles will begin to appear around the edges).

Cool to room temperature. Cover tightly with plastic wrap and refrigerate. Makes 3¾ cups.

Unwrap the cake layers and remove the top "skin," or crust, using a serrated knife if necessary. Using a long serrated knife, divide each layer in half horizontally. Use the trifle bowl as a guide for trimming the layers to fit by inverting it over each layer and cutting away the excess cake. Many trifle bowls are smaller at the bottom than at the top. If this is the case, you will need to trim 3 of the layers slightly more to fit the bowl.

Place the 4 cake layers on a clean work surface and spread each with 2 tablespoons of the raspberry preserves. Place one cake round, jam side down, in the trifle bowl. Brush it evenly with one quarter of the syrup (about ¼ cup). Pour one third (about 1¼ cups) of the crème anglaise over the layer. Sprinkle the crème anglaise with 1 pint of the raspberries.

Continue in the same way with the second and third cake layers, syrup, crème anglaise and raspberries, placing each layer jam side down. Top with the fourth cake layer and brush it with the remaining syrup. Press down gently and cover the bowl tightly with plastic wrap. Refrigerate overnight.

Assembling the Trifle

Refrigerate a mixing bowl and mixer beater for at least 15 minutes.

In a small bowl, place the raspberry jam and whisk in the Chambord or water.

In the chilled bowl, beat the cream and sugar just until beater marks begin to show distinctly in the cream. Add the jam mixture and beat just until stiff peaks form when the beater is raised. Immediately, fill the pastry bag with the jam cream and decorate the trifle: Remove the plastic wrap from the trifle and pipe the jam cream in a shell pattern, starting at the edges of the bowl and working toward the center, mounding it more toward the center. (You may also spread the jam cream on top of the trifle in swirls with a rubber spatula.)

Place a few raspberries decoratively on top. Refrigerate the trifle until 1 to 2 hours before serving time.

Raspberry Jam Cream Topping

- Use superfine sugar for the finest texture. (You can make it by processing granulated sugar in the food processor for a few minutes until fine.)
- Use cake flour without leavening.
- Work quickly once the eggs are beaten so that they do not deflate.
- Fold the flour gently but *thoroughly* into the batter.
- Bake immediately after mixing.
- Use the correct pan size.
- For very even layers, wrap the cake pans with Magi-Cake Strips (available from Maid of Scandinavia, 800-328-6722).

POINTERS FOR SUCCESS

Moist Chocolate Génoise

- The custard must be heated to at least 160°F. to thicken the egg yolks adequately. At temperatures over 180°F. the yolks will start to curdle and the cream may not be smooth.
- When stirring the custard mixture, it is best to use a wooden spoon because a whisk will create air bubbles, making it difficult to judge when the mixture is done.

Crème Anglaise

Bourbon Pecan Butter Balls

This variation on a southern classic is lighter and less sweet than tradition usually dictates. My friend Skip Dye, who grew up in the South, says these are the best he has ever tasted, partly because the bourbon is not overwhelming.

The vanilla essence version can be eaten right away but the marvelous bourbon variety is even more delicious when allowed to mellow for at least a day. If you love the flavor of bourbon as much as Skip and I do, but find it too harsh to drink straight, these are for you.

Makes: 44 balls

Mellowing time: at least 24 hours; up to several weeks

INGREDIENTS *room temperature*	MEASURE *volume*	WEIGHT *ounces*	*grams*
Chocolate Oriolos (page 161) or packaged chocolate wafers*	1 recipe 1½ 9-ounce package	· 13.5 ounces	· 383 grams
pecan halves	1½ cups	5.25 ounces	150 grams
powdered sugar	1¼ cups (lightly spooned into the cup and leveled off)	5 ounces	144 grams
cocoa, preferably Dutch-processed	½ cup (lightly spooned into the cup and leveled off)	1.66 ounces	46 grams
unsalted butter	4 tablespoons	2 ounces	57 grams
corn syrup	¼ liquid cup	3 ounces	82 grams
bourbon (or 3 to 4 tablespoons water + 2 teaspoons pure vanilla extract)	3 to 4 tablespoons	·	·
Topping			
sugar	¾ cup	5.25 ounces	150 grams

*Homemade cookies result in moister, softer and more delicious bourbon balls.

Use a food processor or blender to pulverize the cookies (in several batches) into fine crumbs. Empty them into a large bowl.

Process the pecans with the powdered sugar and cocoa until finely ground. Add the butter and corn syrup and process until combined. Add this mixture to the cookie crumbs.

Food Processor Method

Soften the butter and finely grate the nuts. Sift the powdered sugar and cocoa into the bowl with the cookie crumbs. Add the butter, nuts and corn syrup.

Hand Method

Both Methods | Add 3 tablespoons of the bourbon (or 3 tablespoons of the water and the vanilla) to the cookie crumb mixture. Mix well, adding the remaining tablespoon of liquid if the mixture is too dry to hold together.

Allow the mixture to sit for 30 minutes to absorb the liquid evenly. Add more liquid if necessary.

To roll, use 1 level tablespoon of the mixture and press and roll it between your palms to shape into a ball.

To coat the balls with sugar topping, place the sugar in a small bowl. Add one ball at a time and roll it around in the sugar. The coating is most attractive when the balls are dipped three times. Redip after the sugar starts to disappear.

Place in an airtight container, and allow the balls to mellow for 24 hours or up to several weeks before serving.

Glace de Viande
(Homemade Beef Essence)

I am grateful to Jacques Pépin's La Technique *for introducing me to this indispensable jewel of the kitchen. It is called* glace, *because the broth is so concentrated it becomes a glaze.* Glace *could well be the most important recipe in this book because it will enhance so many things you make without adding either salt or fat, enabling you to control the amount and type of each of these ingredients you desire.*

I make this enrichment stock every two years. In fact, whenever there are meat drippings, I chill them to harden and remove the fat and then freeze them for future use. They are usually salty, though, whereas with glace *there is no salt at all.*

I like to make a large amount as the work is about the same but if you don't have a large enough stock pot, make half the recipe. My enormous hammered copper stockpot, which I brought at the Bridge Kitchenware shop years ago, is my most treasured piece of kitchen equipment. I polish it after I make the stock, and keep it in the living room where I can watch it as the setting sun turns it the most amazing colors. Over the months, the pinkness of newly shined copper gradually oxidizes to a burnished glow. When it dulls, it's a sure sign that it's time to make stock again.

Makes: about 2 cups (18 ounces/510 grams) *glace* or 32 cubes, about 0.5 ounce/16 grams each (1 cube + 1 cup water = 1 cup stock)

EQUIPMENT:
large roasting pan; large stock pot (16 quarts); large fine strainer, cheesecloth; 2-quart or larger saucepan or high-sided skillet, preferably lined with a nonstick surface; bread pan about 8½ inches by 4½ inches, lightly sprayed with nonstick vegetable shortening or lightly oiled

INGREDIENTS *room temperature*	MEASURE volume	WEIGHT ounces/pounds	WEIGHT *grams/kilograms*
chicken bones, veal bones and beef bones (third each), cut into 2-inch pieces	.	10 pounds	4 kilogram, 536 grams
6 carrots, scrubbed, and cut into 1-inch chunks	.	1 pound	454 grams
3 large onions, unpeeled, cut into eighths	.	1½ pounds	680 grams
water, divided	12 quarts	.	.
3 large ripe tomatoes, quartered, seeded and coarsely chopped	.	1½ pounds	680 grams
1 large leek, roots removed, cut in half and thoroughly washed	.	8 ounces	227 grams
3 celery ribs with leaves, cut into 1-inch pieces	.	7 ounces	100 grams
1 small bunch parsley, preferably flat-leafed, tied with string	.	2 ounces	56 grams
2 bay leaves	.	.	.
dried thyme	1 teaspoon	.	.
peppercorns	½ teaspoon	.	.

Place the bones in the roasting pan and brown in a 425°F. oven for 1½ hours, turning the bones once after 45 minutes. Then add the carrots and onions and continue browning for 30 minutes.

With a slotted skimmer or spoon, remove the bones and vegetables to the stockpot. Discard the fat in the roasting pan and set the pan on one or two burners. Add 2 cups of the water and cook over medium heat, scraping to dislodge the browned bits from the bottom of the pan. Pour this liquid along with the browned bits into the stockpot and add the remaining 11½ quarts of water.

Bring the water to a boil over high heat. Reduce the heat to low and simmer for 1 hour, skimming any scum that rises to the surface. Add the remaining vegetables, herbs and spices and simmer for at least 10 hours, adding water as necessary so that the bones and vegetables are always covered by at least 2 inches of water. (It's fine to let it simmer overnight, partially covered, but be sure the heat is at the lowest setting possible so that it never boils.)

Use a slotted skimmer or spoon to remove the bones, vegetables and other solids to a strainer suspended over a large bowl. Press them to remove as much juice as possible and then discard the bones and vegetables. Pour all the sauce through the strainer. You will need several large bowls (or a second large stockpot).

Wash the stockpot and return the strained stock to it. Over high heat, reduce the stock to 3 quarts, about 2½ hours.*

Pour the stock into a bowl and allow it to cool to room temperature, uncovered. Cover it tightly with plastic wrap and refrigerate for several hours or overnight. The fat will congeal on the top; remove and discard it.

Suspend the fine strainer over a 4-quart or larger pot and line it with dampened cheesecloth. Heat the stock and pour it through the strainer into the pot. Over high heat, reduce the stock to 6 cups, stirring occasionally with a greased wooden spoon, 1½ to 2 hours.

Transfer the stock to the 2-quart saucepan or high-sided skillet. Scrape any stock clinging to the stirring spoon into the stock. Reduce the sauce over very low heat, to prevent burning, to about 2 cups, about 1 hour. The bubbling surface will be lighter in color but should not be skimmed. The stock will become a very dark and syrupy essence. Toward the very end of the cooking, large sticky bubbles will form on the surface and break. Remove from the heat.

Pour the concentrated stock (*glace*) into the oiled bread pan, scraping out as much of the stock as possible. Set the saucepan aside. Cool the *glace* to room temperature, cover the pan with plastic wrap and refrigerate it for several hours until firmly set.

Meanwhile, add 2 cups of water to the saucepan and heat, stirring constantly to dissolve any remaining beef essence. Reduce the liquid to 1 cup. Cool and refrigerate it. Use this stock within 3 days.

---

*At this point, if you wish, make the Boeuf à la Ficelle (page 117) before proceeding to the next step. Be sure to skim off as much of the fat as possible from the surface first.

Run a small metal spatula or thin knife between the sides of the bread pan and the *glace* and unmold it onto a cutting board. With a sharp knife, cut it into 32 cubes. (Cut it the short way into eighths, then cut it the long way into fourths.)

When Carl Sontheimer started to market the Cuisinarts pressure cooker, he advised me to buy the largest model available because it was useful for making stock. A 6½-quart pressure cooker makes it possible to do the initial 10-hour cooking of the bones and vegetables in just 1 hour. In a pressure cooker with a 6½-quart liquid capacity you can do half the recipe (half the bones, vegetables, herbs and pepper), using 3 quarts of water; then use a large skimmer to remove the bones and debris and add the remaining half recipe to the same broth. It takes about 30 minutes to bring it up to pressure when the water is cold and about 30 minutes for the pressure to go down. Follow the manufacturer's directions for your pressure cooker. Remove the bones and debris and strain the stock. You will have about 4 quarts. Refrigerate it and proceed as above.

Pressure Cooker Method

The bones need to be well covered with water to remove the maximum amount of gelatin and juices.

The stock must not be allowed to boil or the fat will become bound into the protein and it will not be possible to make the stock entirely fat-free.

A pan with a nonstick lining is ideal for the final reduction as the stock becomes very syrupy and sticky.

The exact amount of *glace* depends on the amount of gelatin in the bones.

Demi-glace (meaning half the concentration) is available in specialty stores. I actually find commercially available *demi-glace* to be one third the concentration of this beef essence. If you use purchased *demi-glace,* use about 3 tablespoons in place of 1 cube.

If you make a smaller quantity of *glace* and have only 1 to 1½ cups, use a 5¾-inch by 3¼-inch 1-pound foil loaf pan, available in supermarkets. Cut the *glace* into eighteen 1-inch by 1-inch by ¾-inch-high cubes (cut the short way into sixths; then cut the long way into thirds).

UNDERSTANDING

Glace de Volaille

(glass duh vohLAHEE)
(Homemade Poultry Essence)

Makes: 2 to 2½ cups (20 ounces/570 grams if 2 cups) *glace* **or 32 cubes, about 0.5 ounce/16 to 18 grams each (1 cube + 1 cup water = 1 cup stock)**

Glace de volaille *offers the complex intensity of* glace de viande *but is somewhat more subtle. Whenever I make a chicken (or any fowl), I save the raw gizzard, neck, heart and feet and as much of the cooked carcass as I can salvage and freeze it in heavy-duty plastic freezer bags. At any given time my freezer is always partially filled with the such bags, waiting for enough to justify making stock. Usually I get motivated to make stock when I need freezer space.*

INGREDIENTS *room temperature*	MEASURE volume	WEIGHT	
		ounces/pounds	*grams/kilograms*
chicken and/or duck parts (feet, necks, gizzards, backs, etc.), cut into 2-inch pieces	·	10 pounds	536 grams
water	12 quarts	·	·
6 carrots, scrubbed, cut into 1-inch chunks	·	1 pound	454 grams
2 medium onions, unpeeled, cut into sixths	·	12 ounces	340 grams
3 large ripe tomatoes, quartered, seeded and coarsely chopped	·	1½ pounds	680 grams
1 large leek, roots removed, cut in half and thoroughly washed	·	8 ounces	227 grams
3 celery ribs with leaves, cut into 1-inch pieces	·	7 ounces	100 grams
1 small bunch parsley, preferably flat-leafed, tied with string	·	2 ounces	56 grams
2 bay leaves	·	·	·
3 cloves	·	·	·
dried thyme	1 teaspoon	·	·
peppercorns	½ teaspoon	·	·

Rinse the chicken pieces under cold running water. Place them in the stock-pot and add the water. Bring to a boil over high heat. Reduce the heat to low and simmer for 30 minutes, skimming any scum that rises to the surface. Add the vegetables, herbs and spices and simmer for at least 4 hours, adding water as necessary so that the bones and vegetables are always covered by at least 2 inches of water. Be sure the heat is at the lowest setting possible so that it never boils.

Use a slotted skimmer or spoon to remove the bones, vegetables and other solids to a strainer suspended over a large bowl. Press them to remove as much juice as possible and then discard the bones and vegetables. Pour all the sauce through the strainer. You will need several large bowls (or a second large stockpot).

Wash the stockpot and return the strained stock to it. Over high heat, reduce the stock to 3 quarts, about 2½ hours.

Pour the stock into a bowl and allow it to cool to room temperature, uncovered. Cover tightly with plastic wrap (preferably Saran brand) and refrigerate for several hours or overnight. The fat will congeal on the top; remove and discard it.

Suspend the fine strainer over a 4-quart or larger pot and line it with dampened cheesecloth. Heat the stock and pour it through the strainer into the pot. Over high heat, reduce the stock to 6 cups, stirring occasionally with a greased wooden spoon, 1½ to 2 hours.

Transfer the stock to the 2-quart saucepan or high-sided skillet. Scrape any stock clinging to the stirring spoon into the stock. Continue to reduce the stock over very low heat, to prevent burning, to about 2 cups, about 1 hour. The bubbling surface will be lighter in color but this should not be skimmed. The stock will become very dark in color and syrupy. Toward the very end of the cooking, large sticky bubbles will form on the surface and break. Remove from the heat.

Pour the concentrated stock (*glace*) into the oiled bread pan, scraping out as much of it as possible. Set the saucepan aside. Cool the *glace* to room temperature, cover the pan with plastic wrap and refrigerate for several hours until firmly set.

Meanwhile, add 2 cups of water to the saucepan and heat, stirring constantly to dissolve any remaining chicken essence. Reduce the liquid to 1 cup. Cool and refrigerate. Use this stock within 3 days.

Run a small metal spatula or thin knife between the sides of the bread pan and the *glace* and unmold it onto a cutting board. With a sharp knife, cut it into 32 cubes. (Cut it the short way into eighths, then cut it the long way into quarters.)

A large pressure cooker makes it possible to do the initial 4-hour cooking of the bones and vegetables in just 1 hour. In a pressure cooker with a 6½-quart liquid capacity you can do half the recipe (half the bones, vegetables, herbs and pepper), using 3 quarts of water; then use a large skimmer to remove the bones and debris and add the remaining half recipe to the same

Pressure Cooker Method

EQUIPMENT:
large stock pot (16 quarts); large fine strainer; cheesecloth; 2-quart or larger saucepan or high-sided skillet, preferably lined with a nonstick surface; bread pan about 8½ inches by 4½ inches, lightly sprayed with nonstick vegetable shortening or lightly oiled

KEEPS:
If refrigerated in an open container, the stock cubes will dry out and harden, losing almost half their weight, and these will keep indefinitely but take longer to reconstitute. (This does not work in a high-humidity refrigerator such as a Traulsen.) If stored airtight in the refrigerator they will keep several months; stored in an airtight container in the freezer, they will keep indefinitely.

broth. It takes about 30 minutes to bring it up to pressure when the water is cold and about 30 minutes for the pressure to go down. Follow the manufacturer's directions for your pressure cooker. Remove the bones and debris and strain the stock. You will have about 4 quarts. Refrigerate it and proceed as above.

UNDERSTANDING

The bones need to be well covered with water to remove the maximum amount of gelatin and juices.

The stock must not be allowed to boil or the fat will become bound into the protein and it will not be possible to make the stock entirely fat-free.

A pan with a nonstick lining is ideal for the final reduction as the stock becomes very syrupy and sticky.

The exact amount of concentrated stock depends on the amount of gelatin in the bones. If you include a large amount of chicken feet, which contain more collagen, you will get more essence of the same concentration.

Poultry *demi-glace* (meaning half concentration) is available in specialty stores.* I actually find the commercially available *demi-glace* to be one third the concentration of this chicken essence. If you use purchased *demi-glace,* use about 3 tablespoons in place of 1 cube.

If you make a smaller quantity of essence and have only 1 to 1½ cups, use a 5¾-inch by 3¼-inch 1-pound foil loaf pan, available in supermarkets. Cut the *glace* into eighteen 1-inch by 1-inch by ¾-inch-high cubes (cut the short way into sixths; then cut it the long way into thirds).

*Duck *demi-glace* is available from D'Artagnan (800-DARTAGN).

Index

About the Author

ROSE LEVY BERANBAUM has her B.S. and M.A. cum laude in food science and culinary arts. In addition to continuing her studies at many of the world's leading cooking schools, she has also studied art and design at the Fashion Institute of Technology in New York City. Rose has received accreditation from the International Association of Culinary Professionals as a food writer and a teacher.

A frequent contributor to all the major food magazines and *The New York Times*, she also writes a syndicated column for the Los Angeles Times Syndicate, is on the board of the Culinary Institute of America and is a consultant to the baking and chocolate industries. For ten years Rose was owner and director of the Cordon Rose Cooking School in New York City.

Rose is the author of the best-selling *The Cake Bible*, 1988, winner of the IACP/Seagram Book of the Year and the National Association for the Specialty Food Trade Showcase Award for the cookbook that has contributed most to the education of the consumer of specialty foods. An Anglicized edition of *The Cake Bible* was published in the United Kingdom in early 1992.

Rose translated from the French and adapted *A Passion for Chocolate*, 1989, winner of the IACP/Seagram Best Book in the Dessert and Baking Category. She published *Rose's Christmas Cookies* in 1990, winner of the James Beard Best Book in the Dessert and Baking Category.

ALSO FROM WILLIAM MORROW

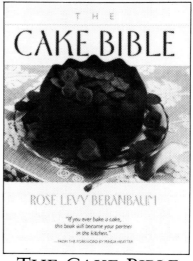

ROSE'S
CHRISTMAS COOKIES

THE CAKE BIBLE

Available at your local bookstore